FROMMER'S

COMPREHENSIVE TRAVEL GUIDE

BARCELONA '93-'94
WITH MAJORCA, MINORCA & IBIZA

D1358118

by F. Lisa Beebe

PRENTICE HALL TRAVEL

NEW YORK • LONDON • TORONTO • SYDNEY • TOKYO • SINGAPORE

FROMMER BOOKS

Published by Prentice Hall General Reference
A division of Simon & Schuster Inc.
15 Columbus Circle
New York, NY 10023

ISBN 0-671-84684-1
ISSN 1045-9324

Design by Robert Bull Design
Maps by Geografix Inc.

FROMMER'S BARCELONA '93–'94

Editor-in-Chief: Marilyn Wood
Senior Editors: Alice Fellows, Lisa Renaud
Editors: Charlotte Allstrom, Thomas F. Hirsch, Peter Katucki, Sara Hinsey Raveret, Theodore Stavrou
Assistant Editors: Margaret Bowen, Lee Gray, Ian Wilker
Managing Editor: Leanne Coupe

Special Sales

Bulk purchases of Frommer's Travel Guides are available at special discounts. The publishers are happy to custom-make publications for corporate clients who wish to use them as premiums or sales promotions. We can excerpt the contents, provide covers with corporate imprints, or create books to meet specific needs. For more information write to Special Sales, Prentice Hall Travel, Paramount Communications Building, 15 Columbus Circle, New York, NY 10023

Manufactured in the United States of America

CONTENTS

LIST OF MAPS

To Dave,

Con Amor

ACKNOWLEDGMENTS

To the many people who contributed their time, expertise, and hospitality to make this guidebook possible, I express my appreciation. Special thanks to the Spanish National Tourist Office, Mònica Colomer of the Barcelona Tourism Board, the Consorci Promoció Turistica de Catalunya, the Conselleria de Turisme del Govern Balear, the Majorcan Tourism Board, the Minorcan Tourism Board, and Don Ramón Ernesto Fajarnés.

INVITATION TO THE READERS

In researching this book, I have come across many wonderful establishments, the best of which I have included here. I am sure that many of you will also come across wonderful hotels, inns, restaurants, guesthouses, shops, and attractions. Please don't keep them to yourself. Share your experiences, especially if you want to comment on places that have been included in this edition that have changed for the worse. You can address your letters to:

F. Lisa Beebe
Frommer's Barcelona '93–'94
c/o Prentice Hall Travel
15 Columbus Circle
New York, NY 10023

A DISCLAIMER

Readers are advised that prices fluctuate in the course of time and travel information changes under the impact of the varied and volatile factors that affect the travel industry. Neither the author nor the publisher can be held responsible for the experiences of readers while traveling. Readers are invited to write to the publisher with ideas, comments, and suggestions for future editions.

SAFETY ADVISORY

Whenever you're traveling in an unfamiliar city or country, stay alert. Be aware of your immediate surroundings. Wear a moneybelt and keep a close eye on your possessions. Be particularly careful with cameras, purses, and wallets, all favorite targets of thieves and pickpockets.

INTRODUCING BARCELONA

Spain's noble city on the Mediterranean, Barcelona is all grace and good looks on the outside and driving ambition within. In fact, the dynamism in the air makes the city's languid palm trees seem somehow out of place. Barcelona aspires to play a vital economic role both within Spain and beyond, and there is no time to waste.

Barcelona has a history of successfully capitalizing on large-scale collective endeavors, such as the World Exhibition of 1888 and the World's Fair of 1929. Thanks to the impetus of the 1992 Summer Olympic Games, the city is now endowed with a new airport that can accommodate 18 million passengers annually, numerous new hotels, and top-notch Olympic facilities that have been turned over to public use. It has also overhauled many architectural heirlooms, plazas, parks, and gardens and added new ones executed by some of the world's leading architects—among them Arata Isozaki, Richard Meier, Gae Aulenti, Norman Foster, Victorio Gregotti, I. M. Pei, and native son Ricardo Bofill. Meier noted this in the August 1989 issue of *Mirabella:* "In no other place in the world is such important work being done to transform a city as in Barcelona. Still, the city has not destroyed its identity." Visitors will now find a new, improved version of what was already a uniquely beautiful metropolis. Though the Olympics were ostensibly the driving force behind the city's robust resurgence, other economic motors will ensure that the revival continues.

In recent years, Catalonia's economy, the most diversified and prosperous of any region in Spain, has been growing even faster than the booming national economy. While Catalonia comprises about 6 percent of Spain's total area, it accounts for 20 percent of the national production. One-quarter of Spain's industrial goods are manufactured here, and one-third of all foreign investment—and virtually all Japanese investment—in Spain comes Catalonia's way, contributing greatly to the region's commercial vigor.

Nicknamed "La Ciudad Condal" for the counts who negotiated its independence in A.D. 874, Barcelona is the Mediterranean's third-largest port and has long been deemed Spain's most "European" city. Until the return of democracy to Spain in the late 1970s, Barcelona had always been the nation's indisputable cultural capital, where art, architecture, design, fashion, and personal style consistently overreached the limits of the imagination. But in the highly competitive post-Franco environment, Madrid, the national capital,

✓ WHAT'S SPECIAL ABOUT BARCELONA

Architectural Highlights

- ☐ Gaudí's Sagrada Familia, an immense modernist cathedral crawling its way to completion.
- ☐ Palau de la Música Catalana, an outstanding example of modernism that's one of the world's finest concert halls.
- ☐ The countless modernist delights along the streets of the Eixample—from the smallest ornamental details to the great explosions of imagination.

Attractions

- ☐ La Rambla, one of the world's most entertaining boulevards.
- ☐ The Gothic cathedral, noted for its cloisters, its *Cristo de Lepanto*, and its tomb of Santa Eulàlia, one of the city's patron saints—especially magical when illuminated on Thursday, Saturday, and Sunday night.
- ☐ The Poble Espanyol, a "village" showcasing Spain's regional architectural styles that's a focal point for nightlife activities ranging from dinner to fine flamenco dancing.

Museums

- ☐ Museu Picasso, home to an enlightening collection of the master's works.
- ☐ Fundació Joan Miró, with more than 10,000 works by this Catalan artist.
- ☐ Museu d'Art de Catalunya, a compendium of regional art that reveals the cultural heritage of the Catalonian region.

Vistas

- ☐ From the top of Montjuïc.
- ☐ From the top of Mount Tibidabo.
- ☐ From the Transbordador Aéreo del Puerto.
- ☐ From Parc Güell.

Park

- ☐ Parc de la Ciutadella, home to the zoo, the Museu d'Art Modern, and many attractive sculptures and fountains.

Neighborhoods

- ☐ Barri Gòtic, a maze of medieval streets sprouting a growing number of shops.

Transportation

- ☐ *Tramvía blau*, running amid the stately modernist mansions of Avinguda Tibidabo.

Excursions

- ☐ Montserrat Monastery, a popular pilgrimage destination that's the home of the Black Virgin, one of Catalonia's patron saints.
- ☐ Sitges, a seaside resort town with elegant modernist villas and two small choice museums, Museu Cau Ferrat and Museu Maricel de Mar, housing fine antiques and works of art.

For the Kids

- ☐ The amusement parks atop Montjuïc and Mount Tibidabo, both offering parents fine panoramic views.

took the initiative in many of these areas, quickly relegating Barcelona to an unwelcome secondary status and heightening the traditional rivalry between the two cities. True to form, Barcelona regrouped, sitting down at the drawing board to make daring designs for the future.

"Barcelona Més Que Mai" ("Barcelona More Than Ever"), "Barcelona, Posa't Guapa" ("Barcelona, Make Yourself Attractive"), and "Barcelona Es Teva" ("Barcelona Belongs to You") are the guiding slogans of this city's rebirth. But, of course, there are drawbacks: more street crime, a burgeoning drug problem, and growing indigence as Barcelona's economic opportunities attract all comers with a dream. Already the city's population of over three million is concentrated in one of the most densely inhabited urban areas in Europe. But Mayor Pasqual Maragall is optimistic. He, too, has a dream, which he calls "Barcelona Gran."

In many ways, Antoni Gaudí's Sagrada Familia is a fitting symbol for this expanding city, suffused with the kind of creative fire that spurred Gaudí to conceive a 20th-century cathedral of medieval proportions. When Norman Foster Associates' radical design for the Olympic telecommunications tower got the go-ahead, architect Kenneth Shuttleworth remarked, "Actually, we didn't expect to win the competition, but Barcelona, we've discovered, is not afraid of progressive ideas" (*Mirabella,* August 1989).

Convenient to coastal beaches, the Penedés wine country, skiing in the Pyrenees, and the Balearic Islands in the Mediterranean, Barcelona is a stepping-stone to a variety of holiday resorts as well as a rich tourist experience in its own right. Nearly 40% of visitors to Spain go to Catalonia. The fact that about 90% of those visitors have been to Catalonia at least twice before speaks well of the region's depth and variety.

1. CULTURE, HISTORY & BACKGROUND

GEOGRAPHY

Barcelona's geographic situation is at once fortuitous and confining. Spread across the plain between the Mediterranean Sea and the Serra del Collserola, the city has always been open to worldly influences through its eastern harbor and somewhat cut off from the rest of Spain by its western mountains. These geographic parameters account for the city's distinctive cosmopolitan manner and high population density. They also account for its scenic appeal. To the northeast Barcelona is bordered by the Besós River and to the southwest by the Llobregat River. Just southwest of the harbor rises Montjuïc, the focal point for the events of the 1992 Summer Olympic Games.

PEOPLE & POLITICS

Even though Barcelona is a city of great cultural, political, and intellectual depth, it has always evinced a mercantile spirit whose emphasis, long before it was fashionable, was on the bottom line.

Not surprisingly, the Catalans are considered among the most savvy of Spanish businesspeople. And although the use of the Catalan language continues to spread, it no longer seems quite the passionate cause célèbre it was several years ago, largely, I suspect, because the pragmatic Catalans understand that their language is not the language of national and international business—and in Barcelona, business is what counts.

The Catalans (along with most other Spaniards, for that matter) have always considered themselves a breed apart. Living close to France and exposed to a diversity of foreign elements through their busy port, the citizens of Barcelona were for centuries more cosmopolitan than their counterparts in other Spanish cities. While Franco was calling all the political, religious, and cultural shots in the country, Barcelona continued to show a certain amount of independence—in some ways it played Hong Kong to the rest of the nation's China. When avant-garde art was denounced in Madrid, Barcelona staged exhibitions that stunned the nation. In effect, it was the national escape valve, both envied and disdained by more straitlaced Spanish cities.

Proud of its strong streak of individualism, Barcelona's citizenry considers itself more European than Spanish. Those familiar with other parts of Spain will detect in the city's inhabitants a reserve and an arrogance more akin to the French temperament. A further indication of the Catalans' sense of separateness are the linguistic politics of the Catalan TV channels, which always refer to Spain as "the Spanish State," thus implying that Catalonia is in a sense a state, too.

The resurgence of the Catalan language is a highly visible manifestation of regional sentiments. A Romance language related to Langue d'Oc and Provençal, it has been spoken since the collapse of the Roman Empire, except during periods of political repression. Of course, it also shares many words with Spanish, and those who are fluent in Spanish, or in both Italian and French, can often readily read and comprehend Catalan. Today, an estimated 6 to 6½ million people actually speak it, making it the largest nonnational language of the European Community. This linguistic currency extends beyond Catalonia to Valencia, where an estimated 50% of the population speaks Catalan, and to the Balearic Islands, where 71% of the population speaks a local version of the vernacular.

Unfortunately, among Catalonia's staunch separatists things have recently taken a turn for the radical. An extremist group called Tierra Lliure (Free Land) is not averse to using violence to focus attention on its vision of a free and independent Catalonia.

Overall, however, the pendulum of regional patriotism seems to be on the downswing as Barcelona (and Catalonia) focuses on its burgeoning economic frontiers. Dynamic in its drive and bold in its vision, Barcelona has *mucho* momentum.

DATELINE

• **3rd century B.C.**
The Carthaginians establish the town of Barcino on the site
(continues)

HISTORY

Barcelona's history goes back at least 2,000 years. Some historic accounts speak of a Phoenician founding and a subsequent Carthaginian identity as "Barcino." Still others allude to the earlier presence of the Laietani, an Iberian Bronze Age tribe. But the port that was to make the city's fortunes began to develop in 201 B.C. under the Romans. Rome's rule was superseded by that of the Visigoths, who in turn were replaced by the Moors and then the Franks.

Just over 1,000 years ago Barcelona became the capital of Catalonia, a region that took shape during the Middle Ages when the Condes de Barcelona (Counts of Barcelona) declared their independence and set up one of Europe's first parliamentary governments. Barcelona reached its peak as an Iberian and a Mediterranean power in the 13th and 14th centuries as the capital of the Kingdom of Catalonia and Aragón. In 1259 it promulgated the first code of European maritime law, which other Mediterranean states used as a model.

With the 1474 marriage of Queen Isabella of Castile to King Ferdinand of Aragón, Catalan independence was quelled for the greater glory of a united Spain. For several centuries, Barcelona was mired in mediocrity. Not until the 18th century did it begin to recover—by 1800 Barcelona was the textile capital of the Mediterranean.

Home to Spain's first industrial-age bourgeoisie, Barcelona embarked in 1859 on a plan of modernization. The old city walls were torn down, and the city expanded into the Eixample, whose grid plan was the pragmatic vision of Catalan engineer Ildefons Cerdà.

Imbued early on with the capitalist spirit, Barcelona was always a staunch defender of democracy, and no doubt its economic fortitude underscored the political audacity that give rise to countless anarchist, republican, and separatist uprisings in the early 20th century. The city was the seat of the Republican government during the Civil War, and its virulent opposition to the Nationalist forces of Franco came home to roost in a heavy-handed post–Civil War repression. The use of the Catalan language and the observance of Catalan traditions were rigorously punished. No wonder that with the return of democracy after Franco's death, Catalonia swelled with supercharged patriotic pride, promptly reinstating Catalan as an official language and reviving most long-suppressed customs.

A longtime rival of Madrid, Barcelona still chafes under the Castilian yoke. But as Spain's principal port and second-largest

DATELINE

of a former Phoenician settlement.

- **201 B.C.** The Romans begin to develop the city's port.
- **A.D. 874** The Counts of Barcelona win local independence.
- **1137** Catalonia merges with the Kingdom of Aragón.
- **1259** The city promulgates the first code of European maritime law.
- **1283** The Catalan parliamentary courts are consolidated.
- **1359** The Generalitat (regional government) is established.
- **13th to 15th century** Barcelona dominates the Mediterranean and builds its Gothic Quarter.
- **1474** Catalan independence comes to an end with the marriage of Queen Isabella of Castile and King Ferdinand of Aragón and the subsequent unification of Spain.
- **1493** Upon his triumphant return from the New World, Columbus is received in Barcelona by the Catholic monarchs.
- **1808–13** The French occupy the city.
- **18th to 20th century** Industrialization leads to the expansion of the city and eventually to the evolution of the modernist architectural tradition.

(continues)

city, it is now carving a new niche for itself not only as an autonomous regional capital but also as a key player in both the national and the international scheme of things. Capitalizing on its long-standing fame as a fashion and design center and as a hotbed of commercial activity, the city is bracing itself for the challenge of a Europe without economic borders.

FAMOUS CITIZENS

José Carreras (1947–   ) A Barcelona-born tenor, Carreras has taken the opera world by storm, acquiring the stature of Pavarotti and Domingo. He has performed in the most prestigious opera houses in the world, including La Scala and the Metropolitan Opera.

Saint Francis of Assisi (1181–1226) Arriving in Barcelona in October 1211, Saint Francis of Assisi soon made a name for himself with a few prophecies that proved true and the fashioning of the world's first Nativity scene at Christmas. He spent a total of about two years in this city.

Antoni Gaudí Cornet (1852–1926) The most effusive, eccentric, and brilliant architect of Barcelona's modernist tradition, Gaudí endowed Barcelona with some of its most enduring landmarks—Casa Milá (a.k.a. "La Pedrera"); Casa Batlló; Parc Güell; and the epic, though unfinished, Sagrada Familia cathedral.

ART, ARCHITECTURE & CULTURAL LIFE

ART Catalonia boasts a strong artistic tradition stretching from the Romanesque marvels found in its rural churches (and to a growing extent in Barcelona's Museu d'Art de Catalunya) to the contemporary works in the city's Museu d'Art Modern. However, this fact is little known beyond the region.

Picasso spent some time in Barcelona at the turn of the century, and the city's inspirational effect on him can be seen first-hand in Barcelona's Museu Picasso.

Catalan artist Joan Miró is also well represented in this city, not only in his own museum on Montjuïc but also in the colorful sidewalk mural dating from 1976 that graces the center of La Rambla near the Gran Teatre del Liceu.

The latest artist to make a striking, and at time controversial, mark is Antoni Tàpies, whose Fundació Antoni Tàpies, founded in 1984, exhibits a comprehensive collection of his own works as well as art from all over the world.

But art in Barcelona has always been more than a mere spectator sport, for the city's artistic sensibilities have continually focused on the aesthetics of daily life. Whether building such parks as the Parc de L'Espanya Indsutrial, or such plazas as the Plaça Reial, or such trendy nightclubs as Velvet and Ticktacktoe, the Barcelonans devote much thought and energy to the creation of complete environments for living. Aesthetics are important here, and as a result the city is very attractive.

ARCHITECTURE The architectural cornerstones of Barcelona are the Gothic Quarter and the Eixample, both the result of periods of urban prosperity. The Gothic Quarter dates from the 13th to the 15th century, when Barcelona was the center of commercial activity in Europe thanks to its Mediterranean port. The Eixample was fueled by the profits of industrialization in the late 19th and early 20th centuries and became a showcase of Catalan modernism. Although part of the worldwide art nouveau movement, modernism in the hands of such masters as Gaudí, Domenech i Montaner, and Puig i Cadafalch demonstrated a distinctively Catalan flair, reflecting in part Spain's strong religious traditions and in part Barcelona's own dare-to-be-different boldness.

A prime example of Barcelona's medieval grandeur is the 14th-century Iglesia de Santa María del Mar, built in the Catalan Gothic style.

Among the modernist masterpieces for which Barcelona is noted worldwide are Domenech i Montaner's Palau de la Música Catalana, Puig i Cadafalch's Casa Amatller, and Gaudí's Casa Milá and Sagrada Familia cathedral.

Gaudí By all accounts, Gaudí was an odd man, moody, unassuming, and quite austere in his personal habits. All effusiveness, it seems, was reserved for his work. An individualist with his own way of doing things, Gaudí took nine years to finish the architectural studies that others typically completed in five. From the beginning he immersed himself in every aspect of the building trade and ultimately designed everything from doorknobs to the towering spires of his highly ambitious 20th-century cathedral, the Sagrada Familia.

Through his relationship with the Güells, a family of industrialists who commissioned him to do numerous works, he gained prestige among Barcelona's bourgeoisie. From 1878 until Eusebi Güell's death in 1918, Güell was Gaudí's principal patron.

> ✪ **Gaudí immersed himself in every aspect of the building trade and ultimately designed everything from doorknobs to the towering spires of his Sagrada Familia.**

Within Catalan modernism, Gaudí's work stands out as singularly organic and brilliantly creative in its use of ornamentation. Gifted as both interior designer and architect, Gaudí was able to integrate all the elements of his structural compositions into organic, unified wholes. Whether he was working with wrought iron, furniture, stained glass, sculpture, mosaics, stone, or brick, he drew his inspiration from nature's forms, colors, and light. "The spirituality of Gaudí's work comes from the material aspect of Nature understood as the work of God, who is the Great Architect of the world," Joan Bassegoda Nonell wrote in *A Guide to Gaudí* (Edicions de Nou Art Thor). A deeply religious man, Gaudí had spiritual and creative convictions that converged most intensely during his involvement with the Sagrada Familia cathedral.

Born Antoni Gaudí Cornet in 1852, he died in 1926 after being struck by a tram, leaving behind no definitive plans for the completion of his masterwork.

CULTURAL LIFE   Although Barcelona is and always has been a business-minded city, it has earned a reputation as a center for fashion, design, culture, and the arts, especially in their more avant-garde forms. Picasso, Miró, Pablo Casals, Gaudí, Montserrat Caballé, and José Carreras are just some of the personalities weaned at the breast of Barcelona's pulsing creativity.

The modernist movement at the turn of the century was Barcelona's initiation into the world's cultural forefront, because it was a movement that flourished not only in architecture and design but also in the sculptures of Josep Llimona and the music of Enrique Granados. Barcelona's Sala Parés, Spain's oldest art gallery, was born to exhibit the artistic outpourings of the period.

More recently the city has again become a center for design. Vinçon in the Passeig de Gràcia carries countless items for the home and office, demonstrating the local flair for conceiving objects that are both functional and fun.

Ever since he designed the Olympic mascot, a jazzy dog named Cobi, Xavier Mariscal has been designing things all over town, including the giant prawn perched atop the Gambrinus restaurant in the Moll de la Fusta and the tipsy bar stools at Maná Maná.

Just have a good look as you walk around town and you'll soon realize that design statements are a Barcelona passion.

RELIGION, MYTH & FOLKLORE   Devotion to the Black Virgin of Montserrat (a.k.a. "La Moreneta") is strong throughout the region of Catalonia but even more so in the city of Barcelona itself. In fact, the figure of La Moreneta in the city's Iglesia de Santa Ana is considered the patron saint of the city's athletes, and her chapel there is adorned with two murals depicting life-size athletes engaged in all manner of sports.

The Christmas crèche and its miniature figures were born in Barcelona thanks to Saint Francis of Assisi, who on Christmas Eve in 1213 displayed the first Nativity scene in Christendom.

Once upon a time Santa Eulàlia was Barcelona's only patron saint. Then along came the friars of the Merced convent, who declared their Virgen de la Merced a patron saint as well. As the legend goes, Santa Eulàlia was so angry that ever since it almost always rains on September 24, the feast day of the usurping municipal patron.

2. FOOD & DRINK

MEALS & DINING CUSTOMS   The Spanish eat later than Americans and other Europeans; most Barcelona restaurants are open daily from 1 to 4pm and 8pm to midnight. In deference to the growing influx of foreign businesspeople and tourists, however, more and more restaurants are keeping longer hours to accommodate both timetables.

IMPRESSIONS

When Charles V, in 1519, came here, he wished to be received, not as a King, but as one of the former counts; 'for,' said he, 'I would rather be Count of Barcelona than King of the Romans.'
—H. O'SHEA, *A GUIDE TO SPAIN*, 1865

Traditionally the Spanish eat their main meal at lunch and have a lighter meal at dinner, but this custom is not as entrenched in the cities, where the demands of business increasingly cut into the custom of the leisurely lunch hour.

Whenever the main meal is eaten, it usually consists of an *entrada* (first course) of salad, vegetables, fish, or an egg dish; followed by a *plato principal* (second or main course) of fish, meat, stew, or game. Coffee is typically taken after, not with, dessert; and any fine meal is incomplete without an after-dinner liqueur, cognac, or *marc de champán* (a kind of local grappa).

THE CUISINE Like the French, the Catalans have always taken their food quite seriously. The first gastronomic manuscript in the Catalan language was written back in 1324, and the first cookbook ever printed in Spain—the *Libre del Coc*—was published in Catalan in 1520.

The cuisine of Barcelona is widely varied, with menus all over town based on what's freshest that day at La Boquería, the famous market in La Rambla. The variety of climates within Catalonia, ranging from the alpine of the upper Pyrenees to the Mediterranean of the coast, provides a wealth of raw ingredients with which to construct a hearty, well-rounded cuisine. Naturally, Barcelona offers a compendium of dishes from throughout the region, many of which have been modified by the influence of other national cuisines.

> ○ **The first gastronomic manuscript in the Catalan language was written back in 1324, and the first cookbook ever printed in Spain was published in Catalan in 1520.**

Primarily Mediterranean in their basic ingredients—such as the greenest of first-press olive oil, lard, almonds, garlic, aromatic herbs, and, more recently, tomatoes—most traditional Catalan dishes consist of what's fresh and closest at hand. Fish, beef, pork, game, poultry, vegetables, and wild mushrooms immediately come to mind. Through Barcelona's open door on the Mediterranean, many other culinary influences have filtered into the regional diet. Both Roman and Moorish presences left their mark, as did the novelties brought by Columbus from the New World—potatoes, tomatoes, peppers, corn, and pineapple. Pastas were added to the Catalan pot in the 18th century when Barcelona restaurants began adapting Italian recipes, and in the 19th century French food also was stirred into the mix.

Given Barcelona's penchant for innovation, it's not surprising that the culinary boundaries of Catalan cuisine are quite elastic. Keeping one eye on tradition, the city's chefs constantly invent new variations on standard themes, making it difficult to affix labels to Barcelona's highly imaginative and ever-shifting culinary currents. But traditional sausages like the *butifarra,* succulent roasts, robust game, delicate seafood, toothsome rice dishes, and savory stews have steadfastly remained the mainstays of Catalan cuisine. Other typical dishes include *paella a la parellada,* with rice, fish, shellfish, chicken, and beef; *zarzuela,* a mixture of fish and shellfish in a rich sauce (some variations on this theme are *suquet de peix* and *caldereta marinera*); *escudella i carn d'olla,* chickpeas or beans stewed with different kinds of sausage, meatballs, chicken, and vegetables; *peus de porc,* or "pig's trotters," cooked in a rich sauce; and faves, broad beans stewed with butifarra. Catalonia is also the land of mushrooms, with over 100 varieties of *setas* (the generic term for wild gourmet mushrooms).

DRINKS   Like Catalan cuisine, Catalan wines vary from one area to another. The *Denominación de Origen* (D.O.), Spain's appellation system, regulates their origin and quality.

Since at least 600 B.C., Catalonia's combination of limestone soil, temperate climate, and moderate rainfall have proved ideal for wine production. Protected by two mountain ranges, the Cordillera Litoral Catalana and the Montes de Garraf, most of the wine-producing region lies in a central depression, which is flat in some places and gently sloping in others. Roughly rectangular in shape, with Barcelona tucked away in the northeastern corner, the Penedés is the principal wine region of Catalonia and is divided into three subregions—the Bajo Penedés, Medio Penedés, and Alto Penedés.

The Bajo Penedés, which hugs the Mediterranean coast, is the hottest of the three zones, with a climate comparable to California's Central Valley. It cultivates mostly Monastrell, Malvasia, Carinena, Garnacha, and Tempranillo grapes to produce traditional, full-bodied reds and some dessert wines.

The Medio Penedés is the source of traditional white wines and classic *cavas*—sparkling wines produced in the manner of champagne but known here as "cava"—made from Xarello and Macabeo grapes. However, the limestone-and-clay soil also permits cultivation of many French varietals. The climate here is comparable to that of Tuscany and the northern part of California's Napa Valley.

The Alto Penedés, in the foothills of the mountains, is cooler and gets more rain, like the regions of Champagne, the Rhine Valley, and the cooler parts of the Napa Valley. This, too, is white wine country, the main grapes being Parellada, Riesling, Gewürztraminer, and Alsace Muscat.

In general, Catalan wine production centers on the whites, which tend to be light and fruity. The reds, produced in smaller quantities, tend to be strong, full-bodied, and of alcohol content sometimes reaching more than 15%.

Recently, Catalan wines have been gaining increasing cachet abroad. The wines of Miguel Torres, a fifth-generation vintner, are found all over the world and have been available in the United States for more than 50 years. The family's California vineyards are managed by his daughter, Marimar. Freixenet, the world's leading seller of cava, has also established wineries in California and in Reims. Codorniu, the other leading cava producer, leads in the high-priced market in both Europe and the United States.

Although the tap water in Barcelona is safe to drink, most locals drink bottled mineral waters famed for their salutary effects. The different brands are countless, and each has its staunch advocates.

Both local and imported beers are widely available; some local brands to look out for are San Miguel, Estrella, and Voll Damm. In the summer, Spaniards consume a wonderfully refreshing drink made from *chufa* nuts (earth almonds) called *horchata*. It is offered at numerous cafeterias, ice-cream shops, and pastry shops around town, but make sure it is fresh and dispensed from a large glass vat because the bottled version is awful.

3. RECOMMENDED BOOKS, FILMS & RECORDINGS

BOOKS

Here is a list of books that may help to prepare you for your trip to Barcelona and Catalonia.

GENERAL

Boyd, Alistair. *The Essence of Catalonia: Barcelona and Its Regions.*
Hooper, John. *The Spaniards.*
Hughes, Robert. *Barcelona.*
Lewis, Norman. *Voices of the Old Sea.*
Michener, James. *Iberia: Spanish Travels and Reflections.*
Morris, Jan. *Spain.*
Plante, David. *The Foreigner.*

HISTORY

Kazantzakis, Nikos. *Spain.*
Orwell, George. *Homage to Catalonia.*

ART

Martinell, Cesar. *Gaudí Designer: His Life, His Theories, His Work.*
Nonell, Joan Bassegoda. *A Guide to Gaudí.*
Penrose, Roland. *Miró.*
Sterner, Gabriele. *Antoni Gaudí.*

FOOD

Casas, Penelope. *The Foods & Wines of Spain.*
Read, Jan, Maite Manjon, and Hugh Johnson. *The Wine & Food of Spain.*

FILMS

Almodóvar, Pedro. "Law of Desire," "Matador," "Women on the Edge of a Nervous Breakdown," "Tie Me Up, Tie Me Down," and "High Heels."
Buñuel, Luís. "El Perro Andaluz" ("Un Chien Andalou"), "L'Age

d'Or," "The Discreet Charm of the Bourgeoisie," and "That Obscure Object of Desire."
Erice, Victor. "The Spirit of the Beehive," and "The South."
Saura, Carlos. "Blood Wedding" and "Carmen."

RECORDINGS

Some popular Spanish musical artists to look for are José Luís Perales, a popular singer of romantic ballads; Joan Manuel Serrat, a native Catalan composer and singer who often celebrates his Mediterranean home in song; Miguel Ríos, a rock singer famous for his rendition of Beethoven's "Ode to Joy"; Ana Belén, a "soft rock" singer whose recent hits include "Puerta de Alcalà"; and the rock group Mocedades.

PLANNING A TRIP TO BARCELONA

With business and tourist traffic to Barcelona on the rise, flights from the United States and Europe are increasing. Nonstop and direct service is available from New York, with easy connections from other major American cities. Once there, you'll find that the city compresses its sightseeing riches into an easy-to-get-to-know ensemble of Old World alleys and broad modern boulevards—all serviced by an efficient public transportation network.

1. INFORMATION, ENTRY REQUIREMENTS & MONEY

SOURCES OF INFORMATION

For information to help you plan your trip, contact the **Spanish National Tourist Office** nearest you. See Chapter 3, "Getting to Know Barcelona," for a list of information sources in Barcelona itself.

New York: 665 Fifth Ave., New York, NY 10022 (tel. 212/759-8822; fax 212/980-1053).

Miami: 1221 Brickell Ave., Miami, FL 33131 (tel. 305/358-1992; fax 305/358-8223).

Chicago: Water Tower Place, Suite 915 East, 845 N. Michigan Ave., Chicago, IL 60611 (tel. 312/944-0216, 944-0225, or 944-0226; fax 312/642-9817).

Los Angeles: 8383 Wilshire Blvd., Suite 960, Beverly Hills, CA 90211 (tel. 213/658-7188 or 658-7193; fax 213/658-1061).

Toronto: 102 Bloor St. West, 14th Floor, Toronto, Ontario M5S 1MB, Canada (tel. 416/961-3131 or 961-4079; fax 416/961-1992).

London: 57–58 St. James' St., London SW1A 1LD, England (tel. 01/499-1169 or 499-0901; fax 01/629-4257).

Sydney: 203 Castlereagh St., Suite 21a (P.O. Box A-685), Sydney South, NSW, 2000 Australia (tel. 612/264-7966; fax 612/267-5111).

ENTRY REQUIREMENTS

DOCUMENTS   For a stay of up to three months, Americans need only a valid passport for travel to Spain. Citizens of most Western European countries need only their national identity cards.

CUSTOMS   You may bring the following into Spain: personal effects; one portable typewriter; one movie camera or two still cameras with ten rolls of film for each; one portable radio or portable tape recorder per person, provided they show signs of use; 200 cigarettes, or 50 cigars, or 250 grams of tobacco; one bottle of wine and one of liquor per person; fishing gear; and two hunting weapons. There is no quarantine in Spain. A certificate stating that an animal is in good health and has been inoculated against rabies (for dogs and cats) is required. This document must be issued by a veterinarian and certified at the nearest Spanish consulate.

MONEY

CURRENCY   The Spanish unit of currency is the **peseta (pta.)**, which is issued in coin denominations of 1, 5, 10, 25, 50, 100, 200, and 500 ptas., and bills of 500 (rare nowadays), 1,000, 2,000, 5,000, and 10,000 ptas. The rate of exchange used to calculate dollar equivalents in this guidebook is 100 ptas. to $1 U.S., but given the constant state of flux of today's economies, prices (in both pesetas and dollars) should be considered as reference points rather than as statements of strict financial fact. The following table should be used only as a guide:

Ptas.	U.S.	Ptas.	U.S.
5	.05	1,500	15.00
10	.10	2,000	20.00
15	.15	2,500	25.00
20	.20	3,000	30.00
25	.25	3,500	35.00
30	.30	4,000	40.00
40	.40	4,500	45.00
50	.50	5,000	50.00
75	.75	6,000	60.00
100	1.00	7,000	70.00
150	1.50	8,000	80.00
200	2.00	9,000	90.00
250	2.50	10,000	100.00
500	5.00	12,500	125.00
750	7.50	15,000	150.00
1,000	10.00	20,000	200.00

TRAVELER'S   CHECKS   &   CREDIT   CARDS   **Traveler's checks** are always the safest way to carry money, but most banks and exchange facilities exact a high minimum commission for their conversion into local currency. As a result, it makes sense to change only substantial amounts of money. Alternatively, you can change your traveler's checks at most four- and five-star hotels; although their exchange rates are not as favorable, their commissions are typically lower or even nonexistent.

Credit cards are accepted at ever-increasing numbers of hotels, restaurants, and stores, but most budget lodgings still won't take them. For assistance or information, call American Express (tel. 3/217-00-70); EUROCARD, VISA, and MasterCard (tel. 3/315-25-12); or Diners Club (tel. 3/302-14-28).

WHAT THINGS COST IN BARCELONA	U.S. $
Taxi from the airport to Hotel Colón	23.00
Metro	1.00
Local telephone call	.20
Double room at the Gran Hotel Havana (deluxe)	300.00–360.00
Double room at the Hotel Colón (moderate)	210.00
Double room at the Hotel Residencia Neutral (budget)	53.00
Continental breakfast	4.95
Lunch for one, without wine, at Flash-Flash (moderate)	15.00
Lunch for one, without wine, at Self Naturista (budget)	7.00
Dinner for one, without wine, at El Dorado Petit (deluxe)	75.00
Dinner for one, without wine, at Tramonti 1980 (moderate)	36.00
Dinner for one, without wine, at Pitarra Restaurant (budget)	20.00
Glass of beer (caña)	1.25–1.50
Coca-Cola	1.40
Cup of coffee	.95
Roll of ASA 100 color film, 36 exposures	5.65
Admission to Museu de Picasso	5.50
Movie ticket	3.65–6.50
Theater ticket	8.60 and up

2. WHEN TO GO — CLIMATE, HOLIDAYS & EVENTS

THE CLIMATE Barcelona's climate is very mild most of the year, with temperatures rarely reaching freezing in the winter. The high humidity can make the dog days (and nights) of July and August rather oppressive, but just do as the Barcelonans do and buy yourself a fan. Rain is infrequent, most likely to fall in the spring and autumn. The following table shows some monthly averages:

Barcelona's Average Daytime Temperatures & Days of Sunshine

	Jan	Feb	Mar	Apr	May	June	July	Aug	Sept	Oct	Nov	Dec
Temp. (°F)	49	51	54	59	64	72	76	76	72	64	57	51
Temp. (°C)	10	11	13	15	18	22	25	25	22	18	14	11
Days of Sun	26	23	22	21	23	24	27	25	23	22	24	25

HOLIDAYS   Local holidays are celebrated with special flair (see the "Barcelona Calendar of Events" below), but life as usual takes a breather on the following days: January 1 (New Year's Day), January 6 (Feast of the Three Kings), Good Friday, Easter Monday, May 1 (Labor Day), June 8 (Pascua Granada), June 24 (Feast of St. John), August 15 (Assumption Day), September 11 (Catalunya Day), September 24 (Fiesta de la Mercè), October 12 (Columbus Day), December 8 (Feast of the Immaculate Conception), December 25 (Christmas Day), and December 26 (Feast of St. Stephen).

BARCELONA CALENDAR OF EVENTS

JANUARY

☐ **Three Kings Parade.** Spain traditionally celebrates the Feast of the Three Kings (January 6), and in anticipation Barcelona stages through its central streets a parade that delights children and adults alike. Usually January 4 or 5.

FEBRUARY–MARCH

☐ **Saló d'Antiquaris de Barcelona.** This annual antiques trade fair is held in the Fira de Barcelona at the foot of Montjuïc. Late February to early March.

MARCH

☐ **Marathon Catalunya.** This marathon starts in Mataró and ends at the Oplymic Stadium of Montjuïc. Usually around the middle of the month.

APRIL

☐ **Festivitat de Sant Jordi and Parades de Llibres i Roses.** On the Feast Day of Sant Jordi, Catalonia's patron saint, it is traditional for Barcelona's citizens to give one another books and roses. April 23.

☐ **Bullfights.** Although they are not quite the passion here that they are in other parts of Spain, they're a national pastime that I recommend you see to gain some insight into the Spanish temperament. Watching the crowd is almost as much as spectacle as the sport itself and will distract you, if you wish, at the "moment of truth"—when the torero zeroes in for the kill. Holy Week in March or April until September.

MAY

☐ **Fira del Llibre de Barcelona.** Barcelona's elaborate book fair usually extends along the Passeig de Gràcia. End of May to early July.

JUNE

☐ **Verbena de Sant Joan.** Barcelona celebrates the Verbena de Sant Joan with bonfires in the city's streets and plazas. It is customary to eat the coca, a special sweet made from fruit and pine nuts, and attend the festivities on Montjuïc, which culminate with an impressive display of fireworks. June 23.

SEPTEMBER

☐ **Fiestas de la Mercé.** The city holds a variety of celebrations in honor of the Virgin de la Mercé, one of the city's patron saints. Barcelona's most important popular festival, it features concerts and theatrical performances in the Plaças de Sant Jaume, de la Catedral, del Rei, Sot del Migdia, Escorxador, and Reial, and parades of giants, devils, dragons, and other fantastic creatures winding through the streets of the old city districts. Marking the end of the festivities is a pageant of music and fireworks. Week of September 24.

NOVEMBER

☐ **Festival Internacional de Jazz de Barcelona.** The dates and venues of this annual jazz festival change from year to year. For information call 3/447-12-90.

3. HEALTH & INSURANCE

HEALTH PREPARATIONS   You will encounter few health problems traveling in Barcelona. The tap water is safe to drink, the milk is pasteurized, and the health services are good. Occasionally, the change in diet may cause some minor diarrhea, so you may want to take some antidiarrhea medicine along.

Bring all your vital medicine in your carry-on luggage and include enough prescribed medicines to sustain you during your stay. Also carry copies of your prescriptions that are written in the generic, not brand-name, form. If you need a doctor, your hotel can recommend one, or you can contact your embassy or consulate. Before leaving, you can also obtain a list of English-speaking doctors from the **International Association for Medical Assistance to Travelers (IAMAT):** in the United States at 417 Center St., Lewiston, NY 14092 (tel. 716/754-4883); in Canada at 40 Regal Rd., Guelph, ON N1K 1B5 (tel. 519/836-0102).

If you suffer from a chronic illness, talk to your doctor before taking the trip. For such conditions as epilepsy, diabetes, and a heart condition, wear a **Medic Alert Identification Tag,** which will immediately alert any doctor to your condition and provide the number of Medic Alert's 24-hour hotline so that a foreign doctor can obtain medical records for you. A lifetime membership costs $35. Contact the Medic Alert Foundation, P.O. Box 1009, Turlock, CA 95381-1009 (tel. toll free 800/432-5378).

INSURANCE   Before purchasing any additional insurance check your homeowner's, automobile, and medical insurance policies as well as the insurance provided by credit-card companies and auto and travel clubs. You may have adequate off-premises theft coverage, or your credit-card company may even provide cancellation coverage if the ticket is paid for with a credit card.

Remember, Medicare covers U.S. citizens traveling only in Mexico and Canada.

Also note that to submit any claim you must always have thorough documentation, including all receipts, police reports, medical records, and the like.

If you are prepaying for your vacation or taking a charter or any other flight that has cancellation penalties, look into cancellation insurance.

The following companies will provide further information:

Travel Guard International, 1145 Clark St., Stevens Point, WI 54481 (tel. toll free 800/826-1300), offers a comprehensive seven-day policy that covers basically everything. It costs $52, including emergency assistance, accidental death, trip cancellation and interruption, medical coverage abroad, and lost luggage. However, there are restrictions that you should understand before you accept the coverage.

Travel Insurance Pak, Travelers Insurance Co., Travel Insurance Division, 1 Tower Square, Hartford, CT 06183–5040 (tel. toll free 800/243-3174), offers illness and accident coverage, costing from $10 to $35 for 6 to 10 days. For lost or damaged luggage, $500 worth of coverage costs $20 for 6 to 10 days. You can also get trip-cancellation insurance for $5.50 per $100.

Mutual of Omaha (Tele-Trip), 3201 Farnam St., Omaha, NB 68131 (tel. 402/345-2400, or toll free 800/228-9792), charges $3 per day (with a 10-day minimum) for foreign medical coverage up to $50,000 that features global assistance and maintains a 24-hour hotline. The company also offers trip-cancellation insurance, lost- or stolen-luggage coverage, standard accident coverage, and other policies.

HealthCare Abroad (MEDEX), 243 Church St. NW, Suite 100D, Vienna, VA 22180 (tel. 703/255-9800, or toll free 800/237-6615), offers a policy good for 10 to 90 days that costs $3 per day and includes accident and sickness coverage of $100,000. Medical evacuation is also included, along with a $25,000 accidental death or dismemberment compensation. Trip-cancellation and lost- or stolen-luggage options can be written into this policy at a nominal cost.

WorldCare Travel Assistance Association, 605 Market St., Suite 1300, San Francisco, CA 94105 (tel. 415/541-4991, or toll free 800/666-4993), features a 9- to 15-day policy that costs $105 and includes trip cancellation, lost- or stolen-luggage protection, legal assistance, and medical coverage and evacuation.

Access America, 6600 W. Broad St., Richmond, VA 23230 (tel. 804/285-3300 or toll free 800/424-3391), has a 24-hour hotline. Medical coverage for 9 to 15 days costs $49 for $10,000 of coverage. If you want medical plus trip cancellation, the charge is $89 for 9 to 15 days. A comprehensive package for $111 grants 9- to 15-day blanket coverage, including $50,000 worth of death benefits.

4. WHAT TO PACK

For most of the year, pack clothing that can be layered in case the weather turns cold at night. In the winter, a lined raincoat and a heavy sweater should keep you sufficiently warm. Since a large part of the old town retains its cobblestone streets, sensible walking shoes are recommended for sightseeing.

Most hotels have 220-volt electrical current, so bring along dual-voltage appliances or a converter as well as the European round-prong adaptor plugs.

Since the Spanish are very clothes conscious, you might want to bring one smart outfit for the theater or that special evening out.

5. TIPS FOR THE DISABLED, SENIORS, SINGLES, FAMILIES & STUDENTS

FOR THE DISABLED Before you go, there are many agencies that can provide advance planning information. For example, contact **Travel Information Service,** Moss Rehabilitation Hospital, 12th Street and Tabor Road, Philadelphia, PA 19141 (tel. 215/456-9900). It charges $5 per package for its data, which contains names and addresses of accessible hotels, restaurants, and attractions. Often these reports are based on firsthand experiences.

You may also want to subscribe to *The Itinerary,* P.O. Box 2012, Bayonne, NJ 07002-2012 (tel. 201/858-3400), for $200 per year. This bimonthly travel magazine is filled with news about travel aids for the disabled, special tours, information on accessibility, and other matters.

It's a good idea to obtain a free copy of "Air Transportation of Handicapped Persons," published by the U.S. Department of Transportation. Write to Free Advisory Circular, No. AC12032, Distribution Unit, U.S. Department of Transportation, Publications Division, M-4332, Washington, DC 20590.

Also, you may want to consider joining a tour for disabled visitors. Names and addresses of such tour operators can be obtained by writing to the **Society for the Advancement of Travel for the Handicapped,** 347 Fifth Ave., New York, NY 10016 (tel. 212/447-7284). Yearly membership dues are $40, or $25 for senior citizens and students. Send a self-addressed stamped envelope.

The **Federation of the Handicapped,** 211 W. 14th St., New York, NY 10011 (tel. 212/206-4200), also operates summer tours for members who pay a yearly fee of $4.

For the blind, the best information source is the **American Foundation for the Blind,** 15 W. 16th St., New York, NY 10011 (tel. toll free 800/232-5463).

FOR SENIORS   Many senior discounts are available, but note that some require membership in a particular association.

For information before you go, send $1 to receive "Travel Tips for Senior Citizens," No. 8970, Superintendent of Documents, U.S. Government Printing Office, Washington, DC 20402 (tel. 202/783-5238). A free booklet called "101 Trips for the Mature Traveler" is available from Grand Circle Travel, 347 Congress St., Suite 3A, Boston, MA 02210 (tel. 617/350-7500, or toll free 800/221-2610).

SAGA International Holidays runs all-inclusive tours for seniors, with insurance included in the net price. Contact SAGA International Holidays, 120 Boylston St., Boston, MA 02116 (tel. toll free 800/343-0273). Membership is $5 per year.

In the United States, the best organization to join is the **American Association of Retired Persons (AARP),** 1909 K St. NW, Washington, DC 20049 (tel. 202/872-4700), which offers member discounts on car rentals, hotels, and airfares. AARP travel arrangements, featuring senior-citizen discounts, are handled by American Express. Call toll free 800/927-0111 for land arrangements or 800/745-4567 for cruises. Flights to and from various destinations are handled by both numbers.

Information is also available from the **National Council of Senior Citizens,** 1331 F St. NW, Washington, DC 20004 (tel. 202/347-8800), which charges $12 per person or $16 per couple. As a member, you receive a monthly newsletter, part of which is devoted to travel tips. Discounts on hotel and auto rentals are available.

Elderhostel, 75 Federal St., Boston, MA 02110 (tel. 617/426-7788), offers an array of university-based summer educational programs for senior citizens throughout the world. Most courses last around three weeks and are remarkable values, considering that airfare, accommodations in student dormitories or modest inns, all meals, and tuition are included. The ungraded courses include field trips, involve no homework, and emphasize liberal arts.

Participants must be over 60, but each may take an under-60 companion. Meals consist of the solid, no-frills fare that's typical of educational institutions worldwide. The program provides a safe and congenial environment for older single women, who make up about 67% of the enrollment.

FOR SINGLES   The unfortunate news for single travelers (some 85 million of them Americans) is that the travel industry is far more geared to duos, so singles often wind up paying the penalty. It makes sense to travel with someone, and one company that helps resolve this problem is **Travel Companion Exchange,** which matches single travelers with like-minded companions. Headed by Jens Jurgen, the company charges between $36 and $66 for a six-month listing in well-publicized records. People seeking travel companions fill out forms stating their preferences and needs and receive a minilisting of potential travel partners. Companions of the same or the opposite sex can be requested. For an application and more information, contact Jens Jurgen, Travel Companion Exchange, P.O. Box 833, Amityville, NY 11701 (tel. 516/454-0880).

Singleworld, 401 Theodore Fremd Ave., Rye, NY 10580 (tel. 914/967-3334, or toll free 800/223-6490), is a travel agency that operates tours for solo travelers. Some, but not all, are for people under 35. Annual dues are $25.

FOR FAMILIES Those traveling with very small children should consult their family doctors and take along such basics as children's aspirin, a thermometer, and Band-Aids.

Airlines do offer special children's meals, but these must be requested at least 24 hours in advance. If your child is still on baby food, bring your own and ask that it be warmed. To make young children more comfortable take along a "security blanket" such as a pacifier or a favorite toy; for older children, a favorite item of clothing or game might do the trick.

If you need cribs, bottle warmers, car seats, or other specific items, be sure to make advance arrangements. If your hotel does not stock baby food (call ahead and check), take some along and buy an additional supply locally.

Before you go, establish strict guidelines regarding bedtime, eating, being in the sun, and other potential problem areas so that children know what is expected of them.

Babysitters can be arranged at most hotels; try to get one with a basic knowledge of English.

Family Travel Times, a newsletter about traveling with children, costs $35 for 10 issues and is available from TWYCH (Travel With Your Children), 80 Eighth Ave., New York, NY 10011 (tel. 212/206-0688). You can also call them with specific questions, Monday through Friday, 10am to noon Eastern standard time.

FOR STUDENTS The largest travel service for students is the **Council on International Educational Exchange (CIEE),** 205 E. 42nd St., New York, NY 10017 (tel. 212/661-1414), which provides details about budget travel, study abroad, working permits, and insurance. It also sells a number of helpful publications, including the *Student Travel Catalog* for $1, and issues to bona-fide students International Student Identity Cards for $10.

For real budget travelers it's worth joining the **International Youth Hostel Federation (IYHF).** For information write to American Youth Hostels (AYH), P.O. Box 37613, Washington, DC 20013-7613 (tel. 202/783-6161). Annual membership costs $25, $10 for those under 18.

Students traveling to Barcelona should be sure to have an **International Student Identity Card** (see above) with them to benefit from discounts offered on travel, lodging, and admission prices.

The **"Youth Card"** issued by the Generalitat of Catalonia makes it easy and cheap for young people to get the most out of their stay. The "Youth Card" guide lists almost 8,000 establishments offering special discounts. For information contact Direcció General de Joventut, Generalitat de Catalunya, Viladomat, 319, 08029 Barcelona (tel. 3/322-90-61), which is open Monday to Friday from 9am to 2pm and from 3 to 7pm.

The following establishments also offer special services and discounts to young travelers: the **Youth Travel Office** (Oficina de Turisme Juvenil—TIVE), Gravina, 1, 08001 Barcelona (tel. 3/302-06-82), open Monday to Friday from 9am to 1pm and from 4 to 5:30pm; and **Information Service and Youth Activities (SIPAJ)**, Rble. Catalunya, 5-Pral., 08007 Barcelona (tel. 3/301-40-46), open Monday to Friday from 5 to 9pm.

6. GETTING THERE

BY PLANE

Because airfares change constantly and special fares can materialize overnight, be persistent. Keep calling the airlines or your travel agent to secure the best possible fare—sometimes you can purchase a discounted ticket at the last minute if a flight is not completely booked. Those averse to such last-minute arrangements should know that fares vary with the season and that special excursion fares are often available. Summer and Easter Week are the peak, and thus the priciest, times to travel to Barcelona. The lowest fares are offered in winter (November through March, excluding Christmas).

THE MAJOR AIRLINES Iberia Airlines (tel. toll free 800/SPAIN-IB), the national carrier of Spain, offers the largest number of flights to Barcelona from Los Angeles, Miami, and New York. Iberia also links Barcelona with many European cities, including Amsterdam, Athens, Brussels, Frankfurt, Geneva, Istanbul, Lisbon, London, Marseilles, Milan, Paris, Stockholm, Vienna, and Zurich.

Iberia has ticket offices on the Plaça de Espanya (tel. 325-73-58); at Mallorca 277 (tel. 215-76-36); in the Hotel Princesa Sofía, Plaça Pius XII 4 (tel. 411-10-85); at Passeig de Gràcia, 30 (tel. 401-33-82); and at El Prat Airport (tel. 370-10-11). For general flight information call **Infoiberia** at 301-39-93; for domestic reservations, call 301-68-00; for international reservations, call 302-76-56.

TWA (tel. toll free 800/892-4141) has direct service to Barcelona via Madrid at comparable full and excursion fares.

Delta Airlines (tel. toll free 800/241-4141) flies daily from Atlanta to Barcelona via Madrid.

Air Europa (tel. 212/888-7010) runs charter flights to Palma de Majorca out of New York, with fares ranging from $700 to $850. For information and reservations contact one of the following: Spanish Heritage Tours, 116–47 Queens Blvd., Forest Hills, NY 11375 (tel. 718/544-2752, or toll free 800/221-2580); or their representative, Club de Vacaciones, 775 Park Ave., Huntington, NY 11743 (tel. 516/424-9600).

From Madrid, Iberia offers frequent, daily shuttle service to Barcelona via the **Puente Aéreo** (literally, "air bridge") as well as frequent nonshuttle flights.

REGULAR AIRFARES Advance-purchase fares, also

known as excursion or APEX fares, are offered by every airline. Restrictions always apply: You have to purchase the ticket at least 14 to 30 days before departure and stay for a certain number of days, usually no fewer than 7 and no more than 21.

Airfares change with amazing rapidity, so always shop around.

Standard, no-strings-attached tickets are sold at **economy, business,** and **first-class fares.** The first is the lowest full-fare ticket and will get you a no-frills seat with the traveling masses. A business-class ticket costs a bit more and gets you some extra leg room, better food, and free bar service. First-class means that you'll travel in style—with tablecloths and several-course meals, more room than in business class, and, depending on the airline, such amenities as toiletry kits and slippers. At this writing, Iberia's round-trip economy, business, and first-class fares between New York and Barcelona were $1,720, $2,822, and $4,788, respectively. Two special Iberia packages are "Barcelona Stop," offering a free 24-hour stopover en route to any other city in Europe, Africa, or the Middle East; and "High Class Weekend," offering business- and first-class travelers a free weekend in Barcelona. Both packages include accommodations, some meals, and entertainment.

Iberia's 60-day "Visit Spain Airpass" is available throughout the year. Purchased in conjunction with a transatlantic ticket, it permits travel to over four cities within the country, including the Balearic Islands, for $249 to $299, depending on the time of year. For an additional $50 you can add the Canary Islands to your list of options.

OTHER GOOD-VALUE CHOICES Bucket Shops Major scheduled airlines regularly make a portion—up to 40%—of their transatlantic seats available to consolidators. They in turn distribute the tickets to the public through discount travel agencies, known as bucket shops, at reductions of about 20% to 30%.

The resulting sharply reduced fares are now the least expensive means of traveling to Barcelona, lower in most instances than charter-flight fares. However, the tickets are restrictive, valid only for a particular date or flight, nontransferable, and nonrefundable except directly from the bucket shop.

Ads for bucket shops are small, usually a single column in width and a few lines long, and most often appear in the Sunday travel sections of major newspapers. Note that while prices for flights available through bucket shops are low, at times they may be eclipsed by special offers from the major airlines.

Leading retail bucket shops selling air transportation to Barcelona include **Access International, Inc.,** 101 W. 31st St., Suite 1104, New York, NY 10107 (tel. 212/465-0707, or toll free 800/825-3633); **Sunline Express Holidays, Inc.,** 607 Market St., 4th Floor, San Francisco, CA 94105 (tel. 415/541-7800, or toll free 800/877-2111); and **Euro-Asia, Inc.,** 4203 E. Indian School Rd., Suite 210, Phoenix, AZ 85018 (tel. 601/955-2742, or toll free 800/525-3876).

Charters The second-cheapest way to get to Barcelona is on a charter flight. Although the ranks of charter airlines have been depleted by competition from the bucket shops and fiercely competitive commercial airline fares, there are still some charter flights to choose from. **Air Europa,** 136 E. 57 St., Suite 1602, New York, NY 10022 (tel. 212/888-7010), is a Spanish charter airline that offers service from New York to Palma de Majorca.

The official U.S. student travel organization, the **Council on International Educational Exchange (Council Charters)**, 205 E. 42nd St., New York, NY 10017 (tel. 212/661-0311, or toll free 800/800-8222), offers charter departures from New York to Barcelona. For detailed information, request the organization's *Student Travel Catalog* for $1.

Like most forms of budget travel, charter offerings come and go. Check the Sunday travel section of any large city newspaper for the latest opportunities. Another comprehensive source of information on charters is *Jax Fax,* the monthly magazine of the air chartering industry. Look through the latest copy in your travel agent's office.

Before booking your charter flight, check the restrictions carefully. You may be asked to purchase a tour package, pay far in advance, change your day of departure or even your destination, pay a service charge, or fly on an airline with which you are not familiar (not typically the case). Finally, you may have to pay harsh penalties if *you* cancel, but you will have to be understanding if the charter company fails to live up to *its* obligation because the charter does not fill up and the flight is canceled anytime up to 10 days before departure. Summer charters fill up more quickly than those at other times of the year and are almost sure to fly.

Standbys   Flying standby is another inexpensive way to get to Barcelona. Many airlines offer standby service from April through November, but eliminate it in the winter. When you call for fare information, ask about standby status. There's always the chance that you won't get on the flight, but if you are at all flexible and have somewhere to stay while waiting for the next flight out, it's an economical way to go.

Going as a Courier   A traveler willing to take on the role of courier stands to save a lot of money in getting to Barcelona. The

---

 FROMMER'S SMART TRAVELER: AIRFARES

1. Shop all the airlines that fly to your destination.
2. Always ask for the lowest fare, not just for a discount fare.
3. Keep calling the airline—the availability of cheap seats changes daily. Airline managers would rather sell a seat than have it fly empty. As your departure date nears, additional low-cost seats may become available.
4. Ask about frequent-flyer programs to gain bonus miles when you book a flight.
5. Check bucket shops for last-minute discount fares that are even cheaper than their advertised slashed fares.
6. Ask about air/land packages. Land arrangements are often cheaper when booked with an air ticket.
7. Check standby fares.
8. Fly free or at a hefty discount as a courier.
9. Look for special promotions offered by major carriers, especially those flying new routes and thus struggling to gain a foothold in the market.

courier company handles the check-in and pickup of packages at each airport, and all you have to do is give up your checked-baggage allowance and make do with carry-on luggage. Expect to meet a courier-service representative at the airport before departure to get the manifest of the checked items; upon arrival, you deliver the baggage-claim tag to a waiting courier agent. The system not only benefits travelers but also works well for companies transporting time-sensitive materials, such as film, blood, or documents for banks and insurance firms.

One drawback (besides the luggage restriction) is that you have to travel alone, since only one person can take advantage of a courier option on any given flight. If there are two of you, try to arrange your departures on consecutive days.

To find a courier service, look in the telephone book *Yellow Pages* or in ads in the travel section of your local newspaper. You may call and arrange your departure as early as a couple of months in advance. You can also contact **Now Voyager Freelance Courier,** 74 Varick St., Suite 307, New York, NY 10013 (tel. 212/431-1616); or **Halbart Express,** 147–05 176th St., Jamaica, NY 11434 (tel. 718/656-8189).

Most flights depart from New York, so you may have to tack on the additional cost to get to the gateway city. Prices change all the time but generally range from low to very low. If a company needs emergency courier service and you can fly immediately, you could even travel for free or next to nothing—say, $50 round trip.

Foreign destinations are booked round trip for specific dates. On occasion, the return flights have no courier delivery on the day of departure, so checked-baggage space is available.

BY TRAIN

For information on national and international train service, call the **Red Nacional de Ferrocarriles Españoles** (R.E.N.F.E.) (tel. 3/490-02-02).

BY SHIP

For general information on ferries and cruises to and from Barcelona, contact **Estació Marítima de Balears,** Moll de Barcelona (tel. 3/317-42-62); **Estació Marítima Internacional,** Moll de Sant Bertrán (tel. 3/301-25-98); or **Compañía Trasmediterránea,** Moll de Barcelona (tel. 3/317-63-11). The last offers service between the Balearic Islands, Barcelona, and Valencia as well as service among the islands themselves. One-way fares to the islands from these cities, varying with the caliber of your seat or cabin, run from 5,500 to 15,000 ptas. ($55 to $150) in high season. Service is curtailed in winter. You can also take along a car for an additional charge.

PACKAGE TOURS

At this writing **Marsans Travel,** 19 W. 34th St., Suite 3302, New York, NY 10001 (tel. 212/239-3880, or toll free 800/777-9110; fax 212/239-4129), offers two-night packages to Barcelona, Ibiza, and Majorca for $115 to $409 (land only, double occupancy). Various package tours to Barcelona and the Balearic Islands also are offered by **Spanish Heritage Tours,** 116–47 Queens Blvd., Forest Hills, NY 11375 (tel. 718/544-2752, or toll free 800/221-2580); **Calvalcade Tours,** 450 Harmon Meadow Blvd., P.O. Box 1568, Secaucus, NJ 07096-1568 (tel. 201/617-8922, or toll free 800/356-2405); and **Isram Travel,** 630 Third Ave., 4th Floor, New York, NY 10017 (tel. 212/661-1193, or toll free 800/223-7460).

CHAPTER 3

GETTING TO KNOW BARCELONA

Because Barcelona is a compact city with a tight core of Old World sights, visitors will soon get their bearings here. The grid-pattern streets of the newer Eixample and a public transport system that is efficient and easy to negotiate further streamline getting acquainted with this city that, above all, invites leisurely exploration on foot.

1. ORIENTATION

ARRIVING

BY PLANE **El Prat Airport** (tel. 3/301-39-93 for general airport information) is 7.5 miles (12km) from the city. A **train** runs between the airport and the Estació Sants every 30 minutes daily between 6am and 11pm. The trip takes about 15 minutes and costs 325 ptas. ($3.25). The convenient, comfortable **aerobus** also runs between the airport and the Plaça Catalunya every 15 minutes from Monday to Friday between 5:30am and 11pm and every 30 minutes on Saturday, Sunday, and holidays from 6am to 10:45pm. The trip takes about 15 minutes and costs 400 ptas. ($4).

With the airport and luggage supplements, a **taxi** into town should run between 1,800 and 2,500 ptas. ($18 and $25).

The bank at El Prat Airport is open daily from 7am to 10pm.

BY TRAIN Most national and international trains arrive at **Estació Sants, Estació França,** or the **Passeig de Gràcia** or **Plaça Catalunya** stations—all centrally located and linked to the municipal metro network.

BY BUS National buses arrive at the **National Terminal,** Estació d'Autobuses Nord-Vilanova. International buses arrive at the **International Terminal,** Estació d'Autobuses Sants, next to the train station Estació Sants.

BY CAR By car you'll arrive via A-7, A-18, or B-10 from the north; via A-17, B-20, or A-19 from the east; or via A-16 or A-2 from the west.

TOURIST INFORMATION

For 24-hour information on what's happening in Barcelona, dial 010.
At the Palau de la Virreina, La Rambla, 99, you'll find a video monitor with detailed information in English about cultural activities, festivals, and much more. It's open Monday to Friday from 9am to 8pm and on Saturday from 10am to 4pm; summer weekend hours are Saturday from 10am to 2pm and from 4 to 8pm and Sunday from 10am to 2pm.

Travessara de Gràcia
Londres
Avinguda
Travessara de Gràcia
Diagonal
Av. de Sant Antoni Maria Claret
Carrer de Còrsega
Carrer de la Industria
Carrer de Rosselló
Carrer de Roger de Flor
Carrer de Provença
Mallorca
Carrer de Mallorca
Pl. de la Sagrada Familia
Carrer de València
Avinguda
Carrer de Muntaner
Carrer d'Aribau
Carrer de Balmes
Ramble de Catalunya
Passeig de Gràcia
Carrer de Pau Claris
Carrer d'Aragó
Diagonal
Carrer del
Consell
de Cent
Carrer de R. Llúcia
Carrer de Girona
Carrer de Bailén
Passeig de Sant Joan
Carrer de Nàpols
Carrer de Sicília
Carrer de Sardenya
Carrer de la Diputació
Carrer de Bruc
Gran via de les Corts Catalanes
Pl. de Tetuan
Carrer de Carles I
Antoni
Carrer de Pelai
Ronda Universitat
Pl. Catalunya
Pl. Urquinaona
Carrer de Casp
Carrer d'Ausias Marc
Passeig de Carles I
del Carme
Ramble
Av. Portal de l'Angel
Ronda de Sant Pere
Carrer d'Ali Bei
Carrer de Ribes
Hospital
Avinguda de la Catedral
Via Laietana
Passeig de Lluís Companys
Pau
BARRI GÒTIC
La Ramble
Carrer de Ferran
Carrer de la Princesa
Passeig de Comerç
Passeig de Pujades
Ramble
Carrer de
Passeig de Picasso
Parc de la Ciutadella
Carrer de Wellington
Carrer Ample
Passeig de Colom
Plaça Portal de la Pau
Estació Barcelons Terme-França
Avinguda d'Icàvia

Church **✝**
Post Office **⊠**
Information **⊖**

The following tourist offices offer basic maps, materials, and timely information on exhibitions and other cultural events: **Estació Sants,** Plaça Països Catalans s/n (tel. 93/410-25-94), open daily from 8am to 8pm; **Ajuntament de Barcelona,** Plaça Sant Jaume, open June 24 to September 30, Monday to Friday from 9am to 8pm and on Saturday from 8:30am to 2:30pm; **Estació de França,** Av. Marqués de L'Argentera, s/n (no number), open daily from 8am to 8pm; the **Centre de Informació,** Palau de la Virreina, La Rambla, 99, open June 24 to September 30, Monday to Friday from 9:30am to 9pm and on Saturday from 10am to 2pm; the **airport information office,** open Monday to Saturday from 9:30am to 8pm and on Sunday and holidays from 9:30am to 3pm; and for information on Barcelona, Catalonia, and the rest of Spain, the **Oficina de Informació Turística,** Gran Via de les Corts Catalanes, 658 (tel. 301-74-43), open Monday to Friday from 9am to 7pm and on Saturday from 9am to 2pm. If you want to phone for information, this last office is your best bet. Or call for tourist information at 490-91-91. For information on cultural activities and museums, call 301-12-21.

CITY LAYOUT

MAIN ARTERIES & STREETS   Although at first glance Barcelona seems every bit an immense metropolis, you'll find that it soon will become a very manageable city that's easily negotiated on foot and via public transportation. Given the city's traffic congestion and paucity of parking space, a car can be an encumbrance.

Barcelona grew around a medieval core, and the constant juxtaposition of its well-preserved past and highly progressive present gives the city a distinctive character that's at once provincial of aspect and cosmopolitan of manner. Between the **harbor** and the ordered grid of the 19th-century Eixample lies the **Ciutat Vella** (old town). Bordered by the **Parc de la Ciutadella** to the northeast and the fortress-topped hill of **Montjuïc** to the southwest, its focal point is the **Barri Gòtic,** the majestic heirloom bequeathed to the city by its medieval prominence.

At the edge of the Barri Gòtic, **La Rambla** bisects the old town. Although five street names designate the different sections that stretch from the Columbus Monument to the Plaça Catalunya, it is really a single, tree-lined boulevard that is one of the city's best-known attractions.

At the port end of La Rambla is the notorious **Barri Xines,** Barcelona's seedy, seaport version of New York's Times Square. Even though the term technically refers to the dowdy, narrow streets west of La Rambla between the harbor and Carrer de l'Hospital, the hookers, sex shows, and drug deals that won it notoriety also abound on the other side of La Rambla. During the day the seediness can be atmospheric, but it's best avoided at night.

Below the Parc de la Ciutadella and east of the harbor is **Barceloneta,** home to many of the city's fishermen and dock workers.

To the north of Plaça Catalunya is the **Eixample,** a grid of wide streets that provide contrast with the density of the old town. Bordered by two arteries that lead out of the city—**Gran Via de les Corts Catalanes** and **Avinguda Diagonal**—it is the product of Barcelona's 19th-century industrialization and concomitant prosperity. Running through it are the parallel thoroughfares **Passeig de Gràcia** and **Rambla de Catalunya,** both teeming with shops, bars, cinemas, art galleries, hotels, restaurants, and bookstores. Perhaps more than other area of the city, the Eixample is divided between business (many offices and corporate headquarters are located here) and pleasure.

North of the Eixample is **Gràcia,** an area of small squares and lively bars that was once a separate village but has now bonded onto Barcelona proper.

FINDING AN ADDRESS In Spain, street numbers *follow* street names and the ° sign indicates the floor. *Dcha.* or *izqda.* following the floor means "right" or "left," respectively. *Baja* refers to the ground floor, and the Spaniard's first floor (1°) is the American's second.

Some Catalan words for street names are different from those in Spanish. Thus you may find a knowledge of the following terms useful when reading maps and street signs in Barcelona (the Spanish word, if different, is in parentheses).

avinguda *(avenida)*	avenue
carrer *(calle)*	street
carretera	road, route
passatge *(pasaje)*	passage, alley
passeig *(paseo)*	boulevard, promenade
plaça *(plaza)*	plaza, square
ronda	outer road, ring road
travessera *(travesía)*	short cross street
via *(vía)*	road, route

STREET MAPS A good map of Barcelona that you may want to purchase before you leave home is "Walks Through Barcelona," available from **VLE Limited,** P.O. Box 547, Tenafly, NJ 07670 (tel. 201/567-5536), or at select bookstores and travel agencies. In Barcelona, pick up the "Barcelona Turística" map published by Pamias and available in most bookstores.

NEIGHBORHOODS IN BRIEF

From the foot of La Rambla to the tip of Mount Tibidabo, Barcelona is a pastiche of distinctive neighborhoods, each with its own unique place in history and prevailing architectural vernacular.

La Rambla The Brechtian parade of humanity that crowds La Rambla is Spain's *paseo* tradition carried to seedy and sublime extremes. Weaving among the kiosks packed with flowers, newspapers, and parakeets and the series of banks, hotels, cinemas, theaters, cafés, bars, and restaurants is a constant stream of passersby that draws the usual contingent of buskers as well as scores of nimble-fingered pickpockets, purse- and chain-snatchers, and other assorted criminal elements. From time to time impromptu markets blossom at the harbor end, which tends to be the diciest section of the street. Recent efforts to gentrify La Rambla and recapture its former cachet are showing definite signs of success, however. Some top hotels are now situated here, the pedestrian area has been enlarged, and most store fronts have undergone a much-needed facelift. As the tenor of this boulevard improves, the incidence of street crime should diminish.

When viewed from the cable car that crosses the port, La Rambla cuts a green swath through what appears to be a dense urban jungle. At ground level, the various lavish mansions of the surrounding streets confirm that this was once the city's poshest address.

Barri Gòtic [Barrio Gótico] Bordered by La Rambla to the west, Passeig de Colom to the south, Via Laietana to the east, and the Ronda de Sant Pere to the north, this quarter is the repository of Barcelona's Roman past and medieval glory days when the city dominated the Mediterranean waters. For some 500 years the Catalan monarchy ruled from this quarter. The historic epicenter is the **Plaça del Rei.** Among other noted landmarks are the **Catedral** and the adjacent Romanesque **Iglesia de Santa Llúcia.** Cobblestone streets, fountains that once served a purpose beyond mere adornment, and buildings so solid that they survived even the devastation of the Civil War complete this slice of history.

As the seat of Catalonia's regional and Barcelona's municipal government, the quarter is as lively as ever. In the summer, music students often fill its narrow streets with the strains of Bach and Mozart. And as you sample the barrio's numerous antique shops, bookstores, eccentric museums, and vest-pocket restaurants, you can easily imagine Columbus striding around the corner full of tales of his recent New World travels: It was here, in the Salón del Tinell, that he delivered his first reports to Queen Isabella.

Barri de la Ribera Adjacent to the Barri Gòtic and stretching east to the Passeig de Picasso, La Ribera was the urban focal point of the great maritime and commercial expansion of the 13th and 14th centuries. After its founding and through the Renaissance years, numerous mansions sprang up along the Carrer Montcada. Two of them—Palau Aguilar and Palau Castellet—now house Barcelona's most-visited museum, the **Museu Picasso.** A new crop of restaurants, bars, and trendy hangouts points to the growing popularity of this long-ignored barrio.

Puerto and Barceloneta Although Barcelona owes its very existence to its port, for centuries the city turned its back on the sea and the unattractive structures of the waterfront. Now, in the same spirit of rehabilitation that spawned New York's South Street Seaport and San Francisco's Ghirardelli Square, the waterfront has been reclaimed, with seaside promenades replacing the largely obsolete cargo piers. A sign of the times is the Moll de la Fusta, a pier with bars, restaurants, and outdoor terraces that offer passersby assorted refreshments with a sea view.

La Barceloneta, born in the 18th century, is a V-shaped area wedged between the port and the sea, with a long stretch of beach along its eastern end. Originally the enclave of sailors and fishermen, the waterfront here now largely caters to citizens and tourists out for some sun, a romp in the waves, or a stroll along the beach. If you walk in a few blocks, though, you'll still find Barcelona's seafaring class going about business as usual.

The Eixample (Ensanche) This area straddles the Passeig de Gràcia north of the Plaça Catalunya and takes its name from the urban expansion plan carried out after the old, binding city walls were torn down in 1860. Comprising a practical grid of perpendicular streets, it was conceived as a bourgeois barrio, its growth coinciding with the evolution of art nouveau (known locally as *modernisme*). Home to Gaudí's **Sagrada Familia** and **Casa Batlló y Mila,** Domenech i Montaner's **Casa Lleó Morera** and **Hospital de Sant Pau,** and Puig i Cadafalch's **Casa Amatller** and **"Les Punxes,"** it is a veritable essay in the Catalan interpretation of that artistic and architectural movement. You'll spot modernism's highly decorative flourishes everywhere, executed in glass, wood, wrought iron, and ceramics.

Montjuic First developed for the 1929 World's Fair and recently remodeled for the 1992 Summer Olympic Games, this sizable hill overlooking the harbor area is one of Barcelona's favorite

IMPRESSIONS

*. . . although the great adventures that befell me there
occasioned me no great pleasure, but rather much grief, I bore
them the better for having seen the city [Barcelona].*
—DON QUIXOTE

urban rest-and-recreation areas. Dedicated to both commercial and leisure activities, it houses convention halls; sports complexes; parks; gardens; an amusement park; museums; and the Poble Espanyol, a village featuring the arts, crafts, and architectural styles of Spain as well as a rich array of daytime and nightlife activities.

Mount Tibidabo This mountain peak to the north of the city is the culmination of the Sierra de Collserola. Below its 1,600-foot (500m) zenith unfolds an urban panorama. Getting there on public transportation is half the fun; a fine restaurant and an amusement park complete the experience.

2. GETTING AROUND

For **general information on public transportation,** call 412-00-00 Monday to Friday from 7:30am to 8:30pm and on Saturday from 8am to 2pm.

BY PUBLIC TRANSPORTATION

DISCOUNT PASSES Two ten-trip cards will save you money. The **Tarjeta T-1,** costing 550 ptas. ($5.50), is valid for the bus, metro, *tramvía blau (tranvía azul),* and Ferrocarrils de la Generalitat (FF.CC.). The **Tarjeta T-2,** costing 500 ptas. ($5), is valid on the metro and FF.CC. Maps of the system are available at most stations.

From the last week in June to the middle of September you can take advantage of the **Bus Turístic.** A single ticket permits unlimited travel on this bus, the tramvía blau, the Montjuïc cable car, and the Tibidabo funicular. This bus makes a sweep of the entire city, passing along La Rambla and Passeig de Gràcia, by the Sagrada Familia, along the Avinguda del Tibidabo and Avinguda Diagonal, by the Estació Sants, through the Parc de Montjuïc, along the Passeig de Colom, and to Pla de Palau. It makes 15 stops along its two-hour route, and you can get on and off as you please and go around as many times as you like. Service is every 20 minutes daily between 9am and 7:30pm. An all-day ticket costs 1,100 ptas. ($11) for adults and 600 ptas. ($6) for children 4 to 12; a half-day ticket, valid after 2pm, costs 600 ptas. ($6) for adults and 400 ptas. ($4) for children ages 4–12. Discounts at various sights around town are also offered in conjunction with the ticket, which can be purchased on the bus.

BY METRO The four metro lines operate on Monday to Thursday from 5am to 11pm; on Friday, Saturday, and holiday eves from 5am to 1am; and on Sunday and holidays from 6am to midnight. The one-way fare is 100 ptas. ($1) on Monday to Friday and 125 ptas. ($1.25) on Saturday, Sunday, holidays, and evenings after 8pm.

BY BUS Buses generally run daily from 6:30am to 10pm, with night buses ("Nitbus") running along the main thoroughfares between 10pm and 4am. The buses are color coded, making it easy for even the first-time visitor to negotiate the network: Red buses originate or pass through the heart of the city; yellow buses cut across the city beyond the central districts; green buses serve the city periphery; and yellow buses ply the night routes and originate or pass through the Plaça Catalunya. The fare is 100 ptas. ($1) on Monday to Friday and 125 ptas. ($1.25) on Saturday, Sunday, and holidays.

The **TOMBBUS** runs a convenient, circular route accessing the city's most important shopping and entertainment districts. Operating between Plaça Catalunya and Plaça Maria Cristina, it seats 18 and comes along about every five minutes on Monday to Friday between 8:45am and 9:20pm and on Saturday between 9:30am and 10pm. The fare is 175 ptas. ($1.75).

BY FERROCARRILS DE LA GENERALITAT These two intracity commuter lines operate Monday to Saturday from 6am to 11pm. The fare is 100 ptas. ($1).

BY TELEFÉRICO, TRAMVÍA BLAU & FUNICULAR The **Transbordador Aéreo del Puerto,** also known as the **Montjuïc Teleferic** (tel. 441-48-20), runs between Barceloneta and Montjuïc, with an intermediate stop on the Moll de Barcelona near the Columbus Monument. These are the hours of operation: October through March on Monday to Friday from noon to 5:45pm and on Saturday, Sunday, and holidays from 11:45am to 7pm; April through June 22 on Monday to Friday from noon to 7pm and on Saturday, Sunday, and holidays from noon to 8pm; June 23 through September 17 on Monday to Friday from noon to 7:30pm and on Saturday, Sunday, and holidays from noon to 8:30pm; September 18 to September 30 on Monday to Friday from noon to 6:45pm and on Saturday, Sunday, and holidays from noon to 7:15pm. Round-trip fares are 675 and 775 ptas. ($6.75 and $7.75), depending on how far you go. Since the Montjuïc stop is far from any sights, take this primarily for the splendid view of the city or perhaps to picnic in the park near the Montjuïc terminus.

The **Montjuïc funicular,** which connects with metro Line 3 at Paral.lel, operates in winter on Saturday, Sunday, and holidays from 11am to 8:15pm and in summer daily from 11am to 10pm. The one-way fare is 175 ptas. ($1.75); the round trip is 300 ptas. ($3). The cable car linking the upper end of the Montjuïc funicular with the hilltop castle operates September through June on Saturday, Sunday, and holidays from 11am to 2:45pm and from 4 to 7:30pm. During the Christmas season it runs daily during those same hours. From June through September it runs daily from 11:30am to 9pm. The one-way fare is 275 ptas. ($2.75).

The **tramvía blau** (blue tram) runs from Passeig de St. Gervasi/Avinguda Tibidabo to the lower end of the Tibidabo funicular. It operates every 30 minutes on Monday to Saturday from 7am to 10pm

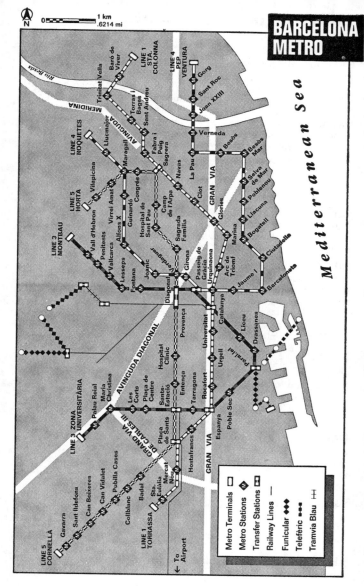

and every 15 minutes on Sunday and holidays from 7:05am to 10:25pm. The fare is 150 ptas. ($1.50).

Continuing where the tramvía blau ends, the **Tibidabo funicular** runs to the top of Mount Tibidabo, 1,600 feet (500m) above sea level. Its hours of operation are every 30 minutes daily from 7:15am to half an hour after the closing of the Tibidabo amusement park. The one-way fare is 250 ptas. ($2.50); the round-trip fare is 450 ptas. ($4.50).

BY TAXI

The standard Barcelona taxi is black and yellow. When available, it displays a "Libre" sign in its window and/or illuminates a green light on its roof. The initial charge is 275 ptas. ($2.75); each additional kilometer is 80 ptas. (80¢). Supplemental charges include 325 ptas. ($3.25) to and from the airport, 100 ptas. ($1) when departing from a train station, and 110 ptas. ($1.10) for each bag. The ride in from the airport should run between 1,800 and 2,500 ptas. ($18 and $25).

You can call for a cab by dialing any of the following numbers: 357-77-55, 358-11-11, 392-22-22, 490-22-22, 433-10-20, 300-38-11, or 263-22-62.

BY CAR

Considering the traffic congestion and the scarcity of parking in Barcelona, I don't recommend driving in the city. Those wanting to travel into the environs, however, might wish to rent a car for an excursion.

RENTALS The following car-rental agencies have in-town and airport offices: **Atesa,** Balmes, 141 (tel. 237-81-40, or 302-28-32 at the airport); **Avis,** Casanova, 209 (tel. 209-95-33, or 379-40-26 at the airport); **Europcar,** Consell de Cent, 363 (tel. 317-58-76, or 379-90-51 at the airport); and **Hertz,** Estació Sants (tel. 490-86-62, or 241-13-81 at the airport).

As an example of **rental rates,** Avis daily rentals at this writing begin at 5,000 ptas. ($50) per day for seven days with unlimited mileage. Add to this a VAT (value-added tax) of 13% and other extras and the bill mounts quickly. Rates change frequently, though, so shop around for the best deal at the moment and don't overlook the local companies. Their brochures can be found in most hotels. If you wish to rent a car with a driver, contact **AutosDriver,** Mallorca, 196 (tel. 253-33-35).

PARKING Parking on inner-city streets is regulated by "blue zones," which require parking tickets purchased locally from ticket machines or the nearest *estanco* (tobacconist). Parking in these areas is limited to an hour and a half and costs up to 250 ptas. ($2.50) per hour. Ample parking in garages is available throughout the city.

DRIVING RULES In Spain motorists drive on the right. Otherwise, the usual rules apply.

BY BICYCLE

Although I advise against riding a bicycle in Barcelona, you can rent one on weekends and holidays at **Bicitram,** Av. Marquéès de l'Argentera, 15 (tel. 792-28-41).

 BARCELONA

Airports See "Orientation" earlier in this chapter.
American Express The local office in Barcelona is at Passeig de Gràcia, 101 (tel. 217-00-70; Metro: Diagonal).

Area Code The telephone area code is **3** when calling internationally but **93** when calling from within Spain.

Babysitters Babysitters are known as *canguros*. Check at your hotel for a reliable sitter or the name of an agency offering babysitting services. Always ask for references and for a sitter who has at least a superficial knowledge of English.

Bookstores The Llibreria Bosch, Ronda Universitat, 11 (tel. 317-53-58), has English-language novels and books about Barcelona. So does the Llibreria Catalonia (a.k.a. Casa del Libro), Ronda de Sant Pere, 3 (tel. 318-91-83), which is open on Monday to Saturday from 10am to 1:30pm and from 4:15 to 8pm. Both are good places to pick up maps of the city, and the rest of the country.

Business Hours Banking hours are generally Monday to Friday from 8:30am to 2pm. If you need to change money on Sunday or a holiday, you can do so at the following locations: Barcelona Estació Sants (tel. 410-39-15), open daily from 8am to 8:30pm (except December 25 and 26 and January 1 and 6); and El Prat Airport (tel. 370-40-05), open daily from 7am to 10pm.

Office hours vary widely, but the norm is Monday to Friday from 9am to 1:30pm and from 4 to 7pm. Some offices have special summer hours from 8am to 3pm.

Shop hours also vary widely, with the norm being daily from 10am to 1:30pm and from 5 to 8pm.

Car Rentals See "Getting Around" earlier in this chapter.

Climate See "When to Go—Climate, Holidays & Events" in Chapter 2.

Currency See "Information, Entry Requirements & Money" in Chapter 2.

Currency Exchange Money can be changed at any bank advertising *"Cambio";* a commission is always charged, which makes cashing small amounts of traveler's checks expensive. When banks are closed (see "Business Hours" above), you can change money at the Estació Sants daily from 8am to 8:30pm (except December 25 and 26 and January 1 and 6). You can change money at the airport daily from 7am to 10pm. If you're really stuck, there are Chequepoint offices at La Rambla, 5, 64, and 130 where you can change money daily from 9am to midnight, although they might charge a hefty commission and/or offer an exchange rate lower than the prevailing rate offered at banks.

Dentists Check with the American consulate for recommendations (see "Embassies/Consulates" below).

Doctors Call 212-85-85 for a doctor or 417-19-94 for a nurse. Or call 061.

Documents See "Information, Entry Requirements & Money" in Chapter 2.

Driving Rules See "Getting Around" earlier in this chapter.

Drugstores When they close, all pharmacies are required to post a notice indicating the nearest pharmacy that is open. For the list of pharmacies open during off-hours on any given day, check *La Vanguardia,* the daily newspaper.

Electricity In most cases, the local electricity is 220–230 volts; however, some hotels have 110–120-volt lines. Although Spain is increasingly standardizing on 220–230 volts, it is advisable to bring along a converter or dual-voltage appliances and adaptor plugs (most outlets accept only round-prong plugs).

Embassies/Consulates The U.S. Consulate is at Passeig Reina Elisenda, 23 (tel. 319-95-50); the Canadian Consulate is at Via Augusta, 125 (tel. 209-06-34); the Consulate of the United Kingdom is at Avinguda Diagonal, 477 (tel. 419-90-44); and the Australian Consulate is at Gran Via Carles III, 98 (tel. 330-94-96).

Emergencies In a medical emergency, call 061. For the police, call 091 or 092. In the event of fire, call 080.

Etiquette It is considered rude to stretch in public in Spain, although allowances are made for foreigners who forget. It is also generally considered rude not to greet people with a "hello" (*hola* or *buenos días*) and to leave them without a "goodbye" (*adiós*). This is true when you enter a shop or merely run into people in the halls of your hotel or hostel. It is also customary to say *adiós* when leaving a bar or restaurant or exiting an elevator.

Eyeglasses There are many opticians around town, so ask at your hotel for the nearest one.

Hairdresser/Barber Women can go to Llongueras in El Cortes Inglés (tel. 302-12-12) on Monday to Saturday from 10am to 9pm; a hair cut and blow dry costs about 6,500 ptas. ($65). Men can go to Toni Galera in El Corte Inglés (same phone and hours); a cut costs about 3,500 ptas. ($35).

Holidays See "When to Go—Climate, Holidays & Events" in Chapter 2.

Hospitals If you require hospital attention, go to Hospital Clínic, Casanova, 143 (tel. 323-14-14); or Hospital de la Cruz Roja, Dos de Maig, 301 (tel. 433-15-51).

Hotline For all consumer complaints and problems call toll free 900/30-03-03 for assistance in English, French, or German.

Information See "Information, Entry Requirements & Money" in Chapter 2.

Language Catalan is the indigenous language of Barcelona and Catalonia and is the second official language of the region. As street, highway, and all other signs increasingly appear either solely in Catalan or in both Catalan and Spanish, you may get confused if your map or other orientation materials are not recent. Throughout this guidebook, as in the city itself, the Catalan term is used primarily; however, at times, street names, important sights, and key terminology appear in Catalan with the Spanish or English indicated in parentheses. Subsequent mentions may be in Catalan or Spanish, depending on the prevailing usage. (Also see the key to Catalan addresses in the "Orientation" section earlier in this chapter.) A good phrasebook to look for locally is the *Conversation Guide YALE* published by Editorial Cantabrica, S.A. A good Catalan-English dictionary is the *Diccionari Català-Inglès* published by Arimany.

Laundry/Dry Cleaning Lavandería/Tintorería Molas, Moles, 8 (tel. 301-20-92), near the Plaça Catalunya, offers both laundry and dry-cleaning services on Monday to Friday from 9am to 2pm and from 4:30 to 8pm and on Saturday from 9am to 2pm. Up to seven kilos of laundry can be washed and dried for about 1,200 ptas. ($12). Autoservicio Lavandería Roca, Raurich, 20 (tel. 231-82-94), in the Barri Gòtic, offers self-service facilities on Monday to Saturday from 8am to 7pm (closed on Saturday in July and August).

Liquor Laws The legal drinking age in Spain is 16.

Lost Property If you've lost something, call 318-95-31 on Monday to Friday from 9:30am to 1:30pm.

Luggage Storage/Lockers You can leave luggage at the

Estació França, Estació Sants, Estació Marítima Internacional, Estació Marítima de Baleares, and R.E.N.F.E. (Passeig de Gràcia).

Mail   Postcards and letters to the United States and Canada cost 90 ptas. (90¢); those to Europe cost 50 ptas. (50¢). You can receive General Delivery mail addressed to you care of "*Lista de Correos*," Barcelona, but you must show your passport to pick it up.

Maps   See "Orientation" earlier in this chapter.

Money   See "Information, Entry Requirements & Money" in Chapter 2.

Newspapers/Magazines   *La Vanguardia* and *El Periódico* are Barcelona's leading daily newspapers. *El País* is the nation's leading paper and offers a Barcelona edition. Most newsstands—and particularly those on La Rambla—sell the *Wall Street Journal*, *USA Today* (yesterday's, of course), *The Times* (of London), *The Daily Telegraph* (London), the *Financial Times* (London), and the *International Herald Tribune*.

Photographic Needs   Panorama, La Rambla, 125 (tel. 317-89-24), is open on Monday to Saturday from 9:30am to 8pm to satisfy most of your photographic needs, including processing. The following Panorama branches offer the same services and hours: Passeig de Gràcia, 4 (tel. 318-37-00) and Calvet 15 (tel. 202-03-30).

Police   Call 091 or 092. The police station at La Rambla, 43 (tel. 301-90-60) offers 24-hour service. You will also see small, roving trailers marked *Oficina de Denuncias* where you can seek assistance or report a crime.

Post Office   Post offices are generally open Monday to Friday from 9am to 2pm. The main post office at Via Laietana, 1 (tel. 302-75-63) is open on Monday to Friday from 8am to 10pm and on Saturday from 8am to 8pm.

Radio   All local radio stations broadcast in Spanish or Catalan. For contemporary music to make you feel at home, tune to Radio-80 Serie Oro (FM 90.5); for classical, traditional Spanish, and jazz, tune to FM 93.0 or 101.5.

Religious Services   Most of the churches in Barcelona are Roman Catholic. Masses are generally held between 7am and 2pm and between 7 and 9pm on Sunday and holidays and between 7 and 9pm on Saturday. This holds true for churches of historical and artistic interest as well. Mass in English is held at 10:30am on the first and third Sunday of the month at Paroisse Française, Anglí, 15 (tel. 204-49-62), and Anglican Mass in English is celebrated every Sunday at 11am and every Wednesday at 11:30am at Saint George Church, Sant Joan de la Salle, 41 (tel. 417-88-67).

Restrooms   There are public pay toilets on La Rambla and near the Sagrada Familia, but I'd suggest trying the nearest hotel or stopping at a bar or restaurant for a rest stop and a drink.

Safety   Whenever you're traveling in an unfamiliar city or country, stay alert. Be aware of your immediate surroundings. Wear a moneybelt and keep a close eye on your possessions. Be particularly careful with cameras, purses, and wallets, all favorite targets of thieves and pickpockets. These are some other helpful hints: Reject any offers of flowers or other objects—often the motive is stealing, not selling. Be on guard against surprise attacks—chain- and purse-snatchers seem to come out of nowhere. If you are part of a group touring by bus, make sure that the driver stays on board to guard any items left inside. Make photocopies of all your personal documents and leave the originals at your hotel.

Shoe Repairs   For a quick fix, go to Rápido López, Plazueleta de Montcada, 5, open Monday to Friday from 9am to 1pm and from 4:30 to 8pm and on Saturday from 9am to 1pm.

Taxes   The value-added tax (VAT) is known as IVA in Spain and runs from 6% on restaurant bills to 33% on luxury items. Recovery of the tax is possible for non-EC residents on single purchases costing over 82,200 ptas. ($822). There are two ways to recover the tax. If you are leaving from Barcelona's El Prat Airport, you can present the store's signed and stamped official bill—along with your passport and the article(s) purchased—for endorsement at Spanish Customs before check-in. The Customs official will return the duly signed blue copy of the bill to you. You then present it to the Banco Exterior de España offices inside the airport terminal, and they will refund the tax to you in the currency of your choice. The other possibility is to mail the blue copy of the bill endorsed by the Customs official to the store and wait for a check to be sent to your home within (one hopes) 60 days.

Taxis   See "Getting Around" earlier in this chapter.

Telephone/Telex/Fax   If you call long distance from your hotel or hostel, expect a hefty surcharge. Most public phone *"cabinas"* have clear instructions in English. Place at least 15 pesetas worth of coins in the rack at the top for a local call, and they will roll in as required.

To make an international call, dial 07, wait for the tone, and dial the area code(s) and number. Note, however, that an international call from a phone booth requires stacks and stacks of heavy 100-pta. coins. As an alternative, international calls can be made at Fontanella 4 on Monday to Saturday from 8:30am to 9pm. You can pay with a credit card, and there is one USA Direct phone that immediately connects you with an AT&T operator.

For collect and credit-card calls, AT&T (tel. toll free 800/874-4000, ext. 359) and MCI (tel. toll free 800/444-3333) have special access numbers that connect you directly with an operator in the United States from virtually any phone in Spain. Call them for full details.

You can send faxes and telexes at the main post office (see "Mail" above).

Television   There are several national channels in Spanish and several regional channels in Catalan. Since Spain recently sanctioned private TV, the offerings in Catalan, Spanish, and other languages are growing by the day.

Time   During most of the year, Barcelona is six hours ahead of the eastern United States. However, Spain switches to and from daylight saving time about a month before the United States, so during most of October and March the time difference is five hours and seven hours, respectively.

Tipping   Tipping is by no means obligatory, and large tips are not expected. A bellhop should get from 100 to 200 ptas. ($1 to $2), depending on the number of bags. Taxi drivers don't get surly if you don't tip them, but 5% to 10% is customary. Virtually all restaurants include a service charge in the bill, so 5% usually suffices. At bars and cafeterias, tipping from 10 to 100 ptas. (10¢ to $1), depending on the amount of the bill, is the norm. Contrary to Stateside practice, the percentage left as a tip decreases as the amount of the bill increases.

Transit Information For general information on public transportation, call 412-00-00 on Monday to Friday from 7:30am to 8:30pm and on Saturday from 8am to 2pm.

Useful Telephone Numbers Airport information (tel. 379-21-51 or 379-24-54); R.E.N.F.E. (Spanish railways) information (tel. 490-02-02).

Water The tap water in Barcelona is safe to drink.

3. NETWORKS & RESOURCES

FOR GAY MEN & LESBIANS Sextienda, Rauric, 11 (tel. 318-86-76), was the first gay shop in Spain and bills itself as the "gay information center." It offers a free map listing bars, discos, restaurants, saunas, and other places around town where gays and lesbians congregate. It's open Monday to Saturday from 10am to 8:30pm and closed on holidays and 10 days in October or November.

FOR WOMEN For all types of information about women's issues, contact the **Associación Catalana de la Dona,** Roger de Flor, 303 (tel. 459-03-98).

FOR SENIORS Senior citizens may find the **Associación Amics de la Gent Gran,** Grassot, 3 (tel. 207-67-73), a useful source of information.

FOR BUSINESS TRAVELERS As one of Spain's leading commercial and industrial cities, Barcelona is becoming an increasingly important destination for business travelers as well as for tourists. In convention and meeting facilities it ranks among the top 10 cities in Europe, and every month the city hosts several large-scale national and international trade fairs and numerous small-scale company meetings and conventions.

The **Barcelona Convention Bureau,** a department of the Patronato de Turismo, helps companies plan successful meetings and conventions. It can also help arrange meeting rooms and auditoriums, hotel rooms in and around the city, banquet facilities, professional services, transportation and excursions, inspection visits, and special programs for companions. For detailed information, contact the bureau at Passeig de Gràcia, 35, 08007 Barcelona (tel. 3/215-44-77; fax 3/215-42-76; telex 59327 PMTB E).

CHAPTER 4

BARCELONA ACCOMMODATIONS

1. EXPENSIVE
- FROMMER'S SMART TRAVELER: HOTELS
2. MODERATE
3. BUDGET

Spurred by the 1992 Summer Olympic Games, numerous Barcelona hotels and hostels have upgraded their facilities and accordingly raised their prices. Consequently, accommodations in the budget category are increasingly difficult to find.

In the past, the slow times for Barcelona's hotels were the winter months, July, and August, but that has changed drastically with the increase in business bookings. Nowadays hotel space is at a premium year round, so you had best make reservations well in advance.

With the exception of a handful of large luxury hotels, most of Barcelona's hostelries are small by American standards—both in the total number of rooms and in the size of the rooms themselves. Except in the luxury hotels, double beds are scarce. If you want one, ask for a *cama de matrimonio* (literally "marriage bed").

Spain's one- to five-star rating system is more a barometer of a hotel's physical dimensions and attributes than of its level of cleanliness or service. Typically, hotels of three stars or fewer don't have restaurants but may have cafeterias or snack bars. Hotels of two stars or fewer often offer breakfast only.

The bulk of Barcelona's hotels cluster along either side of La Rambla and the Passeig de Gràcia south of Avinguda Diagonal, with a few scattered in the city's northern and western reaches. Since this is a compact city, all of the hotels mentioned below are convenient to the major sights. Consequently, they are grouped according to price rather than geographic location. For the purposes of this guide, "expensive" hotels charge 24,000 ptas. ($240) and up for a double room; "moderate" hotels, 10,000 to 23,500 ptas. ($100 to $235); and "budget" lodgings, under 10,000 ($100). Rooms without a shower or bath will usually have at least a washbasin.

Note: Unless otherwise indicated, all accommodations have a private bath or shower and all rates given do not include breakfast or VAT (IVA in Spain).

1. EXPENSIVE

GRAN DERBY HOTEL, Loreto, 28, 08029 Barcelona. Tel. 3/322-20-15. Fax 3/410-08-62. Telex 97429 DEHO E. 40 rms and suites. A/C MINIBAR TV TEL **Metro:** Hospital Clinic.
$ Rates: 21,500 ptas. ($215) single suite or duplex; 24,500–31,000 ptas. ($245–$310) one- or two-bedroom duplex or suite. AE, DC, EURO, MC, V. **Parking:** Across the street at the Hotel Derby.

One of five Derby hotels in Barcelona, the Gran Derby has guest rooms that feature separate sitting areas and wet bars. Many also have their own terraces with views of the lovely interior garden. Most of the rooms are duplexes that are ideal for working businesspeople or those who like the feel of an apartment when they're on vacation. The housekeeping, as in all Derby properties, is impeccable, and the decor, although functional, is inviting and cheery. All in all, this is a solid choice for both business and leisure travelers.

For reservations, contact Marketing Ahead, 433 Fifth Ave., New York, NY 10016 (tel. 212/686-9213; fax 212/686-0271).

Dining/Entertainment: Breakfast is offered at the Hotel Derby across the street.

Services: Room service.

Facilities: Meeting and banquet facilities.

GRAN HOTEL HAVANA, Gran Via C.C., 647, 08010 Barcelona. Tel. 3/412-11-15. Fax 3/412-26-11. Telex 51531 ECBR-E. 145 rms and suites. AC MINIBAR TV TEL **Metro:** Urquinaona.

$ Rates: 26,000 ptas. ($260) single; 30,000–36,000 ptas. ($300–$360) double; 41,000–62,000 ptas. ($410–$620) suite. AE, DC, EURO, MC, V. **Parking:** On premises.

A design statement, this hotel features up-to-the-minute furnishings; gleaming marble baths; and the full complement of amenities, including bathrobes. The hollow atrium center is topped by a glass cupola, and the halls have a slightly nautical feel that will make you think you're on a luxury liner. The guest rooms are on the smallish side, though; they are soundproof and have cassette players with radios. Note the 19th-century clock and the facade, both original to the Casa L. Fradera built here in 1872.

Services: 24-hour room service, turn-down service.

Facilities: Meeting and banquet facilities.

HOTEL ALEXANDRA, Carrer de Mallorca, 251, 08008 Barcelona. Tel. 3/487-05-05. Fax 3/216-06-06. Telex 81107 ALXDR E. 75 rms. A/C MINIBAR TV TEL **Metro:** Passeig de Gràcia.

$ Rates: 19,500 ptas. ($195) single; 24,000 ptas. ($240) double. AE, DC, EURO, MC, V. **Parking:** On premises.

This small hotel, affiliated with the Best Western reservation system, is at once upscale and low key. The vintage facade, torn down and faithfully reconstructed stone by numbered stone, houses a completely modern interior. The sleek lobby and the mezzanine bar, minimalist in their stark lack of paintings and other decorative items, feature sporadic flourishes of art deco. The hotel's design is the work of Joan Pera, an architect of the Gaudí school. The soundproof double rooms are sizable and stylishly appointed. Rooms that face the courtyard have oversize double beds; rooms that face the street have twin beds.

Dining/Entertainment: The breakfast buffet amounts to a first-rate brunch, complete with cava and crema catalana, eggs, sausages, and pastries. At lunch and dinner, the restaurant offers meals prepared with market-fresh ingredients. On Monday to Friday from 7 to 10pm there's live music in the mezzanine bar.

Services: Room service, turn-down service.

Facilities: Meeting and banquet facilities.

HOTEL CLARIS, Pau Claris, 150, 08009 Barcelona.
Tel. 3/487-62-62. Fax 3/487-87-36. Telex 97429 DEHO. 124 rms and suites. A/C MINIBAR TV TEL **Metro:** Passeig de Gràcia.

$ Rates: 19,000–22,000 ptas. ($190–$220) single; 28,000 ptas. ($280) double; 33,000–65,000 ptas. ($330–$650) suite. AE, DC, EURO, MC, V. **Parking:** On premises.

One of Barcelona's newest hotels, the Claris (a Derby hotel) has many marks of distinction that set it apart from its five-star peers. First, it boasts a series of duplex suites adorned with 5th-century Indian art and 18th-century English furnishings; second, it contains a museum exhibiting the collection of ancient Egyptian and pre-Columbian art amassed by Jordi Clos, General Director and owner of the Derby hotels chain; third, there's a roof-top pool; fourth, effective soundproofing ensures optimum silence in the rooms; and fifth, the Claris's interior design features cascading water, glass-encased elevators, and an abundance of daylight penetrating into the hotel's very core. The hotel occupies the 19th-century Palacio Vedruna, whose original facade remains intact. Within all is of the most timely design. Quality materials and design are evident throughout—from the front desk to the marble baths. The guest rooms are spacious, and virtually no two are alike. Two suites feature saunas and Jacuzzis.

For reservations, contact Marketing Ahead, 433 Fifth Ave., New York, NY 10016 (tel. 212/686-9213; fax 212/686-0271).

Dining/Entertainment: The Restaurant Claris features Catalan cuisine; the Caviar Caspio serves only caviar, foie gras, salmon, and carpaccio. On summer evenings there is a roof-top, poolside barbecue.

Services: 24-hour room service, turn-down service.

Facilities: Roof-top pool, sauna, gymnasium, museum.

HOTEL CONDES DE BARCELONA, Passeig de Gràcia, 75, 08008 Barcelona. Tel. 3/487-3737. Fax 3/487-14-42. Telex 51531 ECBR-E. 109 rms and suites. A/C MINIBAR TV TEL **Metro:** Passeig de Gràcia.

$ Rates: 24,500 ptas. ($245) single; 30,000 ptas. ($300) double; 37,000–55,000 ptas. ($370–$550) suite. AE, DC, MC, V. **Parking:** On premises.

Art nouveau outside and mildly art deco inside, this four-star hotel with five-star sophistication and glamour had to ask permission from the real Conde (Count) de Barcelona, King Juan Carlos's father, to use his aristocratic moniker. Housed in the late 19th-century modernist mansion designed by architect Josep Vilaseca for the Batlló family, the hotel retains the original facade and an interior staircase with rose-colored wainscoting.

Each pastel-pretty guest room has a balcony, and street-side rooms have double-glazed windows. The rooms on the fifth floor have wooden floors; all others are carpeted. The premier Suite Barcelona changes its decor every year, except for the pricey silk area rug and the chandelier that architect José Juanpera commandeered from his mother's home. Juanpera also designed all the furniture in the hotel. Reproductions of Picasso, Dalí, and Sorolla are throughout.

Dining/Entertainment: In the lobby area, a small curved bar precedes the small, classically stylish Brasserie Condal, which features special regional dishes, and the Café Condal, where afternoon tea is served and some meals are accompanied by music.

Services: Room service, turn-down service.

Facilities: Access to fitness club one block away.

HOTEL RITZ, Gran Via de les Corts Catalanes, 668, 08010 Barcelona. Tel. 3/318-52-00, or toll-free through Leading Hotels of the World at 800/223-6800 in the U.S. and Canada. Fax 3/318-01-48. Telex 52739. 155 rms, 6 suites. A/C MINIBAR TV TEL **Metro:** Urquinaona.

$ **Rates:** 31,000–45,000 ptas. ($310–$450) single; 46,000–56,000 ptas. ($460–$560) double; 130,000–225,000 ptas. ($1,300–$2,250) suite. AE, DC, EURO, MC, V. **Parking:** On premises.

This has been Barcelona's classic grand hotel since it opened in 1919. A member of the Leading Hotels of the World, it attracts upper-echelon visitors from all walks of life. The public areas are outfitted with all the trappings of old-world elegance—hand-woven woolen rugs, brocaded curtains and upholstery, multicolored marble floors, and twinkling chandeliers.

The guest rooms are somewhat less sumptuous but still stylish and outfitted with all the modern conveniences. Nevertheless, the large baths, reproduction antique furnishings, decorative moldings, and floor-length windows connote another era. The deluxe doubles and suites feature Roman baths, sunken tiled areas, each with two steps leading down into it.

Dining/Entertainment: The back corner of the lobby lounge is devoted daily to high tea. Off the lobby, a winding staircase leads down to a cozy bar. The hotel's palatial Restaurant Diana serves an eclectic assortment of dishes and offers candlelight dinners accompanied by live piano music; it is open daily from 1:30 to 4pm and from 8:30 to 11pm.

Services: 24-hour room service, turn-down service.

Facilities: Meeting and banquet rooms.

HOTEL RIVOLI RAMBLAS, Rambla dels Estudis, 128, 08002 Barcelona. Tel. 3/302-66-43. Fax 3/317-50-53. Telex 99222 RIVO-E. 90 rms and suites. A/C MINIBAR TV TEL **Metro:** Liceu.

$ **Rates:** 20,000 ptas. ($200) single; 25,000–26,500 ptas. ($250–$265) double; 37,000–80,000 ptas. ($370–$800) suite. AE, DC, EURO, MC, V. **Parking:** None.

Located on La Rambla, this hotel dazzles the eye with its abundance of marble. Housed in an art deco building that has been totally modernized, its interior is elegantly uncluttered and boldly accented with splashes of vivid color.

The small but stylish soundproof guest rooms are sunny and bright and outfitted with marble-top tables and desks. The artwork throughout is Catalan contemporary. Rooms on the Rambla side are more expensive and have small balconies; rooms on the Ateneo side face a building that was painted with an abstract design expressly for the visual pleasure of hotel guests. Ask for a room on the seventh floor—it contains the fewest rooms, each boasting a large terrace with a view of the cathedral. The sixth-floor rooms also have spacious terraces. All suites have Minitel PCs, and the Suite Opera boasts antique furnishings, a megaterrace, and a bath with a view.

Dining/Entertainment: In the lobby is the Blue Moon piano cocktail bar. On the mezzanine level, another small bar adjoins Le Brut restaurant, where the menu is a mixture of Catalan and continental.

Services: 24-hour room service, turn-down service.

Facilities: Small fitness center with Jacuzzi, sauna, and tanning table; banquet and meeting rooms.

LE MERIDIEN BARCELONA, La Rambla, 111, 08002 Bar-

BARCELONA ACCOMMODATIONS

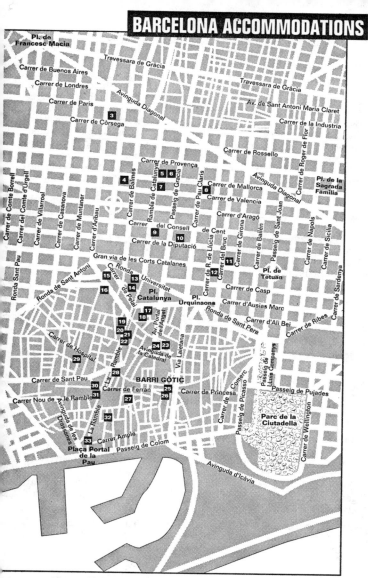

celona. Tel. 3/318-62-00. Fax 3/301-77-76. Telex 54634. 209 rms and suites. A/C MINIBAR TV TEL **Metro:** Liceu.

$ Rates: 27,000 ptas. ($270) single; 40,000 ptas. ($400) double; 45,000–220,000 ptas. ($450–$2,200) superior Club room or suite. AE, DC, EURO, MC, V. **Parking:** On premises.

Just off the upper end of La Rambla is a hostelry where Bruce Springsteen and Michael Jackson once slept. Behind the vintage facade awaits the epitome of modern comfort and luxury.

The guest rooms are decorated in pleasant pastels. Each features a real hairdryer (not one of those boxes mounted on the wall); a constant air-renewal system; a heated bathroom floor; sound insulation; and high-tech communication via radio, TV, video, and direct-dial telephone. For people who work in their rooms, the dimming desk lamps are nice touches. Popular among business travelers are the 28 Club executive rooms on floors 6 to 9, with their own reception area, bar, and restaurant. All sixth-floor rooms have large private terraces. The most sybaritic suite is no. 918 (its dual shower heads are a favorite with honeymooners). No-smoking rooms and special rooms for the disabled are available.

Dining/Entertainment: The lobby bar features live piano music nightly from 7 to 11pm. Adjacent to the bar is the airy (thanks to a skylight) El Patio restaurant, which serves an à la carte and buffet breakfast daily from 7 to 11am and is open for lunch daily from 1 to 4pm and for dinner daily from 8:30 to 11:30pm. The menu is French/Spanish.

Services: 24-hour room service; turn-down service; special Club amenities, including private check-in and check-out, terry-cloth bathrobes, and private elevator.

Facilities: Meeting rooms.

2. MODERATE

HOTEL ASTORIA, Paris, 203, 08036 Barcelona. Tel. 3/ 209-83-11. Fax 3/202-30-08. Telex 81129 ASTEL. 199 rms and suites. A/C MINIBAR TV TEL **Metro:** Diagonal.
$ Rates: 12,000–14,000 ptas. ($120–$140) single; 16,000 ptas. ($160) double; 19,000 ptas. ($190) suite. AE, DC, EURO, MC, V.
Parking: Nearby.

This is one of Barcelona's five Derby hotels, a chain that prides itself on offering fine accommodations at reasonable prices. While meant for businesspeople, their hotels are also ideal for vacationing visitors seeking maximum comfort, cleanliness, quiet, and a convenient location. The Astoria, like most of the others in the group, offers both singles and doubles plus duplex suites (some with terraces), with gardens and greenery wherever they can be inserted. Derby hotels also offer no-smoking rooms.

HOTEL BALMES, Mallorca, 216, 08008 Barcelona. Tel. 3/451-19-24. Fax 3/451-00-49. Telex 81129 ASTEL. 100 rms and suites. A/C MINIBAR TV TEL **Metro:** Diagonal.
$ Rates: 13,000–15,500 ptas. ($130–$155) single; 17,500 ptas. ($175) double; 22,000 ptas. ($220) suite. AE, DC, EURO, MC, V.
Parking: On premises.

Another Derby property with a number of duplex suites, this gem of a hotel is truly an insider's secret. In the back you'll find a lovely garden with a pool. Rooms 219, 220, and 221 have their own terraces. As with all Derby hotels, the service, design, and quality throughout offer great value for the money.

For reservations, contact Marketing Ahead, 433 Fifth Ave., New York, NY 10016 (tel. 212/686-9213; fax 212/686-0271).

FROMMER'S SMART TRAVELER: HOTELS

VALUE-CONSCIOUS TRAVELERS SHOULD NOTE THE FOLLOWING:

1. Accommodations without TV lounges, bars, and private bathrooms are cheaper.
2. Room rates are subject to negotiation depending on the season and current occupancy, so don't be afraid to bargain, especially in the moderate and budget hotels—but even in the high-priced ones.
3. Posted room rates are the maximum an establishment can charge for those rooms—often you'll find that the management charges less.

QUESTIONS TO ASK IF YOU'RE ON A BUDGET

1. Is hot water and a shower included in the price of the room?
2. Are the IVA tax and/or breakfast included in the rate?
3. Can I get a discount, especially in the off-season or for a long stay?

HOTEL COLÓN, Avinguda Catedral, 7, 08002 Barcelona. Tel. 3/301-14-04. Fax 3/317-29-15. Telex 52654 COLÓN E. 164 rms and suites. A/C TV TEL **Metro:** Jaume I.

$ Rates: 13,500 ptas. ($135) single; 21,000 ptas. ($210) double; 40,000 ptas. ($400) suite. AE, DC, EURO, MC, V. **Parking:** Nearby in public parking lot.

Occupying a privileged spot opposite the 13th-century Gothic cathedral, the Colón feels like an amiable country home in both its public areas and its cheery, high-ceilinged guest rooms. The sizes of the rooms vary widely, so if space is important to you, make sure you say so. The suites are especially warm and bright. Although the Colón is located in prime tourist country, numerous business travelers also opt for its special charm. The hotel's grill room offers a comprehensive continental menu.

For reservations, contact Marketing Ahead, 433 Fifth Ave., New York, NY 10016 (tel. 212/686-9213; fax 212/686-0271).

HOTEL DERBY, Loreto, 21–25, 08029 Barcelona. Tel. 3/322-32-15. Fax 3/410-08-62. Telex 97429 DEHO. 117 rms. A/C MINIBAR TV TEL **Metro:** Hospital Clinic.

$ Rates: 15,000–18,000 ptas. ($150–$180) single; 23,000 ptas. ($230) double. AE, DC, EURO, MC, V. **Parking:** On premises. Another Derby offering, this is the first hotel the group opened. In addition to the typically comfortable, clean guest rooms, it offers a coffee shop and a bar with piano music in the evening. This is the only Derby property without any duplex suites.

HOTEL DUCS [DUQUES] DE BERGARA, Bergara, 11, 08002 Barcelona. Tel. 3/301-51-51. Fax 3/317-34-42. Telex 81257 APHO-E. 56 rms and suites. A/C MINIBAR TV TEL **Metro:** Catalunya.

$ Rates: 15,500 ptas. ($150) single; 23,500 ptas. ($235) double; 40,000 ptas. ($400) suite. AE, DC, EURO, MC, V. **Parking:** Nearby.

✪ It is hard to beat this hotel for comfort and convenience. Located just off the Plaça Catalunya, it is intimate, tranquil, and wonderfully central. Its building is modernist, and the hotel's public areas are stylishly gracious. The interior guest rooms are larger and quieter; the fifth-floor rooms have terraces. The hotel cafeteria is open 24 hours, and room service is offered around the clock.

HOTEL GAUDÍ, Carrer Nou de la Rambla, 12, 08001 Barcelona. Tel. 3/317-90-32. Fax 3/412-26-36. Telex 98974 HOGA. 73 rms. TV TEL **Metro:** Liceu.

$ Rates (including breakfast): 9,000 ptas. ($90) single; 11,500 ptas. ($115) double; 15,500 ptas. ($155) triple. Bearers of this book are offered a 10% discount when paying cash and a 5% discount when paying with a credit card. AE, DC, EURO, MC, V. **Parking:** On premises.

Across from Gaudí's Palau Güell, this hotel features splendid views of Gaudí's eccentric roof from some of its streetside rooms. The guest rooms' white floors and light-wood furnishings make them bright and cheery; all those below the third floor have balconies, those from the third floor up have ample terraces. Fourth-, fifth-, and sixth-floor rooms are air-conditioned. Although this is a three-star property, it has a simple, pleasant restaurant offering primarily continental fare.

HOTEL GÒTICO, Carrer Jaume I, 14, 08002 Barcelona. Tel. 3/315-22-11. Fax 3/315-38-19. Telex 97206. 79 rms. A/C TV TEL **Metro:** Jaume I.

$ Rates: 10,000 ptas. ($100) single; 14,000 ptas. ($140) double. AE, DC, EURO, MC, V. **Parking:** Available nearby.

Located on one of the Barri Gòtic's main arteries, the Gòtico is a notch below the Suizo (see below) when it comes to charm and a notch above when it comes to noise. However, the hotel is still a solid choice in the heart of the medieval city.

HOTEL GRAVINA, Carrer Gravina, 12, 08001 Barcelona. Tel. 3/301-68-68. Fax 3/317-28-38. Telex 99370. 60 rms. A/C MINIBAR TV TEL **Metro:** Universitat.

$ Rates: 10,000 ptas. ($100) single; 14,900 ptas. ($149) double. AE, DC, EURO, MC, V. **Parking:** Public parking nearby.

Opened in 1988, this three-star hostelry is now being renovated. It's conveniently situated between the Plaça Catalunya and Plaça de la Universitat, with a classic exterior that houses a bright, modern interior. The guest rooms are small with sparkling marble baths and double-glazed windows on the street side.

HOTEL MESON CASTILLA, Carrer Valldoncella, 5, 08001 Barcelona. Tel. 3/318-21-82. Fax 3/412-40-20. Telegrams CASTILLOTEL. 56 rms. A/C TV TEL **Metro:** Universitat.

$ Rates (including breakfast): 7,000 ptas. ($70) single; 10,000 ptas. ($100) double; 14,000 ptas. ($140) triple. MC, V. **Parking:** On premises.

From the outside, this former apartment building near the Plaça Catalunya looks like a displaced Castillian structure except for its glitzy awning. Each floor features a pleasant sitting area, and the first floor has a large TV room with a beamed ceiling. The furnishings throughout are in the sturdy Castillian vernacular. Some of the guest rooms have large terraces. The buffet breakfast is more substantial than the usual croissants and coffee.

HOTEL MONTECARLO, La Rambla, 124, 08002 Barcelona. Tel. 3/317-58-00. Fax 3/317-57-50. Telex 93345 SRMS-E. 77 rms. A/C TV TEL **Metro:** Liceu.
$ Rates: 8,500 ptas. ($85) single; 12,000 ptas. ($120) double; 15,000 ptas. ($150) triple; 16,500 ptas. ($165) quad. AE, DC, MC, V. **Parking:** On premises.

Beyond the Montecarlo's Felliniesque portal—adorned with chandeliers and imposing statues—await simple, clean, and comfortable guest rooms. Those facing La Rambla have small balconies and double-glazed windows to absorb the noise. Currently the hotel is adding a gymnasium and garden.

HOTEL ORIENTE, La Rambla, 45–47, 08002 Barcelona. Tel. 3/302-25-58. Fax 3/412-38-19. Telegrams ORIENTHOTEL. 150 rms. TV TEL **Metro:** Liceu.
$ Rates: 7,800–10,000 ptas. ($78–$100) single; 12,000–15,000 ptas. ($120–$150) double; 16,800–20,000 ptas. ($168–$200) triple. AE, DC, EURO, MC, V. **Parking:** Public parking nearby.

This 150-year-old hotel is conveniently located, but you should request a room away from La Rambla for peace and quiet. The guest rooms are comfortable, though rather dimly lit, and the baths are modern. Unlike most three-star hotels, the Oriente has a restaurant, a vestige of the hotel's five-star days when La Rambla was Barcelona's most prestigious neighborhood. Both the restaurant and the large, somewhat palatial TV/sitting room retain the grandeur of those glory days.

HOTEL REGENCIA COLÓN, Carrer Sagristans, 13–17, 08002 Barcelona. Tel. 3/318-98-58. Fax 3/317-28-27. Telex 98175. 55 rms. A/C MINIBAR TV **Metro:** Urquinaona or Jaume I.
$ Rates (including breakfast): 9,500 ptas. ($95) single with shower, 11,000 ptas. ($110) single with bath; 16,800 ptas. ($168) double with bath; 22,500 ptas. ($225) triple with bath. AE, DC, MC, V. **Parking:** Nearby.

The Regencia Colón's proximity to the cathedral and its bright, cheerful, sound-insulated rooms make it a fine choice. Forty rooms have tubs, and the remainder have only showers. Related to the Hotel Colón (see above)—and virtually next door—the Regencia Colón is attractive to tour groups.

For reservations, contact Marketing Ahead, 433 Fifth Ave., New York, NY 10016 (tel. 212/686-9213; fax 212/686-0271).

HOTEL REGENTE, Rambla de Catalunya, 76, 08008 Barcelona. Tel. 3/215-25-70. Fax 3/487-32-27. Telex 51939. 78 rms. A/C MINIBAR TV **Metro:** Passeig de Gràcia.
$ Rates: 13,500–18,500 ptas. ($135–$185) single; 20,000–23,500 ptas. ($200–$235) double; 26,000–31,000 ptas. ($260–$310) triple. AE, DC, EURO, V. **Parking:** Nearby.

In a pleasant Eixample location, the Regente is a solid choice that's unusual because it offers a small swimming pool and sunbathing area on the roof. The inviting lobby has Tiffany touches and an etched-glass doorway leading to a charming bar. The guest rooms are compact and modern, with double beds available in singles only. If you don't mind a bit of noise, consider a room with a terrace.

HOTEL REGINA, Carrer Bergara, 2–4, 08002 Barcelona. Tel. 3/301-32-32. Fax 3/318-23-26. Telex 59380 HREG. 103 rms. A/C MINIBAR TV TEL **Metro:** Catalunya.

$ Rates: 10,500 ptas. ($150) single; 15,500 ptas. ($155) double. AE, EURO, MC, V. **Parking:** Public parking nearby.

Near the Plaça Catalunya, this Best Western affiliate is a very comfortable choice at a moderate price. Its guest rooms are quite large, although the baths are a bit small. Doubles on the street side have balconies; doubles in the back have small sitting areas.

HOTEL RIALTO, Carrer de Ferran, 40–42, 08002 Barcelona. Tel. 3/318-52-12. Fax 3/315-38-19. Telex 97206. 130 rms. A/C TV TEL **Metro:** Jaume I.

$ Rates: 10,000 ptas. ($100) single; 14,000 ptas. ($140) double. AE, DC, EURO, MC, V. **Parking:** Available nearby.

The Gargallo group of hotels offers three solid three-star choices in the Barri Gòtic (the Gótico, see above; this one; and the Suizo, see below). All feature distinctively Spanish furnishings in the guest rooms and attractive, comfortable public areas. The Rialto is the most spacious of the three. In fact, the rooms here are larger than those of most hotels in this category. Keep in mind, though, that the exterior rooms with balconies are noisier than the interior rooms.

HOTEL ROYAL, La Rambla, 117, 08002 Barcelona. Tel. 3/301-94-00, or 3/318-73-29 for reservations. Fax 3/317-31-79. Telex 97565 RYAL-E. 108 rms. A/C MINIBAR TV TEL **Metro:** Catalunya.

$ Rates: 14,000 ptas. ($140) single; 18,000–26,500 ptas. ($180–$265) double. AE, DC, EURO, MC, V. **Parking:** On premises.

At the lower end of the luxury scale in terms of price, this hotel offers a comfortable complement of amenities (such as room service, medical service, and turn-down service) in a modern setting at the upper end of La Rambla. The guest rooms are attractive and pleasant. The dining facilities include a bar, a cafeteria-pizzeria, and the El Racó restaurant with an open grill and a mixed menu of Catalan and international cuisine. Also, the Royal offers banquet and meeting rooms.

HOTEL SUIZO, Plaça del Angel, 12, 08002 Barcelona. Tel. 3/315-41-11. Fax 315-38-19. Telex 97206 HSUI. 48 rms. A/C MINIBAR TV TEL **Metro:** Jaume I.

$ Rates: 10,000 ptas. ($100) single; 14,000 ptas. ($140); double; 18,750 ptas. ($187.50) triple. AE, DC, EURO, MC, V. **Parking:** Available nearby.

This is my favorite of the Gargallo group. All its rooms feature new wood furnishings and have small balconies with sound-insulated sliding glass doors. The cafeteria-bar next to the reception area offers breakfast and tapas in a charming bistro atmosphere with a wooden bar, etched glass, brass fixtures, and marble-top tables.

3. BUDGET

HOSTAL MARITIMA, La Rambla, 4, 08001 Barcelona. Tel. 3/302-31-52. 16 rms (all with sink, 3 with shower). **Metro:** Drassanes.
$ Rates: 1,900 ptas. ($19) single; 3,000 ptas. ($30) double; 4,000 ptas. ($40) triple; 4,800 ptas. ($48) quad. No credit cards.

Ⓢ Exuberant Italian proprietor Vittorio Rosellini runs a clean, disciplined establishment on the lower Rambla near the Wax Museum. The high-ceilinged rooms are bare-bones basic but still somehow friendly. This is a favorite with young travelers. There are laundry facilities on the premises, and you can have a load done for 650 ptas. ($6.50). Note that the hostel is several flights up—there's no elevator.

HOSTAL-RESIDENCIA OLIVA, Passeig de Gràcia, 32, 4°, 08007 Barcelona. Tel. 3/488-01-62. 16 rms (10 with bath). **Metro:** Passeig de Gràcia.
$ Rates (including IVA): 2,400–3,500 ptas. ($24–$35) single with sink; 4,700–6,900 ptas. ($47–$69) double with sink, 6,000–8,300 ptas. ($60–$83) double with shower or full bath; 2,400 ptas. ($24) per person additional in triple or quad. 375 ptas. ($3.75) per shower or bath if room doesn't have one. No credit cards.

⭐Ⓢ Located in a beautiful, vintage Eixample building with a correspondingly beautiful, vintage elevator, the Oliva offers comely, high-ceilinged guest rooms with tile floors and lace curtains. Ten of the rooms have full baths; the remaining six have half baths. Though you could hardly find a more central spot to bed down than the Oliva, the feeling here is one of intimacy and tranquility. Those who enjoy small hostelries with lots of character will be very happy here.

HOTEL CATALUÑA, Carrer de Santa Anna, 24, 08002 Barcelona. Tel. 3/301-91-50. Fax 3/302-78-70. 40 rms. TEL **Metro:** Catalunya.
$ Rates (including breakfast and IVA): 4,700 ptas. ($47) single; 8,300 ptas. ($83) double. AE, DC, MC, V.
About a block east of the upper Rambla, this spotless budget choice offers complete baths in all the guest rooms (some with truncated tubs). Colorful rugs brighten the halls. The rooms are furnished simply, but everything is well maintained.

HOTEL CORTÉS, Carrer de Santa Anna, 25, 08002 Barcelona. Tel. 3/317-91-12. Fax 3/302-78-70. 54 rms. TEL **Metro:** Plaça Catalunya.
$ Rates (including breakfast and IVA): 5,400 ptas. ($54) single; 9,000 ptas. ($90) double. AE, DC, MC, V.
Just off La Rambla, the Cortés is popular with American students on youth tours. All the clean guest rooms have modern tile baths and are being renovated.

HOTEL COSMOS, Carrer dels Escudellers, 19, 08002 Bar-

celona. **Tel. 3/317-18-16.** Fax 3/412-50-39. 67 rms (25 with shower only). TEL **Metro:** Drassanes.

$ Rates: 3,200 ptas. ($32) single; 5,000 ptas. ($50) double; 6,800 ptas. ($68) triple. No credit cards.

Located near the lower end of La Rambla, the Cosmos offers no-frills budget digs amid undecorated halls. The white walls of the guest rooms themselves, however, do much to brighten the clean but rather cramped quarters.

HOTEL RESIDENCIA INTERNACIONAL, La Rambla, 78–80, 08002 Barcelona. Tel. 3/302-25-66. Fax 3/317-61-90. 60 rms. TEL **Metro:** Liceu.

$ Rates (including breakfast and IVA): 7,200 ptas. ($72) single; 9,500 ptas. ($95) double; 13,000 ptas. ($130) triple; 15,000 ptas. ($150) quad. Prices higher in Aug and during trade fairs, but bearers of this book get a 10% discount if they show it when checking in. AE, DC, MC, V.

The Internacional has harbored many Frommer's readers over the years. It offers a great location (across from the Liceu Theatre), cleanliness, and newly refurbished rooms that are bright and cheery (if a bit functional) and feature ample baths. The large, friendly breakfast room overlooks La Rambla, where in the summer the hotel runs an al fresco café.

HOTEL RESIDENCIA NEUTRAL, Rambla de Catalunya, 42, 08007 Barcelona. Tel. 3/487-63-90. 28 rms (25 with bath or shower). TEL **Metro:** Passeig de Gràcia.

$ Rates: 2,700 ptas. ($27) single with shower; 4,000 ptas. ($40) double with shower, 5,300 ptas. ($53) double with bath; 5,500 ptas. ($55) triple with shower, 7,000 ptas. ($70) triple with bath. No credit cards.

A budget choice in a luxury area, the Neutral has an entrance that's one flight up. Colorful antique floor tiling helps brighten the high-ceilinged guest rooms, which are furnished with assorted odds and ends. The guest rooms are small, but the breakfast room, with its impressive coffered ceiling, and the adjacent TV room are spacious.

HOTEL SAN AGUSTIN, Plaça Sant Agustí, 3 (at Carrer Hospital), 08001 Barcelona. Tel. 3/318-16-58. Fax 3/317-29-28. 77 rms. A/C TV TEL **Metro:** Liceu.

$ Rates (including breakfast): 5,600–6,000 ptas. ($56–$60) single; 8,300–8,900 ptas. ($83–$89) double; 10,000–10,500 ptas. ($100–$105) triple; 12,500–15,500 ptas. ($125–$155) quad; 17,500–18,300 ptas. ($175–$183) quintuple. AE, EURO, MC, V.

Close to La Rambla but at a quiet remove, this was once a convent and has been a hotel for over 100 years now. It sports a new, inviting entrance; gleaming-white walls; and rustic ceiling beams. Its large, commendable restaurant offers daily fixed-price lunch and dinner menus with a choice of appetizers, entrees, and desserts.

BARCELONA DINING

Catalan cuisine in all its diversity is the culinary highlight of Barcelona. Drawn from areas whose climates and topographies run from the alpine in the Pyrenees to the Mediterranean along the coast, the Catalan kitchen employs a wide variety of fresh ingredients and is complemented by a similarly wide variety of regional wines.

Cuisines from other areas of Spain, however, are also well represented in the city. And when it comes to foreign fare, Italian and French restaurants predominate, although there are a smattering of Middle Eastern and Asian offerings, as well as a few vegetarian restaurants. Cafeterias and snack bars typically offer extensive and varied menus and a selection of economical *platos combinados* composed of meat, a potato, a vegetable, and usually a fried egg.

Many of the more prestigious establishments around town have recently taken to charging a "cover" (*pan y cubierto*) of 100 ptas. ($1) or more for bread and, it seems, the sheer privilege of eating there—a regrettable practice that appears to be spreading throughout Spain's restaurants. Sometimes the menu lets you know whether this is the case, but sometimes it doesn't. Although restaurants are increasingly offering menus in English, this practice is not yet widespread. Those eateries most frequented by tourists, of course, have always provided English menus, while the city's luxury restaurants have polylingual waiters to do the translating for you.

For the purposes of this guide, entrees at an "expensive" restaurant can be as high as 5,000 ptas. ($50) or more; at a "moderate" restaurant, as high as 3,500 ptas. ($35) but usually a bit lower; and in a "budget" restaurant, as high as 2,500 ptas. ($25) but as low as 500 ptas. ($5). As with the hotels, service is usually included in the prices; however, VAT (IVA in Spain) is *not*. Many restaurants offer very economical fixed-price three-course lunches, including bread and house wine. At cafeterias, tapas bars, and other informal establishments, it often costs less to eat at the bar than at a table.

1. EXPENSIVE

BOTAFUMEIRO, Gran de Gràcia, 81. Tel. 218-42-30.
Cuisine: SEAFOOD. **Reservations:** Required. **Metro:** Fontana.

$ Prices: Appetizers 1,500–2,500 ptas. ($15–$25); main courses 3,500–7,500 ptas. ($35–$75); four-course tasting menu 5,300 ptas. ($53). AE, DC, EURO, MC, V.
Open: Tues–Sat 1pm–1am; Sun 1–4pm. **Closed:** Holy Week and Aug.

★ Botafumeiro, housed in a modernist building of the late 19th century, is truly a contender for best seafood restaurant in the land. Among its repeat clientele is the King of Spain. As you enter, you can appraise the fresh marine life, flown in primarily from Galicia in northern Spain. An appropriate nautical decor prevails, and patrons may eat at the long wooden bar (complete with tablecloth) if they wish. The lobsters, shrimp, mussels, and other assorted shellfish are usually served steamed, boiled, or grilled. Some of the fish, however, do come with their own delicate sauces, such as the mero al champagne (grouper in champagne) and the lubina à la sidra (sea bass in cider sauce). The menu is in half a dozen languages.

EL DORADO PETIT, Dolors Monserdá, 51. Tel. 204-51-53.
Cuisine: MEDITERRANEAN. **Reservations:** Required. **FF.CC.:** Sarrià.
$ Prices: Appetizers 975–3,700 ptas. ($9.75–$37); main courses 1,800–4,000 ptas. ($18–$40); six-course tasting menu 7,500 ptas. ($75). AE, EURO, MC, V.
Open: Lunch Mon–Sat 1–4pm; dinner Mon–Sat 9pm–midnight. **Closed:** Several weeks in Aug, Fri–Mon of Holy Week, and Christmas.

★ Perhaps the restaurant with the most inviting entranceway in all of Barcelona, El Dorado Petit is situated in the northern reaches of the city in a fin-de-siècle house that was once a summer retreat from the heat of the city. Owner Luis Cruañas characterizes the seasonal menu as Mediterranean since it is based on the finest and freshest ingredients the area has to offer. For starters, there's shrimp salad with champagne vinegar, remarkable for the tenderness and sweetness of the shrimp, brought in from Cruañas's home village on the Costa Brava. The menu is highly imaginative — with canelones de cigalas à la crema de russinyols (cannelloni stuffed with prawns and topped with a wild-mushroom sauce), ravioli stuffed with shrimp and Iranian caviar, and dishes built around baby squid and baby octopus. Also recommended is the San Pedro (a Mediterranean fish) baked with rosemary and served with a dry white-wine sauce. Hard to resist is the tantalizing selection of unique ice creams, sorbets, and pastries.

Cruaña's son now runs a New York outpost of El Dorado Petit at 47–49 West 55th Street (tel. 212/586-3434).

LA ODISEA, Carrer Copons, 7. Tel. 302-36-92.
Cuisine: MEDITERRANEAN. **Reservations:** Recommended. **Metro:** Urquinaona.
$ Prices: Appetizers 1,000–3,600 ptas. ($10–$36); main courses 1,500–3,600 ptas. ($15–$36). DC, V.
Open: Lunch Mon–Fri 1:30–4pm; dinner Mon–Sat 9pm–midnight. **Closed:** Holidays and Aug.

As its name suggests, La Odisea is an adventure. Chef Antonio Ferre Taratiel is also a part-time poet, and the restaurant's decor is sophisticatedly bohemian—the attractive contemporary art on the walls is the work of talented friends. At lunch, businesspeople abound; at dinner, there are numerous artists and writers.

A native of Aragón, Taratiel carefully studied Catalan cuisine to create a menu that he calls Mediterranean. Although the offerings vary, some standard dishes include crema de cangrejos (cream of crab), solomillo villetes con hortalizas al Calvados (steak filet with vegetables in a Calvados sauce), and hígado de pato con manzana (duck liver with apple). The extensive wine list includes a large selection of regional cavas (sparkling wines) and French champagnes, as well as numerous Rioja reds.

OROTAVA, Carrer de Consell de Cent, 335. Tel. 487-73-74.

Cuisine: SEAFOOD/GAME. **Reservations:** Required. **Metro:** Passeig de Gràcia.

$ Prices: Appetizers 375–3,000 ptas. ($3.75–$30); main courses 2,200–5,000 ptas. ($22–$50). AE, DC, MC, V.

Open: Lunch Mon–Sat 1–4pm; dinner, Mon–Sat 8pm–midnight.

This Eixample restaurant has character—both in the decor and in the ingratiating exuberance of its owner, José María Luna. The successful legacy of Luna's father, the restaurant features an opulent 19th-century–style decor laden with brocades and highlighted by several original Miró paintings dedicated to the restaurant and its honored owners. In the downstairs dining area several Picasso ceramics are on casual display.

Billing itself as "the small restaurant for the grand gourmet," Orotava has an ample menu concentrating on seafood and game. Standard dishes include partridge with wild mushrooms and venison in a delicate cream sauce, served with raspberry and apple marmalades. Luna is especially proud of his Cobonoff, a kind of seafood tartare he invented and calls "a symphony of seafood that is a guaranteed aphrodisiac." Blending seven kinds of fish, Cobonoff is topped with caviar and served with whole-wheat bread. Vieira al cava (scallops with a dash of sparkling cava wine) is another culinary trademark, as is baby octopus prepared with garlic and parsley, which was once served to Prince Juan Carlos before he became King of Spain. Guests are treated on Tuesday to a magic show during dinner and on Friday and Saturday to live piano music (no additional charge).

RESTAURANT PASSADÍS DEL PEP, Plaça del Palau, 2. Tel. 310-10-21.

Cuisine: SEAFOOD. **Reservations:** Required. **Metro:** Barceloneta.

$ Prices: Meals average 7,500 ptas. ($75) without wine. AE, DC, EURO, MC, V.

Open: Lunch Tues–Sat 1:30–3:30pm; dinner Mon–Sat 9–11pm. **Closed:** Holidays and 3 weeks in Aug.

No sign indicates the presence of this "insider's" restaurant at the end of a corridor leading off a large portal. Located in the port area, Passadís del Pep is small, with a decor devoid of pretentious frills. The lack of fanfare extends to the menu and the wine list as well—there are none. Both at lunch and at dinner you are simply presented with that day's offering of fine fresh fish and

seafood, and there is never a doubt that it will be superb. The selection of wines is ample and equally reliable.

RESTAURANT QUO VADIS, Carrer del Carme, 7. Tel. 302-40-72.

Cuisine: CATALAN/CONTINENTAL. **Reservations:** Recommended. **Metro:** Liceu.

$ Prices: Appetizers 1,000–2,500 ptas. ($10–$25); main courses 1,100–3,200 ptas. ($11–$32). AE, DC, EURO, MC, V.

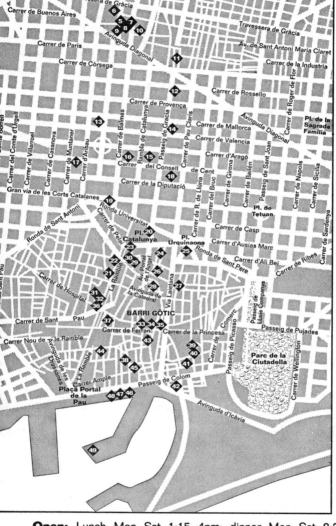

Open: Lunch Mon–Sat 1:15–4pm; dinner Mon–Sat 8:30–11:30pm. **Closed:** Aug.

Quo Vadis was founded 34 years ago by the father of the current owner, Marti Forcada. The understated elegance of the polished-wood bar and the dining areas lend the place the atmosphere of a men's club. A single flower on each table adds a grace note. Lone travelers will be interested to know that there are some tables for one.

Located near the Bouquería Market, Quo Vadis builds its meals around the day's prime produce. The menu is mainly Catalan, with some representative dishes from other parts of Spain—for example, cochinillo tostado (suckling pig)—and more universal fare such as grilled chateaubriand and chuletitas de cabrito lechal à la milanesa ("suckling lamb" chops). House specialties include potpourri de setas (wild mushrooms sautéed with garlic and parsley) that's usually available from September to January, filete de toro (yes, that's right, from the bull), and espaldita de cabrito asado (roasted lamb's back). Look for game in the fall.

RESTAURANTE RENO, Tuset, 27. Tel. 200-91-29.

Cuisine: CATALAN/FRENCH. **Reservations:** Required.
Metro: Diagonal. **FF.CC.:** Gràcia.
$ Prices: Appetizers 1,300–4,300 ptas. ($13–$43); main courses 2,500–4,500 ptas. ($25–$45); six-course fixed-price meal 8,000 ptas. ($80). AE, DC, EURO, MC, V.
Open: Lunch daily 1–5pm (kitchen closes at 4pm); dinner daily 8:30pm–1am (kitchen closes at 11:30pm).

One of Barcelona's top restaurants, Reno was founded in 1954 by Antonio Juliá Rafecas, father of the current proprietors. Its decor is fashionably contemporary, with lots of wood, plants, and black-leather benches and chairs. The china is Villeroy & Boch.

Chef-owner José Juliá Bertrán describes his cuisine as "rooted in Catalan but prepared in the French manner." Many of his dishes are a cross between the two cuisines or common Catalan recipes spruced up for a night on the town. Although he abhors categories, he places his menu between the classical and the nouvelle because he believes in sauces that are light and subtle. The seasonal menu changes four times a year. For an appetizer, try cold langostinos (prawns) from the Catalan region—they're succulent and sweet. As a main course, pick pimientos con salsa negra (red peppers in a delicate black sauce with a base of squid's ink), arroz con chipirones (a juicy rice dish with baby squid in a fish-broth–based sauce), or the distinctive solomillo (filet mignon) served with a sweet-and-sour sauce of honey and sherry vinegar. In summer, there's a green-bean salad topped with thinly sliced lobster and dressed with delicate olive oil that has been steeped with truffles for two weeks to give it a distinctively delicate flavor. The tartare de salmon is made of raw salmon with a pinch of smoked salmon (prepared in-house) and salmon roe. The extensive wine list embraces over 400 different vintners, with the emphasis on Catalan and French wines, in keeping with the cuisine. A squadron of attentive waiters virtually makes a ritual of the meal.

ROIG ROBI, Séneca, 20. Tel. 218-92-22.

Cuisine: CATALAN/FRENCH. **Reservations:** Required.
Metro: Diagonal.
$ Prices: Appetizers 950–2,300 ptas. ($9.50–$23); main courses 2,500–6,200 ($25–$62). AE, DC, MC, V.
Open: Lunch Mon–Fri 1:30–4pm; dinner Mon–Sat 9–11:30pm.
Closed: Holidays.

Tucked away on an afterthought of an alleyway north of Avinguda Diagonal, Roig Robi is a fine place to dine. Chef-owner Mercé Navarro draws from the Catalan and French kitchens—and even more so from her own imagination—to offer menus commensurate with the seasons.

A popular favorite is merluza al Roig Robi (hake prepared with a tomato sauce and topped with lightly fried zucchini strips). For an appetizer, try fideos rossos con almejas (thin noodles fried and cooked in savory fish broth and served dry with small clams). Another fine appetizer, a variation of the traditional Catalan esqueixada, is the salad of raw codfish and pasta. All the desserts are homemade.

2. MODERATE

BRASSERIE FLO RESTAURANTE, Carrer Junqueres, 10. Tel. 319-31-02.

Cuisine: FRENCH. **Reservations:** Recommended. **Metro:** Urquinaona.

$ Prices: Appetizers 525–3,000 ptas. ($5.25–$30); main courses 1,200–3,500 ptas. ($12–$35). AE, DC, EURO, MC, V.

Open: Lunch daily 1–4:30pm; dinner daily 8:30pm–1am.

Near the Palau de la Música and not far from the Catedral, a passage flanked by Spanish tiles and fresh seafood on ice leads to a bit of Paris at the Brasserie Flo. The wooden floor, plants, statues and busts, and vintage French posters and photos combine to create a bistro ambiance. The specialties here are duck pâté and choucroûte.

CAFÈ DE L'ACADEMIA, Carrer Lledó, 1 (Plaça Sant Just). Tel. 315-00-26.

Cuisine: CATALAN. **Reservations:** Strongly recommended. **Metro:** Jaume I.

FROMMER'S SMART TRAVELER: RESTAURANTS

1. The menu del día at lunch, which usually comprises a first course of vegetables or salad, a main course of meat or fish, and sometimes dessert and coffee but always bread and wine, is a good budget choice.
2. If a restaurant is filled with Spaniards, that usually means the food is authentic and tasty.
3. Try the money-saving tapas bars in the evening, where, if you choose carefully, you can enjoy a complete and balanced meal.
4. Standing up to eat or drink costs less than eating at a table. Many establishments have two prices: *mesa* (table) and *barra* (bar).
5. Some restaurant prices include VAT (IVA in Spain); some don't. If you're on a budget, check the menu carefully.
6. Be aware that the bread and butter and such extras as olives that appear as a matter of course will also most likely appear on your bill later.

$ Prices: Salads 575–1,800 ptas. ($5.75–$18); main courses 900–1,600 ptas. ($9–$16); menu del día 1,300 ptas. ($13). AE, EURO, V.

Open: Breakfast Mon–Fri 9am–1pm; lunch Mon–Fri 1:30–4pm; dinner Mon–Fri 9–11pm. **Closed:** Aug.

Off a quiet plaza in the Barri Gòtic, ensconced within Gothic walls of amber stone, L'Academia is very popular with the government officials who work nearby. Although the menu is exclusively in Catalan, it's well worth struggling with the language to savor the low-priced gourmet fare.

Empredat de fesolets amb tonyina (white-bean–and–tuna salad) and pollastre de pagès (a typical Catalan dish of roast chicken with prunes and pine nuts) are highly recommended. The luscious desserts are on tempting display. Since the place has only about a dozen tables, reservations are strongly recommended; however, unannounced patrons are happily accommodated with place settings at the bar.

LOS CARACOLES, Carrer dels Escudellers, 14. Tel. 302-31-85.

Cuisine: SPANISH. **Reservations:** Recommended. **Metro:** Drassanes.

$ Prices: Appetizers 650–2,500 ptas. ($6.50–$25); main courses 1,000–3,700 ptas. ($10–$37). AE, EURO, MC, V.

Open: Daily 1pm–midnight.

Los Caracoles is to Barcelona restaurants what La Rambla is to Barcelona sights—a must for the visitor. It is located just off the Rambla and full of the kind of character that comes only with time. Run by the same family since it was established in 1835 as a bodega selling snails (caracoles) and wine—the original barrels are part of the current decor—it evolved into a restaurant. Outside, you'll see chickens roasting over a wood fire; as you enter, you'll pass through the kitchen, where snails and mussels simmer in large pots. The snails and spit-roasted chicken are, of course, the house specialties. But there is much, much more, and it's all good. Among the patrons whose photos line the walls are John Wayne, President Nixon, Dalí, Christian Dior, and Cole Porter.

LA DENTELLIERE, Ample, 26. Tel. 319-68-21.

Cuisine: FRENCH. **Reservations:** Recommended. **Metro:** Barceloneta.

$ Prices: Appetizers 525–1,300 ptas. ($5.25–$13); main courses 650–1,700 ptas. ($6.50–$17); menu del día at lunch and dinner from 1,200–3,000 ptas. ($12–$30). EURO, MC, V.

Open: Lunch Tues–Sun 1–4pm; dinner Tues–Sat 8:30pm–midnight.

This is one of my favorite Barcelona restaurants because the ambiance is cozy, the food fabulous, and the value terrific. Beneath rustic wood-beamed ceilings are a dozen or so lace-draped tables. The confit de pato is a long-standing specialty always executed with tasty perfection. Other specialties include fondues and, among the scrumptious home-made desserts, the various crêpes.

DURÁN DURÁN, Alfonso XII, 39–41. Tel. 201-35-13.

Cuisine: CATALAN. **Reservations:** Recommended. **Metro:** Diagonal.

$ Prices: Appetizers 650–2,500 ptas. ($6.50–$25); main courses 1,300–3,000 ptas. ($13–$30). AE, EURO, MC, V.
Open: Lunch Mon–Fri 1–4pm; dinner, Mon–Sat 8:30–11:30pm.
Closed: Holidays and 2 weeks in Aug.

Slightly off the beaten track, Durán Durán is worth seeking out. Although the owner, Señor Durán, dislikes culinary labels, he characterizes his menu as Catalan-French (with some Italian overtones).

The house specialties are amanida de salmó fumat i poma (smoked-salmon–and–apple salad); timbal d'alberginies, panses, pinyons i crema de pebrot (a savory pastry with eggplant, raisins, pine nuts, and sweet-pepper sauce); homemade duck pâté; veal filet with duck-liver pâté; magret of duck with sweet-and-sour figs; and roast leg of lamb. Durán is especially proud of his botifarra dolça amb allioli de codonys (sweet Catalan sausage with quince allioli), a traditional Catalan dish rarely found in Barcelona. When this sausage is cooked, its sugar caramelizes, making for a crispy sweet entree. Durán Durán is also one of the few Barcelona restaurants to offer a selection of gourmet coffee and tea.

ESCOLA DE RESTAURACIO I HOSTALATGE BARCELONA, Carrer Muntaner, 70–72. Tel. 453-29-03.

Cuisine: CATALAN. **Reservations:** Recommended. **Metro:** Universitat or Hospital Clínic.
$ Prices: Appetizers 950–2,000 ptas. ($9.50–$20); main courses 1,500–2,500 ptas. ($15–$25). AE, V.
Open: Lunch Mon–Fri 1:30–3pm; dinner Mon–Fri 9–10:30pm.
Closed: Holidays and Aug.

A nonprofit organization that is a joint effort of the city's hotel and restaurant guilds, the Escola runs this friendly, modern, moderate-size restaurant as a training ground for the chefs, bartenders, waiters, and sommeliers of tomorrow. Here these professionals-to-be practice what they have already learned very well, carefully supervised by the professors. Behind the restaurant are the actual classrooms, where the students study their respective arts for three years.

The menu is seasonal: In summer it includes such dishes as sopa frappe de mar i muntanya (gazpacho enriched with seafood) and macedonia de mars sobre salsa d'eriço (a seafood medley over sea-urchin sauce); in winter and fall look for such game as venison, rabbit, and partridge; in spring there's the freshest of vegetables. Even the breads and desserts—including the ice cream—are made here.

FLASH-FLASH, La Granada del Penedés, 25. Tel. 237-09-90.

Cuisine: CATALAN. **Reservations:** Not required. **Metro:** Diagonal.
$ Prices: Tortillas 475–1,300 ptas. ($4.75–$13); main courses 700–2,500 ptas. ($7–$25). AE, DC, EURO, MC, V.
Open: Lunch daily 1:30–5pm; dinner daily 8:30pm–1:30am.
Closed: Christmas.

A trendy spot where the Barcelona elite meet to grab an informal bite, Flash-Flash is at the business end of town. Primarily this is a tortillera, a restaurant specializing in omelets. You can have yours with potatoes ("à la española"), beans, capers, butifarra (Catalonian sausage), sweetbreads, all manner of vegetables, shrimp, cod, tuna, or various combinations thereof. Team your omelet choice with a salad for a perfect light meal. Heartier eaters can select among steak, veal, hamburgers, and half a dozen daily specials.

GIARDINETTO NOTTE, La Granada del Penedés, 22. Tel. 218-75-36.

Cuisine: ITALIAN. **Reservations:** Not required. **Metro:** Diagonal.

$ Prices: Appetizers 750–2,000 ptas. ($7.50–$20); main courses 1,200–2,600 ptas. ($12–$26). AE, MC, V.

Open: Dinner only, Mon–Sat 9pm–2:30am. **Closed:** Aug.

This "night garden" is intimately lit and features an abundance of wood and dark-green walls and upholstery. The menu is a blend of Catalan, traditional Spanish, and Italian influences. The pasta dishes include tagliatelle with tuna, tomato, capers, olives, and oregano. The risotto with crab and shrimp and the carpaccio are good, too.

EL GRAN COLMADO, Carrer de Consell de Cent, 318. Tel. 488-17-04.

Cuisine: CONTEMPORARY CATALAN. **Reservations:** Recommended. **Metro:** Passeig de Gràcia.

$ Prices: Appetizers 600–1,700 ptas. ($6–$17); main courses 1,250–2,500 ptas. ($12.50–$25). AE, DC, MC, V.

Open: Lunch Mon–Sat 1:30–4pm; dinner Mon–Sat 7pm–midnight. **Closed:** Holidays.

Colmado is Catalan for "grocery store," and in part that's what this is. The other part is a very fine restaurant—the tables are set in the grocery-store aisles. The Catalan chef seemingly invents new dishes daily, but all are firmly rooted in the regional culinary traditions. The long oval table seating more than a dozen people is popular with single diners who don't wish to eat alone. If you're interested in a picnic, purchase your provisions here and head for the Parc de la Ciutadella.

MORDISCO, Carrer de Roselló, 265 (at the corner of Passeig de Gràcia). Tel. 218-33-14.

Cuisine: SPANISH. **Reservations:** Not required. **Metro:** Diagonal.

$ Prices: Salads 500–1,000 ptas. ($5–$10); main courses 675–2,000 ptas. ($6.75–$20). MC, V.

Open: Mon–Fri 8:30am–2am; Sat 1:30pm–2am. **Closed:** Aug.

Mordisco's decor of rust-yellow walls and avant-garde art seems slightly tongue-in-chic. Two long, narrow tables accommodate singles who don't mind dining in the company of strangers. The management considers its cuisine "capricious" and states plainly on its calling card that it's not in the Michelin guide.

The specialties here include a variety of salads and stuffed rolls—hot and cold—and local bread toasted with tomato and topped with sausage, cheese, or ham. Beyond that, there's the usual roundup of meat entrees. This place is great for off-hour snacking.

NETWORK, Avinguda Diagonal, 616. Tel. 201-72-38.

Cuisine: CONTINENTAL. **Reservations:** Not required. **Metro:** María Cristina.

$ Prices: Appetizers 650–1,800 ptas. ($6.50–$18); main courses 700–1,900 ptas. ($7–$19). AE, V.

Open: Lunch daily 1–4pm; dinner daily 7pm–2:30am.

Network is a trendy spot that bills its fare as *cocina mundana* (literally "worldly cuisine"). Those who read Spanish will enjoy the self-directed wry humor sprinkled throughout the menu. Rock music permeates the cavelike atmosphere, which is punctuated with TVs at each table and several more suspended over the large central bar. Dishes include tempura, guacamole and shrimp, German potato salad, chicken-curry salad, burgers, barbecued chicken, fettuccine, filet mignon, spareribs, chicken wings, and carpaccio. Downstairs are a bar and billiard tables. Rather quiet at lunch, Network gains momentum as the night goes on.

PARADIS BARCELONA, Passeig Manuel Girona, 7. Tel. 203-76-37.

Cuisine: CATALAN. **Reservations:** Recommended. **Metro:** María Cristina.

$ Prices: Fixed-priced buffet from 2,500–3,000 ptas. ($25–$30), not including drinks. AE, MC, V.

Open: Lunch daily 1–4pm; dinner Mon–Sat 8:30–11:30pm.

Located in a modern business-district building, Paradis Barcelona offers outstanding buffet dining in a gracious, cafetarialike setting. This buffet includes the meat of your choice grilled before your eyes and the full gamut of salads, side dishes, vegetables, and desserts. The presentation and the quality of the fare are excellent.

In 1989 Paradis Barcelona opened its first foreign outpost, in New York at 145 E. 50th St. (tel. 212/754-3333), where the service is à la carte and the stylish decor is largely imported from Catalonia.

LA PERLA NERA, Via Laietana, 32–34. Tel. 310-56-46.

Cuisine: ITALIAN. **Reservations:** Not required. **Metro:** Jaume I.

$ Prices: Pizzas 750–950 ptas. ($7.50–$9.50); pasta 700–1,200 ptas. ($7–$12); main courses 950–2,500 ptas. ($9–$25). AE, DC, V.

Open: Lunch, Thurs–Tues 1–4pm. Dinner Thurs–Tues 8–11pm. **Closed:** Several days at Christmas.

Imagine a rustic Italian trattoria installed in a modern cafeteria and you have a good idea of La Perla Nera. Its specialty is pizza prepared in a wood-burning oven, with the standard array of pasta dishes as well.

REIAL CLUB MARITIM DE BARCELONA, Moll d'Espanya, s/n (no street number). Tel. 315-02-56.

Cuisine: NOUVELLE CATALAN. **Reservations:** Required. **Transportation:** Take a taxi; it should cost about 375 ptas. ($3.75) from Plaça Catalunya.

$ Prices: Appetizers 825–2,200 ptas. ($8.25–$22); main courses 1,700–3,300 ptas. ($17–$33). EURO, MC, V.

Open: Lunch Tues–Sun 1:30–4pm; dinner Tues–Sat 9–11:30pm. **Closed:** Holy Week and Aug.

You must take a taxi to this restaurant located at the end of a pier next to the nautical club. Despite its location, it attracts many businesspeople at lunchtime. But then again, it's always worth going out of your way for a good meal with a fine view, and this is the only public restaurant with a view of the harbor, the Columbus Monument, and lots of luxurious yachts.

The restaurant offers an abbreviated standard menu of grilled fish and meats and an extensive daily menu that is market fresh. The innovative dishes are grounded in the Catalan kitchen but have a nouvelle twist—the prawn flan with tarragon vinaigrette is a tasty example.

RESTAURANT CAN CULLERETES, Carrer Quintana, 5. Tel. 317-30-22.

Cuisine: CATALAN. **Reservations:** Recommended. **Metro:** Liceu.

$ Prices: Appetizers 600–750 ptas. ($6–$7.50); main courses 850–1,800 ptas. ($8.50–$18). EURO, MC, V.

Open: Lunch Tues–Sun 1:15–4pm; dinner Tues–Sat 9–11pm. **Closed:** Two weeks in Aug.

✪ Founded in 1786, this restaurant tucked away in a forgotten alley of the Barri Gòtic serves fine Catalan fare at very reasonable prices. The dining room's beautiful tiles and rustic chandeliers impart a historic charm.

RESTAURANT CAN PESCALLUNES, Carrer Magdalenes, 23. Tel. 318-54-83.

Cuisine: CATALAN/FRENCH. **Reservations:** Not required. **Metro:** Urquinaona.

$ Prices: Appetizers 700–1,300 ptas. ($7–$13); main courses 1,550–2,400 ptas. ($15.50–$24). EURO, MC.

Open: Lunch Mon–Fri 1–3:30pm; dinner Mon–Fri 8:30–10:30pm. **Closed:** Holidays and Aug.

The French bistro decor of Can Pescallunes echoes the French accents of its otherwise largely Catalan menu. (The menu, by the way, is available in English.) Brandada de bacalao (puréed codfish with raisins and pine nuts), steak tartare, and jarret de ternera con setas (veal stew with wild mushrooms) are some of the dishes available year round. Other house specialties include monkfish with clams and tomatoes, chateaubriand with béarnaise sauce, sole cooked in cider, and dessert crêpes with Cointreau.

RESTAURANTE EL CUS-CUS, Plaça Cardona, 4. Tel. 201-98-67.

Cuisine: NORTH AFRICAN. **Reservations:** Not required. **FF.CC.:** Muntaner.

$ Prices: Appetizers 400–1,200 ptas. ($4–$12); main courses 700–3,000 ptas. ($7–$30). MC, V.

Open: Lunch Tues–Sun 1:30–3:30pm; dinner Tues–Sun 8:30pm–midnight.

Chef-owner Omar Difallah, a native of Algiers, has created a Moorish outpost in Barcelona with blue, white, and yellow tiles; woven rugs; leather cushions; brassware; photos; and Algerian art. Couscous served with vegetables or a selection of meats is the main attraction, seconded by grilled meats.

RESTAURANT FONT DEL GAT, Passeig Santa Madrona, s/n (no street number), Montjuïc. Tel. 424-02-24.

Cuisine: CATALAN/CONTINENTAL. **Reservations:** Recommended. **Transportation:** Take a taxi; it should cost about 575 ptas. ($5.75) from the Plaça Catalunya.

$ Prices: Appetizers 550–1,200 ptas. ($5.50–$12); main courses 1,000–3,000 ptas. ($10–$30). AE, DC, V.

Open: Lunch daily 1–4pm; dinner daily 8–10pm.

Housed in a 100-year-old building built by Puig i Cadafalch, the Font del Gat purveys Catalan and continental cuisine. Posted at the doorway is an extensive "standard" menu (in Spanish only); a separate menu with English translations offers seasonal dishes. For an appetizer, try the habas à la catalana (Catalan beans). As a main course, the zarzuela is a good choice, or perhaps sole prepared as you like it. For a special treat, in season, consider the rabbit ampurdan style, grilled with white beans.

Note: If you don't have a car, you'll have to call for a taxi to take you back to the center of town, as taxis don't cruise the Montjuïc area. The nearest bus stop is also quite a hike.

RESTAURANT 7 PORTES, Passeig de Isabel II, 14. Tel. 319-30-33.

Cuisine: SPANISH. **Reservations:** Recommended, especially if you're in a hurry. **Metro:** Barceloneta.

$ Prices: Appetizers 600–2,200 ptas. ($6–$22); main courses 800–3,300 ptas. ($8–$33). AE, MC, V.

Open: Daily 1pm–1am.

Founded in 1836, this Barcelona institution buzzes at midday with brokers from the nearby stock exchange; at night, you'll find just about everybody else. It's a classic place, complete with high ceilings and waiters wearing the long white aprons of yore. Paella in several variations (with rabbit, with sardines, or spicy) is the specialty of the house, but the extensive menu goes on to offer a broad selection of meat and fish dishes as well. The wine list contains a healthy sampling of regional cavas.

TRAMONTI 1980, Avinguda Diagonal, 501. Tel. 410-15-35.

Cuisine: ITALIAN. **Reservations:** Required. **Metro:** María Cristina.

$ Prices: Appetizers 850–1,600 ptas. ($8.50–$16); pasta 900–1,400 ptas. ($9–$14). AE, V.

Open: Lunch, daily 1–4pm. Dinner, daily 9pm–midnight.

Closed: Christmas.

Named after the Italian home village of the owner, Giuliano Lombardo, and his brother, Franco, the chef, this is one of the best Italian choices in the city. White wrought-iron furnishings impart an outdoor feel to the dining area. The clientele includes many artists and athletes, and most of the eccentric knickknacks and works of art on display are gifts from patrons. The spaghetti with sepia en su tinta (cuttlefish in its own ink) is a hybrid Italian-Catalan dish.

Ⓕ FROMMER'S COOL FOR KIDS: RESTAURANTS

Orotava (see p. 57) keeps children entertained with a magic show on Tuesday nights.

Foster's Hollywood (see p. 68) will make American kids feel right at home with its selection of hamburgers, onion rings, and spareribs. It also features a special children's menu.

Henry J. Bean's Bar and Grill (see p. 69) is another slice of home.

3. BUDGET

CAN TRIPAS, Carrer Sagues, 16. Tel. 200-85-40.
Cuisine: SPANISH/CATALAN. **Reservations:** Not required.
Metro: María Cristina.
$ Prices: Appetizers 550–1,400 ptas. ($5.50–$14); main courses 750–1,900 ptas. ($7.50–$19). AE, MC, V.
Open: Lunch, Mon–Sat 1–4pm. Dinner, Mon–Sat 9pm–midnight. **Closed:** Holidays.

This superbudget bet is the place to go for mom's cooking done in Catalan style. Quaintly furnished with decorative tiles and plaid tablecloths, it's rustic and friendly. The savory escudella is a cross between soup and stew with garbanzos, other beans, and potatoes.

LA FINESTRA, Carrer de les Moles, 25. Tel. 317-58-66.
Cuisine: CATALAN. **Reservations:** Not required. **Metro:** Plaça Catalunya.
$ Prices: Daily specials 450–1,700 ptas. ($4.50–$17); menu del día 1,000 ptas. ($10). No credit cards.
Open: Mon–Fri 8am–5pm.

This quaint, charming eatery adorned with tiles and flowers offers primarily set menus and daily specials at very reasonable prices in a very central location. It makes a good breakfast choice, too.

FOSTER'S HOLLYWOOD, Avinguda Diagonal, 493. Tel. 405-34-87.
Cuisine: AMERICAN. **Reservations:** Not required. **Metro:** Hospital Clinic.
$ Prices: Appetizers 350–850 ptas. ($3.50–$8.50); hamburgers 600–775 ptas. ($6–$7.75); main courses 800–1,600 ptas. ($8–$16); children's menu with hamburgers and sandwiches from 300–500 ptas. ($3–$5). No credit cards.
Open: Sun–Thurs 1pm–1:15am; Fri–Sat 1pm–2:15am.

Foster's is a taste of home. Hamburgers come in quarter- and half-pound versions served with coleslaw, onion rings, and french fries. Also offered are spareribs, filet mignon, shish kebab, and a children's menu.

GOVINDA, Plaça Villa de Madrid, 4–5. Tel. 318-77-29.
Cuisine: INDIAN/VEGETARIAN. **Reservations:** Not required.
Metro: Plaça Catalunya.
$ Prices: Pizzas 750–1,200 ptas. ($7.50–$12); Indian dishes 950–1,100 ptas. ($9.50–$11). AE, DC, MC, V.
Open: Breakfast Mon–Sat 9:30am–noon; lunch Mon–Sat 12:30–4pm; dinner Mon–Sat 8:30pm–midnight. **Closed:** Most of Aug.

Located in a quiet plaza east of the upper Ramblas, this rather curious restaurant is strictly vegetarian and largely Indian; however, on its menu are also an enchilada, numerous pizzas, and a Spanish menu del día. The house specialty is the thali, a tray of various Indian dishes that constitute a meal. Other fine features are a very appetizing salad bar, a selection of Indian breads and desserts, and a variety of fresh fruit and vegetable juices. The "natural" breakfast includes sandwiches and cereals.

HENRY J. BEAN'S BAR AND GRILL, La Granada del Penedés, 14–16. Tel. 218-29-98.

Cuisine: AMERICAN. **Reservations:** Not required. **Metro:** Diagonal.

$ Prices: Appetizers 250–1,100 ptas. ($2.50–$11); pizzas 1,300–2,200 ptas. ($13–$22); hamburgers 900–1,100 ptas. ($9–$11). AE, DC.

Open: Sun–Thurs 12:30pm–1am; Fri–Sat and holiday eves 12:30pm–1:30am. Happy hour daily 7–9pm.

Step right up here and see a culinary culture warp—an Englishman's idea of an American bar and grill set in the heart of Barcelona. The atmosphere is English pub, the cuisine American fast food, and the clientele multinational and lively. Celebrity photos and assorted American posters and ads from the 1950s grace the walls. At the bar, Budweiser and American tapas (nachos, potato skins, garlic bread, and breaded mushrooms) are served. The salad bar—a rare find in Spain—offers less variety than Americans are used to, but Henry J.'s hamburgers, barbecued ribs, and spicy chili con carne will make you feel at home. The desserts include mud pie, pecan pie, and cheesecake. During the daily happy hour, the drinks and tapas are half price.

MÁNA MÁNA, Passeig de Gràcia, 7. Tel. 215-63-87.

Cuisine: PIZZA/PASTA/SALADS. **Reservations:** Not required. **Metro:** Passeig de Gràcia.

$ Prices: Sandwiches from 300 ptas. ($3); pizzas 750–950 ptas. ($7.50–$9.50); pastas 850–1,150 ptas. ($8.50–$11.50); main courses 900–2,200 ptas. ($9–$22); menu del día 1,300 ptas. ($13). EURO, MC, V.

Open: Lunch daily 1–4pm; dinner daily 9pm–midnight.

Mána Mána specializes in sandwiches, pizzas, pastas, ice cream, sorbet, and a delicious assortment of coffee concoctions. The unusual bar stools are a Xavier Mariscal (creator of the Olympic mascot) design.

MOKA RESTAURANT CAFETERIA, La Rambla, 126. Tel. 302-68-86.

Cuisine: CONTINENTAL. **Reservations:** Not required. **Metro:** Plaça Catalunya.

$ Prices: Salads and pizzas 650–1,100 ptas. ($6.50–$11); main courses 1,000–3,000 ptas. ($10–$30); menu del día 1,400–1,800 ptas. ($14–$18); menu turística 950 ptas. ($9.50). No credit cards.

Open: Sun–Fri 8am–1:30am; Sat 8am–2pm. Christmas 7pm–1:30am.

This clean, airy, well-lit place features salads, pizzas, pastas, and platos combinados. The regular entrees cover the full range of fish and meats.

PITARRA RESTAURANT, carrer D'Avinyó, 56. Tel. 301-16-47.

Cuisine: CATALAN. **Reservations:** Not required. **Metro:** Liceu, Drassanes, or Jaume I.

$ Prices: Appetizers 550–990 ptas. ($5.50–$9.90); main courses 700–2,500 ptas. ($7–$25). AE, DC, MC, V.

Open: Lunch Mon–Sat 1–4pm; dinner Mon–Sat 8:30–11pm.
Closed: Aug.

Pitarra occupies the former home and watch shop of the prolific and prized Catalan playwright and poet, Federic Soler Hubert (whose pseudonym was "Pitarra"). The atmosphere is friendly, the service attentive, and the food very good. The menu is seasonal—look for game in the winter.

LA PIZZA NOSTRA, Carrer Montcada, s/n (no street number) (at the corner of Arc de St. Vincenç). Tel. 319-90-58.
    Cuisine: PIZZA/PASTA. **Reservations:** Not required. **Metro:** Jaume I.
$ Prices: Salads 500–1,100 ptas. ($5–$11); pizzas 850–1,450 ptas. ($8.50–$14.50); pasta 950–1,290 ptas. ($9.50–$12.90). MC, V.
    Open: Lunch Tues–Sun 1:30–4pm; dinner Tues–Sun 8:15pm–midnight.

This cozy pizzeria near the Museu Picasso occupies the romantic confines of a medieval mansion. Its pizzas, served with a choice of exotic toppings, are some of the best in town. Those who can't make up their minds about the toppings can have half the pizza topped one way and the other half another way. The desserts here are also a star attraction. Pizza Nostra is a good place for familiar food in a distinctive local setting.

RESTAURANTE EGIPTE, La Rambla, 79. Tel. 317-95-45.
    Cuisine: CATALAN/SPANISH. **Reservations:** Not required. **Metro:** Liceu.
$ Prices: Appetizers 650–1,500 ptas. ($6.50–$15); main courses 750–2,000 ptas. ($7.50–$20); menu del día 1,000 ptas. ($10). AE, V.
    Open: Lunch, Mon–Sat 1–4pm. Dinner, Mon–Sat 8pm–midnight.

Despite this restaurant's name, its cuisine is primarily Spanish and Catalan. The daily lunch menu includes a choice of appetizers and main courses. The gazpacho and chicken with mustard-herb sauce are very good.

Two other branches at Jerusalem, 3 (tel. 317-74-80), and Jerusalem, 12 (tel. 301-62-08), are somewhat cheaper, each offering a menu del día at about 850 ptas. ($8.50).

RESTAURANT LLIVIA, Carrer Copons, 2. Tel. 318-10-78.
    Cuisine: CATALAN. **Reservations:** Not required. **Metro:** Urquinaona.
$ Prices: Menu del día 950 ptas. ($9.50), plus supplemental charges for substitutions ranging from 350–900 ptas. ($3.50–$9). AE, EURO, MC, V.
    Open: Lunch Mon–Sat 1–4pm; dinner Mon–Sat 8–11pm.
Closed: Holidays.

The menu here is drawn up daily and offered at a fixed price unless you want to substitute some more expensive entrees. The food is a good value for the money. Downstairs you can have tapas at the small bar.

SELF NATURISTA, Carrer de Santa Anna, 11–15. Tel. 318-23-88.

Cuisine: VEGETARIAN. **Reservations:** Not required. **Metro:** Plaça Catalunya.

$ Prices: Appetizers 150–550 ptas. ($1.50–$5.50); main courses 300–700 ptas. ($3–$7); menu dei día 700 ptas. ($7). No credit cards.

Open: Mon–Sat 11:30am–10pm. **Closed:** Holidays.

Off the upper Rambla, this self-service vegetarian restaurant is extremely cheap and extremely good. The ample selection of salads, main courses, and desserts varies daily, and there is a healthy choice of fresh fruit juices. Seating is McDonald's style.

4. SPECIALTY DINING

NEIGHBORHOOD DINING
LA BOQUERÍA

It's only fitting that in this fine market, along La Rambla near the Gran Teatre del Liceu, there should be two fine Barcelona eateries.

BAR PINOCHO, La Boquería. Tel. 317-17-31.

Cuisine: CATALAN. **Reservations:** Not required. **Metro:** Liceu.

$ Prices: Appetizers and main courses 150–1,100 ptas. ($1.50–$11). No credit cards.

Open: Mon–Sat 6am–6pm. **Closed:** Holidays and 2 weeks in Aug.

As you enter the market, take a right at Frutos Secos Morilla to get to this restaurant. There is no sign—just a picture of Pinocchio. There is also no menu. The owner, Juanito, will gladly let you sample what's on the stove, which has been conjured from the abundant fresh ingredients all around. Even a simple amanida (salad) is a treat here. As there is room for only eight on the counterside stools, you'll probably have to eat and run. This is also a good place to come for breakfast.

RESTAURANTE GARDUÑA, Carrer Morera, 17–19 (located at the back of the market). Tel. 302-43-23.

Cuisine: CATALAN. **Reservations:** Not required. **Metro:** Liceu.

$ Prices: Appetizers 450–1,500 ptas. ($4.50–$15); main courses 550–2,600 ptas. ($5.50–$26). AE, DC, EURO, MC, V.

Open: Lunch Mon–Sat 1–4pm; dinner Mon–Sat 8pm–midnight.

At the entrance to this market eatery is a tapas bar. Inside, a casual rusticity prevails, with half a dozen tables with checkered tablecloths downstairs and two more formal dining rooms upstairs. The downstairs walls are filled with autographed photos of satisfied celebrity customers. The menu includes a selection of grilled seafood and over a dozen daily specials—again, all is market fresh. There is also a sampling of rice and pasta dishes and a respectable wine list.

MOLL DE LA FUSTA

The Moll de la Fusta once was a pier where wood (*fusta*) was loaded and unloaded. Now it's a waterfront promenade with a choice of eateries, three of which I've described below.

LA BRASSERIE DEL MOLL, Moll de la Fusta. Tel. 310-32-68.

Cuisine: SEAFOOD. **Reservations:** Recommended. **Metro:** Barceloneta or Drassanes.

$ **Prices:** Appetizers 525–2,500 ptas. ($5.25–$25); main courses 1,200–3,500 ptas. ($12–$35); menu del día 3,000 ptas. ($30). AE.

Open: Daily 9am–3am. **Closed:** Oct–Apr.

An offspring of the Brasserie Flo (see above), this seaside outpost offers many of the same specialties as its parent restaurant—with the added option of enjoying it all outdoors.

CERVECERIA DEL MOLL, Moll de la Fusta. Tel. 319-89-97.

Cuisine: SNACKS/SANDWICHES. **Reservations:** Not required. **Metro:** Barceloneta.

$ **Prices:** Appetizers 250–1,200 ptas. ($2.50–$12); sandwiches 750–1,000 ptas. ($7.50–$10); main courses 600–2,000 ptas. ($6–$20). V.

Open: Daily noon–3am.

This is a good seaside choice for drinks, snacks, sandwiches, and light meals—which can be enjoyed either outdoor or indoors.

GAMBRINUS, Moll de la Fusta. Tel. 310-55-77.

Cuisine: SEAFOOD. **Reservations:** Not required. **Metro:** Barceloneta.

$ **Prices:** Appetizers 700–1,300 ptas. ($7–$13); main courses 850–4,000 ptas. ($8.50–$40). AE, EURO, MC.

Open: Summer, daily noon–3am (kitchen open noon–4:30pm and 8pm–2:30am). Winter, daily noon–1am (kitchen open noon–4:30pm and 8pm–1am).

The most notable among Moll de la Fusta restaurants is Gambrinus, at the eastern end. You can't miss it: Just look for the wavy roof topped by the giant prawn designed by Olympic-mascot creator Xavier Mariscal. In summer you can eat al fresco; in winter you must limit yourself to the indoor restaurant with a bar that resembles the prow of a ship complete with a plastic "smokestack." English-language menus are available. For a start, try the toasted bread with tomato and cured ham; half a dozen oysters; or one of the cold salads, such as octopus, seafood, or smoked salmon. You can also come here just to sit and have a drink by the sea.

TAPAS

ALT HEIDELBERG, Ronda Universitat, 5. Tel. 318-10-32.

Cuisine: TAPAS. **Reservations:** Not required. **Metro:** Universitat.

$ **Prices:** Tapas 175–750 ptas. ($1.75–$7.50); sandwiches 350–800 ptas. ($3–$8). No credit cards.

Open: Mon–Sat 8:30am–2am; Sun noon–midnight.

Near Plaça de la Universitat, this tapas bar/restaurant is quite popular and rightly so—its food is good and very reasonable. It offers an extensive selection of tapas and a large variety of sandwiches, including hamburgers and hot dogs (known here as "frankfurts"). As the name suggests, the emphasis is on German specialties, such as Bratwurst, German salads, and choucroûte (sauerkraut) with bacon, sausage, and potatoes. The choice of beers includes Guinness.

CERVESERIA JOSÉ LUIS, Avinguda Diagonal, 520. Tel. 200-83-12.
  Cuisine: TAPAS. **Reservations:** Not required. **Metro:** Diagonal.
$ **Prices:** Tapas 175–700 ptas. ($1.75–$7). AE, MC, V.
  Open: Mon–Fri 9am–1am; Sat 10am–1am; Sun and holidays noon–1am. **Closed:** Christmas.

If you don't mind paying as much for tapas as some people pay for a meal, you'll probably appreciate the sophistication of this place, where you can readily pick from the first-rate display of tempting tapas lining the blond-wood bar. Understandably, José Luis attracts the same kind of upscale crowd here as do its counterparts in Madrid and Seville.

TASCO MARCELINO, Enric Granados, 41. Tel. 453-10-52.
  Cuisine: TAPAS. **Reservations:** Not required. **FF.CC.:** Provença.
$ **Prices:** Tapas 250–900 ptas. ($2.50–$9). AE, MC, V.
  Open: Mon–Sat 7:30am–midnight. **Closed:** Aug.

There are many tapas bars by this name in Barcelona, and all are loosely affiliated and comparable in terms of prices and fare. Generally, the atmosphere is congenial and rustic, and the quality of the tapas high.

EL XAMPANYET, Carrer Montcada, 22. Tel. 319-70-03.
  Cuisine: SEAFOOD TAPAS. **Reservations:** Not required.
  Metro: Jaume I.
$ **Prices:** Plate of tapas averages 350 ptas. ($3.50). No credit cards.
  Open: Lunch Tues–Sun noon–4pm; dinner Tues–Sat 6:30–11:30pm. **Closed:** Aug.

This small, very inexpensive place near the Museu Picasso serves a sparkling wine, from which it gets its name, and specializes in anchovie tapas and a variety of canned seafood tapas from various parts of Spain.

DEPARTMENT-STORE DINING

CAFETERIA, in El Corte Inglés, Plaça Catalunya. Tel. 302-12-12.
  Cuisine: INTERNATIONAL. **Reservations:** Not required.
  Metro: Plaça Catalunya.
$ **Prices:** Salads 650–950 ptas. ($6.50–$9.50); sandwiches 350–800 ptas. ($3.50–$8); lunch buffet 2,500 ptas. ($25). AE, DC, EURO, MC, V.
  Open: Lunch only, Mon–Sat 12:30–4pm.

This ninth-floor department store cafeteria offers an extensive and appetizing luncheon buffet. An added treat is the view of the city—in summer you can eat on the outdoor terrace. There is also counter service for snacks, drinks, and sandwiches.

LAS TREBEDES, in El Corte Inglés, Plaça Catalunya. Tel. 302-12-12.
  Cuisine: SPANISH. **Reservations:** Recommended. **Metro:** Plaça Catalunya.
$ **Prices:** Appetizers 800–2,300 ptas. ($8–$23); main courses 1,700–2,900 ($17–$29). AE, DC, EURO, MC, V.

Open: Lunch only, Mon–Sat 1–4pm.

More formal dining is offered in this restaurant adjacent to the main El Corte Inglés cafeteria mentioned above (sorry, there's no view).

FAST FOOD

McDonald's has three Barcelona outposts: Carrer de Pelai, 62, near Plaça Catalunya (tel. 318-29-90); La Rambla, 62; and Portal De L'Angel, 36—all are open daily from 11am to 11pm and offer hamburgers from 175 to 375 pesetas ($1.75 to $3.75).

Burger King also has two locations: La Rambla, 135, near Plaça Catalunya (tel. 302-54-29); and Passeig de Gràcia, 4, on the opposite side of Plaça Catalunya (tel. 317-18-57)—both are open on Monday to Thursday from 11am to midnight, on Friday and Saturday from 11am to 1:30am, and on Sunday from noon to midnight.

BREAKFAST

Breakfasting in Spain means grabbing a cup of coffee and a croissant or roll. If you want a full breakfast with eggs and toast, you'll have to stick to the hotels.

FORN DE SANT JAUME, Rambla de Catalunya, 50. Tel. 216-02-29.

Cuisine: CROISSANTS. **Reservations:** Not required. **Metro:** Passeig de Gràcia.

$ Prices: Pastries and croissants 80–325 ptas. (80¢–$3.25); sandwiches 325–525 ptas. ($3.25–$5.25); coffee 100–250 ptas. ($1–$2.50). No credit cards.

Open: Mon–Fri 9am–9pm; Sat 9am–1pm and 5–9pm.

Located in the Eixample, this place specializes in croissants served plain or stuffed with your choice of chocolate, cheese, foie gras, or ham.

MESON DEL CAFE, Llibretería, 16. Tel. 315-07-54.

Cuisine: COFFEE BAR. **Reservations:** Not required. **Metro:** Jaume I.

$ Prices: 150–500 ptas. ($1.50–$5); pastries 125–200 ptas. ($1.25–$2). No credit cards.

Open: Mon–Sat 7am–11:30am. **Closed:** Holidays and Aug.

This café dispenses the best coffee at the best prices in town. For breakfast or a quick pick-me-up during the day, stop in at this tiny place near the cathedral in the Barri Gòtic. Founded in 1909, it looks like a bar but specializes in coffee and cappuccino with whipped cream instead of steamed milk. There are few stools, so you'll most likely have to enjoy your food standing up.

XOCOLATERÍA SANTA CLARA, Plaça Sant Jaume. No phone.

Cuisine: COFFEE BAR. **Reservations:** Not required. **Metro:** Jaume I.

$ Prices: Coffee and drinks 90–200 ptas. (90¢–$2); croissants and pastries 200–300 ptas. ($2–$3). No credit cards.

Open: Daily 8am–9:30pm.

Just down the street from Meson del Cafe (see above) in Plaça Sant Jaume, this establishment offers cappuccino and a wonderfully rich, thick hot chocolate (topped with whipped cream, if you want). For breakfast or a snack, you can select among the tasty pastries on the counter.

FOR THE SWEET TOOTH

GELATERIA ITALIANA PAGLIOTTA, Carrer Jaime I, 15. Tel. 310-53-24.
    Cuisine: ICE CREAM. **Metro:** Jaume I.
$ **Prices:** Ice cream 150–1,300 ptas. ($1.50–$13); horchata 150–275 ptas. ($1.50–$2.75). No credit cards.
    Open: Mar–Oct (more or less), daily 8am–11pm or later if there is sufficient clientele. **Closed:** Fri from Mar to June and in Sept.
This shop in the Barri Gòtic makes its own ice cream (some in a "light" version) and has the best horchata (a refreshing drink made from the chufa nut) in town. It also serves cappuccino.

LATE-NIGHT DINING

You can dine late at **Mordisco, Flash-Flash, La Pizza Nostra,** and **Set Portes** (see their listings above) and at **Ticktacktoe** (see "Barcelona Nights" in Chapter 6). **Laie,** Pau Claris, 85 (tel. 302-73-10), serves cheese, salads, and pâtés; it's open daily from 1pm to 2am.

PICNIC FARE & WHERE TO EAT IT

Stock up at the incomparable La Boquería market in La Rambla and head for the Parc de la Ciutadella or the park at the Montjuïc end of the Transbordador del Puerto.

CHAPTER 6

WHAT TO SEE & DO IN BARCELONA

Barcelona consistently gets rave reviews from visitors enthralled with the sheer spectacle of its everyday life. Even if you don't set foot in a single museum or take in any of the must-see sights, the city will charm you with its impressive architectural displays and its unmistakable Mediterranean flair.

As elsewhere in the Mediterranean, life in Barcelona unfolds in the streets. Foremost among them is La Rambla, the central tree-lined boulevard where life *is* pure street theater. But while Barcelona is an extremely attractive city capable of entertaining passersby for hours on end, it is much more than a pretty urban face. Its ranks of monuments and museums reveal great historic depth and cultural complexity; its trendy "designer" bars and enduring opera house demonstrate a flair for fun of all kinds; and its chic shops and boutiques convey a cosmopolitan sense of style and cutting-edge design that point the way to tomorrow.

SUGGESTED ITINERARIES

IF YOU HAVE ONE DAY   First, stroll along La Rambla, where Spain's *paseo* tradition runs from the seedy to the sublime. Starting from the lower end, you'll be able to take in the Columbus Monument, La Boquería market, and the Gran Teatre del Liceu (see below for limited tour hours). In the afternoon, visit the Museu Picasso and the Catedral.

IF YOU HAVE TWO DAYS   Spend your first day as suggested above. The next morning, visit the Sagrada Familia and stroll along Passeig de Gràcia to see some of the masterpieces of modernist architecture. In the afternoon, head for Montjuïc and visit the Museu d'Art de Catalunya and Museu d'Art Modern in the Palau Nacional, the Fundació Miró, and the Poble Espanyol.

? DID YOU KNOW . . . ?

- After his first voyage to the New World, Columbus returned to Barcelona to report to Queen Isabella.
- Raising the roof of the Palau Sant Jordi took 12 cranes and 10 days.
- The world's first submarine was immersed in the port of Barcelona on September 23, 1859.
- Barcelona hosted the 1992 Summer Olympic Games after unsuccessful bids for the 1924, 1936, and 1972 Games.
- The 268-meter Torre de Comunicaciones de Collserola (the communications tower atop Mount Tibidabo) is Spain's tallest structure.
- Since 1980, almost 100 squares and parks, both large and small, have been created or redesigned in Barcelona.

IF YOU HAVE THREE DAYS Spend your first two days as described above. On your third morning, visit the Museu-Monestir de Pedralbes and Museu de Ceràmica. Spend the afternoon wandering leisurely around the Barri Gòtic and visiting the Saló del Tinell, Capilla de Santa Agueda, Museu Frederic Marès, and Museu de l'Historia de la Ciutat.

IF YOU HAVE FIVE DAYS OR MORE After spending your first three days as described above, explore the Ribera barrio, visiting its Santa María del Mar Church and Museu Textil i d'Indumentària. Then stroll through the Parc de la Ciutadella and visit the zoo. Have lunch along the Moll de la Fusta and then either stroll along the waterfront promenade, stroll or sunbathe at the beach in Barceloneta, or take a trip to the breakwater in Las Golondrinas.

On your fifth day, tour the modernist works of the Eixample (see Walking Tour 3 in "Strolling Around Barcelona" below) and visit Parc Güell in the morning. For lunch, go to the top of Mount Tibidabo and spend the afternoon enjoying the views and the amusement park if you have children (be sure to call first and see if it's open). One night be sure to see the Fuentes de Montjuïc, which are illuminated from October to May on Saturday and Sunday from 8 to 11pm (9 to 10pm with music) and from June to September on Thursday, Saturday, and Sunday from 9pm to midnight (10 to 11pm with music). The music truly enhances the experience.

1. THE TOP ATTRACTIONS

MUSEU PICASSO, Montcada, 15–19. Tel. 319-63-10.

★ This is Barcelona's most popular attraction, and with good reason—it reveals much about this multitalented artist that many of us never knew. Here you will see the evolution of a boundless artistic vision from adolescence through a long and prolific career, with a creative span extending well beyond the cubist style. All of us have seen bits and pieces of Picasso's oeuvre over the years, but here the scope of his work is presented as a coherent whole, and the man and his art take on greater depth.

Ensconced in two Gothic mansions, this intimate museum of small rooms and cozy corners invites you to linger over the paintings, drawings, engravings, ceramic creations, and other assorted artistic reflections, which are displayed chronologically to trace the artist's development.

Among the individual highlights are the portrait of Picasso's aunt, Tía Pepa, and sketches of his friends Sabartés and Junyer, all of which reveal something more of Picasso the man; *Science and Charity,* a strikingly vivid work produced by the artist at age 16, using his father as a model for the doctor; the famed "Las Meninas" series; and interesting works from his blue period.

Admission: 550 ptas. ($5.50) adults; children under 16 free.

Open: Tues–Sat 10am–8pm; Sun and holidays 10am–3pm. **Metro:** Jaume I. **Bus:** 16, 17, 22, or 45.

CATEDRAL, Plaça de la Seu, s/n (no street number). Tel. 315-35-54.

⭐ This Gothic cathedral reflects the splendor of medieval Barcelona. Construction began at the end of the 13th century and was completed around the middle of the 15th (except for the main facade, which dates from the 19th century). Built atop the remains of a Roman temple, a Moorish mosque, and a Romanesque cathedral, it contains three artistically lit naves, 29 side chapels, a central choir impressively adorned with medieval and Renaissance designs, soaring Gothic arches, and 10 columns around the main altar. Steps lead from the altar down to the crypt of Santa Eulàlia, Barcelona's patron saint, whose white alabaster sepulchre is of 14th-century Italian craftsmanship. In the Chapel of the Most Holy Sacrament, to the right of the main entrance, is the *Cristo de Lepanto,* whose twisted torso is reportedly the result of dodging a bullet during the Battle of Lepanto, when the figure graced the prow of Juan de Austria's flagship. Along one of the cathedral's lateral walls are the sepulchres of Ramón Berenguer I, the Count of Barcelona, and his wife, Almodis, founders of the city's Romanesque cathedral in 1058.

In the Sala Capitular of the cathedral's cloisters is a small museum whose focal point is Bartolomé Bermejo's late 15th-century painting *La Pietat* (The Pietà). The museum is open daily from 11am to 1pm; admission is 50 ptas. (50¢).

The vaulted galleries of the cloisters themselves enclose a garden with palm trees, magnolias, and medlars; an unusual fountain erupting from a moss-covered rock; and a small gaggle of geese.

Note: Even though you can enter the cathedral in jeans and modest shorts, bare shoulders must be covered with a shawl, a sweater, or a jacket.

Admission: Free.

Open: Daily 7:45am–1:30pm and 4–7:45pm. **Metro:** Jaume I. **Bus:** 16, 17, 19, 22, or 45.

SAGRADA FAMILIA, Mallorca, 401. Tel. 455-02-47.

⭐ This unique modernist building is perhaps Barcelona's best-known landmark. An ambitious work-in-perpetual-progress, it will be Europe's largest cathedral if ever finished. Work began in 1882; two years later Gaudí took over, conceiving a monumental temple of immense proportions (the dome is slated to be 525 feet high) and profound religious symbolism. The ornamentation—composed of symbols within symbols, crosses within crosses, and motifs drawn from nature—drips down the facades like caramelized sugar. But to date, the Sagrada Familia is still only a shell, and controversy swirls around what's missing. When Gaudí died in 1926, he left no detailed plan for the cathedral's completion. Ever since, construction has continued by fits and starts, financed by donations. Some people claim that no one can imitate Gaudí's free interpretation of Gothic motifs—and that no one should even try; it's rather like having Zubin Mehta complete Schubert's *Unfinished Symphony*, they say. But the cranes have become a permanent fixture and the work continues. Within one of the towers is an elevator that ascends to a magnificent urban panorama; the charge for the elevator is 150 ptas. ($1.50).

Installed in the cathedral's crypt is the Museo del Templo Expiatorio de la Sagrada Familia, which chronicles the cathedral's evolution in blueprints, models, and drawings. Admission here is 250 ptas. ($2.50).

Admission: 450 ptas. ($4.50).
Open: Sept–Mar, daily 9am–7pm. Apr–June, daily 9am–8pm. July–Aug, daily 9am–9pm. **Metro:** Sagrada Familia. **Bus:** 19, 34, 43, 50, 51, or 54.

MUSEU NACIONAL D'ART DE CATALUNYA, Palau Nacional, Parc de Montjuïc.

Currently being redone, this museum will share the Palau Nacional with the Museu d'Art Modern. As work will not be completed until sometime in 1993, no details are available at this writing. Contact one of the tourist offices (see "Orientation" in Chapter 3) for full details when you arrive.

FUNDACIÓ JOAN MIRÓ, Plaça Neptú, Parc de Montjuïc. Tel. 329-19-08.

Acclaimed for artistic expression both outside and inside, this museum was designed by Josep Lluís Sert to house in permanent tribute the work of the prolific Catalan abstractionist Joan Miró. The nucleus of the collection follows his work from 1914 to 1978 and includes many highly original sculptures, paintings, and multimedia tapestries. The Mediterranean feel of the boxy white building gives added punch to Miró's exuberant use of primary colors. Temporary exhibitions of other contemporary artists are also featured here on a regular basis.

Admission: 450 ptas. ($4.50) adults; 250 ptas. ($2.50) students and children.
Open: Tues–Wed and Fri–Sat 11am–7pm; Thurs 11am–9pm; Sun and holidays 10:30am–2:30pm. **Transportation:** Montjuïc funicular or bus no. 61 from Plaça Espanya.

2. MORE ATTRACTIONS

MUSEUMS & GALLERIES

PALAU GÜELL, Nou de La Rambla, 3. Tel. 317-39-74.

Gaudí built this mansion in the 1880s for his patron, Eusebi Güell. It is very Gothic, melodramatic, and even somewhat foreboding; the carved ceilings are especially notable. The building houses a library of the theater arts.

FROMMER'S FAVORITE BARCELONA EXPERIENCES

Strolling on La Rambla No matter how many times you wander up and down this captivating boulevard, you'll find it impossible to become bored with the ever-changing, ever-surprising spectacle.

Meandering through the Streets of the Barri Gòtic The narrow, winding ways of this medieval neighborhood have the power to take you back centuries, while the new shops and boutiques occupying the old structures are a tantalizing taste of the here and now.

Fuentes de Montjuïc [Montjuïc Fountains] These present a dazzling display of dancing colored waters.

The Tramvía Blau This colorful, vintage streetcar traverses a neighborhood of fine modernist mansions en route to the base of the funicular that accesses the top of Mount Tibidabo.

A Performance at the Palau de la Música Catalana Any production staged at this magnificent modernist theater is significantly enhanced by the spectacle of the theater itself.

A Performance at the Gran Teatre del Liceu Attending an opera, a concert, a ballet, or a recital at this opulent opera house is well worth the price of admission.

Admission: 225 ptas. ($2.25).
Open: Mon–Fri 11am–2pm and 5–8pm; Sat–Sun and holidays 4–8pm. **Metro:** Liceu or Drassanes.

FUNDACIÓ TÀPIES, Aragó, 255. Tel. 487-03-15.

This museum permanently displays the work of Antonio Tàpies—a provocative contemporary artist born in Barcelona in 1923—and stages temporary exhibitions of contemporary works from around the world. The tangle of wire that crowns the facade is a work by Tàpies entitled *Cloud and Chair.*
Admission: 450 ptas. ($4.50).
Open: Tues–Sun 11am–8pm. **Metro:** Passeig de Gràcia.

MUSEU D'ART MODERN, Parc de la Ciutadella. Tel. 319-57-28.

The Museu d'Art Modern primarily contains the work of modern Catalan painters. Especially eye-catching is the courtyard sculpture of wooden poles and mobiles by Josep Guinovart i Bertran. You will also find modernist furniture, with some particularly nice pieces by Puig i Cadafalch. When work on Montjuïc's Palau Nacional is completed in 1993, this museum will share that building with the Museu Nacional d'Art de Catalunya.
Admission: 550 ptas. ($5.50).
Open: Mon 3–7:30pm; Tues–Sat 9am–7:30pm; Sun and holi-

days 9am–3pm (ticket sales stop half an hour before closing). **Metro:** Ciutadella.

MUSEU DEL CALÇAT ANTIC [MUSEUM OF ANTIQUE SHOES], Plaça Sant Felip Neri. Tel. 302-26-80.

Founded by the local shoemaker's guild, this fascinating museum contains extraordinary samples of footwear—ranging from a 1st-century A.D. Roman slave's sandal to shoes donated by modern-day celebrities.

Admission: 175 ptas. ($1.75).

Open: Tues–Sun 11am–2pm. **Metro:** Jaume I or Liceu.

MUSEU DE CERA, Passatge de la Banca. Tel. 317-26-49.

This wax museum and its sibling, **Expomuseu,** are located just off La Rambla and offer 300 wax figures to marvel at.

Admission: 475–575 ptas. ($4.75–$5.75) adults; 325–375 ptas. ($3.25–$3.75) children 5–11; children under 5 free.

Open: Mon–Fri 10am–1:30pm and 4–7:30pm; Sat–Sun and holidays 10am–8pm. **Metro:** Drassanes.

MUSEU FREDERIC MARÉS, Plaça de Sant Iu. Tel. 310-58-00.

Alongside the Catedral, this museum houses the collection of Frederic Marés, a Catalan sculptor who, at this writing, is in his 90s. At the far end of the exterior courtyard is a section of Roman wall. The museum's lower floors contain Punic, Hellenic, and Roman artifacts; a vast array of religious carvings and sculptures from the 12th to the 16th century; and assorted Gothic and baroque objets d'art. As you ascend to the upper floor, you go from the solemn to the frivolous: Here is a collection of items so vast and varied that one wonders how the man could have amassed it all in a mere nine decades. On display is virtually everything from cigar wrappers to cameras, clocks, parasols, belt buckles, and tiaras.

Admission: 275 ptas. ($2.75).

Open: Tues–Sat 9am–2pm and 4–7pm; Sun and holidays 9am–2pm. **Metro:** Jaume I.

MUSEU DE L'HISTÒRIA DE LA CIUTAT, Veguer, 2. Tel. 315-11-11.

This museum is housed in the 15th-century Casa Clariana Padellás, which was moved stone by stone from its original site on Carrer Mercaders. Inside, below ground level, are the excavated remains of the Roman and Visigothic cities that were the seeds of Barcelona, along with mosaics, statuary, and pediments of those eras and a model of the supposed layout of the city. The museum's upper floors are a veritable maze of municipal memorabilia, with some dioramas of Barcelona as it looked in days gone by.

Admission: 275 ptas. ($2.75).

Open: Tues–Sat 9am–8pm; Sun and holidays 9am–1:30pm. **Metro:** Jaume I.

MUSEU MARÍTIM [MUSEO MARITIMO], Porta de la Pau 1. Tel. 301-64-25.

The Maritime Museum is installed in the Drassanes (medieval shipyards of the 13th century). The most outstanding among the collection of seafaring paraphernalia is a reconstruction of Don Juan de Austria's *La Galería Real,* which took part in the Battle of Lepanto, and a map from the hand of Amerigo Vespucci.

Admission: 175 ptas. ($1.75).
Open: Tues–Sat 9am–1pm and 4–7pm; Sun and holidays 10am–2pm. **Metro:** Drassanes.

MUSEU MONESTIR DE PEDRALBES, Baixada del Monestir, 9. Tel. 203-92-82 or 204-27-47.

A jewel of Catalan Gothic art, this monastery was founded in 1326 by Queen Elisenda of Montcada and her husband, King Jaume II. Among its more noteworthy features are the three-story cloisters and the chapel's outstanding mural paintings by Ferrer Bassa.
Admission: 275 ptas. ($2.75) adults; children under 13 free.
Open: Tues–Sun 9:30am–2pm. **Bus:** 22, 64, or 75.

MUSEU DE CERÁMICA, Palau de Pedralbes, Avinguda Diagonal, 686. Tel. 280-16-21.

Within a vintage 1920s palace is the Museu de Cerámica, whose collection (considered the most important of its kind in Europe) traces the history of Spanish ceramics from the 13th century to today.
Admission: 300 ptas. ($3) adults; children under 18 free.
Open: Tues–Sun 9am–2pm. **Closed:** Holidays. **Metro:** Palau Reial. **Bus:** 7 or 75.

MUSEU TEXTIL I D'INDUMENTÀRIA, Montcada, 12. Tel. 310-45-16.

Occupying two 13th-century Gothic palaces near the Museu Picasso, this museum contains a fascinating collection of textiles. Ancient pieces (Egyptian and Spanish-Arabic) as well as a spectrum of fabrics, garments, and accessories dating from the Gothic period to the 20th century can be found here. Particularly impressive is the assemblage of clothing and accessories from the 18th to the 20th centuries and the interesting lace collection (including a lovely array of Chantilly lace shawls) stretching from the 16th century on.
Admission: 275 ptas. ($2.75).
Open: Tues–Sat 9am–2pm and 4:30–7pm; Sun and holidays 9am–2pm. **Metro:** Jaume I.

TORRE DE COLLSEROLA, on Mount Tibidabo. No phone.

From the viewing platform (at 560 meters above sea level) of this communications tower built for the 1992 Summer Olympic Games, you call behold all of Barcelona at your feet.
Admission: 550 ptas. ($5.50).
Open: Hours have not yet been determined at this writing. Call one of the tourist offices for information. **Directions:** Take the FF.CC. to Avinguda del Tibidabo, then catch the tramvía blau and continue on in the Tibidabo funicular.

PARKS & OUTDOOR AMUSEMENTS

FUENTES DE MONTJUÏC (Montjuïc Fountains), located below the Museu d'Art de Catalunya at the base of Montjuïc.

One of Barcelona's most unique spectacles is the Fuentes de Montjuïc when illuminated. A masterpiece of engineering by Carles Buigas, the fountains were built for the 1929 World's Fair. Make an effort to see them with the musical accompaniment—it transforms the play of water and colored lights (in 50 different and extraordinary formations) into a dramatic ballet.

Admission: Free.
Open: Fountains are illuminated Oct–May, Sat–Sun 8–11pm (9–10pm with music); June–Sept, Thurs and Sat–Sun 9pm–midnight (10–11pm with music). **Metro:** Plaça Espanya.

PABELLON MIES VAN DER ROHE, Montjuïc. Tel. 423-40-16.

Reconstructed several years ago on its original site, this pavilion was designed by Mies van der Rohe as the German entry to the 1929 World's Fair. It features a bronze copy of a Georges Kolbe sculpture and the famous "Barcelona chair," also designed by the architect.
Admission: Free.
Open: Winter, daily 8am–9pm. Summer, daily 8am–midnight.
Bus: 61.

PARC DE LA CIUTADELLA, at the southeast corner of the Barri de la Ribera.

Occupying the former site of the city's citadel, Parc de la Ciutadella packs a lot into a small space. Its noteworthy attributes include some remnants of its military past—among them a chapel, the governor's palace, and the arsenal—the zoo (see "Cool for Kids" below), the Museu d'Art Modern (see "Museums & Galleries" above), and a lake with rowboats.

Last remodeled for the Universal Expo of 1888, the park's grand cascade, lake, flower beds, and abundant trees make a tranquil sanctuary within a dense metropolis. Here, too, installed in the Domenech i Montaner building that housed the 1888 Expo's café-restaurant, is the Museo de Zoología (exactly what it sounds like—a zoological museum). Another modernist touch is Llimona's *El Desconsol* sculpture in the middle of the pool in front of the Parliament. But the park's most monumental feature is the effusive fountain (you can't miss it) by Gaudí.
Admission: Free.
Open: Oct–Mar, daily 8am–8pm. Apr–Sept, daily 8am–9pm.
Metro: Ciutadella.

PARC GÜELL, Olot, s/n, Gràcia. Tel. 424-38-09.

From 1910 to 1914, Gaudí worked here to compose a garden suburb of 60 homes and such requisite supporting services as roads, markets, and schools. Commissioned by the financier Eusebi Güell, the project was aborted after only two houses and a smattering of public areas had been built. In 1922 the city acquired the land and turned it into a park. One of the two finished houses, where the architect lived from 1906 to 1926, is devoted to the Casa-Museo Gaudí and contains a selection of furniture designed by him. The house itself, however, is the work of Ramón Berenguer.

The entrance stairway to the park itself is adorned with a colorful lizard fountain, and once inside you *must* visit the surrealistic Hall of a Hundred Columns (all Doric and slightly askew) and the proposed market area above it (ringed with benches covered with mosaics fashioned of broken ceramics). From here you can see Barcelona stretch away to the sea.
Admission: Parc Güell free; Gaudí Museum 175 ptas. ($1.75).
Open: Par Güell: Winter, daily 10am–6pm. Summer, daily 9am–9pm. Gaudí Museum: Winter, Sun–Fri 11am–2pm and 4–7pm. Summer, Sun–Fri 10am–2pm and 4–6:30pm. **Directions:** Bus no. 25, but my advice is to take a cab.

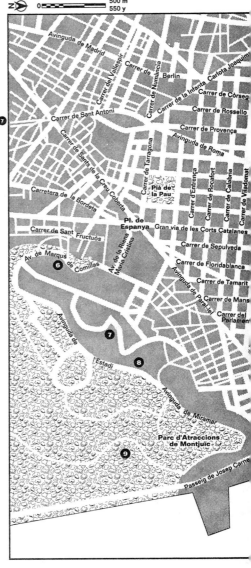

POBLE ESPANYOL [PUEBLO ESPAÑOL], Montjuïc. Tel. 325-78-66.

⭐ This microcosm of Spain was conceived for the 1929 World's Fair and constructed as a permanent open-air museum of Spanish architecture and handcrafts. As you look around, you'll find it hard to believe that most of what you see is simulated stone, brick, and rock. But nowadays the Poble Espanyol is much more than a museum. In fact, it's almost a village in its own right,

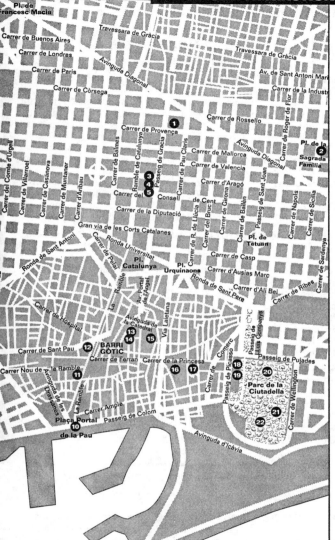

with artisans working in their shops and frequent "fiestas" that evoke the spirit of local village fairs. In recent years it has also become a favored leisure retreat for Barceloneses, who especially flock here on summer evenings to enjoy the cooler Montjuïc air and the various nightclubs, music bars, flamenco performances, jazz "caves," and restaurants—in short, over 40 different nightspots.

Admission: 550 ptas. ($5.50) adults; 275 ptas. ($2.75) children 7–14; children under 7 free.

Open: Daily 9am–past midnight. **Directions:** From Plaça Espanya, take the free double-decker bus that shuttles visitors back and forth.

HISTORIC BUILDINGS & MONUMENTS

COLUMBUS MONUMENT, at the harbor end of La Rambla. Tel. 302-52-24.

This Barcelona landmark commemorates Columbus's triumphant return after his first successful expedition to the New World. After sailing into the harbor, he delivered reports of his discoveries to Queen Isabella in the Gothic Quarter's Salon de Tinell.

The monument itself contains a small tubular elevator that ascends 200 feet (60m) to Columbus's feet, where a tiny platform offers a partially obstructed view of the sea and city.

Admission: 225 ptas. ($2.25) adults; 125 ptas. ($1.25) children 4–12 and senior citizens over 60; children under 4 free.

Open: June 24–Sept 24, daily 9am–9pm. Rest of year, Tues–Sun 10am–2pm and 3:30–6:30pm. **Metro:** Drassanes.

GRAN TEATRE DEL LICEU, Sant Pau 1 bis. Tel. 318-91-22.

Barcelona's majestic opera house dates from the 19th century and nowadays often resounds with the native talents of Montserrat Caballé and José Carreras. A study in Victorian opulence, the theater features blue silk walls in the entrance hall, a sweeping staircase leading to a salon of mirrors, and one of Europe's largest stages. Enter at Sant Pau 1 bis, around the corner from the main facade on La Rambla.

Tours: Guided half-hour tours in English Mon–Fri at 11:30am and 12:15pm for 225 ptas. ($2.25).

Metro: Liceu.

SANTA MARÍA DEL MAR, Passeig del Born, 1. Tel. 310-23-90.

This is not a church you need go out of your way for, but since it's close to the Museu Picasso, you might as well drop in and see its lovely rose window and stained-glass display.

Admission: Free.

Open: Mon–Fri 9am–12:30pm and 5–8pm. **Metro:** Jaume I.

3. COOL FOR KIDS

GOLONDRINAS, on the Barcelona Pier. Tel. 412-59-44.

Both children and adults enjoy the 30-minute round-trip boat ride from the Barcelona Pier (in front of the Columbus Monument) to the breakwater.

Fare: 325 ptas. ($3.25).

Open: Winter, Mon–Fri 11am–5pm; Sat–Sun 11am–6pm. Summer, daily 11am–9pm.

PARC D'ATRACCIONS [AMUSEMENT PARK], Montjuïc. Tel. 441-70-24.

For children there are 40 rides and open-air concerts in summer; for adults there is a panoramic view of the city and port.

Admission: 550 ptas. ($5.50); global ticket good for all rides 1,700 ptas. ($17).

Open: Sept 15–Mar 31, Sat–Sun and holidays noon–8pm. Apr 1–June 20, Sat–Sun and holidays noon–10pm. Jun 21–Sept 14, Mon–Thurs 6pm–midnight; Fri–Sat 6pm–2am; Sun and holidays noon–midnight. (*Note:* Hours of operation vary greatly from season to season and year to year, so call before you go.) **Directions:** Take the funicular from the Paral.lel Metro stop.

PARC D'ATRACCIONS LA MUNTANYA MÁGICA [AMUSE-MENT PARK], Cumbre del Tibidabo, s/n (no street number). Tel. 211-79-42.

This park features more rides for the kids and another spectacular view for the parents.

Admission (including 9 attractions): 900 ptas. ($9); global ticket good for all rides 1,800 ptas. ($18).

Open: Summer, Mon–Thurs 6pm–2:30am; Fri–Sat 6pm–3:30am; Sun noon–11pm. Christmas and Easter school vacations also open weekdays. (*Note:* The hours are as unpredictable here as at the Montjuïc park, so call before you make the trek.) **Directions:** Take the FF.CC. to Avinguda del Tibidabo, then the tramvía blau to the Tibidabo funicular (an amusing ride in itself!).

ZOO, Parc de la Ciutadella. Tel. 309-25-00.

If you think that you've seen it all as far as zoos are concerned, you'll be pleasantly surprised by Copito de Nieve, the only albino gorilla in captivity and the headliner among this zoo's outstanding cast of primates. With over 7,000 animals in residence plus a petting zoo, children will find hours of educational entertainment here.

Admission: 750 ptas. ($7.50); children under 3 free.

Open: Winter, daily 10am–5pm. Summer, daily 9:30am–7:30pm. **Metro:** Ciutadella.

---

4. ORGANIZED TOURS

BUS TOURS **Julià Tours,** Ronda Universitat, 5 (tel. 317-64-54), and **Pullmantur,** Gran Vía de les Corts Catalanes, 635 (tel. 318-02-41), offer a variety of guided bus tours in English. The daily half-day city tour costs 3,500 ptas. ($35). The full-day city tour, including lunch (offered Tuesday to Sunday), costs 8,500 to 10,000 ptas. ($85 to $100). Another daily tour features Barcelona by night and a flamenco performance for 6,500 to 9,500 ptas. ($65 to $95), depending on whether you have just a drink or dinner.

AERIAL TOURS Both the Montjuïc cable car and the Transbordador del Puerto that crosses the harbor from Montjuïc to Barceloneta are fine ways to survey the city, sea, and surrounding mountains from on high. The former, as you approach the castle, provides a partial glimpse of the Olympic installations on your right behind the Palau Nacional, while in the distance the Sagrada Familia rises like a crown from the urban landscape. The latter provides a view of La Rambla and the port.

For a look at the city and the sea from the mountains, go to the top of Mount Tibidabo. The ascent combines a number of different transports, beginning with the **Ferrocarrils de la Generalitat** from the Plaça Catalunya station (use your T-2 ticket) to Avinguda del Tibidabo. Next, the quaint, colorful **tramvía blau** (also T-2 ticket), an old-fashioned streetcar that travels Avinguda del Tibidabo with its stately mansions (many now house offices or luxury apartments). After the tramvía blau, you continue in the funicular to the amusement park (see "Cool for Kids" above), Sacred Heart Church, and a nice overlook. To the left of the main altar in the church is access to the elevator that will take you to the base of the Christ statue, the highest vantage point of all. The **Bar Tibidabo** here serves good sandwiches, or, if you wish, go around the back to **Restaurante La Masía** (tel. 417-63-50), whose moderately priced menu offers quality Catalan fare with entrees averaging 1,600 ptas. ($16); it's open in winter on Monday to Saturday from 1 to 4pm, in June to September on Monday to Saturday from 1 to 4pm and 8:30 to 11:30pm, and all year on Sunday from 1 to 4pm.

5. STROLLING AROUND BARCELONA

WALKING TOUR 1 — La Rambla

Start: Columbus Monument.
Finish: Plaça de la Vila de Madrid.
Time: Allow 1–2 hours.
Best Times: Weekdays.
Worst Times: Sunday.

La Rambla, one of the world's most fascinating promenades, not only attracts the full spectrum of humanity but also offers numerous architectural and cultural tidbits.

Begin at the port, at the base of the:

1. **Columbus Monument** (see "More Attractions" above). To the left as you look up La Rambla is the:
2. **Museu Marítim,** installed in the medieval Drassanes shipyards and containing an interesting collection of maritime objects (see "More Attractions" above).

   Now continue along **La Rambla,** a long boulevard that ascends to Plaça Catalunya in five seamless segments. The first is the Rambla de Santa Monica, the seedier end of La Rambla, lined with sex shops, assorted soothsayers, and a smattering of respectable newspaper kiosks and terrace bars.

   To the right down the Passatge de la Banca is the:
3. **Museu de Cera (Wax Museum),** as well as the related **Expomuseu** (see "More Attractions" above). At Plaça del Teatre begins the Rambla dels Caputxins, where the terrace bars continue and more souvenir shops appear.

   To the left down Nou de La Rambla is the:
4. **Palau Güell,** a fortresslike Gaudí structure (see "More Attractions" above).

   On the other side of La Rambla is the:

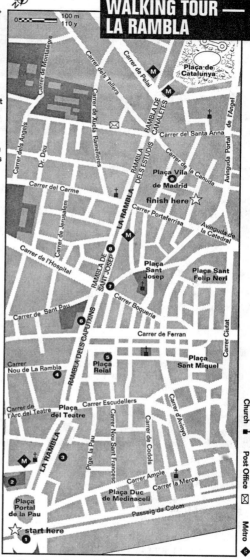

BARCELONA

La Rambla

1 Columbus Monument
2 Museu Marítim
3 Museu de Cera
4 Palau Güell
5 Plaça Reial
6 Gran Teatre del Liceu
7 Casa Bruno Cuadros
8 La Boquería
9 Plaça de la Vila de Madrid

5. Plaça Reial, its yellow facades and courtyard palms reminiscent of Seville. Along its periphery are numerous cafés; at its center is a fountain with surrounding lamps designed by Gaudí. Take care here at night—it's an unsavory area filled with pickpockets, prostitution, and drugs.

Back on La Rambla, you'll notice some white chairs lined up along the curbs. If you decide to sit, you may be asked to pay a token fee.

A little farther on the left is the:

6. Gran Teatre del Liceu, Barcelona's premier opera house, built in 1847 and then, after a fire, rebuilt from 1861 to 1862. Although it's modest outside, inside it's a glittering feast of Victorian gilt, glass, velvet, and blue silk walls. Especially masterful are the ceiling paintings (see "More Attractions" above).

REFUELING STOP Opposite the opera house is the **Cafetería de La Opera,** which is over 100 years old. The café's former cachet lingers in the etched mirrors and elaborate mural paintings adorning its walls, but as with La Rambla itself, the original luster has tarnished considerably. Once a hotbed of intellectual discussion, it is now a place where people of diverse classes and ages come to sip coffee side by side.

The Rambla de Sant Josep, primarily dedicated to the sale of plants and flowers, begins at the Plaça de la Boquería, where on the right you'll find:

7. Casa Bruno Cuadros, a modernist building designed by Josep Vilaseca and dating from the 1890s. It features a protruding green dragon and other Asian designs. In the center sidewalk of the Plaça de la Boquería is a mosaic by Miró.

A little farther up on the left is:

8. La Boquería (Mercat Sant Josep), one of the world's great produce markets.

The Rambla dels Estudis, where birds and fish and an occasional large turtle are sold, begins at Carrer del Carme (on the left) and Carrer de la Portaferrissa (on the right). The fifth and final section, the Rambla de Canaletes, lined with banks, better shops, and an abundance of snack bars, begins its brief sprint to the Plaça Catalunya at the Carrer del Santa Anna.

Take Carrer Canuda leading off to the right to the:

9. Plaça de la Vila de Madrid, where you'll find some steps leading down to Roman tombs.

WALKING TOUR 2 — BARRI GÒTIC (GOTHIC QUARTER)

Start: Plaça Nova.
Finish: Museu del Calçat Antic.
Time: Allow 2 hours.
Best Times: Weekdays.
Worst Times: Weekends.

The Barri Gòtic is an enclave of narrow medieval streets paved with cobblestones and suffused with an imposing sense of history.

Begin your tour at the:

1. Plaça Nova, where several circular and square towers incorporate Roman bases made up of large stone blocks. The upper portions, constructed of smaller stones, date from the 12th century. As you pass from the plaza onto Carrer de Bisbe (toward the port), you cross the threshold that was the city's oldest entrance gate.

The first building on the right is the:

2. Palau Episcopal (Bishop's Palace), whose 18th-century

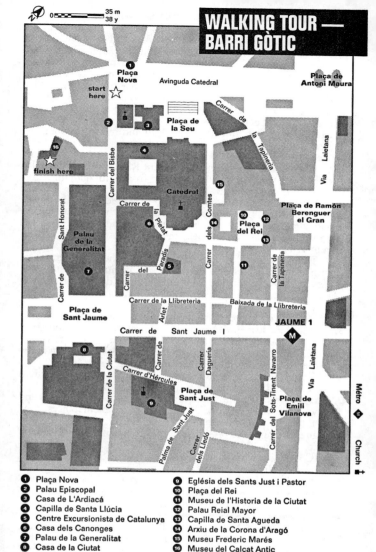

**WALKING TOUR —
BARRI GÒTIC**

Avinguda Catedral

Plaça Nova

start here

Plaça de Antoni Maura

Carrer de

la Tapineria

Via Laietana

finish here

Plaça de la Seu

Carrer del Bisbe

Catedral

Carrer de

la Pietat

Palau de la Generalitat

Carrer de

Sant Honorat

Carrer de

Paradís

del

Plaça de Ramón Berenguer el Gran

Plaça del Rei

Carrer

dels Comtes

Carrer de la Tapineria

Plaça de Sant Jaume

Carrer de la Llibreteria

Baixada de la Llibreteria

Arlet

Carrer de Sant Jaume I

JAUME 1

M

Carrer de la Ciutat

Carrer d'Hércules

Carrer de

Carrer Daguería

Plaça de Sant Just

Carrer del Sots-Tinent Navarro

Plaça de Emili Vilanova

Via Laietana

Métro

Palma de Sant Just

Carrer dels Lledó

Church

① Plaça Nova
② Palau Episcopal
③ Casa de L'Ardiacá
④ Capilla de Santa Llúcia
⑤ Centre Excursionista de Catalunya
⑥ Casa dels Canonges
⑦ Palau de la Generalitat
⑧ Casa de la Ciutat
⑨ Església dels Sants Just i Pastor
⑩ Plaça del Rei
⑪ Museu de l'Historia de la Ciutat
⑫ Palau Reial Mayor
⑬ Capilla de Santa Agueda
⑭ Arxiu de la Corona d'Aragó
⑮ Museu Frederic Marés
⑯ Museu del Calçat Antic

---

portal opens onto an attractive courtyard with Romanesque construction below and Gothic above. At the top of the stairway leading off the courtyard is a patio with a 13th-century Romanesque mural and a splendid coffered ceiling. The courtyard is open to the public daily from 10am to 1:30pm, but even if the gate is closed you can peek into the courtyard and see the incongruous central fountain that dates from this century.

Leaving the Palau Episcopal and walking straight ahead onto Carrer Santa Llúcia, you'll see the:

3. Casa de L'Ardiacá on your left. Although it was originally built atop the Roman wall, it exhibits a Gothic-Renaissance styling dating from its 15th-century reconstruction and expansion. You can visit the courtyard here, which contains a single palm tree, a murmuring fountain, and beautiful *azulejos* (tiles) that, despite their addition as recently as 1920, do not detract from the overall sense of history. Once the archdeacon's residence, this structure now houses the city archives. It's open Monday to Friday from 10am to 1pm and from 4 to 6pm. Across the way on the right is the:

4. Capilla de Santa Llúcia, a vestige of the 11th-century Romanesque cathedral built by Count Ramón Berenguer I. It's open daily from 8am to 1:30pm and from 4 to 7:30pm.

Exiting the chapel at the far side, you'll find yourself in the **cathedral cloisters,** whose moss-covered fountain, white geese, and soaring palms possess a singular charm. Entering the cathedral through the door by the fountain, you'll find the **tombs** of Count Ramón Berenguer I and his wife, Almodis, on your right.

Upon exiting the cathedral through the main entrance, turn right up Carrer dels Comtes. Look up and you'll see some classic Gothic gargoyles. As you turn right down Carrer de la Pietat behind the cathedral, the medieval atmosphere intensifies.

Leading off to the left is Carrer Paradís, where at no. 10 is the:

5. Centre Excursionista de Catalunya, whose courtyard contains four remaining columns of the city's largest Roman temple, honoring Augustus (a model of which can be seen in the Museu de la Historia de la Ciutat).

Return to Carrer de la Pietat and continue to the left behind the cathedral. On your left you'll pass:

6. Casa dels Canonges, the former residence of the canons and now home to a number of regional government offices. One of them, no. 8, with an entrance on Carrer Bisbe, is the official residence of the president of the Generalitat, but it is rarely used.

Continuing along Carrer Bisbe to Plaça de Sant Jaume, you'll pass along the Gothic side of the:

7. Palau de la Generalitat, seat of the regional Catalan government; the main 16th-century Renaissance facade faces the plaza itself and displays a distinctive statue of Sant Jordi.

REFUELING STOP In the Plaça de Sant Jaume is the **Xocolatería Santa Clara,** a fine place for coffee, hot chocolate, horchata (in summer), and pastries (see Chapter 5 under "Specialty Dining" for full details).

Across the plaza from the Palau de la Generalitat is the:

8. Casa de la Ciutat (City Hall), whose 19th-century neoclassical facade supersedes a Gothic one. Again, the side wall along Carrer de la Ciutat is older and more interesting in its Gothic styling. Above its doorway is an unusual image of the Archangel San Rafael sprouting bronze wings. Inside both of these governmental buildings are magnificent salons that were once open to the public but are now off-limits for security reasons.

To the left off Carrer de la Ciutat runs the narrow Carrer d'Hercules, which leads into Plaça Sant Just and its:

9. **Església dels Sants Just i Pastor.** On Saturday and Sunday the main entrance of this church is open to the public from 9am to 1pm and from 5 to 9pm. If you wish to go inside on other days, you must go around to the gate at the back of the church (at the end of the brief Carrer de Rera Sant Just); ring the bell if no one is there to open the door for you. The same visiting hours apply. This church was built above an older one in the 14th century and contains a single nave with side chapels. Most notable is a curious Byzantine capital with a Greek inscription and the 16th-century retablo in the San Félix chapel. An image of the Virgen de Montserrat presides at the altar.

Back in the Plaça Sant Just, notice the upper-crust 18th-century houses with their decorative reliefwork.

REFUELING STOP   Stop in at the **Café de L'Academia** for coffee or a lunch of good Catalan fare (see Chapter 5 under "Moderate" for full details).

Now turn onto Carrer Daguería and cross Carrer Jaume I and Carrer de la Llibrería and continue along Carrer Frenería. Turning right onto the Baixada de Santa Clara, you'll soon find yourself in the remarkable:

10. **Plaça del Rei,** lined with palatial medieval structures that will make you feel you've stepped back in time.

To do so within the context of a museum, turn right on Carrer del Veguer and go to the:

11. **Museu de l'Historia de la Ciutat** (see "More Attractions" above).

You can enter the:

12. **Palau Reial Mayor,** the former residence of the Condes de Barcelona and the kings of Aragón, through the Museu de l'Historia de la Ciutat. Begun in the 11th and 12th centuries, the palau evolved to its present aspect by the end of the 14th century. Rumor has it that one wing was once given over to the Inquisition, but we do know for certain that in its majestic **Salón del Tinell,** Queen Isabella and King Ferdinand received Columbus—with six Native Americans in tow—upon his return from the New World. The palau is open Tuesday through Saturday from 9am to 8pm, on Sundays and holidays from 9am to 1:30pm.

Adjacent to the palau is the:

13. **Capilla de Santa Agueda,** built atop the Roman wall and distinguished by a slender bell tower that is an extension of a Roman tower. Within, the chapel's single nave is adorned with polychromatic wood, its altar with a beautiful 15th-century retablo. Behind the altar you'll find the "Big Clock of Barcelona" dating from the 16th century.

Returning to the Plaça del Rei, go back to the Baixada de Santa Clara and turn right on Carrer dels Comtes. On the right you can enter the courtyard of the:

14. **Arxiu de la Corona d'Aragó** in the old **Palacio del Lugarteniente.** Note the elaborate coffered ceiling above the stairs.

Alongside the cathedral in the Plaça de Sant Iu is the:

15. **Museu Frederic Marés,** which contains the enormous and eclectic collection of sculptor Frederic Marés—on display is everything from Roman artifacts to modern cameras (see "More Attractions" above).

    If you're not too tired by now, go back around the cathedral via Carrer de la Pietat and Carrer Bisbe and make a left onto Carrer Sant Sever. Make your first right on Carrer Sant Felip Neri into the plaza of the same name, where you'll find the:

16. **Museu del Calçat Antic (Museum of Antique Shoes).** Founded by the shoemaker's guild, the museum contains samples of footwear through the ages (see "More Attractions," above).

WALKING TOUR 3 — Modernist
Barcelona

Start: Casa Lleó Morera.
Finish: Casa Terrades (also known as Casa de les Punxes).
Time: Allow 1–2 hours.
Best Times: During business hours.
Worst Times: Holidays and weekends.

Americans know it as art nouveau, the Germans call it *Jugendstil,* the Finns call it National Romantic, and the Spanish (more specifically, the Catalans) call it modernism. All these terms refer to an essentially organic architectural vernacular that's loosely grounded in the Gothic tradition and inspired by forms found in nature.

The best way to survey the broad scope of forms and fantasy embraced by this turn-of-the-century genre is to have a look at the numerous examples of modernist architecture sprinkled throughout Barcelona's Eixample area. The city's three most important modernist stylists were Domenech i Montaner, Antoni Gaudí, and Puig i Cadafalch. Because most of their buildings are now apartment houses or offices, they are not readily accessible to the general public; however, a discreet glance at their interiors is often possible.

One representative work by each of these architects can be seen along Passeig de Gràcia between Carrer Consell de Cent and Carrer Provença. The first, at Consell de Cent, is the:

1. **Casa Lleó Morera,** designed in 1905 by Domenech i Montaner in a floral mode. Today it houses the Patronato de Turismo and the chic store Loewe, which recently restored the facade to reveal many of its original modernist elements. Enter portal no. 35 next to Loewe for a look at the floral decoration of the staircase.
    Now continue on to the:

2. **Casa Amatller,** at Passeig de Gràcia 41 (tel. 216-01-75). Dating from 1900, it is the work of Josep Puig i Cadafalch superimposed on an older structure and combines grace notes of Dutch Gothic (note the finish of the facade) with elements of Catalan architecture (note the style of the arches) and the typical naturalist elements of modernism (note the sculptures, ceramics, and wrought iron). Enter the **Institut Amatller d'Art Hispanic** (Amatller Institute of Hispanic Art) on the first floor for a look at

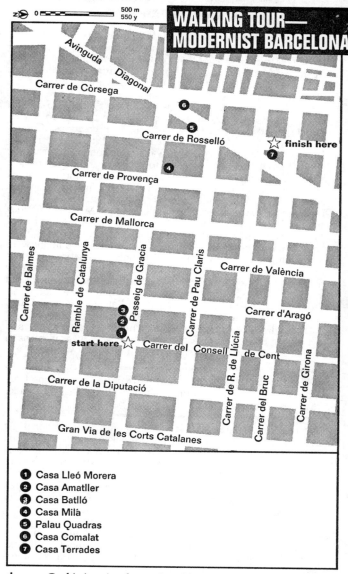

0 | 500 m
500 y

z

Avinguda Diagonal

Carrer de Còrsega

Carrer de Rosselló

☆ **finish here**
7

6
5

Carrer de Provença

4

Carrer de Mallorca

Carrer de Balmes

Ramble de Catalunya

Passeig de Gracia

Carrer de Pau Claris

Carrer de València

Carrer d'Aragó

3
2
1

start here ☆ Carrer del Consell de Cent

Carrer de R. de Llúcia

Carrer del Bruc

Carrer de Girona

Carrer de la Diputació

Gran Via de les Corts Catalanes

1 Casa Lleó Morera
2 Casa Amatller
3 Casa Batlló
4 Casa Milà
5 Palau Quadras
6 Casa Comalat
7 Casa Terrades

the neo-Gothic interior decoration. It's open Monday to Friday from 10am to 2pm and from 4 to 8pm; admission is free.

Next door is the:

3. Casa Batlló, built by Gaudí between 1905 and 1907 on top of an existing structure. A fine example of the integration of natural forms into architecture, it rises like an organic structure from its stone base through the bony forms of its windows to a rolling crown. The impact is enhanced by the brilliant polychromatic exterior, which takes on an added sheen on rainy mornings. Now it's occupied by an insurance company, but you can still go in and catch a discreet glimpse of the sinuously molded interior staircase off the entranceway, as well as other decorative Gaudí flourishes beyond the double doors to the left.

At the corner of Carrer Provença is the:

4. **Casa Milá** (popularly known as "La Pedrera") (tel. 215-33-98), the butt of many jokes in its youth but now considered one of Gaudí's—and modernism's—most singular creations. Gaudí's last completed work, it was built between 1905 and 1910 and resulted in a lawsuit by Señora Milá, who complained that the finished product did not conform to the plans she'd been shown. The house, which evolved according to Gaudí's improvisational whims, takes the use of curved forms to the limit in its endless interior and exterior undulations. Free half-hour guided visits of La Pedrera in various languages are offered on Monday to Friday at 10 and 11am, noon, and 1, 4, 5, and 6pm; on Saturday at 10 and 11am, noon, and 1pm; and on Sunday at 11am, noon, and 1pm. Since a maximum of 25 people may visit at once, you might want to call ahead. Currently you may visit only the interior patio and the roof (six floors up) with its singular assemblage of chimney turrets—some clustered like small squadrons of helmeted knights, others spiraling upward in a twisting mosaic of stone. From here you also have a good view of Barcelona and, as Gaudí no doubt intended, the Sagrada Familia.

La Pedrera now houses an assortment of apartments and offices, but the Caixa de Catalunya, which now owns it, plans to restore it and open up much of it as a museum.

REFUELING STOP Stop in at **Mordisco** for anything from coffee and a sandwich to a full-fledged meal (see Chapter 5 under "Moderate" for full details).

Continue along Passeig de Gràcia to Avingunda Diagonal. At Diagonal 373 is Puig i Cadafalch's castlelike:

5. **Palau Quadras** (1904), which now houses the Museu de la Música. The elaborate sculpturing of the facade lends a hint of baroque to the overall Gothic and naturalist tenor of the design. If you want to pay the 300 ptas. ($3) to enter the museum (open Tuesday to Sunday from 9am to 2pm), you can see the hand of Cadafalch in the decorative elements on the first floor.

Just across the way at no. 442 is the:

6. **Casa Comalat,** the work of Salvador Valeri, dating from 1911. The back of the building on Carrer Córsega is more interesting, with its bulging undulations and colorful ceramics clearly inspired by Gaudí.

A little farther east along Avingunda Diagonal, at the corner of Roselló, is the:

7. **Casa Terrades,** also known as the **Casa de les Punxes.** It is a Puig i Cadafalch structure dated from 1904 to 1905, with brickwork and spires that are reminiscent of those at Eero Saarinen's National Museum in Helsinki.

Although the walking tour ends here, Gaudí devotees might want to take Metro Line 3 to Fontana to have a look at **Casa Vincens,** Carrer Carolines 22. This was Gaudí's first important work after graduating as an architect and shows the Arab influence characteristic of his early work. As it is a private home, you can view it only from the outside.

6. SPORTS & RECREATION

For workouts of all kinds, contact the **Estadi Joan Serrahima,** Segura 27 (tel. 332-60-48). As there are many fitness centers around town both in hotels and otherwise, ask your hotel for the center nearest you. This goes for swimming pools and tennis courts as well. At this writing, plans were to open the Olympic installations of Montjuïc to the public for various sports and fitness activities. Contact one of the tourist offices for details.

The **bullfight season** runs from Holy Week to September; ask at your hotel or at one of the tourist offices for information regarding times and tickets.

7. SAVVY SHOPPING

Fashion and design have long been in the forefront of Barcelona's cultural and commercial activities, and the city, always open to foreign influences through its Mediterranean gateway, cultivated a notably strong streak of independence and boldness during the Franco years. Today the ranks of local designers of clothing, furnishings, and complete interior environments are growing quickly. Although Barcelona is no Paris when it comes to designer-name recognition and sheer numbers of shops, what you'll find here is the best of the latest and a glimpse of what awaits on the horizon.

In a city with Barcelona's historic pedigree, one would expect the emphasis to be on the arts and crafts of yesteryear, yet quite the opposite is true. Barcelona's aim is to look for the newest of the new. In fact, innovative design is such a vital aspect of city life that the *Guía del Ocio,* in its listing of bars, often cites the designers responsible for shaping their distinctive atmospheres. And as you stroll along any of the main shopping thoroughfares mentioned below, you'll see stores not only selling the latest designs in everything from coffeemakers to couches but also applying this designing vision to their window displays and installations.

THE SHOPPING SCENE

HOURS Most shops are open daily from 10am to 1pm and from 4:30 to 8pm. However, department stores and certain shopping centers and stores, especially in the city center, no longer close at lunch.

SALES Although consumer prices in Barcelona have catapulted in recent years, the annual sales, which run from the second week of January to the end of February and during July and August, provide ample opportunity for bargain hunting.

TAXES Most purchases are subject to a VAT (value-added tax), here called IVA, ranging from 6% to 33%, depending on the degree of luxury of the item. Nonresidents can recover this tax under certain circumstances, but it's a cumbersome and protracted process (see "Fast Facts: Barcelona" in Chapter 3).

SHOPPING AREAS The main shopping streets in the old town are La Rambla, Avinguda Portal de l'Àngel, Carrer Portaferrissa, Carrer del Pi, and Carrer Pelai. In the Eixample, they are Passeig de Catalunya, Passeig de Gràcia, and Rambla de Catalunya. In the northern reaches of town, they are Avinguda Diagonal, Plaça Francesc Macia, Bori i Fontesta, Valvet, Via Augusta, Travessera de Gràcia, Carrer de Balmes, and Carrer Muntaner. Antiques shops are concentrated in Carrer dels Banys Nous and Carrer del Palla.

SHOPPING A TO Z
AN ART GALLERY

SALA PARES, Petritxol, 5. Tel. 318-70-20.
Since 1877 this gallery has had its finger on the pulse of the art world. As Spain's oldest gallery, it displayed the works of Picasso, Dalí, and Toulouse-Lautrec when it was not yet fashionable to do so. Open on Monday to Saturday from 10:30am to 2pm and from 4:30 to 8:30pm, Sunday from 11am to 2pm; closed Sunday in July and August. Metro: Liceu.

CHOCOLATES & SWEETS

ESCRIBÀ, Rambla de les Flors, 83. Tel. 301-60-27.
For four generations Escribà has been handcrafting unusual chocolate creations, which it offers for sale here and at its original store at Gran Vía C.C., 546 (tel. 254-75-35). It also sells wines, preserves, and tempting homemade pastries. Here you're in for double treat, though, because all the sweetness awaits behind a striking modernist facade. Open on Tuesday to Sunday from 9am to 2:30pm and from 5 to 8:30pm. Metro: Liceu.

FORN DE SANT JAUME, Rambla de Catalunya, 50. Tel. 216-02-29.
This shop offers homemade ice cream, cookies, pastries, and chocolates. There is also a cafeteria next door (see "Specialty Dining" in Chapter 5) offering fine horchata. Open daily from 9am to 9pm; closed on Christmas night. Metro: Passeig de Gràcia.

LANELLES-DONAT, Portal L'Angel, 25. Tel. 301-70-96.
This place specializes in *turrones,* a tempting concoction of almonds and honey introduced to Spain by the Moors. There are many varieties, and you'll have fun trying them all. Open on Monday to Saturday from 10:15am to 2pm and from 4 to 8pm; closed in August. Metro: Catalunya.

CRAFTS

ARTESPAÑA, Rambla de Catalunya, 75. Tel. 215-61-46.
Artespaña is a national network of stores promoting Spain's great variety of quality handcrafts. Typically, these stores offer everything from ceramics to furniture, but this one features furniture and decorative items for the home. The quality is first class and the styling

most attractive. Open on Monday to Saturday from 10am to 2pm and from 4:30 to 8:30pm. Metro: Passeig de Gràcia.

LA MANUAL ALPARGATERA, Aviño, 7. Tel. 301-01-72.

For almost 50 years, this store has been purveying baskets, handbags, hats, and other assorted articles woven of straw, palm, or reeds. In the back at a table brimming with spools of ribbon sits a woman making some of the wares for sale. Judging by the way they are overflowing the shelves, she must be very productive indeed. As you walk in, you'll see the left wall stacked to the ceiling with espadrilles, which you can have made to order in as little as one day or as much as a week, depending on the intricacy of the styling. Proudly displayed above the cashier's counter is the photo of one celebrated customer—Jack Nicholson. Open on Monday to Saturday from 9am to 1:30pm and from 4:30 to 7:30pm; closed on holidays. Metro: Liceu.

MILS, Passeig de Gràcia, 11. Tel. 412-17-94.

This rather chic shop carries crystal, fine cutlery, and Lladró, featuring some of the more elaborate figurines in the line. The entrance is in Condal Corner, an upscale shopping mall near Plaça Catalunya. Open on Monday to Friday from 9:30am to 1:30pm and from 4 to 8pm, Saturday from 10am to 1:30pm and from 5 to 8:30pm. Metro: Catalunya.

MOLSA, P1 Sant Josep Oriol, 1. Tel. 302-31-03.

Molsa sells beautiful ceramic ware, both old and new, primarily from Spain and France. Open on Monday to Friday from 10am to 2pm and from 4 to 8pm, on Saturday from 10am to 2pm and from 4:30 to 8:30pm. Metro: Liceu.

PARAGUAS, S.A., La Rambla, 104. Tel. 301-33-26.

Considering that it doesn't rain all that much in Barcelona, this specialty shop selling umbrellas of its own manufacture (see them being made in the back of the store) seems out of place. For 100 years it has been selling not only umbrellas (which you can have custom-made) but also canes and flirtatious Spanish fans and parasols. Open on Monday to Saturday from 9:30am to 1:30pm and from 4 to 8pm; closed on holidays. Metro: Liceu.

SARGADELOS, Provenza, 274. Tel. 215-01-79.

The distinctive Sargadelos ceramic ware of Galicia in northwestern Spain is the specialty at this shop. The pieces are characterized by the use of strong geometric designs and the colors blue and white and sometimes red. Open on Tuesday to Friday from 9:30am to 1:30pm, Monday to Friday from 4:30 to 8pm, and Saturday from 10:30am to 1:30pm and from 4:30 to 8pm. Metro: Passeig de Gràcia.

DEPARTMENT STORES

EL CORTE INGLÉS, Plaça Catalunya, 14. Tel. 302-12-12.

This is Barcelona's biggest department store, offering everything from souvenirs to soup dishes. Another branch is located at Avinguda Diagonal, 617–619 (tel. 419-28-28). Open on Monday to Saturday from 10am to 9pm. Metro: Catalunya.

GALERIAS PRECIADOS, Avinguda Portal de l'Angel, 19–21. Tel. 317-00-00.

The other big department store in Barcelona also offers everything imaginable. A second location is Avinguda Diagonal 471–473 (tel. 322-30-11). Open on Monday to Saturday from 10am to 9pm. Metro: Catalunya.

FASHION & DESIGN

ADOLFO DOMÍNGUEZ, Passeig de Gràcia, 89. Tel. 215-13-39.

Those who used to watch "Miami Vice" will recognize the designing hand of Adolfo Domínguez, who dressed Don Johnson to kill during that show's second season. Although most noted for redefining the "classic" look of today's chic male, Domínguez also offers designs for women on the upper floor of this store, whose angular, unadorned decor echoes the stark lines of the fashions. Open on Monday to Saturday from 10am to 2pm and 4:30 (5pm on Saturday and Monday) to 8pm. Metro: Passeig de Gràcia or Diagonal.

ARAMIS, Rambla de Catalunya, 103. Tel. 215-16-69.

If your tastes run to the classically traditional and money is no object, Aramis can dress you in Ungaro and Valentino, among other elite designer signatures for both men and women. The store's Ralph Lauren–esque decor tells the fashion story. King Juan Carlos has been known to shop here while in town. Open Monday to Friday from 10:30am to 2pm and from 4:30 to 8:15pm, Saturday from 10:15am to 2pm and from 4:30 to 8:30pm. Metro: Passeig de Gràcia.

B.D. EDICIONES DE DISEÑO, Mallorca, 291. Tel. 258-69-09.

Installed in a turn-of-the-century modernist building designed by Lluís Domenech i Montaner, b.d Ediciones de Diseño is a notable showcase for Barcelona design both inside and out. Spread over two vast floors are the latest statements in furniture, lamps, and other household accoutrements by leading contemporary Spanish and foreign designers. Among them are Britisher Jane Dillon; Italians Vittorio Gregotti, Ettore Sottsass, and Alessandro Mendini; Portuguese Alvaro Siza Vieira; American Robert Stern; and Spaniards Miguel Milá, Enric Soria, Jorid Garcés, André Ricard, Pep Bonet, Cristián Cirici, Lluís Clotet, Pepe Cortés, Xavier Mariscal, Pete Sans, Oscar Tusquets, and Mireia Riera. But b.d Ediciones is also in the business of manufacturing reproductions of historic furniture by such masters as Gaudí, Domenech i Montaner, Terragni, MacKintosh, and Schindler. Apart from its own production, b.d imports and distributes exceptional design objects, including works by Alvar Aalto, Josef Hoffman, Le Corbusier, Mies van der Rohe, and Breuer. (Some of the designs are on permanent exhibition in the Philadelphia Museum of Art, the Victoria and Albert Museum in London, and New York's Museum of Modern Art.) B.d will ship purchases home for you. Open on Monday to Friday from 10am to 1:30pm and from 4 to 8pm, Saturday from 10am to 1:30pm; closed in August and on holidays. Metro: Verdaguer.

BEVERLY FELDMAN, Mallorca, 259, next door to the Hotel Condes de Barcelona. Tel. 487-03-83.

If you're really into shoes (women's only), you'll have to set foot in here. Feldman is an American shoe designer who has lived and worked in Spain for over 20 years and whose shoes also sell Stateside at such upmarket outlets as Neiman Marcus, I. Magnin, and Saks

Fifth Avenue (where, by the way, they are considerably cheaper). Here, however, you can select from her entire collection of up-to-the-minute footwear fantasies. Open on Monday to Friday from 10am to 8pm, Saturday from 10:30am to 2pm and from 5:30 to 8pm. Metro: Passeig de Gràcia.

LOEWE, Passeig de Gràcia, 35. Tel. 216-04-00.

Loewe is Spain's upscale purveyor of luxury leather goods and elegant clothing and chic accessories for men and women. There are two other, smaller branches in Barcelona—one for men at Avinguda Diagonal 570 (tel. 200-09-20) and one for women at the Hotel Princesa Sofía (tel. 202-31-50). The first two shops are open on Monday to Saturday from 9:30am to 2pm and from 4:30 to 8pm; the shop in the Hotel Princesa Sofía is open on Monday to Saturday from 9am to 9:30pm and Sunday and holidays from 10am to 8pm. Metro: Passeig de Gràcia.

VINÇON, Passeig de Gràcia, 96. Tel. 215-60-50.

A vast emporium of the latest design innovations in housewares of all kinds, Vinçon carries some 10,000 products conceived by designers both domestic and international. Open on Monday to Saturday from 10am to 2pm and from 4:30 to 8:30pm. Metro: Diagonal or Passeig de Gràcia.

MALLS & SHOPPING CENTERS

EL BULEVARD DELS ANTIQUARIS, Passeig de Gràcia, 55. Tel. 215-44-99.

Located above the cornucopia of consumer abundance that is El Bulevard Rosa (see below), El Bulevard dels Antiquaris offers over 70 shops selling art and antiques, including paintings, jewelry, ivories, bronzes, furniture, toys, watches, porcelains, silver, dolls, African art, and coins. Open in summer on Monday to Friday from 9:30am to 8:30pm; in winter on Monday from 4:30 to 8:30pm and on Tuesday to Saturday from 10:30am to 8:30pm. Although the gallery itself is open all day, some shops do close for three hours at midday. Metro: Passeig de Gràcia.

EL BULEVARD ROSA, Passeig de Gràcia, 55. Tel. 309-06-50.

This was Barcelona's pioneer shopping mall, and suffice it to say that a shopping mall is a shopping mall is a shopping mall—wherever it may be. Its 102 diverse shops are open on Monday to Saturday from 10:30am to 8:30pm.

Not surprisingly, El Bulevard Rosa proved popular enough to spawn offspring at Avinguda Diagonal, 470 and Avinguda Diagonal, 611–615 (same phone as above), next door to El Corte Inglés. The former has some 40 shops; the latter, some 100 establishments. Metro: Passeig de Gràcia.

DIAGONAL CENTER, Avinguda Diagonal, 584. Tel. 209-65-97.

This is another popular shopping gallery, with 59 stores. Open Monday to Saturday from 10:30am to 2pm and from 4:30 to 8:30pm. Metro: Diagonal.

THE DRUGSTORE, Passeig de Gràcia, 71, near the Hotel Condes de Barcelona. Tel. 215-70-74.

The Drugstore is not a pharmacy but a complex of 12 shops that are open 24 hours daily. It contains a restaurant, a cafeteria, a bar, a supermarket, a tobacco shop, a bookstore, a gift shop, a photographic shop, and an area of video games. Metro: Passeig de Gràcia.

VIP'S, Rambla de Catalunya, 7. Tel. 301-48-05.
Over 20 establishments comprise this shopping gallery, which is similar to The Drugstore (see above). VIP'S is open Monday to Thursday and Sunday from 9am to 2am and Friday, Saturday, and holiday eves from 9am to 3am. Metro: Catalunya.

MARKETS

LA BOQUERÍA, La Rambla near the Gran Teatre del Liceu. No phone.
Also known as the Mercat de Sant Josep, this is one of the world's cleanest, most extensive, and most fascinating produce markets—as such, it's a Barcelona sight in its own right. Beyond great gates of glass and iron dating from 1914 await aisle upon aisle of attractively displayed produce from both sea and land, as well as all manner of prepared provisions, vying for the attention of a highly discerning and demanding clientele. Within the market itself are some choice places to have a meal or a snack (see "Specialty Dining" in Chapter 5). Metro: Liceu.

MERCADO GÒTICO DE ANTIGUEDADES (Gothic Antique Market), Plaça del Pi. Tel. 317-19-96.
Antiques lovers will enjoy this open-air market that springs up every Thursday from 10am to 10pm, except during August. Here you'll find everything from antique buttons and lace to vintage armoires. Remember to bargain. Metro: Liceu.

STAMPS & COINS

AURELIANO MONGE, Boters, 2. Tel. 317-94-35.
Collectors will want to pay a visit to this prestigious shop near the cathedral, where the hushed atmosphere suggests a consummate professionalism. Open on Monday to Saturday from 9am to 1:30pm and from 4 to 8pm. Metro: Catalunya.

8. BARCELONA NIGHTS

While Barcelona offers the full range of evening entertainment—from plays to cabarets—those who don't speak Spanish will find their options somewhat restricted by the language barrier. Even movies are typically dubbed rather than subtitled. Of course, ballets, operas, and concerts transcend the language barrier, and the season for these events runs from September to early July.

On a trendier note, "designer" bars have been the rage in Barcelona for several years now, with each new offering aspiring to ever-greater heights of originality and creative chutzpah. Of course, drinks in these ultratrendy bars cost several times what they do in the down-home bar next door. Since many of these chic spots come and go in the flicker of a neon light, ask around for the shining star of the moment.

For the most comprehensive listing of evening activities, including restaurants, TV programming, clubs, and discos, pick up a copy of the weekly *Guía del Ocio* at any newsstand. Although it's in Spanish, such readily recognizable cognates as "Cocteles," "Bares," and "Champañerías" should help you negotiate a path through the night. A more upscale guide to nightlife is the monthly *Vivir en Barcelona.* For a guide to the thriving gay scene, pick up a map of gay Barcelona with a list of bars, clubs, hotels, and contacts at **Sextienda** (see "More Entertainment" later in this chapter).

Barcelona's nightlife often greets the dawn, and some semilegal clubs actually open on Saturday and Sunday between 5 and 9am.

THE PERFORMING ARTS

Barcelona has long been fertile ground for the performing arts. In 1603 it boasted its first theater, and in 1847 its magnificent opera house, the Gran Teatre del Liceu, opened. Modernism, which fomented all manifestations of culture and the arts, endowed the city with its magnificent Palau de la Música, where the mere act of attending a performance is a truly cultural experience. In addition to the classical arts of ballet, opera, and concerts, Barcelona enjoys a special reputation for fostering the avant-garde, especially in the realm of theater.

OPERA, CLASSICAL MUSIC & BALLET

For the latest information on concerts and other musical events around town, call the **Amics de la Música de Barcelona** (literally, Barcelona's "Friends of Music") at 302-68-70 on Monday to Friday from 10am to 1pm or from 3 to 8pm.

Opera and classical music performances by local companies and orchestras are offered regularly at the Gran Teatre del Liceu and Palau de la Música Catalana. Check the *Guía del Ocio* or call the theaters themselves for the latest schedule of events.

You may want to catch a performance by one of the following companies while you're in Barcelona. The **Associación D'Etnografia i Folklore** specializes in cultural and folkloric theatrical presentations. For information on performances by the **Ballet Contemporaneo de Barcelona,** call 322-10-37. The **Art-Companyia de Dansa** specializes in neoclassical dance, and

---

THE MAJOR CONCERT/PERFORMANCE HALLS

Gran Teatre del Liceu, Sant Pau 1 bis. Tel. 318-91-77, or 318-97-80 for information.
Mercat de les Flors, Lleida, 59. Tel. 325-06-75, or 318-85-99 for reservations.
Palau de la Música Catalana, Amadeu Vives, 1. Tel. 268-10-00.
Teatre Condal, Avda. Paral.lel, 91–93. Tel. 442-85-84.
Teatre Llantiol, Riereta, 7. Tel. 329-90-09.
Teatre Lliure, Montseny, 47. Tel. 218-92-51.

jazz dance highlights the repertoire of the **Companyia de Bailes Jazz.**

MAJOR CONCERT HALLS & AUDITORIUMS

GRAN TEATRE DEL LICEU, Sant Pau 1 bis. Tel. 318-92-77, or 318-97-80 for information.

This 2,000-seat 19th-century opera house is a splendid setting for opera, classical music, and ballet performances, as well as a sight in itself (see "More Attractions" earlier in this chapter). The opera season runs from early February to June, and ballet performances are held in October and November. Metro: Liceu.

The box office is open on Monday to Friday from 10am to 1pm and from 4 to 7pm, on Saturday from 10am to 1pm. Evening performances begin at 9pm, matinees at 5pm.

Prices: Tickets 350–9,500 ptas. ($3.50–$95).

PALAU DE LA MÚSICA CATALAN, Amadeu Vives, 1. Tel. 268-10-00.

This magnificent 2,000-seat modernist concert hall is among the world's finest. The work of Catalan architect Lluís Domenech i Montaner, it was inaugurated in 1908 and is considered his most important structure. Its distinctive facade is a tour de force of brick, mosaic, and glass recalling in part the sensuous, rhythmic flow of Arab art. But it is the drama and elegance inside that truly set this hall apart from its peers worldwide. The harmonious interplay of ceramic mosaics, colored crystals, and a central skylight build to the stunning crescendo of carvings that frame the stage. Throughout the year a variety of concerts and recitals by leading orchestras and artists are held here. Metro: Urquinaona.

Tours: Guided one-hour tours of the building available by arrangement Tues, Thurs, and Sat for 250 ptas. ($2.50).

Prices: Tickets 450–4,000 ptas. ($4.50–$40).

THEATERS

Ticket prices vary greatly in each theater, depending on the work and the caliber of the company. The average range of prices is 500 ptas. ($5) to 3,000 ptas. ($30). Virtually all performances are either in Spanish or in Catalan.

The **Teatre Condal,** Avda. Paral.lel, 91–93 (tel. 442-85-84; metro: Paral.lel), presents mostly contemporary works, often in Catalan. Similar in its offerings is the **Teatre Llantiol,** Riereta, 7 (tel. 329-90-09; metro: Paral.lel or Liceu). The **Mercat de les Flors,** Lleida, 59 (tel. 325-06-75, or 318-85-99 for reservations), presents all types of performances from theater to dance and concerts; located at the foot of Montjuïc, it is accessible from Metro Plaça Espanya and by bus nos. 9, 27, 30, 50, and 57. The **Teatre Lliure,** Montseny, 47 (tel. 218-92-51; metro: Fontana), famed for its avant-garde ventures, boasts its own Companyia Teatre Lliure.

LOCAL CULTURAL ENTERTAINMENT

The *sardanas* is a sedate regional folk dance that's very popular with the local citizenry, who gather regularly to keep the tradition alive. Watch them in Plaça Catedral on Saturday at 6:30pm and on Sunday at noon; at Plaça Sant Jaume on Sunday and holidays at 7pm in summer and 6:30pm in winter; at Plaça Eivissa on Sunday at noon;

at Plaça Sant Felip Neri on the first Saturday of the month at 6pm; at Parc de l'Escorxador on Sunday at noon; and at Parc de la Guineueta on Sunday at noon.

THE CLUB & MUSIC SCENE
NIGHTCLUBS, CABARETS & DISCOS

EL MOLINO, Vila Vilà, 99. Tel. 441-63-83.

Since 1916, this establishment has been offering piquant burlesque entertainment to enthusiastic audiences. The nudity and sexual innuendo are all in good fun, and the vaudeville-style presentation now borders on parody. El Molino is open Tuesday to Sunday, with shows on Tuesday through Friday and on Sunday at 6pm and 11pm. Saturday shows are at 6 and 10:30pm and 1am. Metro: Paral.lel.

Admission (including one drink): 3,200 ptas. ($32).

LA PALOMA, Tigre, 27. Tel. 301-68-97.

Both accomplished ballroom dancers and those with two left feet will enjoy this most campy of dance halls with a ponderous baroque decor dating from 1915. Since 1903 it has been catering to hoofers from all walks of life. The large central chandelier, even unlit as it usually is, imparts a certain nostalgic elegance to the cavernous space. The music is always provided by live orchestras. Local tradition calls for Barcelona wedding parties to make a stop here sometime during the night; other celebrations, from birthday parties to bachelor parties to retirement parties, are regularly announced between dance numbers. Even if you don't like dancing, stop in for the local color. Open on Thursday to Sunday, holiday eves, and holidays with sessions from 6 to 9:30pm and 11:30pm to 3:30am. The first session features softer, more tranquil music; the latter is a little more lively. Metro: Universitat.

Admission: 450–700 ptas. ($4.50–$7), depending on day and time.

TANGO, Diputación, 94. Tel. 325-37-70.

A typically dark nightspot with two bars and a large dance floor, Tango features live orchestras playing Latin rhythms interspersed with recorded music of diverse rock vintages. Open daily from 6 to 9:45pm and 11:30pm to 4am (until 4:30am on Friday night and from 11pm to 4:45am on Saturday night). Metro: Rocafort.

Admission (including one drink): 1,000–1,700 ptas. ($10–$17) men; 1,200–1,500 ptas. ($12–$15) women.

FLAMENCO

EL TABLAO DE CARMEN, Poble Espanyol, Arcos, 9. Tel. 325-68-95.

This is unquestionably the best flamenco show in town. The performances are of a consistently high caliber, and the food is good, the atmosphere intimate, and the service friendly. The club is open Tuesday to Sunday from 9pm to 3am, with shows on Tuesday to Friday and Sunday at 10:30pm and on Saturday at 11pm and 1am. Directions: From Plaça Espanya, take the free double-decker bus that shuttles visitors back and forth to the Poble Espanyol.

Admission: Dinner and show 7,000 ptas. ($70); drink and show 4,200 ptas. ($42); reduced admission for the second show on Sat.

JAZZ

L'EIXAMPLE JAZZ, Diputació, 341. Tel. 201-84-41.
This is basically a place for jazz but features tangos on Monday and flamenco on Thursday. Live performances are featured nightly, except Sunday, when there's recorded music only. Open daily from 11:30pm to 5:30am. Metro: Girona.
Prices: First drink from 650–1,600 ptas. ($6.50–$16) and subsequent drinks from 800–1,000 ptas. ($8–$10), depending on the cachet of the performers.

HARLEM JAZZ CLUB, Comtessa Sobradiel, 8. Tel. 310-07-55.
A hole-in-the-wall filled with aficionados who come for the fine jazz, the Harlem Jazz Club is open on Tuesday to Thursday from 8pm to 3am, on Friday and Saturday from 8pm to 4am, and on Sunday from 8pm to 2am. There are live performances Tuesday through Thursday at 10 and 11:30pm and on Sunday at 9:30 and 11pm. Metro: Jaume I or Liceu.
Admission: Free.

THE BAR SCENE

BARS

In summer, the lower end of the Rambla de Catalunya blossoms with café-bars and their umbrella-shaded tables lining its central sidewalk. Drinks, snacks, and assorted ice-cream treats are served until the wee hours—great for late-afternoon coffee klatsches or late-night drinks. Here are some more suggestions:

BOADAS COCKTAIL BAR, Tallers, 1. Tel. 318-88-26.
Since 1933 this bar has been dispensing a long list of sophisticated cocktails. They are shaken, stirred, and at times poured from on high in such a way that having a drink here becomes a theatrical event. Also, there is always a featured "cocktail of the day" bound to educate even the most worldly of palates. Open on Monday to Saturday from noon to 2am and holiday eves and holidays from noon to 3am. Metro: Catalunya.

NICH HAVANNA, Roselló, 208. Tel. 215-65-91.
Touted as "the ultimate bar," this has long been a staple of Barcelona nightlife. Like Ticktacktoe (see below), it is a *multiespacio* (literally, "multispace") experience—that is, there's something here for everyone. Open on Monday to Thursday from 8pm, Friday to Sunday from 6pm; closing time is somewhere in the wee hours. Metro: Diagonal.

EL PARAIGUA, Paso de la Eseñanza, 2. Tel. 317-14-79.
A Barcelona institution, this pleasant two-story bar with modernist overtones specializes in exotic concoctions, not all of them alcoholic. Downstairs is particularly romantic. Open on Monday to Friday from 8:30am 2am and Saturday 5pm to 2am; closed during August. Metro: Jaume I.

TICKTACKTOE, Roger de Llúria, 40. Tel. 318-99-47.

This multidimensional, ultramodern nightspot is part bar, part restaurant, and part billiard hall. The prime attraction, however, is Manuel Ybargüengoitia's ingenious decor, featuring unique lamps, an abstract marble whale behind one bar, and another bar contoured like a woman's breast. The patrons, mostly in their mid-20s to mid-30s, are drawn from the fashion and sports worlds as well as from the VIP heights of other walks of life.

The moderately priced restaurant has a menu that varies daily with the market offerings. Upstairs, when you stand at the sinks in the bathroom, you'll get a surprising view of the bar below. Open on Monday to Thursday from 7pm to 2:30am, Friday and Saturday from 7pm to 3am; the restaurant serves from 1:30 to 4pm and 8:30pm to 1am. Closed on holidays and most of August. Metro: Urquinaona.

UNIVERSAL, Maria Cubí, 182-184. Tel. 201-46-58.

In the vanguard of avant-garde designer displays, Universal's postmodern punk decor is so minimalist that it seems threatened with extinction. Stark, dark, and severe in its sparseness, the high-ceilinged space calls to mind a converted warehouse. The music is loud, and the visual sense is stimulated by slides projected on the far brick wall. The crowd is young, but the wooden theater seats lining the walls are old. Open daily from 11pm to 3am. FF.CC.: Passeig de Gràcia.

VELVET, Balmes, 161. Tel. 217-67-14.

Installed in a modernist structure, the ultrachic Velvet has a small dance floor and two bars lined with buttock-shaped bar stools. There is no sign marking its dual entrances—one an arched pavement dotted with plants and the other a ramp.

The crowd here varies with the day of the week and the time of the year, but it is primarily older and seasoned with the occasional celebrity. Alfredo Arribas is the architect behind this distinctive design statement, where again even the bathrooms are worth a visit. Open on Monday to Thursday from 7:30pm to 4:30am, Friday and Saturday from 7:30pm to 5am, and Sunday from 7pm to 4:30am. Metro: Diagonal.

CHAMPAÑERÍAS

These establishments specializing in cavas from Catalonia and foreign champagnes run from the very sophisticated to the mundane.

LA CAVA DEL PALAU, Verdaguer i Callis, 10. Tel. 310-09-38.

This establishment has evolved from a small place specializing in *cava catalana* to a very sophisticated space carrying 40 different regional cavas; 40 French champagnes; and some 350 different appellation wines from Spain, France, and Chile. Connoisseurs of sparkling wines will want to try the *brut natures,* elaborated without the traditional *licor de expedición* and thus, as the name suggests, the driest and most natural of all cavas.

La Cava del Palau also serves a choice selection of *raciones* (somewhat larger than tapa portions) of Spanish and foreign cheeses, French pâtés, and caviar for up to 4,000 ptas. ($40) per plate. Most raciones, however, average about 1,500 ptas. ($15) per plate, and the cava, served in fine fluted glasses, averages about 600 ptas. ($6) per glass.

Although this bar can accommodate up to 300, its multilevel

layout provides intimacy no matter where you sit. It usually fills up after 11pm and is especially packed after concerts at the nearby Palau de la Música. Open on Monday to Saturday from 7pm to 2:30am, with live piano music starting at 11:30pm; closed during Holy Week and in August. Metro: Urquinaona.

LA XAMPANYERÍA, Provença, 236, at the corner of Enric Granados. Tel. 253-74-55.
The "blue lagoon" of champagne bars, this place attracts a lively mixed crowd, especially after midnight on weekends. Twinkling above its undulating marble-top bar are small lights that suggest stars. In addition to over 40 types of cavas—including half a dozen French champagnes—it serves pâtés, cured ham, and chocolates averaging about 1,100 ptas. ($11) per racion. A glass of cava averages 500 ptas. ($5). Open on Monday to Saturday from 7pm to 3am; closed on holidays and in August. FF.CC.: Provença.

MORE ENTERTAINMENT
THE GAY SCENE

Sextienda, Carrer Rauric, 11 (tel. 318-86-76), was the first gay shop in Spain and bills itself as the "gay information center." It offers a free map listing bars, discos, restaurants, saunas, and other places around town where gay men and lesbians congregate. Open on Monday to Saturday from 10am to 8:30pm; closed holidays and 10 days in October or November.

A traditional place to stay and meet companions is the Hotel California, Carrer Rauric, 14 (tel. 317-77-66). Some "in" spots of the moment are the Metro Disco, Sepulveda, 185 (tel. 323-52-27); the Sauna Condal, Condal, 18 bis (tel. 301-96-80); and Sauna Casanova, Casanova, 57 (tel. 323-78-60).

MOVIES

Most first-run movies are dubbed into Spanish. The following cinemas often show English-language movies. Check the *Guía del Ocio* for the shows, times, and nearest metro stop.

Mainstream Movies

ARKADIN, Trav. de Gràcia, 103 (tel. 218-62-42).
CASABLANCA I & II, Passeig de Gràcia, 115 (tel. 218-43-45).
MALDA, Pi, 5 (tel. 317-85-29).
VERDI, Verdia 32 (tel. 237-05-16).

X-Rated Movies

SALA X, Plaça de Urquinaona, 5 (tel. 301-70-94).
SALA X, La Rambla, 17 (tel. 317-70-58).

A CASINO

GRAN CASINO DE BARCELONA, Sant Pere de Ribes. Tel. 893-36-66.
About 25 miles (40.25km) out of Barcelona near Sitges, this casino is housed in a romantic 19th-century structure and offers the full range of games of chance in a grand setting studded with elegant

rugs, chandeliers, and scalloped curtains. The sedate, sophisticated atmosphere is completely devoid of the boisterous frenzy found in most American gambling dens. In the casino's restaurant you can enjoy a meal averaging about 5,000 ptas ($50). After dinner on Friday and Saturday you can enjoy the downstairs disco. Open June through August, daily from 6pm to 5am; September through May, on Sunday to Thursday from 5pm to 4am and on Friday, Saturday, and holiday eves from 5pm to 5am. Closed on Christmas Eve.

Admission: You'll need your passport to get in and admission is 600 ptas. ($6), even if you're planning only to have dinner or go to the disco. Jeans and sneakers not permitted. Restaurant reservations recommended Fri–Sat and throughout Aug. **Directions:** Take the Autovía Castelldefels and Túneles de Garraf, exiting toward Vilanova.

CHAPTER 7

EASY EXCURSIONS FROM BARCELONA

1. MONTSERRAT MONASTERY & ENVIRONS
2. CAVA COUNTRY
3. GIRONA (GERONA)
4. TARRAGONA
5. SITGES

Beyond Barcelona is the Catalan region it captains. Home to some six million inhabitants (about half of whom live in the greater Barcelona area), it offers great scenic variety, with 365 miles (580km) of Mediterranean coastline, impressive mountain ranges, and inland plains. Bordered by France to the north, Aragón to the west, and Valencia to the south, it is slightly larger than Belgium. Its geographic parameters hark back to the counties created by Charlemagne along the southern edge of his empire in the late 8th century, as a buffer against Muslim incursions.

Two hundred years after Charlemagne, the Catalan counts, consolidating around the House of Barcelona, broke with the French kings. In 1137 Catalonia merged with the Kingdom of Aragón. And in the following century James I brought Mallorca and Valencia into the Catalan fold. In 1283 the parliamentary courts were consolidated, and in 1359 the Generalitat, Catalonia's permanent political delegation, was instituted.

Regional expansion continued to the 15th century, embracing Sicily, Athens, Sardinia, and Naples. In the latter half of the 15th century, Mediterranean dominance waned and Catalonia-Aragón joined with Castilla—but without relinquishing its own political integrity. In the early 18th century, however, that integrity was abrogated by Philip V. Not until 1931 was the Generalitat revived under the Second Spanish Republic, only to be annihilated again in the aftermath of the brutal Spanish Civil War (1936–39).

During the ensuing 40 years of Franco's rule, all manifestations of Catalan identity were rigorously suppressed; but with the rebirth of the Generalitat at the head of the newly autonomous regional Catalan government in 1979, Catalan patriotism resurfaced with a good deal of pent-up zeal. Catalan once again became an official language, and the historic Catalan flag with four red stripes on a yellow background (which Catalans say was the inspiration for the flag of Spain) was resurrected.

As Catalonia rode the tumultuous tides of its political history, its artistic and cultural traditions were fed by the hybrid mix of conquerors and merchants carried here by the Mediterranean Sea. Thus Tarragona is today a showcase of Roman remains, and the medieval heart of Girona (Gerona) reflects the passing presence of Romans, Moors, and Jews. Marvelous monasteries and cathedrals, financed by the fruits of vigorous trade, rose up throughout the region, their crowning glory the Monastery of Montserrat, spiritual home of Catalonia.

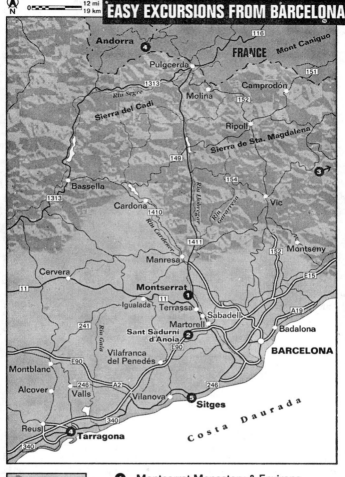

❶ Montserrat Monastery & Environs
❷ Cava Country
❸ Girona (Gerona)
❹ Tarragona
❺ Sitges

In the 11th and 12th centuries, masterpieces of Romanesque art began to dot the countryside, and in the 13th, the Gothic style, essentially an urban phenomenon, echoed in stone the general economic and cultural prosperity of its time. Eclipsed by other centers of European power during the Renaissance and baroque eras and then swallowed up by a greater Spain, Catalonia offers but a smattering of artistic specimens from these and the neoclassical periods. But as the 20th century dawned, Catalan culture boldly reasserted itself in the modernist tradition, fueled by the innovative visions of such architectural geniuses as Antoni Gaudí and Domènech i Montaner. Carrying the rekindled torch of Catalan culture through the 20th century were such grand artistic talents as Salvador Dalí, Joan Miró, and Antoni Tàpies.

Touring Catalonia by car allows you to combine some of its principal destinations with visits to interesting sidelights along the way, so the itineraries below are geared toward travelers with their own set of wheels. However, the major cities and sights mentioned can also be reached by train or bus, so information on these alternative travel options is given.

AL-ANDALUS EXPRESO In July, the *Al-Andalus Expreso,* Spain's luxury train, cruises from Barcelona to the Rioja wine region and Pamplona; in August, it travels from Barcelona to Santiago de Compostela, following in part the medieval pilgrimage route of St. James and stopping in Hemingway's Pamplona and in Burgos (famed for its cathedral and proximity to the birthplace of El Cid). A stunning eyeful of Lalique glass, gleaming brass, meticulous marquetry, and art deco glamour, the *Al-Andalus* actually outclasses the fabled *Orient Express*—it's wider; has showers, a cellular phone, video entertainment, and air conditioning; and makes sightseeing stops.

These four-day/three-night train journeys cost about 50,000 ptas. ($500) per person per day in a deluxe double cabin, including all guided sightseeing visits and meals on the train. In the off-season, the *Al-Andalus* offers special holiday excursions and is available for charter. For information and reservations call toll free 800/323-7308.

1. MONTSERRAT MONASTERY & ENVIRONS

38 miles (60km) W of Barcelona

GETTING THERE By Train The FF.CC. de la Generalitat (commuter train line) from Plaça d'Espanya station will take you to the cable car serving the top of the mountain; a round-trip combined ticket costs about 1,300 ptas. ($13). For details, call FF.CC. de la Generalitat at 205-15-15.

By Bus Pullmantur, Gran Vía les Corts Catalanes, 635 (tel. 318-02-41), and **Julià Tours,** Ronda Universitat, 5 (tel. 317-64-54), offer half-day bus tours to Montserrat Monastery leaving daily all year long at 9:30am, and from April 1 to October 15 daily at 3:30pm as well. The cost is 4,500 ptas. ($45).

By Car If you go by car, you'll be able to add to your itinerary a visit to an interesting Gaudí church in Santa Coloma de Cervelló, about 12.5 miles (20km) from Barcelona, and lunch at a converted Catalan country mansion. To visit Gaudí's crypt of the parish **Church of the Sacred Heart,** follow the Avinguda Diagonal out of town in the direction of the airport until it becomes the A-2 heading toward Tarragona. Take the "Cinturó Litoral" exit toward Sant Boi de Llobregat and then follow the road toward Sant Vincenç dels Horts. Just before the railroad crossing, take a left (a sign on the side of the building points to the Cripta Güell). Continue straight for about half a mile, and when you come to a small incline, you'll find the church on the right. (If you want to visit just the church and not continue on to the Montserrat Monastery, you can take the FF.CC. de la Generalitat from Plaça d'Espanya to Santa Coloma de Cervelló.)

To travel on to the monastery, retrace your route to the railroad tracks on the San Vincenç dels Horts road (which becomes the N-11) and continue straight on through that village and through Martorell for a total of about 24 miles (38km). At this point you'll see a sign indicating Manresa and Montserrat to the right. Up until now you will have been traveling through a highly industrialized area, but here the scenery changes abruptly. The 9 miles (14km) leading up to the monastery wind through pine forests and eerie rock formations resembling sculptured towers. Those familiar with the Meteora in Greece will notice a scenic similarity. In all, it's about 32 miles (52km) from the Colonia Güell to the monastery, and the drive takes just over an hour in light traffic.

WHAT TO SEE & DO

EN ROUTE TO THE MONASTERY

CHURCH OF THE SACRED HEART, in Santa Coloma de Cervelló.

Here in the village of Santa Coloma de Cervelló, the financier Güell and several associates established a velvet factory and constructed a village for the workers, commissioning Gaudí to design its church. After eight years the project was abandoned; only the crypt of the church was finished. Nevertheless, it is one of Gaudí's most admired and studied works and includes many elements that he would later use for his Sagrada Familia.

Perched atop a small hill amid pine trees, this round, mostly brick structure with a portico of sloping columns and vaults today functions as the village church. In the cavelike interior, the flower-shaped stained-glass windows shine like stars. In reinterpreting the traditional Catalan vault, Gaudí rendered it in the form of hyperbolic paraboloids. Of special note inside are the unique benches of wood and wrought iron also of Gaudí design.

Since this is a functioning church, be discreet if services are going on. However, even if you can't get inside when you get there, the exterior is well worth the slight detour en route to the Montserrat Monastery.

Admission: Free.

Open: Mon–Sat 10:15am–1:30pm and 4–8pm; Sun and holidays 10am–2pm.

MONTSERRAT MONASTERY

The complex of the Montserrat Monastery is vast, containing a basilica with the venerated Black Madonna, a museum, numerous hostels for pilgrims, restaurants, and a wealth of souvenir shops and food stalls. For many, the trip to Montserrat is a pious pilgrimage; for others, it's a day's diversion—especially on Sunday, when the throngs of visitors and vendors give the place the feel of a religious Disneyland.

The jagged mountain (*Montserrat* means "serrated mountain") is 7 miles (10km) long and 3.5 miles (5km) wide. Its highest peak, Sant Jeróni, is 4,075 feet (1,235m). The monastery itself is situated at 2,393 feet (725m). One of its noted institutions is the 50-member Boys Choir (Escolanía), established in the 13th century. If you time your visit right, you can hear them sing the Salve and the Virolai (the hymn of Montserrat) at 1pm or the Montserratine Salve at 7:10pm.

About 80 Benedictine monks make their home at the monastery, which cannot be visited. What can and should be visited, however, are the basilica, the Chapel of the Virgin, and the museum. Parking at the monastery costs 350 ptas. ($3.50), and on Sunday, when the mountaintop is awash with day-trippers and faithful worshippers, you may have a bit of a walk from your car.

THE BASILICA AND THE CHAPEL OF THE VIRGIN. No phone.

The basilica dates from the 16th century, although its facade, memorable for the sculptures of Jesus and the 12 Apostles, was not completed until the turn of our century. Inside, all is rather heavy and dark. The main altar is made of rock from the mountain, and suspended from a baldachin above it is a beautiful 16th-century ivory Christ-image of Italian origin, mounted on a modern cross.

To see the image of the revered **La Moreneta (Black Madonna)** of Montserrat, Catalunya's patron saint, you must exit the basilica and re-enter through the side door on the right. The image, housed in a splendid chapel adorned with glittering mosaics, is of the Virgin and Child.

Admission: Free.

Open: Daily 6am–8pm.

MONTSERRAT MONASTERY MUSEUM. Tel. 835-02-51.

The museum is made up of two parts. The old section contains religious paintings of the old Italian and modern Catalonian schools; a biblical collection containing Egyptian, Roman, and Arab archeological artifacts; and a display of Jewish liturgical items, including Torahs from the 17th and 18th centuries. The new section houses secular paintings of the 19th and 20th centuries, primarily by such Catalan artists as Raurich and Urgell, although there are a Sorolla and three Picassos here as well.

Admission: 325 ptas. ($3.25).

Open: Old section: Daily 10:30am–2pm and 3–6pm. New section: Daily 3–6pm.

SANT JOAN. Tel. 835-04-80 for information.

IMPRESSIONS

Catalonia is undoubtedly the best cultivated, the richest, and most industrious province or principality in Spain; and the King, who has the sun for his hat (for it always shines in some part of his dominions), has nothing to boast of, equal to Catalonia.
—PHILIP THICKNESSE, *A YEAR'S JOURNEY THROUGH FRANCE AND SPAIN*, 1789

Beyond the human-made sights, there is the mountain itself, Sant Joan, crisscrossed with numerous funiculars and paths leading to some 13 uninhabited hermitages and numerous shrines—or simply to spectacular views. For a soaring vista, take the funicular up to the summit.

Prices: Round-trip ticket for funicular 700 ptas. ($7).

Open: Funiculars run every 20 minutes daily 10am–5:35pm.

WHERE TO DINE

CAN AMAT, Urbanización Can Amat, Crta. N-II, km. 585. Tel. 771-40-27.

Cuisine: CATALAN. **Reservations:** Recommended, especially on weekends.

$ Prices: Appetizers 975–2,500 ptas. ($9.75–$25); main courses 2,000–3,500 ptas. ($20–$35). AE, MC, V.

Open: Sun–Fri 1–4pm; Sat 1–4pm and 9pm–midnight.

Installed in a magnificent Catalan mansion dating from 1890, this flagship of the Paradis group of restaurants exudes an atmosphere of cozy elegance. A large number of daily specials are offered, along with a fixed menu heavily weighted with seafood (including over half a dozen ways to prepare bacallà, or cod). The turbot in a cava-cream sauce is sinfully tasty. But long before you have a chance to study the menu, your table will fill up with olives, bread with tomato, and snails to *abrir el apetito* (open the appetite) in case the menu itself doesn't do the trick. Then, before dessert, you will be served muscatel in a *porrón,* a flask with a pointed spout that must never touch your lips as you lift it up and pour the golden elixir down your throat. (*Note:* If you've never done this before, ask for a demonstration and an extra napkin to tuck under your chin.) Besides the appetizing homemade desserts on the display cart, the house specializes in exotic home-made ice-cream.

To get here, take the Monistrol/Manresa road back down from the monastery to see the other side of the mountain. When you get to the bottom, take the road toward Barcelona and Martorell for about 15.5 miles (25km) to the turnoff for Can Amat, located at kilometer 585 on the N-II. Here you'll turn into an industrial park. Go straight for about a kilometer, then follow the sign to the left for the restaurant.

EN ROUTE BACK TO BARCELONA

It's about 19 miles (30km) back to Barcelona via the N-II, which leads into the A-2, which eventually becomes Barcelona's Avinguda Diagonal.

2. CAVA COUNTRY

Sant Sadurní d'Anoia, about 25 miles (40km) W of Barcelona

GETTING THERE By Train Trains run daily to Sant Sadurní d'Anoia (the station is right next to the Freixenet bodega) from Barcelona's Estació Sants. To visit the Codorniu winery, however, you need a car, because taxis from the train station are unreliable. For train information and fares call R.E.N.F.E. at 490-02-02.

By Bus From Barcelona, **Pullmantur,** Gran Vía les Corts Catalanes, 635 (tel. 318-02-41), and **Julià Tours,** Ronda Universitat, 5 (tel. 317-64-54), offer a full-day excursion to a cava winery, the Museu del Vi, and Sitges from May 1 to September 30 on Tuesday and Thursday for 8,000 ptas. ($80).

By Car To get to Sant Sadurní d'Anoia from Barcelona, take the A-2 (Exit 27).

The Penedés wineries that produce the fine sparkling wines known as *cavas* in Spain are principally found in the area of Sant Sadurní d'Anoia. From here you can make an afternoon of it by the sea in Sitges (discussed fully later in this chapter), about 14 miles (22 km) away, before returning to Barcelona.

WHAT TO SEE & DO

CODORNIU, 08770 Sant Sadurní d'Anoia. Tel. 891-01-25.

Spain's oldest cava producer (since 1872) is proud to show visitors around its extensive and remarkably immaculate facilities, both above and below ground—down to 95 feet (29m). About 160,000 visitors annually take the one- to two-hour guided tour, which is conducted in several languages. A brief audiovisual presentation precedes the tour, which includes the modernist, cathedral-like Hacienda Codorníu designed by Josep Puig i Cadafalch and the 10 miles (16km) of underground wine cellars where the sparkling wines are produced by the "champenoise" method. (This endless maze of multilevel cellars must really be seen to be believed.) The old pressing section has been converted into a museum, and the whole complex has been declared a national monument. Codorniu produces some 40 million bottles of cava annually, making it the world's largest cava vintner (it now also produces cava in California's Napa Valley). At any one time, there are about 100 million bottles in stock. The tour concludes with a tasting.

The most interesting time to visit is during the grape harvest in September and October; the least interesting time is in August, when most of the production facilities are shut down for vacation.

Tours: Free. Since hours vary widely throughout the year, it's best to call before you go.

FREIXENET, 08770 Sant Sadurní d'Anoia. Tel. 891-07-00.

This winery presents a half-hour video followed by a one-hour tour detailing the production of its wines. In business since 1889, it has recently also acquired vineyards in California's Sonoma Valley and in France. Although this is not as much a showpiece vineyard as Codorniu (see above), the tour, including a tasting, is every bit as informative as Codorniu's and again is conducted in various languages.

Tours: Free. Since hours vary widely throughout the year, it's best to call before you go.

MUSEU DEL VI [WINE MUSEUM], Plaça Jaume (near the cathedral), Vilafranca del Penedés. Tel. 890-05-82.

You can enhance your oenological knowledge still further with a visit to this museum, about 6 miles (10km) from Sant Sadurní d'Anoia. Surprising in its scope—not only does it have exhibits relating to wine production, storage, and consumption throughout the ages, but also it has impressive collections of art, ceramics, and geological and archeological items—this museum calls itself "the ethnological museum of Vilafranca and of the Penedés . . . the 'Musée de l'Homme' on a Penedés scale." Upon the conclusion of your visit, you are offered a sample of a local white, red, or rose wine.

Admission: 225 ptas. ($2.25).

Open: Oct 1–May 31, Tues–Sun 10am–2pm and 4–7pm. June 1–Sept 30, Tues–Sun 10am–2pm and 4:30–7:30pm.

---

3. GIRONA (GERONA)

60 miles (96km) N of Barcelona

GETTING THERE **By Train** Trains run daily between Girona and Barcelona's Estació Sants station. Call R.E.N.F.E. for schedule and fares at 490-02-02.

By Bus **Pullmantur,** Gran Vía les Corts Catalanes, 635 (tel. 318-02-41), and **Julià Tours,** Ronda Universitat, 5 (tel. 317-64-54), offer a full-day tour from Barcelona to Girona and the Teatre-Museu Dalí in Figueres from May 1 to September 30 on Wednesday and Friday for 9,000 ptas. ($90).

By Car From Barcelona, take the A-2 north to the A-7.

ESSENTIALS Tourist information is available in Girona from the Patronato de Turismo Costa Brava–Girona, Pujada Sant Martí, 5, 17004 Girona (tel. 72/208-401; fax 72/221-570).

Located at the confluence of the rivers Ter and Onyar, Girona (Gerona) is a provincial capital with a 2,000-year pedigree.

A key city along the Roman Via Augusta, Girona is still today one of Catalonia's most important cities. It lived its most splendid moments in the Middle Ages and was a focal point for the Jews of the region. Numbering up to 300 strong in its day, Girona's Jewish community—the second largest in Catalonia, after Barcelona's—established the first Cabalistic school on the Iberian Peninsula during the first half of the 12th century.

WHAT TO SEE & DO

As you cross the Onyar River, which divides the old and new towns, you will see its banks lined with colorful houses dating from the late Middle Ages. These border on Girona's old town, which retains its cobblestone streets (bring sensible shoes) and a network of narrow alleys and steep, staircased streets that seem immune to the passing of time. Once inside the old town, take note of the sturdy walls and the tower that date from Roman times but were reconstructed during the Middle Ages.

From 890 to 1492, Girona's Carrer de la Força was the backbone of the *Call* (Jewish Quarter). Periodic tensions between the Christian and Jewish communities caused successive modifications in the configuration of the quarter, but nevertheless it remains one of the best-preserved Jewish ghettoes in Western Europe. The tiny Carrer de Sant Llorenç and Carrer de Cúndaro are other vestigial arteries of the Call.

Girona's **Passeig Arqueològic** is a 20th-century walk skirting a large section of the old city ramparts. The stroll is pleasant and punctuated with scenic views of the city. Just off it near the cathedral are the **Jardins de la Francesa,** which lie within the city wall and offer a view of the impressive bulk of the cathedral and the outskirts of Girona.

GIRONA CATHEDRAL AND MUSEUM, Plaça Catedral. Tel. 972/21-44-26 for the museum.

Dominating the old town from its perch at the top of an impressive 17th-century baroque staircase (90 steps) is the city's unusual **cathedral.** Considered one of the most beautiful examples of Catalan baroque, it is, however, rooted in the Romanesque style and blends a variety of architectural themes. Its nave has the widest unsupported Gothic arch in the world, measuring 75 feet (22.98m). In fact, it is the widest nave of any style except for that of St. Peter's Basilica in Rome. The cathedral's Romanesque cloisters feature well-preserved carvings representing the creation of man and his fall from grace.

The cathedral **museum** contains two pieces of singular importance. The first is the *Tapestry of the Creation,* a unique piece of 11th- to 12th-century Romanesque embroidery fashioned from colored wool whose hues have remained remarkably vibrant. The second is the *Codex del Beatus,* a 10th-century illuminated manuscript of commentary on the Book of the Apocalypse, which was illustrated by a nun, Sister Eude.

Admission: Cathedral free; museum 175 ptas. ($1.75).

Open (both): Mar 1–June 30, daily 10am–1pm and 3:30–7pm. July 1–Sept 30, daily 10am–7pm. Oct 1–Nov 3, daily 10am–1pm and 3–6pm. Nov 4–Feb 28, Sat–Sun and holidays 10am–1pm.

ISAAC EL CEC CENTER, Carrer de Sant Llorenç. Tel. 972/21-67-61.

This former synagogue now houses a center dedicated to presenting exhibitions relating to the Jewish presence in Girona.

Admission: Free most of the time; admission charged to certain exhibitions.

Open: Tues–Sat 10am–2pm and 4–7pm. **Closed:** Holiday afternoons.

MUSEU ARQUEOLÒGIC DE SANT PERE DE GALLIGANTS, Santa Llúcia, 1. Tel. 972/20-26-32.

This 12th-century Benedictine monastery is the home of the archeological museum. A noteworthy example of Catalan Romanesque architecture, the monastery contains an important collection of prehistoric objects together with items from the Greek and Roman periods, all of which were found in the province of Girona. Of special historic interest are the 21 Jewish tombstones with Hebrew inscriptions found in the small Romanesque cloister.

Admission: 125 ptas. ($1.25).

Open: Tues–Sat 10am–1pm and 4:30–7pm; Sun and holidays 10am–1pm.

MUSEU D'HISTORIA DE LA CIUTAT, Carrer de la Força, 27. Tel. 972-20-91-60.

This is another museum "must." Installed in an 18th-century convent, it traces the city's evolution from the ancient settlers of Puig d'en Roca, Catalonia's oldest prehistoric site, to the present day. Among many other exhibits, it displays the apparatus that first illuminated the streets of Girona, the first city on the Iberian Peninsula to have electric street lights. Additional displays of tools, technical materials, and the accoutrements of passing lifestyles make up a kind of municipal résumé. Also on proud display are the works of the local *noucentista* sculptor, Fidel Aguilar. From the original Capuchin convent there remains the cemetery used for drying corpses before mummifying them (one of the three of this type left in the world).

Admission: Free.

Open: Tues–Sat 10am–2pm and 5–7pm; Sun and holidays 10am–2pm.

MUSEU D'ART DE GIRONA, Pujada de la Catedral, 12, Palau Episcopal. Tel. 972/20-95-36.

This museum occupies the former episcopal palace, which preserves a number of Romanesque and Gothic features inside and a Renaissance facade and entrance courtyard outside. Outstanding among its collection of art stretching from the Romanesque period to the present day are the 15th-century altarpiece of Saint Pere of Púbol by Bernat Martorell and that of Saint Michael of Cruïlles by Lluís Borrassa, two exemplary works of Catalan Gothic painting; the 10th- to 11th-century altarstone of Saint Pere of Roda, depicting figures and legends carved of wood and stone and covered in embossed silver; the 12th-century Romanesque biga de Cruïlles (Cruïlles timber) in polychrome wood; a carved alabaster image of Our Lady of Besalú from the 15th century; and a glazier's table from the 14th century, which shows how Gothic stained glass was prepared.

Admission: 125 ptas. ($1.25).

Open: Tues–Sat 10am–1pm and 4:30–7pm; Sun and holidays 10am–1pm.

BANYS ARABS [ARAB BATHS], Ferran al Católic. No phone.

These are a Romanesque copy of Moorish models and were heavily restored in 1929. In their prime, they were the setting for parties and merriment just beyond the city walls, with areas for hot baths, steam baths, and cold baths.

Admission: 125 ptas. ($1.25).

Open: Tues–Sat 10am–1pm and 4:30–7pm; Sun and holidays 10am–1pm.

L'ESGLESIA DE SANT FELIU, Pujada de Sant Feliu. No phone.

The eight pinnacles of this church distinctively mark the Girona skyline and signal a structure of artistic importance. Dating from the 14th to the 17th century, Romanesque pillars and arches support a central Gothic-style nave surrounded by an elegant triforium. Note the 14th-century reclining Christ sculpted in alabaster by Aloi de Montbrai; it demonstrates a naturalism unusual in Catalan Gothic. Also exceptional are the eight pagan and Christian sarcophagi set in the walls of the presbytery on either side of the high altar. The two oldest are from the 2nd century and are in a late Roman style: One depicts Pluto carrying Proserpina off to the depths of the earth in a chariot; the other shows a lion hunt.

Admission: Free.

Open: Most of the time (but no set hours).

TEATRE-MUSEU DALÍ, Plaça de Salvador Dalí i Gala, s/n (no street number), Figueres. Tel. 972/50-56-97.

After a morning's sightseeing in Girona, consider heading to Figueres, about 23 miles (37km) north, to see the Teatre-Museu Dalí. Installed in the former municipal theater, it is every bit as eccentric as the man who conjured it; among Spanish museums, it is second only to the Prado in the number of visitors. The museum contains paintings, sculptures, jewelry, drawings, and sketches by the artist himself; works from his private collection; and various "constructions" from different periods of his career. Dalí would permit no catalog of its contents to be prepared, however, believing his museum to be not an intellectual experience but a spiritual one.

Truly a celebration of one man's unbridled imagination, this artistic funhouse is replete with optical illusions and sleights—not of hand but of mind. Some of it is even done with mirrors. In the courtyard, drop a coin into the slot and the vintage Cadillac will drench its trailing plastic plants with water. Drop a coin into the viewer on the ground floor and a painting of Gala looking at the sea becomes a representation of Abraham Lincoln. Surprises in every nook and cranny are the order of the day here.

Admission: 350 ptas. ($3.50).

Open: Oct 1–June 30, daily 11:30am–5:30pm. July 1–Sept 30, daily 9am–8:30pm.

WHERE TO DINE

BRONSOMS, Avinguda Sant Francisco, 7. Tel. 972/21-24-93.

Cuisine: CATALAN. **Reservations:** Not required.

$ Prices: Appetizers 200–900 ptas. ($2–$9); main courses 600–2,200 ptas. ($6–$22). No credit cards.

Open: Mon–Fri 1–4pm and 9–11pm; Sat–Sun and holidays 1–4pm. **Closed:** Third Sun of every month and 3 weeks in Aug.

An excellent place for lunch, this restaurant serves regional specialties with home-cooked goodness. One eye-catching feature in its otherwise plain decor is a collection of menus that owner-chef Josep Bronsoms has worked hard to assemble. Try the chipirones or the pulpitos to start, then perhaps follow with a fish dish or a tender veal filet.

---

4. TARRAGONA

68 miles (110km) S of Barcelona

GETTING THERE   By Train   Trains run daily to Tarragona from Barcelona's Estació Sants. For schedule and fares call R.E.N.F.E. at 490-02-02.

By Bus   For information on bus connections to Tarragona call **Bacoma,** Estació de Autobuses Norte-Vilanova (tel. 231-38-01).

By Car   Head out of town on the A-2, passing through cava country en route. Although it's physically longer and more costly to go via the A-2 and then the A-7 than via the N-340, it's faster.

ESSENTIALS   For tourist information in Tarragona, go to the Patronato Municipal de Turismo de Tarragona, Rambla Nova 46, 43004 Tarragona (tel. 77/232-143).

Just before Exit 33 into Tarragona along the A-7, you'll see on your right the **Pont del Diable,** part of the Roman aqueduct that served this city, whose origins hark back to the arrival of the Romans around 218 B.C. Recognizing that the rocky bluff at the edge of the sea was a perfect natural defense for the port below, the Romans established Tarraco as a base for conquering the peninsula. Soon it blossomed into the most elegant and cultured city of the Roman Spanish provinces and became one of Rome's four Catalonian capitals. Later, the emperors Augustus and Hadrian each put his architectural stamp on the city, which was then both an administrative center and a favored holiday resort.

WHAT TO SEE & DO

Today Tarragona is Catalonia's second-largest city, with the attendant industrialization and ugly outskirts to prove it. The ancient and medieval walled city sits on high, while the modern urban expanse radiates beyond the 19th-century town below, whose Rambla Nova is a showpiece promenade lined with fashionable shops and cafés. The Rambla Vella, running parallel to the Rambla Nova to the east, marks the limits of the old town. Vestiges of Tarragona's Roman days are scattered throughout both areas of the city.

Try to get to Tarragona by about 10am, when things open up. Park near the cathedral or Plaça del Rei (you may have to ask directions because the signs are poor).

STROLLING THROUGH TOWN

To explore the sights listed below, I suggest the following walking tour, which should take you righ+ through lunch.

Begin at the **Museu Nacional Arqueològic** on the Plaça del Rei. Then visit the **Museu d'Història de Tarragona,** located next door. Continue down the Passeig de Sant Antoni to take in the view from the Balcó de Mediterrani above the **Roman amphitheater,** located on the beach at the foot of the beautifully terraced Milagro Park. Next, cross over the Passeig de les Palmeres and enter the Rambla Vella; on the right is the entrance to the **Voltes del Circ.**

Now head back up to Carrer Nau leading off the Museu d'Història and take a right on Carrer Major, a pedestrian passageway leading to the **cathedral,** which you enter through the cloister. Once you have toured the cathedral, return to Carrer Nau and follow its continuation, the Carrer Cavallers, to the **Casa-Museo Castellarnau.** Continue along Carrer Cavallers to Plaça del Pallol, where the structures top Roman remains with Gothic motifs. Go through the arch at the far end of the plaza to enter the **Passeig Arqueològic.**

After lunch, visit the remains of the **Roman forum** wedged between Carrer Lleida and Carrer Soler in the new town. The last major sight before leaving Tarragona is the **Museu Necropolis Paleocristians** on the Passeig de la Independéncia.

ATTRACTIONS

MUSEU NACIONAL ARQUEOLÒGIC, Plaça del Rei. Tel. 977/23-62-06.
Built atop part of the ancient Roman city wall, this museum features attractive displays of Roman artifacts, mosaics, statuary, pottery, and architectural fragments that date primarily from ancient Tarraco.
Admission: 125 ptas. ($1.25).
Open: Summer, Tues–Sat 10am–1:30pm and 4:30–8pm; Sun and holidays 10am–2pm. Winter, Tues–Sat 10am–1:30pm and 4–7pm; Sun and holidays 10am–2pm.

MUSEU D'HISTORIA DE TARRAGONA, Escales de Sant Hermenegild. Tel. 977/23-21-26.
Here you can continue to follow the history of the city through its Visigothic, Moorish, and medieval periods while exploring the Roman Praetorium in which the museum is installed. Just wandering through these impressive vaults is worth the price of admission. Ask for an English-language brochure to help explain the displays, which are labeled in Catalan. Usually you can visit the upper terrace of this structure, which provides a panoramic view of the city. A set of exterior stairs leads you back to the Plaça del Rei while giving you a good look at the 3rd-century B.C. Roman walls that circled the old city. Only about one-fourth of the original wall remains today.
Admission: 125 ptas. ($1.25).
Open: Summer, Tues–Sat 10am–1pm and 4:30–8pm; Sun and holidays 10am–2pm. Winter, Tues–Sat 10am–1:30pm and 4–7pm; Sun and holidays 10am–2pm.

ROMAN AMPHITHEATER, Milagro Park.
You can view the amphitheater (and the city) from the Balcó del Mediterrani above. Dating from the end of the 1st century or the first half of the 2nd century B.C., the amphitheater took advantage of the natural slope of the bedrock for part of its tiered seats.
Admission: Free.
Open: Oct–Mar, Mon–Sat 10am–6pm; Sun and holidays 10am–2pm. Apr–Sept, Sun–Fri and holidays 10am–2pm; Sat 10am–8pm.

VOLTES DEL CIRC, Rambla Vella.
Venue for the Roman chariot races, these ruins were uncovered not too long ago and are still under excavation. The ongoing work might disrupt the viewing hours; nevertheless, even when it's closed you can see a good deal through the fence.
Admission: Free.
Open: Oct–Mar, Mon–Fri 10am–1pm; Sat 10am–6pm; Sun 10am–2pm. Apr–Sept, Mon–Fri 10am–2pm.

CATEDRAL, Carrer Major. Tel. 977/23-72-69.

The cathedral's construction spanned the 12th to 14th centuries and combines the Romanesque and Gothic vernaculars. The main doorway is pure Gothic, while the doors of the lateral naves flanking it are Romanesque. Above the transept rises a notable octagonal dome with beautiful Gothic rose windows set on either side. Worthy of your attention are the Chapel of the Holy Sepulchre, whose sculpture of Christ lies on a 4th-century Roman sepulchre; the open choir, which is Gothic with plateresque chairs dating from the beginning of the 16th century; and the numerous items on display in the Chapel of Corpus Christi, including medieval utensils for making Communion hosts.

The cathedral's square cloister illustrates the transitional Romanesque style with six ogival arches along each side divided into three semicircular arches. Take time to observe the capitals depicting a variety of biblical and mythical scenes and a curious procession of rats.

Admission: Free.

Open: Nov–Mar, daily 10am–1pm and 4–6pm. Apr–Oct, daily 10am–7pm.

CASA-MUSEO CASTELLARNAU, Carrer Cavallers, 14. Tel. 977/23-69-46.

This is a former noble house whose distinguished guest in 1542 was none other than the emperor, Charles I. The mezzanine floor contains archeological, ethnological, and historical objects from Tarragona, including a collection of coins dating from the time of the Roman conquest to the early 20th century, numerous Roman ceramics, and an array of Catalan tiles dating from the 17th to the 19th century. The upper level is a veritable palace—with floors of typical geometric Catalan tiling; trompe l'oeil wall and ceiling paintings; and a remarkable assemblage of furnishings in the Elizabethan, Empire, and Louis XV and XVI styles. Over the billiard table hangs an elaborate lamp in the turn-of-the-century modernist tradition.

Admission: 125 ptas. ($1.25).

Open: Mon–Sat 10am–1pm and 4–7pm; Sun and holidays 10am–1pm.

PASSEIG ARQUEOLÒGIC, Plaça del Pallol.

This half-mile walkway along the old Roman wall is attractively landscaped, perfumed with cypress, and punctuated with sporadic overviews of the city. Of special note along the way are the Minerva tower and its adjacent Roman gate and the Cyclopean doors in the megalithic base of the wall, distinguished by enormous stone

---

IMPRESSIONS

Tarragona has a cathedral that is grey and austere, very plain, with immense, severe pillars; it is like a fortress; a place of worship for headstrong, violent, and cruel men. The night falls early within its walls and then the columns in the aisles seem to squat down on themselves and darkness shrouds the Gothic arches. It terrifies you. It is like a dungeon.
—W. SOMERSET MAUGHAM, *DON FERNANDO,* 1935

blocks believed to have been laid down by pre-Roman Iberian inhabitants.

Admission: 125 ptas. ($1.25).

Open: Oct–Jan, Mon–Sat 10am–1pm and 3–5pm; Sun and holidays 10am–2pm. Feb–June, daily 10am–1pm and 3–6:30pm. July–Sept, daily 10am–8pm.

ROMAN FORUM, Carrer Lleida and Carrer Soler.

The reconstructed columns and skeletal excavations here are so attractively set off with greenery that they create a small parklike oasis in the heart of the lower town. In the 19th century, that park grew beyond the old city walls and now contains numerous examples of modernist architecture.

Admission: Free.

Open: Oct–June, Tues–Sat 10am–1pm and 3–6pm. July–Sept Tues–Sat 10am–1pm and 4–7pm.

MUSEU NECROPOLIS PALEOCRISTIANS, Passeig de la Independéncia, s/n (no street number). Tel. 977/21-11-75.

This ancient burial ground, conserved in situ, came to light in 1923 when the new tobacco factory was built. It comprises an open-air excavation area and an indoor museum. Its great importance lies in the broad historic scope of its more than 2,000 pagan and Christian tombs—they date from the late Roman period through the 5th century.

Admission: 125 ptas. ($1.25).

Open: Summer, Tues–Sat 10am–1pm and 4:30–8pm; Sun and holidays 10am–2pm. Winter, Tues–Sat 10am–1:30pm and 4–7pm; Sun and holidays 10am–2pm.

WHERE TO DINE

SOL RIC, Via Augusta, 227. Tel. 977/23-20-32.

Cuisine: CATALAN. **Reservations:** Recommended.

$ Prices: Appetizers 350–1,500 ptas. ($3.50–$15); main courses 800–2,500 ptas. ($8–$25). AE, EURO, MC, V.

Open: Lunch Tues–Sun 1:30–4:30pm; dinner Tues–Sat 8:30–11:30pm. **Closed:** Dec 15–Jan 8.

One of the finest restaurants in Tarragona, Sol Ric offers typical Catalan seafood dishes as well as some creative inventions of chef Simón Tomàs. The pastries and ice creams are homemade. The selection of wines is vast.

EN ROUTE BACK TO BARCELONA

Later in the day, after you've seen all the sights, take a more leisurely route back to Barcelona along the N-350. You'll catch glimpses of the sea as well as pass by the **Torre dels Escipions** on your left about 4 miles (6km) out of town. This funerary monument possibly dates from the first half of A.D. 1. Some 12.5 miles (20km) out of town, you'll find the **Arc de Berá,** built at the beginning of the 2nd century, right in the middle of the road. As you near Barcelona, you might want to take the turn off toward Sitges to have dinner and try your luck at the Gran Casino de Barcelona (see "Barcelona Nights" in Chapter 6).

5. SITGES

27 miles (43km) SW of Barcelona

GETTING THERE By Train Trains run daily to Sitges from Barcelona's Estació Sants. For schedule and fares call R.E.N.F.E. at 490-02-02.

By Bus See the entry in "Cava Country" earlier in this chapter.

By Car At the end of the Garraf coast, Sitges is about a 45-minute drive away along the C-246, the coastal road leading off the Plaça d'Espanya.

ESSENTIALS The Patronato Municipal de Turismo de Sitges is located in the bus terminal Oasis, Plaça Villafranca, s/n, 08870 Sitges (tel. 894-4700).

Popular with both Barceloneses and travelers from less sunny climes, this seaside village was once an elite retreat for wealthy Catalan merchants and industrialists and such prominent artists as Dalí, Rusiñol, and Casas. Of late it has begun to attract the young, trendy set and has gained increasing popularity among the gay community. On a summer weekend and during July and August, it bursts at the seams with a polyglot population of fun-seekers from all over Europe. By mid-October it retreats into hibernation.

You'll want to wander the town's winding narrow streets lined with bright whitewashed houses or perhaps head for the beach. Of special note at the western end of town are the numerous turn-of-the-century mansions (some in modernist style) lining the Passeig Marítim. The Platja de St. Sebastiá, east of the old town, is among the more tranquil of the centrally located beaches.

WHAT TO SEE & DO

CAU FERRAT, Fonollar, s/n (no street number). Tel. 93/ 894-03-64.
One of two charming museums perched on a promontory in the village's old quarter, Cau Ferrat is the legacy of the well-known Catalan painter Santiago Rusiñol, who lived and worked in this 19th-century house that combined two 16th-century fishermen's homes. When he died in 1931, Rusiñol left his house and his choice collection of paintings (including several small Picassos, two El Grecos, and many of his own works), wrought iron, tiles, and archeological artifacts to the town.
Admission: 175 ptas. ($1.75).
Open: Tues–Sat 9:30am–2pm and 4–6pm; Sun 9:30am–2pm.

MUSEU MARICEL DE MAR, Fonollar, s/n (no street number). Tel. 93/894-03-64.
This museum is right next door to Cau Ferrat (see above) and is the legacy of Dr. Perez Rosales, whose impressive collection of furniture, porcelain, lamps, and tapestries draws largely from the medieval, Renaissance, and baroque periods. But there are also Romanesque frescoes and an entire 14th-century chapel! One particularly impressive room contains murals by Josep M. Sert i Badía with allegorical depictions of World War I. Originally painted when the

house was owned by an American, these murals traveled back to the United States with the owner and were auctioned after his death. A series of subsequent auctions took them to several countries before Dr. Rosales purchased them and installed them once again in their original spot.

Admission: 175 ptas. ($1.75).

Open: Tues–Sat 9:30am–2pm and 4–6pm; Sun 9:30am–2pm.

WHERE TO DINE

West of the old town, along **Passeig de la Ribera,** is a dense concentration of restaurants and bars, and in the streets behind it are numerous trendy shops. The **Gran Casino de Barcelona** (see Chapter 6 for more information) is just 3 miles (5km) from Sitges along the C-246.

CHAPTER 8

INTRODUCING MAJORCA, IBIZA & MINORCA

1. CULTURE, HISTORY & BACKGROUND

2. PLANNING A TRIP TO THE BALEARIC ISLANDS

Majorca, Ibiza, and Minorca—ask most people where they are, and you'll probably be told they're somewhere off the Mediterranean coast of Spain. But ask those people where the Balearic Islands are and they'll probably draw a blank. Los Baleares (in Spanish) are an uncommon set of islands stretching along the eastern coast of Spain from Valencia to Barcelona. An archipelago comprising three sizable tourist islands and several smaller islets, the Baleares allegedly derive their collective name from *balaro,* the Phoenician term given to the slingshots the aboriginal population handled so expertly—on occasion against the armies of Hannibal.

Since February 25, 1983, the Balearic Islands have been autonomously governed by the Govern Balear, headquartered in the regional capital of Palma de Majorca, on the largest island of the group. Next in size is Minorca, 35 miles (56km) northeast of Majorca, and then Ibiza, 46 miles (74km) south of Majorca. There are also several smaller islands and islets—among them, Formentera (a tourist extension of Ibiza), Cabrera, and Dragonera (uninhabited).

What these islands have in common are lots of lazy white-sand beaches; vibrant aquamarine waters; countless coves sheltered by towering cliffs; and a history dating back thousands of years before Christ. What they don't have in common is just about everything else. Their personalities, temperaments, and touristic miens are as different from one another as they are from the Spanish mainland.

Majorca is the most touristy of the three. Jaded in part by overexploitation, it nevertheless offers a goodly number of off-the-beaten-track pleasures.

Ibiza, feisty and footloose, is unabashed, uninhibited, and carefree. A passionate nonconformist, this island appeals to free spirits who wish for nothing more than sand and sea and the opportunity to do exactly as they please.

Minorca is the shy, serene member of the group. It yields its most beguiling charms only to those willing to search them out, to travel a few rough miles for a deserted beach or a glorious vista.

To preserve such natural endowments, the Balearics recently adopted regulations to protect the environment from the kind of damage inflicted upon parts of Majorca and Ibiza in earlier, less enlightened decades. Under the new provisions, 34.8% of the islands' territory is now protected from rampant, haphazard exploitation. Bravo!

Easily tacked onto a Barcelona holiday or undertaken as a stand-alone, island-hopping experience in their own right, the Balearics offer something for every vacationer's taste.

1. CULTURE, HISTORY & BACKGROUND

MAJORCA Nicknamed "La Isla de Calma" ("the tranquil island"), Majorca can be just that in its quiet coves, but it can also be quite lively in the bustling center of its capital, Palma. Long a haven for package-tour vacationers from Britain, Germany, and northern European countries, the island has grown rather tired of throwing cheap holiday bashes for the multitudes. The time has come, some local officials say, to upgrade the offerings and to expand with the greatest of care. The sentiment is commendable, and we should wish them well, because beach resorts are a dime a dozen and Majorca has the potential for a good deal more.

Scattered throughout the countryside are crumbling megalithic monuments suggesting habitation by the prehistoric Talayotic civilization, which existed from the 13th century B.C. until the arrival of the Romans. The earliest settlers that can be positively identified were the Phoenicians, followed over the centuries by the Greeks, Carthaginians, Romans, Vandals, Byzantines, and Moors. In 1229 James I, King of Aragón, captured Majorca for his realm. After a brief period of independence, it returned to the crown of Aragón in 1343 and became part of Spain when the Catholic kings unified the nation at the end of the 15th century.

Palma de Majorca and Alcudia are the island's oldest existing settlements, founded by the Romans and dating from 123 B.C. Of all the subsequent conquering presences, however, the 327 years of Moorish rule left the most enduring mark. Although most of the monumental structures of that period have been razed by the destructive hand of conflict, the traditional green-and-blue (Islam's sacred colors) trim on the houses and the practice of keeping one's home shut to the outside world with "jalousied" shutters are quotidian vestiges of Muslim custom.

In the 19th century, well before tourism was an industry on the island, Majorca attracted numerous painters, writers, and other artists in search of peace and inspiration. In fact, the island is still dining out on the brief presence of George Sand and Frédéric Chopin during the winter of 1838 to 1839. More recently, Majorca proved the location of choice for author Robert Graves, who made his home in Deyá, and Catalan artist Joan Miró, who established his home and studio in Cala Mayor.

Of all the Balearic Islands, Majorca offers the greatest scenic contrast and impact. In the north, rugged mountains shield the island from cold winds and shelter valleys verdant with orange and lemon trees. In the west, quiet coves are embraced by dramatic cliffs, some

FRANCE

Bay of Biscay

Castro-Urdiales
Bermeo
Guernica
Lekeitio
Fuenterrabia
San Sebastián/Donostia
Roncesvalles
Vitoria/Gasteiz
Pamplona
Estella
Sangüesa
Logroño
Jaca
Calahorra
Olite
Sos del Rey Católico
Tudela
Huesca
Tarazona
Calatayud
Zaragoza
Nuévalos
Piedra

SPAIN

Teruel

Cuenca

Valencia

Gulf of Valencia

Benidorm
Eiche
Alicante
Murcia

Cartagena

COSTA CALIDA

COSTA BLANCA

COSTA DEL AZAHAR

Tarragona
Sitges
BARCELONA
Montserrat

Pyrenees
ANDORRA

Gulf of Lions

Cadaqués
Figueras
Girona
COSTA BRAVA
Tossa de Mar
Lloret de Mar

Balearic Sea

Minorca

Majorca

Ibiza

BALEARIC ISLANDS

Formentera

Mediterranean Sea

ALGERIA

of which are still topped by the ominous ruins of watchtowers built to foil the pirates who plagued Majorca in centuries gone by. In the island's center, almond blossoms color the plains pink and white in January and February and picturesque windmills relieve the flatness of the terrain. Along the coast, olive trees twisted and tangled with age survey the soothing blue waters of the Mediterranean. Like all the Balearics, however, Majorca lacks a river and suffers from a chronic scarcity of water.

Among Majorca's population of 585,000 are some 30,000 English-speaking residents, including many Europeans who have established second homes here. At times referred to as the "California of Europe," Majorca does bear a certain scenic and climatic resemblance to that state. No doubt native Majorcan Friar Junípero Serra, who in the 18th century established numerous missions in California, thought so, too.

Included in the ranks of frequent visitors to the island are the Spanish royal family and their friends among the British royalty. But it is, of course, the "commoners" of this world who make Palma de Majorca's airport one of Europe's busiest in summer. Annually, over four million regular folks descend on the island for recreation and relaxation.

In addition to being a holiday haven, Majorca engages in substantial agricultural activity, its main crops being almonds, oranges, lemons, carob, olives, pears, apples, grapes, and melons. The production of simulated pearls and the fabrication of fine leather goods are also important economic activities. Among the island's leading handcrafts are wrought-iron work, ceramics, glass, and furniture.

Culinary accomplishments include the *calderetas* (fish stews) commonly found along the coast, the *ensaimada* (a spiral pastry), the *sopas mallorquinas* (made from a mixture of pork and vegetables whose broth is soaked up with slices of bread), *tumbet* (a vegetable dish similar to ratatouille), and *sobrasada* (a slightly piquant pork sausage).

Most visitors to Majorca come for the Mediterranean sun and sea and remain oblivious to its inland riches. If you make the trip, take some time off from tanning to dip into the till.

IBIZA   The Carthaginians called it Ibosim; the Greeks, Ebysos; the Romans, Ebusus. Once the coin of the realm bore the name Aivis, and the Arabs called it Yebisah. We now call it Ibiza, and the locals increasingly insist on Eivissa. But by any name, it's the same enchanting holiday retreat.

Ibiza is a spellbinding island: The tally of its myriad beaches, boutiques, pine-clad hills, and remote coves is an inadequate measure of its ineluctible enchantment. Ibiza is, above all, a celebration of individualism, a place where humankind's diversity can do, within the limits of respect for others, precisely as it pleases. "Laid back" and "mellow" may be California concepts, but they suit Ibiza to a "T."

Basking in the Mediterranean some 175 miles (280km) from Barcelona and 85 miles (137km) from Palma de Majorca, Ibiza is the third largest of the Balearic Islands, with an area of 230 square miles (572 square km). Along with the island of Formentera, it marks the southernmost extension of the archipelago.

Once upon a distant time the Phoenicians, the earliest-known foreigners to arrive on the scene, made Ibiza a focal point for commerce. Its strategic position along the Mediterranean's prime trade routes subsequently attracted the Carthaginians, Greeks, Romans, Vandals, Byzantines, and Moors. In the 8th century, the struggle between the Christians and the Moors began, ending in Arab victory at the beginning of the 10th century. In 1235, however, the island reverted to Christianity under the crown of Aragón. Ever since, its fate has been linked with that of the Spanish mainland.

From the 14th to mid-18th century, piracy was rampant. In the

18th and 19th centuries Ibiza's corsairs defended their home and surrounding seas against that seafaring menace. Today a monumental tribute to those swashbuckling heroes of yesteryear stands in the Port of Ibiza.

Ibiza's topography is irregular and varied, with many pine forests tinged a startlingly vibrant chartreuse. In fact, Ibiza and Formentera were called by the Greeks the *pitiusas*, or "piny," islands, and the nickname is still used today. To the Romans, Ibiza was a sacred isle because it was (and still is) devoid of any poisonous flora or fauna. In fact, many of imperial Rome's prominent citizens were brought here for burial.

One curious note of animal lore is the Ibizan hound. Most often reddish brown and white, with a slender snout and erect pointed ears, this breed of dog, prized for its excellent hunting instincts, dates back to the time of the Pharaohs and is conserved purebred in the Ibizan countryside. Unlike most small islands, whose resources are quickly exhausted, Ibiza seems rather to offer more and more as you get to know it. The more you immerse yourself in its freewheeling spirit, the richer, deeper, and more textured the place becomes. Ibiza can be whatever you want it to be, for it is many islands in one: remote and reclusive or highly social and trendy. Define your vacation terms, and the island will oblige.

Although it's been over 20 years, everyone here still talks about the halcyon hippie days of the 1960s, when Ibiza evolved its distinctive ad-lib, ad-libitum, "ad-libido" ethic. The idea remains to "go with the flow." Time is unstructured; plans are best left to tomorrow . . . or next week . . . or next year. People come for vacation and stay forever. Former flower children, now often dressed to the affluent nines, keep coming back for a dose of nostalgia, while today's New Age youth constructs their own version of Ibiza for the 1990s.

Although the juggernaut of mass tourism has considerably altered the island during the last 25 years, traditions struggle to survive, at least in the interior villages. In the 1950s the population was 30,000 and the island was very poor. Since the dawn of mass tourism, the population has more than doubled, including several thousand foreigners, among them many writers and artists. Supplementing the current population of over 70,000 are well over one million tourists annually, primarily from Europe. Because Ibiza's climate is somewhat warmer than Majorca's, it is a better choice for a winter escape, although many tourist facilities do shut down.

After tourism, the island's second most important industry is fashion. Lagging well behind are agriculture (cultivation includes olives, citrus fruit, almonds, and ground crops) and the handcrafting of leather goods, ceramics, tapestries, jewelry, lace, and embroidery. The oldest industry on the island is salt production. Begun by the Romans in the 3rd century B.C., it has continued relatively unchanged up to the present day on the 400 acres known as Las Salinas.

Today some 100 Ibiza families still make their living from fishing. Red mullet, grouper, stone bass, scorpion fish, pilchard, and white bream are some of the more popular species abounding in this part of the Mediterranean. Among the island's more unusual seafood fare are *ratjada* (skate or ray) and *dentón*.

MINORCA   To poorly paraphrase Robert Frost, this is the Balearic Island less traveled—and that makes all the difference. It also makes it a little duller than its more developed siblings. But there are those among us who might prefer it that way.

Minorca's most striking departure from the Balearic fold lies in its British legacy. A hundred years of British rule have left their imprint in the overall tenor of the island, which tempers Spanish exuberance with British reserve. Although physically larger than Ibiza—measuring some 9 miles (14km) wide by 30 miles (48km) long—Minorca seems smaller, in part because its windswept scenery stoops defensively low to the ground and in part because its limited network of roads necessarily curtails the number of places one can go.

As with the other islands of the group, Minorca's history has been a collaborative effort of the Greeks, Phoenicians, Carthaginians (Mahón, the capital, owes its name to the Carthaginian general Magon), Romans, and Muslims (they built the stone walls that crisscross the countryside)—as well as the British and the Spanish. The Romans called it Menorca ("the little one") in contrast to Majorca ("the big one"). In 1287 Minorca became part of the Kingdom of Aragón and was inducted into the linguistic and cultural community of Catalonia, many of whose inhabitants came to repopulate the island.

In 1535 Redbeard ("Barbarossa" in Spanish) devastated Maó (Mahón), prompting the city to retreat within defensive walls. Their only present-day remnant is the Pont de Sant Roc, one of the city gates. In 1713 Spain ceded the island to England under the Treaty of Utrecht. Throughout that century, the struggle for dominion of Minorca flared continuously among the English, French, and Spanish. In 1802, under the Treaty of Amiens, the Spanish repossessed the island.

Economic activity thrived under the British, and the modern outline of the current capital was established. Many important buildings, including the main barracks, the Town Hall, and the principal churches, date from this period. The British also introduced the art of distilling juniper berries into Minorcan gin (Xoriguer, Beltra, and Nelson are some local brands to look for), which advocates claim is superior to all others. You be the judge.

Somewhat surprisingly, Minorca for a long time enjoyed the highest standard of living in all of Spain, rooted not in tourism but in the shoe and costume-jewelry industries. Today, much of the population of 67,000 (many of whom speak excellent English) still participate in the production of costume jewelry and leather goods, as well as cheese, cured sausages, and assorted handcrafts. Recently, however, tourism has begun to eclipse all other economic enterprises on the island—something of great concern to many locals. Tourists number slightly over half a million annually, but to date the island still retains much of its virgin beauty both along the coast and inland, and one can only hope that Minorca takes to heart the lessons harshly learned in parts of Majorca and Ibiza.

In addition to sand, sea, sun, and dramatic coastal cliffs, Minorca offers many interesting archeological remains, and—although this might sound strange—an unusual moon. Somehow that earth-orbiting orb seems closer, bigger, and more commanding here. I was not alone in noting this and urge visitors to keep an eye out for this curious phenomenon. For those tired of life in the fast lane, Minorca's singular moon and palette of white houses, green hills, and blue sea and sky paint a soothing portrait of escape.

2. PLANNING A TRIP TO THE BALEARIC ISLANDS

Most of the information you need to help you plan your trip is in the first two chapters of this book. However, this section has information that specifically pertains to the Balearic Islands.

CLIMATE   First and foremost, the Balearic Islands tally about 300 sunny days a year. In winter, the water temperatures remain moderate, and hearty souls can still enjoy a swim. The norm in summer is warm, sunny days with mild evenings; in winter, there are mild days with cool to chilly nights. The average maximum daily temperature is 70°F (21°C); the average minimum is 57°F (14°C). On rare occasions the mercury may approach the freezing point, but it will almost never cross that climatic threshold. The sun is spelled by brief showers now and then, mostly in autumn and early winter. April, May, September, and October are often the best months for moderate weather and moderate crowds. July and August are hot and thick with tourists. Bearing in mind that Ibiza is slightly warmer and Minorca slightly windier, use the monthly averages for Palma de Majorca shown in the table as a barometer of the Balearic climate throughout the year.

Palma de Majorca's Average Daytime Temperatures and Days of Sunshine

	Jan	Feb	Mar	Apr	May	June	July	Aug	Sept	Oct	Nov	Dec
Temp. (°F)	50	52	54	59	63	71	76	76	73	65	58	53
Temp. (°C)	10	12	13	15	18	22	25	25	23	19	14	12
Days of Sun	23	22	23	24	26	27	30	28	25	22	22	22

WHAT TO PACK   In late spring, summer, and early fall, pack for the beach and take a light shawl or jacket for the occasional cool evening. In the winter, take clothes that can be layered at night for warmth and peeled off stratum by stratum as the sun warms the day.

HOLIDAYS   The following holidays are celebrated on all the Balearic Islands: January 1 (New Year's Day), January 6 (Feast of the Three Kings); Good Friday, Easter Monday, May 1 (Labor Day), May 15 (Feast of the Pentecost), June 24 (Feast of St. John), August 15 (Assumption Day), October 12 (Columbus Day), November 1 (All Souls' Day), December 6 (Constitution Day), December 8 (Feast of the Immaculate Conception), December 25 (Christmas Day), and December 26 (Feast of St. Stephen).

COST   While package tours (especially out of London) to any of the Balearic Islands can prove very economical, the cost of eating out, going out at night, and buying things can, on the other hand, be very high. Prices are pretty much on a par among the three islands, with Minorca, perhaps, being the least costly overall.

GETTING THERE Flights from Barcelona and between the islands are offered on **Iberia, Aviaco,** and **Mediterranean Air** and can be booked through Iberia (tel. toll free 800/SPAIN-IB). At this writing, one-way fares from Barcelona to Palma, Maó, and Ibiza were $80, $83, and $91, respectively. In August the system is taxed to the limit and often breaks down, so make sure you have confirmed reservations for both transportation and accommodations during that month.

CHAPTER 9

PALMA DE MAJORCA

Capital of Majorca and the Balearic Islands, Palma de Majorca is part medieval still life and part bustling modern metropolis. Clustered around the majestic cathedral are the well-worn mementoes of centuries gone by—cobblestone streets, narrow alleys, and stoic stone structures. Along the Paseo Marítimo are the contemporary trappings of commerce and tourism: high-rise hotels, sophisticated restaurants, and a plethora of nocturnal diversions.

Located about 50 miles (80km) from Barcelona, Palma's airport is one of the busiest in Europe, able to accommodate 30 million passengers annually.

Among Majorca's most prominent annual visitors is the Spanish royal family. Every Easter and summer they come to stay at the Palacio de Marivent, between Palma and Illetas, where they are often joined by British royalty.

Palma's sweeping bay, stretching 30 miles (48km) cape to cape, is one of the largest in the world. Unfortunately, haphazard construction has somewhat scarred the municipal waterfront. Still, the city—especially the old town—is attractive. Endowed with all the cosmopolitan trappings one would expect of a city of 315,000 inhabitants, Palma bustles year round and is a good base from which to enjoy the nearby beaches and explore the rest of the island.

During the Moorish domination of Majorca from the 9th through the 11th century, the old city of Palma was a walled casbah, or fortified city. After Jaime I of Aragón brought the island into the Catalan fold in 1229, Palma steadily climbed to the pinnacle of riches and prominence it enjoyed in the 15th century as the main port of call between Europe and Africa. In 1928, with the building of Palma's first hotel, the island embarked on a new career as a purveyor of vacation pleasures. Today there are over 1,000 hotels throughout the island, most of them in Palma itself and the surrounding holiday communities strung along the island's southwestern coast.

1. ORIENTATION

GETTING THERE

BY PLANE From Madrid, Barcelona, the other Balearic Islands, and many major European cities, there is frequent regular and charter

✔ WHAT'S SPECIAL ABOUT MAJORCA

A Monument
☐ Palma's 14th-century Bellver Castle, with its beautiful view.

Nightlife
☐ The exotic drinks and decor of Palma's Abaco bar.

Shopping
☐ Leather goods and Majorica pearls.
☐ The posh boutiques of Palma's Avenida Jaume III.
☐ The pedestrian shopping streets of the old town.

Beaches
☐ Es Trenc, a secluded, undeveloped stretch of silky sand near Palma.

Vistas
☐ The scenic overlooks along the west coast and on the Formentor Peninsula.
☐ The bay at Port de Pollença viewed from the terrace bar of the Hotel Illa D'Or.

☐ The Majorica pearl factory in Manacor.

air service. Barcelona is the major gateway, with several daily flights in summer. Both **Iberia** (tel. toll free 800/SPAIN-IB) and **Aviaco** (same phone) fly to Palma from Barcelona, Valencia, and Madrid, with Aviaco operating the bulk of the interisland flights.

From May through October **Air Europa,** 136 E. 57th St., Suite 1602, New York, NY 10022 (tel. 212/888-7010), offers charter flights from New York to Palma de Majorca through Spanish Heritage Tours (tel. 718/544-2752, or toll free 800/221-2580); fares run from $700 to $850 round trip.

BY FERRY & HYDROFOIL Regular ferry service and limited hydrofoil service (more frequent in summer) links Majorca with the other Balearic Islands, Barcelona, and Valencia. Contact any travel agent for details (see "Getting There" in Chapter 2).

ARRIVING

BY PLANE The **airport tourism office** (tel. 26-08-03) is open on Monday to Saturday from 9:30am to 8pm and on Sunday from 9:30am to 2pm in winter, later in summer. You can change money 24 hours a day (except New Year's Eve and Easter) at the airport office of the Banco Exterior de España or at most hotels.

Buses from the airport to the Plaça España, in the center of Palma, run every 30 minutes and cost about 175 ptas. ($1.75) during the day and 225 ptas. ($2.25) at night and on holidays. The **taxi** fare from the airport to the Paseo Marítimo is about 1,800 ptas. ($18).

BY BOAT If you come by boat, the passenger port is some 2.5 miles (4km) west of town. There is bus service on Bus 1 into town, but to catch the bus you have to walk about half a kilometer. Buses to the Paseo des Born run every half hour; however, service may be curtailed on Sunday and late at night.

TOURIST INFORMATION

See "Arriving" above for details on the airport's information office. The two **municipal tourist offices** in town are located at Carrer Santo Domingo 11 (tel. 72-40-90) and Plaça España, s/n (no street number) (tel. 71-15-27); both are open on Monday to Friday from 9am to 8:30pm and on Saturday from 9am to noon (closed holidays). The **tourist office of the Govern Balear,** at Avenida Jaume III, 10 (tel. 71-22-16), dispenses information on all the Balearic Islands; it's open on Monday to Friday from 9am to 2:30pm and from 3 to 8pm and on Saturday from 10am to 1:30pm (closed holidays).

Note: If you arrive without a hotel reservation, contact the **Central Booking Office,** Mallorca Hotel Federation (tel. 20-84-59 or 20-97-17) daily between 9am and 2pm and 6:30 and 7:30pm.

CITY LAYOUT

In town, the area around the cathedral, the heart of "old" Palma, is known as the **Portela Quarter.** Beyond its cluster of alleyways the city expands into broader, more ordered avenues. Leading up from the sea beside the cathedral is the **Paseo des Born,** a broad boulevard lined with shops and offices. At the top of the hill at the end of Carrer Jaume II is the **Plaça Mayor,** a focal point of tourist activity.

Along the bay west of the old town stretches the six-lane, 2-mile-long (3km-long) **Paseo Marítimo,** lined with hotels, restaurants, discos, and souvenir shops. The streets behind it, offering more of the same, comprise the **El Terreno** district, which is noted for its nightlife.

GETTING AROUND

Since tourist activity is centered in the rather compact old town or along the Paseo Marítimo, you can do a good deal of sightseeing and shopping **on foot** or by making limited use of taxis.

BY BUS   Municipal buses serve the city of Palma and surrounding areas for fares ranging from 100 to 150 ptas. ($1 to $1.50). Full information on lines and hours is available from the tourist offices (see "Tourist Information" above) or the E.M.T. (tel. 29-08-55). Since bus service to other parts of the island is offered by a variety of private companies, again contact the tourist offices for full information or call the central bus station in Plaça España (tel. 75-22-24); to find out about special service for the handicapped, call 29-57-00.

BY TAXI   Taxi rates are 125 ptas. ($1.25) for the flagfall and 75 to 125 ptas. (75¢ to $1.25) for each additional kilometer depending on the time of day; the airport supplement is 350 ptas. ($3.50) and the per bag supplement is 75 ptas. (75¢). For a radio taxi, call 75-54-40, 40-14-14, or 71-04-03.

BY CAR   Having your own car can be a hindrance because of the scarcity of parking, especially in high season, and the stringent application of parking rules. In the city of Palma the parking restriction plan "ORA" is in effect on Monday to Friday from 9:30am

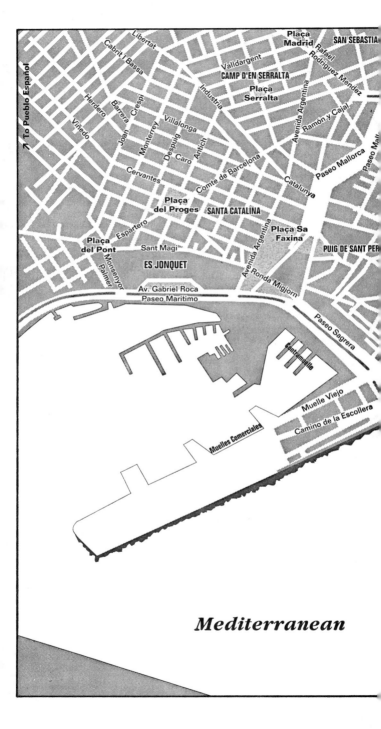

PALMA DE MAJORCA

Jesus

Via Alemania

Avenida Conde Sallent

Via Portugal

Foni y Monteros

Via Roma

Train Station

Olmos

Avenida Juan March

Avenida Alejandro Rosello

Plaça España

La Rambla

San Juane

San Miguel

Zanoguera

Concepción

Rey Jaime III

de la Uno

Plaça Weyler

Navarra

Plaça Major

Sindicato

Paseo des Born

Plaça Cort

Plaça de la Reina

Conquistador

Victoria Almudaina

Morey

SA CALATRAVA

Socorro

Pasaje Manel Mateo Enrique Lledo

V. Antonio Maura

Sol

Catedral
Plaça Almirante Moreno

Paseo Uruguay

Plaça Porta d'es Camp

Parque de la Mar

Plaça Llorenc Villalonga

Autopista de Levante

Sea

Information

to 1:30pm and from 5 to 8pm and on Saturday from 9:30 to 1:30pm. These zones are usually indicated by blue lines delineating the parking spaces. You must purchase a ticket valid for 30, 60, or 90 minutes in any *estanco* (tobacconist shop) or from a ticket vending machine and display it visibly on your dashboard. At this writing 90 minutes' parking cost 75 ptas. (75¢).

BY TRAIN   For information on trains to Inca, a famed leather goods center with factory outlet stores, contact **FEVE,** Central Station, Plaça España (tel. 75-22-24), Monday to Friday from 8am to 5pm. For information on trains to Sóller, contact **Train Sóller Railway Company,** Eusebio Estada Street (tel. 75-20-28), daily from 8am to 1pm and from 3 to 7:45pm.

BY FERRY   Ferry information and tickets can be obtained at any travel agency or from **Trasmediterránea,** Muelle Viejo, 5 (tel. 72-67-40), open on Monday to Friday from 9am to 1pm and from 5 to 7pm.

FAST FACTS PALMA DE MAJORCA

For information on currency, electricity, tipping, and so forth, see "Fast Facts: Barcelona" in Chapter 3.

Airport Information   For airport information call 26-46-24 on Monday to Friday from 8am to 8pm; in summer, on Saturday and Sunday 24 hours a day; winter hours vary greatly.

The Iberia office, Paseo des Born, 10 (tel. 72-43-49), is open on Monday to Friday from 9am to 1:45pm and from 4 to 6:45pm and on Saturday from 9am to 12:15pm. For Iberia reservations, call 71-80-00; for flight information, call the airport office at 26-26-00 daily 24 hours. The airport ticket office is open daily from 6am to 11pm.

Area Code   The area code for all the Balearic Islands when calling from other parts of Spain is 971. When calling from outside the country, dial 71.

Business Hours   Shop hours are generally Monday to Friday from 9:30am to 1:30pm and from 4:30 to 8pm and on Saturday from 9:30am to 1:30pm. Department stores are open Monday to Saturday from 10am to 9pm. Restaurant hours are generally daily from 1:30 to 4pm and from 8 to 11pm. Normal banking hours are Monday to Friday from 9am to 2pm.

Bear in mind, however, that hours vary greatly throughout the year as the islands move in and out of peak and shoulder tourist seasons. Even during peak seasons, the hours and closing days of shops and restaurants often fluctuate with demand. If business is booming, they may well stay open beyond their regular posted hours, but if business is lagging, you may find the doors unexpectedly closed.

Consulates   The U.S. Consulate, at Avenida Jaume III, 26 (tel. 72-26-60), is open on Monday to Friday from 4 to 7pm; if you call at other times you can leave a message on the answering machine. In the event of an emergency, contact the American Consulate General in Barcelona at 93/319-95-50.

The Consulate of the United Kingdom, at Plaça Mayor, 3 (tel.

71-24-45), is open in summer on Monday to Friday from 9am to 2pm and in winter on Monday to Friday from 9am to 3pm.

Emergencies   For the police, dial 092 or 28-16-00. For an ambulance, call 20-65-65 or 75-51-38; in case of fire, call 75-12-34. In a medical emergency go to the Medical Center, Nuredduna, 4 (tel. 46-06-06).

Holidays   Local holidays include June 29 (Feast of St. Peter, patron saint of fishermen), when the Port of Alcudia stages from 6 to 7pm a boat procession that can be viewed from either land or sea. July 16 (Feast of the Virgin of Carmen, patron of fishermen—apparently they need all the celestial assistance they can get!—and sailors) is celebrated in all of Majorca's port towns but especially in Port de Andraitx, which holds a special procession of decorated boats and a children's parade, and in Cala Ratjada and Port de Sóller, where the nighttime processions feature boats illuminated with torches and flares. August 2 (Feast of Our Lady of the Angels) is observed in Pollença with a mock battle between Moors and Christians.

Language   As in Barcelona and throughout Catalonia, Catalan is the second official language (along with Spanish) of all the Balearic Islands, so signs and streets names may appear in one or the other or both. Most newer maps will have all the names in Catalan, but you may find the actual street names and other signs still in Spanish. Although the Catalan language is common to all the islands, there are dialectical variations on each. Most different of all is the Mallorquín dialect of Majorca. While throughout this guidebook I refer to "Majorca" and "Minorca," their Spanish spellings are "Mallorca" and "Menorca."

Newspapers   The *Diario de Mallorca, Baleares,* and *Última Hora* are Spanish-language dailies covering not only Majorca but also the Balearic region. The *Majorca Daily Bulletin* is the English-language daily. *Majoric Tourist Information* is a bimonthly newspaper with the latest information of interest to visitors. Beyond that, newspapers and magazines from all over the world are ubiquitous.

Post Office   The central post office, Carrer Constitució, 6 (tel. 72-18-67), is open on Monday to Friday from 9am to 7pm and Saturday 9am to 2pm. You can also send faxes and telexes from here on Monday to Saturday from 8am to 9pm. For postal rate information, see "Fast Facts: Barcelona" in Chapter 3.

Safety   Whenever you're traveling in an unfamiliar city or area, stay alert. Be aware of your immediate surroundings. Wear a moneybelt and keep a close eye on your possessions. Be particularly careful with cameras, purses, and wallets, all favorite targets of thieves and pickpockets.

Telephone   The surcharged laid on by most hotels is a case of highway robbery (anywhere from 20% on), so check before making any calls from your room. There are numerous telephone offices around town, but beware of those that are not run by *Telefónica,* Spain's national telephone company, because sometimes their surcharges are as high as or higher than those of the hotels (many of these private operations are found at the beaches as well).

The most economical choice is always a Telefónica locutório. The one in Palma at the corner of Paraires and Plaça de la Reina is open on Monday to Saturday from 9:30am to 8:30pm and Sunday and holidays from 10am to 2pm. For dialing information, see "Fast Facts: Barcelona" in Chapter 3. The base rate for calls to the United States and Canada is about 500 ptas. ($5) per minute; to Great Britain, about 190 ptas. ($1.90) per minute.

Television/Radio   There are 30,000 English-speaking residents on Majorca served by an English-language radio station. Radiocadena Española, Radio Majorca, and Radio Popular also offer foreign-language programs. There are several national Spanish-language TV stations, a couple of regional stations broadcasting in Catalan, and via satellite hookup numerous channels in English and various European languages.

2. ACCOMMODATIONS

The bulk of Majorca's hotels are in Palma and the surrounding beach areas, where most offer your garden variety, tour-group brand of accommodations. The low-price, vacation-package business has fallen off in recent years, however, and Majorca now aspires to upgrade its overall hotel offering to attract more upscale travelers. This is not to say that there aren't already a number of fine hotels for the independent traveler. In fact, there are quite a few, and a number of them are very select indeed. You will find them below, along with the mass-market hotels that offer room, board, sand, sun, and sea at bargain-basement rates (always subject to further negotiation).

The posted rates at most lodgings are the official maximums the place can charge. Often you can negotiate at least a 10% discount— sometimes more in the off season. For the purposes of this guide, "expensive" hotels charge 15,000 ptas. ($150) and up for a double room; "moderate" hotels, 6,000 to 13,000 ptas. ($60 to $130); and "budget" lodgings, 3,000 to 6,000 ptas. ($30 to $60).

Note: Unless otherwise indicated, all accommodations have private bath or shower, all hotels are open year round, and all rates given include service charge but *not* breakfast and IVA.

SOL HOTELS   The Sol Group, headquartered in Palma and with over 120 properties in Spain, is Spain's largest hotel company. Its "Meliá" hotels are five-star properties, while the "Sol" line comprises three- and four-star hotels geared to mass tourism but with higher standards of quality than the usual hotels of that ilk.

For information or reservations at any Meliá or Sol hotel, call toll free 800/336-3542 or contact Meliá Hotels at Coral Plaça Building, Suite 402, 2100 Coral Way, Miami, FL 33145 (tel. 305/854-0990, or toll free 800/446-3542).

EXPENSIVE

BELLVER SOL, Paseo Marítimo, 11, 07014 Palma de Majorca. Tel. 971/73-51-42. Fax 971/73-14-51. Telex 69643. 393 rms. A/C TV TEL **Bus:** 1.

$ Rates (including breakfast): 9,700–12,000 ptas. ($97–$120) single; 16,500 ptas. ($165) double. AE, DC, EURO, MC, V. **Parking:** Nearby.

A Sol hotel, the Bellver is conspicuous for its tiers of scalloped white terraces. The marble lobby and large public areas have been stylishly refurbished. The spacious guest units have carpeting, terraces (one-third with views of the bay), and roomy baths.

Dining/Entertainment: In addition to a cafeteria, there is a restaurant that serves a buffet breakfast and has a mixed buffet and à la carte service at lunch and dinner. On Sunday to Friday from 9pm to midnight there is live musical entertainment in the bar.

Services: Room service until midnight.

Facilities: Pool.

HOTEL SARATOGA, Paseo Majorca, 6, 07012 Palma de Majorca. Tel. 971/72-72-40. Fax 971/72-73-12. 189 rms. A/C MINIBAR TV TEL **Bus:** 3, 7, or 21.
$ Rates: 7,300–8,100 ptas. ($73–$81) single; 14,400–16,000 ptas. ($144–$160) double; 17,000–20,000 ptas. ($170–$200) double with sitting room. MC, V. **Parking:** On premises.

Near the medieval moat of the old city's fortifications, the Saratoga has been completely redone and features an airy, inviting reception area and bright, charming, modern, comfortable, sound-insulated guest rooms, most with pretty balconies and wonderful views. The hotel has two pools—one on the roof and one at lobby level—a top-floor bar with more great views, and a large terrace-garden beyond its lobby-level pool.

HOTEL SON VIDA, Urbanización Son Vida, Palma de Majorca. Tel. 971/79-00-00, or toll free 800/223-6800 through Leading Hotels of the World. Fax 971/79-00-17. Telex 68651. 171 rms, 13 suites. A/C MINIBAR TV TEL **Bus:** 7.
$ Rates: 21,000–28,000 ptas. ($210–$280) single; 27,500–35,000 ptas. ($275–$350) double; 48,000–50,500 ptas. ($480–$505) suite. AE, DC, EURO, MC, V. **Parking:** On premises.

This is a princely haven for the well-heeled traveler looking for luxury, beauty, and tranquillity. The list of visiting royalty, statesmen, artists, and celebrities is long and impressive—including Prince Ranier and Princess Grace, John Lennon, and John Wayne. Built around the core of a castle given by King Jaime I to the Marquis de la Torre, it is a sumptuous property set in the Son Vida hills several miles outside the city and offers panoramic views of Palma and the Mediterranean. The modern extension, done in a traditional Spanish style, looks more like a noble hacienda than a hotel. The grounds include a golf course, well-manicured gardens, and several outdoor terraces.

Inside, the palatial public areas are drenched in fine fabrics and sprinkled with Oriental rugs and wrought-iron chandeliers. Although the guest rooms are not as palatial as the public areas, they are large and have private terraces or balconies.

Dining/Entertainment: The hotel restaurant has an extensive selection of international dishes and fine wines. After dinner, a glass of port or cognac in the piano bar tops off a perfect evening.

Services: 24-hour room service.

Facilities: Outdoor pool; tennis (two of the four courts are illuminated); golf; health center with sauna, Turkish bath, massage, solarium, gymnasium, and covered pool with whirlpool.

MELIÁ VICTORIA HOTEL, Avenida Joan Miró, 21, 07014

Palma de Majorca. Tel. 971/73-43-42. Fax 971/45-08-24. Telex 668558. 167 rms. A/C MINIBAR TV TEL **Bus:** 1, 4, or 21.
$ Rates: 13,000–22,000 ptas. ($130–$220) single; 24,000–27,000 ptas. ($240–$270) double; 31,000–46,000 ptas. ($310–$460) suite. AE, DC, EURO, MC, V. **Parking:** On premises.

⭐ This is a gracious five-star choice smack in the center of things along the Paseo Marítimo. A member of the Sol Group of hotels, whose first-class properties carry the name "Meliá," this one dates from 1905 but is constantly being refurbished.

All the spacious carpeted guest rooms have terraces. Doubles have sea views; singles have castle views. The junior suites have small sitting rooms and king-size beds. Each room is furnished uniquely, with the occasional antique piece here and there contributing a charming grace note of distinction.

Dining/Entertainment: The hotel restaurant serves regional, national, and international dishes and a wonderful buffet breakfast (a trademark of the Sol group). Before and after dinner the piano bar attracts both guests and locals. In summer, the outdoor terrace becomes a dance floor with live music.

Services: 24-hour room service.

Facilities: Business center, indoor and outdoor pools, sauna, hairdresser, solarium, fitness center, massage.

SOL PALAS ATENEA, Paseo Ingeniero Gabriel Roca, 29 (next door to the Meliá Victoria), 07014 Palma de Majorca. Tel. 971/28-14-00. Fax 971/45-19-89. Telex 69644 HPAT. 370 rms. A/C MINIBAR TV TEL **Bus:** 1.
$ Rates (including breakfast): 11,000–14,000 ptas. ($110–$140) single; 18,000 ptas. ($180) double. AE, DC, EURO, MC, V.
Parking: Nearby.

This four-star Sol hotel is modern and businesslike, although somewhat past its prime. All the carpeted guest rooms have terraces. Those facing the bay have wonderful views but are noisier than the ones in the back overlooking Bellver Castle.

Dining/Entertainment: The hotel restaurant serves an ample breakfast buffet and dinner. There are also an outdoor terrace bar and an indoor piano bar.

Services: Club Elite floors for executives; room service until 10pm.

Facilities: Indoor and outdoor pools, sauna, solarium, Jacuzzi, massage, beauty parlor, shops.

VALPARAISO PALACE/HOTEL, La Bonanova, 07015 Palma de Majorca. Tel. 971/40-04-11. Fax 971/40-59-04. Telex 68754. 150 rms and suites. A/C MINIBAR TV TEL **Bus:** 4.
$ Rates: 17,500 ptas. ($175) single; 22,000 ptas. ($220) double; 26,000 ptas. ($260) suite. AE, DC, EURO, MC, V. **Parking:** On premises.

⭐ ⓢ *Sybaritic* is the word that best describes the pampering pleasures of this oasis perched on a hill in a tranquil residential area overlooking Palma Bay. From the tapestried walls and colorful wool carpets of its halls to the elegantly modern restaurant with a view of the city and sea below, it is the pride and joy of the Majorcan proprietors who live in its upper reaches. Its grounds include not only lovely gardens but also a man-made lake with a rowboat and swans.

The soundproof guest rooms are refuges of comfort, all tastefully appointed and equipped with large terraces and sea views. The decor differs from room to spacious room, but the beds in each are situated in a raised alcove. The electricity is dual voltage (125 and 200 volts).

Dining/Entertainment: The hotel restaurant offers Spanish and international cuisine. One of the hotel's four bars is open 24 hours and features nightly musical entertainment.

Services: 24-hour room service.

Facilities: Indoor and outdoor pools, mini-golf, tennis, sauna, hairdresser, art gallery, laundry, gymnasium, shops, solarium, garage. The hotel offers special discounts at four island golf courses.

MODERATE

HOTEL COSTA AZUL, Paseo Marítimo, 7, 07014 Palma de Majorca. Tel. 971/73-19-40. Fax 971/73-19-71. Telex 69479. 125 rms. TEL **Bus:** 1.

$ Rates (including breakfast): 5,300 ptas. ($53) single; 7,500–8,300 ptas. ($75–$83) double. AE, DC, EURO, MC, V. **Parking:** Nearby.

If you can't find a room elsewhere, the spacious—but rather worn and barren—guest rooms here are an acceptable fall-back option. Both the lobby-level bar and restaurant, which offers buffet service at all meals, are cozy in their traditional Spanish styling. The very small pool on the third floor is covered and heated in winter.

HOTEL JAIME III SOL, Paseo Majorca, 14B, 07012 Palma de Majorca. Tel. 971/72-59-43. Fax 971/72-59-46. 88 rms. TV TEL **Bus:** 4, 7, or 21.

$ Rates (including breakfast): 7,500–8,100 ptas. ($75–$81) single; 9,500–10,200 ptas. ($95–$102) double. AE, DC, EURO, MC, V. **Parking:** Not available.

Right at the end of Palma's main shopping street, this is a good choice for those who prefer to stay in the urban heart of things and commute to the beaches. Its double guest rooms are large and carpeted, with big baths. The air-conditioned restaurant serves an ample buffet-style breakfast and dinner, which for those on the half-board plan costs an additional 1,300 ptas. ($13) daily. The hotel's cafeteria is popular with both visitors and locals.

HOTEL MAJORICA, Carrer Garita, 3, 07015 Palma de Majorca. Tel. 971/40-02-61. Fax 971/40-33-58. Telex 69309. 153 rms. TEL **Bus:** 3, 4, or 21.

$ Rates: 4,000–7,800 ptas. ($40–$78) single; 6,000–13,000 ptas. ($60–$130) double. AE, DC, EURO, MC, V. **Parking:** Not available.

Located in the hills above Palma Bay at the far western end of Avenida Joan Miró, the Majorica exudes a cozy Spanish charm and has nice, bright rooms. Off the lobby is a small, friendly bar; another bar serves sunbathers. The facilities include a pool, and the hotel offers minibus service into town and to the beach on weekdays.

HOTEL MIRADOR, Paseo Marítimo, 10, 07014 Palma de Majorca. Tel. 971/73-20-46. Fax 971/73-39-15. 78 rms. TV TEL **Bus:** 1.

$ Rates: 4,300–6,000 ptas. ($43–$60) single; 6,500–9,500 ptas. ($65–$95) double. AE, DC, EURO, MC, V. **Parking:** Nearby.

A charming hostelry hiding behind a very humble facade, the Mirador dates from the late 1950s and retains the gracious charm of an era when hotels were less homogeneous and more homey. Throughout the lobby, lounges, and guest rooms are beautiful handcrafted furnishings made by local Majorcan artisans.

The oversize, sound-insulated guest rooms feature lots of fine dark wood—as do some of the vintage elevators—and the halls have parquet flooring. The baths are a bit passé in styling but not in comfort. All in all, this is a good value.

Meals in the restaurant are buffet style; there are also a cafeteria and a bar. Guests enjoy the tiny rooftop pool and token sunbathing deck.

HOTEL-RESIDENCIA ALMUDAINA, Avenida Jaume III, 9, 07012 Palma de Majorca. Tel. 971/72-73-40. Fax 971/72-25-99. 80 rms. A/C TV TEL **Bus:** 3, 7, or 21.

$ **Rates** (including breakfast): 5,200–6,000 ptas. ($52–$60) single with shower; 5,600–6,500 ptas. single with bath; 8,500–9,500 ptas. ($85–$95) double; 10,500–12,200 ptas. ($105–$122) triple. AE, EURO, MC, V. **Parking:** Free when available on premises.

They don't come any more central than this. Smack in the middle of the city's central shopping street, the Almudaina nevertheless offers peace and quiet in most of its large, bright, recently renovated guest rooms, some of which have views of the cathedral and port. Owner Mateo Cabrer Parera takes good care of the place and loves to chat with guests.

BUDGET

HOSTAL RITZI, Carre dels Apuntadors, 6, 07012 Palma de Majorca. Tel. 971/71-46-10. 19 rms. (with a variety of in-room plumbing facilities). **Bus:** 1, 3, 4, or 7.

$ **Rates** (including IVA): 1,500 ptas. ($15) single with sink but no WC; 2,700 ptas. ($27) double with sink but no WC; 3,000 ptas. ($30) double with shower but no WC; 3,200 ptas. ($32) double with complete bath. No credit cards. **Parking:** Not available.

This very central, in-town hostel has an inviting, plant-laden entryway. The guest rooms spread across three floors (no elevator), and all are different in decor and a bit worn, although not without a certain déshabille charm. This is a great place for students on a budget.

HOTEL APARTAMENTOS BOSQUE SOL, Camilo José Cela, 5, 07014 Palma de Majorca. Tel. 971/73-44-45. Fax 971/73-34-44. 284 apts. TEL **Bus:** 3, 4, 21, or 22.

$ **Rates** (including breakfast): 3,500–4,700 ptas. ($35–$47) single; 4,300–4,950 ptas. ($43–$49.50) double. AE, DC, EURO, MC, V. **Parking:** Nearby.

Just off Avenida Joan Miró a block behind Paseo Marítimo, this member of the Sol group offers small studio apartments where the daytime sofas in the sitting rooms become beds at night. Each unit has a fully equipped kitchenette and terrace. Gradually, they are all being renovated. Try to get one that's been rejuvenated, but don't worry if you don't—the old ones are quite acceptable.

The restaurant serves buffet breakfasts and dinners only; the bar serves snacks. Facilities include indoor and outdoor pools, laundry, and sauna.

HOTEL BORENCO, Avenida Joan Miró, 61, 07015 Palma de Majorca. Tel. 971/73-23-47. 70 rms. TEL **Bus:** 3, 4, 21, or 22.

$ Rates (including breakfast): 3,000 ptas. ($30) single; 4,500 ptas. ($45) double. No credit cards. **Parking:** Nearby.

The Borenco's functionally furnished guest rooms have terraces with views of either Bellver Castle or the Paseo Marítimo and the sea. The air-conditioned dining room offers Spanish and international fare. The adjoining TV room is rather shabby, but a small pool and sunbathing area on the roof that overlooks the port makes up for it.

HOTEL HORIZONTE SOL, Vista Alegre, 1, 07015 Palma de Majorca. Tel. 971/40-06-01. Fax 971/40-07-83. Telex E-69113. 199 rms. TEL **Bus:** 3 or 4.

$ Rates (including breakfast): 3,200–4,000 ptas. ($32–$40) single; 4,200–6,300 ptas. ($42–$63) double. AE, DC, EURO, MC, V. **Parking:** Not available.

A block away from the Hotel Majorica (see above) on a parallel street, the Horizonte is another reliable Sol property. Most of its ample guest rooms have terraces and sea views. Although this is only a two-star hotel, the extensive buffets at breakfast, lunch, and dinner uphold the high standards of the Sol group. The facilities include a pool and sunbathing areas.

HOTEL ROSAMAR, Avenida Joan Miró, 74, Palma de Majorca. Tel. 971/73-27-23. Fax 971/28-38-28. 40 rms. TEL **Bus:** 3, 4, 21, or 22.

$ Rates (including IVA): 3,000–5,200 ptas. ($30–$52) single; 4,600–5,200 ptas. ($46–$52) double. AE, DC, EURO, MC, V. **Parking:** Nearby.

The Rosa Mar is a clean, inexpensive option about two blocks behind the Paseo Marítimo. Half the guest rooms, which have been recently redone, have sea views. A games room features a billiard table, and there is also a TV room. Off to one side is the bar.

3. DINING

The cuisine of Majorca, and to a great extent that of the other Balearic Islands, relies heavily on pork products. Two of Majorca's culinary trademarks are *ensaimada* and *sobrasada*. Every morning many Majorcans enjoy the former, a type of pastry prepared with lard, with their morning coffee. Ranging from breakfast-roll size to pizza size for family celebrations, ensaimada can be plain or filled with cream, custard, or shredded pumpkin. Sobrasada is a savory sausage composed primarily of pork and red pepper.

Among the Balearic Islands, Majorca is the only one that produces a commercial quantity of wine. Of its three wine-producing areas—Binissalem, Porreres, and Felanitx—the first produces the best wines (most notable are the reds). The local *Palo* is an apéritif composed of sweet wine enriched with iodine, sugar, and herbs. A rather thick drink, it is usually served cold with a dash of soda.

The rustic *celleres* of Majorca, found mostly in the countryside, are traditional eateries located in vaulted, cavelike confines. They typically feature such traditional dishes as *lechona* (roast suckling pig), *frit* (a mixture of all sorts of animal innards fried together with herbs and hot peppers), *sopas mallorquines* (a hearty bread-and-vegetable soup), pork tenderloin in cabbage leaves, or, in winter, thrush wrapped in cabbage. All the meals are accompanied by a wine likely to come from the barrels flanking the walls.

In Palma, Paseo Marítimo and Avenida Joan Miró are lined with all types of snack bars, restaurants, pizzerias, and bars.

The Spanish eat later than Americans and other Europeans. Typical restaurant hours are 1 to 4pm and 8pm to midnight. As with the hotels, service is usually included in the prices, but IVA is *not*. Many restaurants offer very economical three-course luncheon menus, including bread and house wine. At cafeterias, tapas bars, and other informal eating establishments, it often costs less to eat at the bar than at a table. You'll also find in many restaurants that bread, butter, and perhaps an appetizer (olives or canapés) arrive automatically, but you'll be charged additionally for them—anywhere from 75 to 200 ptas. (75¢ to $2).

EXPENSIVE

ES RECÓ D'EN XESC, Paseo Marítimo, 17, next to the auditorium. Tel. 45-21-12.
   Cuisine: SEAFOOD/MAJORCAN. **Reservations:** Not required. **Bus:** 1.
$ Prices: Appetizers 600–1,100 ptas. ($6–$11); main courses 1,000–1,700 ptas. ($10–$17); menu del día (IVA included) 1,100 ptas. ($11). V.
   Open: Lunch Tues–Sun 1–4pm; dinner Tues–Sun 8pm–12:30am. **Closed:** Feb.

Situated in a small, indented plaza along the waterfront, Es Recó d'en Xesc offers both indoor and outdoor dining amid splashes of greenery.

Seafood is the house specialty. Some outstanding selections include pescado mallorquín prepared with spinach, potatoes, and tomatoes, and caldereta de langosta, which comprises the soup broth, then the lobster that was cooked in it. An unusual house offering is gambas al "Xesc," shrimp in a spicy sauce prepared according to an old recipe that owner-chef Nicolas Bonnin's father, Xesc (Francisco), found in a book given him by Rafael Pomar, the artist who did most of the paintings covering the restaurant's walls. Among the meat dishes, solomillo al rey (filet mignon with an almond sauce served with mashed potatoes and mushrooms) is recommended. Meals will be more expensive if you order the pricey caldereta or shellfish dishes. For dessert, try the *tarta de manzana* (apple tart) made fresh and served warm (place your order at the beginning of the meal).

MEDITERRANEO 1930, Paseo Marítimo, 33, next to the Hotel Melià Victoria. Tel. 45-88-77.
   Cuisine: SEAFOOD. **Reservations:** Recommended. **Bus:** 1.

$ Prices: Appetizers 650–5,000 ptas. ($6.50–$50); main courses 1,100–4,500 ptas. ($11–$45). AE, EURO, MC, V.
Open: Lunch daily 1–4pm; dinner daily 8pm–1am (live piano music begins at 9pm).

Mediterraneo 1930 is a chic art deco dining experience with a Mediterranean flair. Specializing in seafood, it prominently displays the catches of the day. Owners Juan and Mary Martí offer more than two dozen seafood dishes and a dozen or so meat entrees.

PORTO PI, Carrer Joan Miró, 174, or Carrer Garita, 25. Tel. 40-00-87.
Cuisine: GAME. **Reservations:** Required. **Bus:** 3, 4, 21, or 22.
$ Prices: Appetizers 1,000–2,500 ptas. ($10–$25); main courses 2,000–3,500 ptas. ($20–$35). AE, EURO, MC, V.
Open: Lunch Mon–Fri 1:30–3:30pm; dinner Mon–Sat 8:30–11:30pm. **Closed:** Holidays.

Installed in a turn-of-the-century house, Porto Pi's dining rooms and outdoor terrace are intimate and elegantly simple. The restaurant has two entrances—the one on Garita is the main one and offers the best possibilities for parking.

Porto Pi's menu varies greatly with the season and is studded with unusual dishes, such as pigeon salad, kokotxas de merluza (the gills of the hake), and lubina (sea bass) with a green-pepper-and-tequila sauce. Another house specialty is grilled magret fileted and draped appetizingly over puff pastry that's filled with spinach and pears. In winter, game is the culinary gambit.

RESTAURANTE ZARZAGAN, Paseo Marítimo, 13. Tel. 73-74-47.
Cuisine: SEAFOOD. **Reservations:** Recommended for dinner. **Bus:** 1.
$ Prices: Appetizers 900–7,500 ptas. ($9–$75); main courses 1,000–7,700 ($10–$77). AE, DC, EURO, MC, V.
Open: Lunch Mon–Fri 1–3:30pm; dinner daily 8–11:30pm. **Closed:** Usually in July.

This modern, sophisticated eatery has large picture windows overlooking the port and an ambiance of casual elegance.

The specialty of the house, as evidenced by the tank full of live specimens, is lobster. But among the numerous outstanding seafood dishes on the menu, perhaps the most innovative is centro de merluza al estilo waleska (hake topped with lobster medallions and a white cream sauce). Another fine selection is parrillada, an abundant array of grilled seafood. There is also a fine choice of meat dishes, including suckling lamb Segovia style and filet mignon prepared half a dozen different ways.

TRISTAN, Port Portals, Portals Nous. Tel. 13-25-00.
Cuisine: NOUVELLE CUISINE. **Reservations:** Required for dinner. **Bus:** 22.
$ Prices: Appetizers 1,200–2,700 ptas. ($12–$27); main courses 2,300–5,000 ptas. ($23–$50). AE, DC, EURO, MC, V.
Open: Lunch Tues–Sun 1–3:30pm; dinner Tues–Sun 8:30–11pm. **Closed:** Mid-Nov to mid-Dec.

Tristan hosts the yachting crowd whose boats are docked in the swanky marina of Port Portals. Just inside the restaurant entrance is a purple-topped circular bar surrounded by purple wicker chairs. Elsewhere all is white-linen elegance.

The menu varies markedly from day to day, depending on what's best in the market. The selection is largely international nouvelle cuisine, with some dishes reflecting Spanish and Majorcan influences.

MODERATE

DIPLOMATIC, Carrer Palau Reial, 5. Tel. 72-64-82.
   Cuisine: CONTINENTAL. **Reservations:** Recommended at lunch. **Bus:** 1, 3, or 15.
$ Prices: Appetizers 750–2,100 ptas. ($7.50–$21); main courses 900–2,300 ptas. ($9–$23); menu del día 1,200 ptas. ($12). AE, EURO, MC, V.
   Open: Lunch Mon–Sat 1–4pm; dinner Mon–Fri 8–11pm.

Located near the cathedral in the center of Palma, this is an excellent choice for anything from a sandwich or tapas at the bar to a full-fledged meal. As you move from the outdoor terrace to the inner recesses of this medieval structure with beamed ceilings and white stucco walls, the atmosphere becomes increasingly formal and intimate. Similarly, the wall decor runs from rustic knickknacks to sophisticated artwork.

The menu is a compendium of international dishes. Some house specialties are pâté with green peppercorns, sole with almonds, filet mignon in port wine, and steak tartare. Wine connoisseurs should note that owner Juan Contesti is particularly proud of his wine cellar and will happily show it to any interested parties.

LONJA DEL PESCADO (commonly known as Casa Eduardo), Muelle Viejo, s/n (no street number). Tel. 72-11-82.
   Cuisine: SEAFOOD. **Reservations:** Required for dinner in summer. **Bus:** 1 or 4.
$ Prices: Appetizers 1,000–1,400 ptas. ($10–$14); main courses 1,000–2,500 ptas. ($10–$25); menu del día 2,500 ptas. ($25). AE, EURO, MC, V.
   Open: Lunch Tues–Sat 1–3:30pm; dinner Tues–Sat 8–11pm.
   Closed: Last 2 weeks in Dec and first 3 weeks in Jan.

At this no-frills wharfside restaurant, the fish pass directly from the fishermen's boats at the front door to the kitchen. Don't be put off by the warehouselike entrance—the restaurant is one flight up. High-ceilinged and of modest decor, it is utterly devoid of pretensions, preferring to put its stock in the day's catch. The house specials include zarzuela (a local interpretation of bouillabaisse), a delicious seafood paella, and lobster. Beyond this, there is an extensive menu with a heavy Majorcan accent. If you don't want fish, though, go elsewhere.

MESON LOS RAFAELES, Paseo Majorca, 28. Tel. 71-77-96.
   Cuisine: SPANISH. **Reservations:** Recommended. **Bus:** 3, 7, or 21.
$ Prices: Appetizers 600–2,600 ptas. ($6–$26); main courses 775–2,200 ptas. ($7.75–$22). AE, EURO, MC, V.
   Open: Lunch Mon–Sat 12:30–4:30pm; dinner Mon–Sat 8pm–12:30am.

This small family-style place is popular with locals, who come for the handful of quality meat entrees and the varied selection of fresh seafood on appetizing display behind the bar and priced according to the day's market.

RESTAURANTE CABALLITO DE MAR, Paseo Sagrera, 5. Tel. 72-10-74.
   Cuisine: SEAFOOD. **Reservations:** Recommended. **Bus:** 1, 4, or 21.
$ Prices: Appetizers 850–2,400 ptas. ($8.50–$24); main courses 1,800–6,000 ptas. ($18–$60). AE, DC, EURO, MC, V.
   Open: Lunch daily noon–4pm; dinner daily 7:30pm–midnight.
The emphasis at this indoor/outdoor restaurant near the water is on food, not frills. To start, try the datiles (thin, long, mussel-like creatures that are sweetly succulent) and shrimp. For a main course, the lubina (sea bass) baked in sea salt is tender, juicy, and very traditional. Other house specialties include bouillabaisse and sea bass with fennel. Some nonfish dishes complete the offering. Leave room for the almond ice cream or cake, both typical Majorcan desserts.

RESTAURANTE LA LUBINA, Muelle Viejo. Tel. 72-33-50.
   Cuisine: SEAFOOD. **Reservations:** Recommended. **Bus:** 1, 4, or 21.
$ Prices: Appetizers 650–2,700 ptas. ($6.50–$27); main courses 1,500–5,000 ptas. ($15–$50). AE, DC, EURO, MC, V.
   Open: Lunch daily 12:30–4pm; dinner daily 8pm–midnight.
La Lubina greets you with a pretty tiled bar surrounded by a few tables and chairs for sipping apéritifs before dinner. For dining there are two informal terraces (one enclosed) that look out on the sea, the source of most of what you'll find on the menu.

They have, however, some unique ways of preparing their marine goods. Caldereta, for example, is lobster (fresh from their tanks) prepared in a broth flavored with almonds. Arroz a banda is rice cooked with fish in a broth; then the fileted fish and rice are served separately. Likewise with the bullavesa: The fish is first cooked in the broth and then the two are served separately. The menu also includes fish prepared the traditional Majorcan way, en papillote (encrusted with salt—the end result is in no way salty, however), or served with allioli (garlic mayonnaise).

BUDGET

BON LLOC, San Feliu, 7. Tel. 71-86-17.
   Cuisine: VEGETARIAN. **Reservations:** Not required. **Bus:** 1, 4, 15, or 21.
$ Prices: Four-course menu del día 1,050 ptas. ($10.50). No credit cards.
   Open: Tues–Sat 1–4pm; Fri also 9–11:30pm.
Installed in a noble house where Carlos V is said to have spent some time, Bon Lloc is a commendable vegetarian restaurant near Paseo des Born. Its decor is simple. Except on Friday night, when you can order à la carte, Bon Lloc offers only a four-course menu del día with a limited choice for each course. The menu varies daily, and the dishes are consistently savory.

C'AN PELUT, Paseo Marítimo, 30. Tel. 23-26-00.
   Cuisine: ITALIAN. **Reservations:** Not required. **Bus:** 1.

$ Prices: Appetizers 500–850 ptas. ($5–$8.50); pasta 525–725 ptas. ($5.25–$7.25); pizzas 500–900 ptas. ($5–$9); main courses 900–1,800 ptas. ($9–$18). AE, EURO, MC, V.
Open: Lunch Wed–Mon 1–4pm; dinner daily 8pm–midnight.
Closed: Tues evening in winter and Feb.

This is one of the seemingly thousands of places in Palma offering pizza and pasta. The advantage here is that you can sit at a sidewalk table on a sunny day and watch the passing parade along the paseo.

C'AN SALVADOR, Federico García Lorca, 21. Tel. 28-60-41.

Cuisine: SALADS/PASTAS/SNACKS. **Reservations:** Not required. **Bus:** 1.
$ Prices: Appetizers 650–1,600 ptas. ($6.50–$16); pasta 700–900 ptas. ($7–$9); pizzas 700–950 ptas. ($7–$9.50); main courses 800–2,000 ptas. ($8–$20). DC, MC, V.
Open: Mon–Sat 8:30am–1am (lunch served 1–4pm, dinner served 8pm–midnight).

At the top of Carrer S'aigo Dolça behind the Hotel Sol Palas Atenea, this is the place to come when you're not sure what you want or if you just want to pick. Either indoors amid hints of art deco styling or outdoors on the terrace, you can enjoy everything from a refreshing glass of horchata (a national drink made from the earth almond) to a limited à la carte menu. In addition, you can choose from among a small selection of fine tapas, assorted sandwiches made with crusty French bread, croissants, pastas, and pizzas.

LA CASITA, Avenida Joan Miró, 68. Tel. 73-75-57.

Cuisine: FRENCH/AMERICAN. **Reservations:** Not required. **Bus:** 3, 4, 21, or 22.
$ Prices: Appetizers 275–925 ptas. ($2.75–$9.25); main courses 700–1,425 ptas. ($7–$14.25); menu del día 850 ptas. ($8.50). EURO, MC, V.
Open: Lunch Tues–Sun 1–4pm; dinner Tues–Sun 7pm–midnight. **Closed:** Aug.

La Casita advertises French and American specialties, but the American accent is barely discernible. What *is* accented, however, is economy. The prices here are reasonably right, and the half a dozen tables are set in a friendly atmosphere punctuated by lazy ceiling fans and a soupçon of artwork. Among the French specialties are onion soup, pepper steak, and trout almondine; among the American dishes are chopped chicken liver pâté and potato pancakes.

RESTAURANTE EBOLI, Carrer Joan Miró, 17. Tel. 28-59-38.

Cuisine: PIZZA/FLAMBÉS. **Reservations:** Not required. **Bus:** 4, 20, or 21.
$ Prices: Appetizers 450–900 ptas. ($4.50–$9); pasta 700–750 ptas. ($7–$7.50); pizzas 450–650 ptas. ($4.50–$6.50); main courses 750–1,200 ptas. ($7.50–$12). AE, DC, EURO, MC, V.
Open: Lunch daily noon–4pm; dinner daily 7:30pm–midnight.

Eboli projects a slightly rustic image with lots of wood and checkered tablecloths. If you're eating inside you can watch the tropical fish in the aquarium as you savor the pizza or flambéed meat dishes that are the house specials. Meat fondue is on the menu, too. All flambés are prepared tableside.

RESTAURANTE MARIO'S, Carrer Bellver. Tel. 28-18-14.
　　Cuisine: ITALIAN. **Reservations:** Not required. **Bus:** 3, 4, 21, or 22.
$ Prices: Appetizers 450–1,250 ptas. ($4.50–$12.50); pasta 700–800 ptas. ($7–$8); main courses 1,000–1,700 ptas. ($10–$17). AE, DC, EURO, MC, V.
　　Open: Lunch Thurs–Mon 1–3:30pm; dinner Wed–Mon 8pm–midnight.

A block off the bustling Avenida Joan Miró, Mario's offers peaceful outdoor dining on an ivy-rimmed terrace amid all the trappings of a trattoria—white stucco, abundant wrought iron, and checkered curtains and tablecloths. Pasta is the main attraction here.

LA VECCHIA TRATTORIA, Carrer Robert Graves, 10. Tel. 73-79-86.
　　Cuisine: ITALIAN. **Reservations:** Not required. **Bus:** 3, 4, 21, or 22.
$ Prices: Appetizers 350–750 ptas. ($3.50–$7.50); pasta 500–850 ptas. ($5–$8.50); pizzas 525–1,050 ptas. ($5.25–$10.50); main courses 625–1,000 ptas. ($6.25–$10); menu del día 950 ptas. ($9.50). AE, EURO, MC, V.
　　Open: Lunch Wed–Mon 1–4pm; dinner Wed–Mon 8pm–12:30am.

This eatery features an extensive and inexpensive selection of pastas and above-average pizzas in a checkered-tablecloth atmosphere. Next door at its companion restaurant, **Ten** (with the same menu), the decor is more contemporary.

SPECIALTY DINING

TAPAS

ALBORADA RESTAURANT (also known as Casa Gallega), Plaça Weyler, 2. Tel. 72-46-20.
　　Cuisine: TAPAS. **Reservations:** Not required. **Bus:** 1, 14, or 15.
$ Prices: Tapas 550–1,100 ptas. ($5.50–$11); appetizers 500–1,900 ptas. ($5–$19); main courses 550–1,700 ptas. ($5.50–$17). MC, V.
　　Open: Lunch daily 1–4pm; dinner daily 8pm–midnight.

Tucked away in a niche just off the Plaça Mayor in the heart of Palma, the Alborada is a local favorite for tapas at the bar served beneath dangling beer mugs, garlic strands, and gourds, or for full-fledged meals served at one of a handful of simple tables. Many of its more than two dozen tapa selections are flown in from Galicia.

At its sibling establishment, the **Alborada Mar,** Paseo Marítimo 25 (tel. 28-49-74), you'll find much the same menu but a fancier setting.

BODEGA LA RAMBLA, Rambla, 15. Tel. 71-61-06.
　　Cuisine: TAPAS. **Reservations:** Not required. **Bus:** 1, 14, or 15.
$ Prices: Tapas 250–550 ptas. ($2.50–$5.50). No credit cards.
　　Open: Lunch Thurs–Tues 10am–2:30pm; dinner Thurs–Tues 7–10pm. **Closed:** Aug.

This is a 50-year-old fixture in central Palma devoted to tapas; you can get a small or large plate of mixed tapas, too. The place is small and you'll have to eat standing at the bar—there aren't even any bar stools. Overhead hangs an eccentric assortment of shells, pine cones, hooks, gourds, and more. The very friendly owner, Roberto, has been in charge for over 40 years.

MESON LAS TINAJAS, Berengario de Tornamira, 13, behind Galerias Preciados. Tel. 71-33-89.
   Cuisine: TAPAS. **Reservations:** Not required. **Bus:** 1, 4, or 21.
$ **Prices:** Tapas 450–1,000 ptas. ($4.50–$10); appetizers 400–1,000 ptas. ($4–$10); main courses 1,000–4,300 ptas. ($10–$43); menu del día 1,050 ptas. ($10.50). AE, EURO, MC, V.
   Open: Mon–Fri 10:30am–11pm; Sat 10:30am–4:30pm (meals served from 12:30pm). **Closed:** Holidays.

Both a tapas bar and a restaurant, Las Tinajas specializes in several varieties of paella, duck drumsticks in champagne sauce, and seafood. The selection of tapas is ample and tasty. If you're in the mood for a sweet snack, the cakes and pies here are homemade (try the lemon meringue).

EL PILON, Carrer San Cayetano, 12 (just off Paseo des Born). Tel. 21-75-90.
   Cuisine: SPANISH/MAJORCAN. **Reservations:** Not required. **Bus:** 1, 4, or 21.
$ **Prices:** Tapas 250–1,300 ptas. ($2.50–$13); appetizers 700–1,300 ptas. ($7–$13); main courses 1,000–2,900 ptas. ($10–$29). AE, EURO, MC, V.
   Open: Mon–Sat 9:30am–midnight. **Closed:** Feb.

This place offers good food at a good price in very pleasant surroundings, and thus it is one of my favorite in-town spots to snack or sup. Sometimes you'll find among the tapas such local dishes as *tumbet* (a mixture of fried peppers, eggplant, potatoes, garlic, and more, topped with tomato sauce) or *coca* (a kind of Majorcan pizza topped with a vegetable mixture similar to that of the tumbet).

DESSERT

Dating from 1700, **Ca'n Juan de S'aigo,** Carrer Sans, 10 (tel. 71-07-59), is the oldest ice-cream parlor on the island. Correspondingly elegant and Old World, it serves its homemade ice creams (try the almond), pastries, cakes, ensaimadas, fine coffee, and several kinds of hot chocolate amid marble-top tables, lots of wood, beautiful tile floors, and an indoor garden with a fountain. This is a place not to be missed. A cup of ice cream will run 160 ptas. ($1.60). Open Wednesday to Monday from 8am to 9pm.

There is also a branch at Baró Sta. María del Sepulcre, 5 (near Galerias Preciados; tel. 72-57-60), open the same hours but with slightly higher prices.

FAST FOOD

There's a **McDonald's** in Palma, smack in the center at Plaça Pio XII, 7 (tel. 71-84-85). Open on Monday to Thursday from 10am to midnight, Friday and Saturday from 10am to 1am, and Sunday and holidays from 11am to midnight. A Big Mac runs about 400 ptas. ($4).

4. WHAT TO SEE & DO

Horse-drawn carriages line up daily all year long along Paseo de Sagrera and Avenida Antonio Maura near the Muelle Viejo and offer a 45-minute circuit along the Paseo Marítimo or in the old town of Palma. The cost is about 3,300 ptas. ($33).

CATHEDRAL, Carrer Palau Reial, 29. Tel. 72-31-30.

Dominating the heart of Palma, this intricate limestone construction known locally as "La Seu" evolved in a largely Renaissance style from the 13th to the 16th century and was built in gratitude for James I of Aragón's victory over the Moors on December 31, 1229. Noteworthy are the Gaudí reformations within—moving the choir behind the altar and adding a baldachin over it. The window over the altar is one of the largest in the world.

As you exit the cathedral, you'll see a glass floor revealing three subterranean Roman columns discovered during a recent renovation.

The cathedral's museum and treasury contain many silver and gem-encrusted religious objects and reliquaries, some 15th- and 16th-century Gothic paintings, the tomb of the 14th-century antipope (who, curiously enough, was demoted to bishop by the real pope), and two human-size 18th-century baroque silver candelabra (500 lbs. each) depicting mythical figures supporting a world of gambolling cherubs.

Admission: Cathedral free; museum and treasury 225 ptas. ($2.25).

Open: Cathedral daily 8am–6pm; museum and treasury Mon–Fri 10am–12:30pm and 4–6:30pm, Sat 10am–1:30pm. **Closed:** Holidays. **Bus:** 1.

PUEBLO ESPAÑOL, Capitán Mezquida Veny, 39. Tel. 23-70-75.

Like Barcelona's, this is an assemblage of scaled-down replicas of Spain's important architectural highlights. Unlike Barcelona's, it is not a focal point for nightlife.

Admission: 375 ptas. ($3.75) adults; 275 ptas. ($2.75) children under 12.

Open: Daily 9am–8pm. **Directions:** Take a taxi since no buses pass by here.

BELLVER CASTLE, between Palma and Illetas. No phone.

Built in 1309, Bellver ("beautiful view") Castle is the former summer palace of Majorca's King James II. After his death it was turned into a fortress with the addition of a double moat. It is Europe's only round castle; its sandstone construction looks eternally new. During the Civil War it served as a prison; now it houses the Municipal Museum, containing archeological relics and old coins. Its chief attraction, however, is the 360° panorama of Palma, the sea, and the distant mountains from its upper terrace.

Admission: 160 ptas. ($1.60).
Open: Oct–Mar, daily 8am–6pm. Apr–Sept, daily 8am–8pm.
Museum and halls closed on Sun. **Bus:** 3, 4, 21, or 22.

BAÑOS ARABES [MOORISH BATHS], Carrer Serra, 3. Tel.72-15-49.

These baths in the narrow streets of the old quarter east of the
cathedral are the only completely Moorish constructions remaining
in Palma. Although it is impossible to determine when they were
built, most experts agree that it was probably the 10th century. While
they are less impressive than the Arab baths of Granada or Girona,
they have an interesting room whose dome is supported by 12
columns with diverse capitals. The tables and chairs in the garden
area outside will tempt you to linger.
Admission: 125 ptas. ($1.25).
Open: Daily 10am–1:30pm and 4–6pm. **Bus:** 1.

PALAU DE LA ALMUDAINA, Carrer Palau Reial. Tel. 71-43-68.

Another structure with Moorish roots, the Palau de la
Almudaina is opposite the cathedral (see above). Originally a
fortress, it contains the trademark gardens and fountains of the
Moors and was converted into a royal residence during the brief
reign of the Majorcan kings. Now one of the most popular
attractions of Palma, its museum gathers together antiques, arts, suits
of armor, and several Gobelin tapestries.
Admission: 450 ptas. ($4.50).
Open: Mon–Sat 9:30am–1:30pm; also Mon–Fri 4–6:30pm.
Bus: 1.

LA LONJA, Paseo Sagrera, s/n (no street number). Tel. 71-17-05.

This former commodities exchange of the 15th century is a
strikingly innovative rendition of the Gothic.
Admission: Free.
Open: Only during exhibitions (check the local papers) Tues–Sun
11am–2pm and 5–9pm. **Bus:** 1.

PLAÇA DE TOROS. Tel. 75-16-39.

Bullfights are held very sporadically these days because there is an
ever-diminishing local and foreign audience. Typically the *corridas*
are held Sunday at 5:30pm during July and August. Although they're
not of the caliber you'll find on the Peninsula, go see one if this is your
only opportunity.
Admission: Varies greatly with seat and renown of the
toreros—anywhere from 1,000–5,000 ptas. ($10–$50).
Directions: Take a cab because no buses pass by here.

5. SAVVY SHOPPING

Palma's prime shopping streets are **San Miguel, Carrer
Sindicato** (the street of bargains in shoes, clothing, and spices such
as saffron), **Avenida Jaume III** (the poshest shopping street),

Carrer Jaume II (for modern boutiques), and the warren of winding narrow streets between the Paseo des Born and Plaça Mayor (with a veritable outburst of boutiques).

Palma's lone department store is **Galerías Preciados,** Avenida Jaume III, 15 (tel. 71-10-10); open on Monday to Saturday from 10am to 9pm. It offers tourists special discounts and services with its free Passport Service Card. To obtain one simply go to the Customer Service Department.

One of Majorca's main industries is leather; another is simulated pearls. Both are quite visible in Palma's shops.

ADOLFO DOMÍNGUEZ, Carrer Bonaire, 2. Tel. 71-23-83.

This shop features the oversize, angular fashions for both men and women of this trendy Spanish designer, who outfitted Don Johnson during the second season of "Miami Vice." He also has shops in Madrid and Barcelona (see Chapter 6). Open Monday to Saturday from 10am to 1:30pm and from 4:30 to 8:15pm; closed Saturday evenings in summer. Bus: 3 or 4.

LOEWE, Paseo des Born, 2. Tel. 71-52-75.

This is another outpost of Spain's premier purveyor of fine leather goods and chic fashion for both men and women. Open on Monday to Friday from 9am to 1:30pm and from 4:30 to 8pm, Saturday from 9am to 1:30pm. **Bus:** 1, 4, 7, or 21.

PASSY, Avenida Jaume III, 6. Tel. 71-33-38.

The location above—plus shops at San Miguel, 53 (tel. 72-56-86), and Tous y Ferrer, 8 (tel. 71-73-38)—offers quality, locally made shoes and handbags. Open on Monday to Friday from 10am to 1:45pm and from 4:30 to 8pm, Saturday from 10am to 1:45pm; closed on Saturday in August. Bus: 3 or 4.

PERLAS MAJORICA, Avenida Jaume III, 11. Tel. 72-52-68.

This factory store (see "The Eastern Coast" in Chapter 10) offers a wide selection of Majorica pearl rings, necklaces, bracelets, and brooches produced on the island at Manacor. Authorized Majorica retailers display the sign "Majorica Simulated Pearls Official Agent." The authenticity of the product is signaled by a red label with the gold inscription "Perlas Majorica," on the back of which you'll find a quality-control number. An international certificate of guarantee is also attached ensuring free replacement of any pearl showing a defect within 10 years of the date of purchase; simply take the certificate and faulty pearl to an official agent anywhere in the world. In addition to pearl creations, this store offers some fine gold and silver jewelry. Open on Monday to Friday from 9:30am to 1:30pm and from 4:30 to 8pm, Saturday from 9:30am to 1:30pm. Bus: 3 or 4.

PINK, Plaça Pio XII, 3. Tel. 72-73-51.

At the above location and at the shop at Avenida Jaume III no. 3 (tel. 72-23-33), Pink offers luxury leather-goods in exclusive, highly imaginative designs that can be custom-made. Open on Monday to Friday from 10am to 1:30pm and from 4 to 8pm, Saturday from 10:30am to 1:30pm. Bus: 3 or 4.

YANKO, Carrer Unión, 3. Tel. 72-27-88.

Yanko is a classic, high-fashion, high-quality leather-goods store for both men and women. You'll get your money's worth here. Open on Monday to Saturday from 9:45am to 1:30pm and from 4:30 to 8pm. Bus: 3 or 4.

---

6. EVENING ENTERTAINMENT

Palma is the focal point for island nightlife, but much of it is of the pounding-music in the cavernous-and-crowded disco variety or the topless peep-show variety. Most of the bars, cabarets, topless clubs, and discos are in the El Terreno district stretching along Avenida Joan Miró behind Paseo Marítimo. These places tend to come and go with great rapidity, but below are some that have been around for awhile.

CLUBS

BROADWAY NIGHT CLUB, Avenida Joan Miró, 36. Tel. 28-52-73.
This club appeals to the prurient interest with a series of shows that get increasingly risqué as the night grinds on. The last show of the night is quite explicit and not recommended for demure viewers. The club is open nightly from 10pm to 5:30am; the first of two shows starts at midnight. Bus: 3, 4, 21, or 22.
Admission (including one drink): 2,300 ptas. ($23).

CASINO MALLORCA, Urbanización Sol de Mallorca, Costa de Calva. Tel. 13-00-00 or 45-45-08.
Casino Mallorca offers both gambling and a Las Vegas–style nightclub show complete with sexy ladies in sequins and feathers, dance numbers, singers, and so on. You can call the above phone numbers on Monday to Saturday from 9am to 1:30pm and 4 to 7:30pm for show information and reservations. The casino is open Monday, Tuesday, and Thursday to Saturday from 8pm to 5am. To get there, take the Cala Figuera exit off the autopista to Andraitx.
Admission: Casino 600 ptas. ($6), and you must have your passport to get in. Show and one drink 4,300 ptas. ($43); show and dinner 5,700–6,500 ptas. ($57–$65), including wine, champagne, casino admission, and IVA.

TITO'S PALACE, Plaça Gomila, 3. Tel. 23-58-84.
One of the shopping-mall breed of discos for today's youth, Tito's spreads across many floors and offers numerous bars. There is also an entrance via elevator from Paseo Marítimo. Tito's is open daily from 10:30pm to 5am. Bus: 1.
Admission (including one drink): 1,700 ptas. ($17).

ZHIVAGO, Robert Graves, 18. Tel. 23-15-82.
This dark dance hall with fringed lamps over the bar acknowledges the Russian theme. Two orchestras play a selection of music of all eras, including tangoes, salsas, waltzes, and rock. This is the place for those who like to hold their partners while dancing. March

through November it's open daily from 10pm to 4:30am; December to February it's open only on Friday and Saturday from 10pm to 4:30am. Bus: 3, 4, 21, or 22.

Admission (including one drink): 1,000 ptas. ($10).

BARS

ABACO, San Juan, 1. Tel. 21-49-39.

Installed in a 17th-century house near the cathedral, this place for exotic drinks is a bacchanalian feast for the eyes, with decadent displays of fruits and flowers by the bushel and heaps of candles dripping wax wantonly. It is said that the florist's bill alone runs $500 per day! Dozens of tables share an inner courtyard with exotic caged birds, fountains, sculptures, and more flowers, fruits, and candles. Upstairs are several small rooms with antique furnishings and an old-fashioned kitchen. The long downstairs bar is made of stone; cocktails as overpowering as the decor (one combines whiskey, rum, Grand Marnier, and fruit juice) are served. Abaco is open daily from 9pm to 3am. Drinks run about $12. Bus: 1, 4, 15, or 21.

AZZURRO, Paseo Marítimo, 30, near the Sol Palas Atenea. Tel. 58-80-75.

This sophisticated piano bar draws an older crowd appreciative of its more sedate musical offerings. It's open daily from 7:30pm to 3:30am (to 4:30am on weekends); live music begins at 10pm. There's no cover, but drinks cost about 20% more after 10pm (about $9 per cocktail). Bus: 1.

BAR MAM'S, Avenida Joan Miró, 39. No phone.

This hole-in-the-wall watering hole is popular with English-speaking tourists from many nations. Posters of Marilyn Monroe, Humphrey Bogart, and James Dean keep company with the stand-up drinkers. Chili con carne (450 ptas. [$4.50]) and burgers (400 ptas. [$4]) are served. Open May through October daily from 6:30pm to 5am, November through April daily from 1pm to 3am. A beer runs about 175 ptas. ($1.75). Bus: 3, 4, 21, or 22.

7. EASY EXCURSIONS FROM PALMA DE MAJORCA

PLATJA DE PALMA, C'AN PASTILLA & ARENAL

On either side of Palma along Majorca's southwestern coast are popular beach resorts. The largest and best known is Platja de Palma, a 4¼-mile (7km) uninterrupted flow of fine white sand and crystalline blue water skirting the "hotel forests" of C'an Pastilla and Arenal, about 7½miles (12km) east of Palma.

In recent years the place has grown to the point where sometimes you can't see the beach for the people. In July and August this group-tour resort area is packed with young people; in winter it's a haven for senior citizens. Just before and after the peak summer season it seems to appeal primarily to families. The crowd is mostly European.

Unfortunately, the hotel offerings are not on a par with the natural beauty of the setting. The hotel, restaurant, and nightlife offerings are more or less homogeneous all along the beach without great fluctuations in quality or price. All the hotels are close to, if not on, the beach, and their facilities are geared to mass tourism, with half- and full-board buffet meals and organized sports activities and entertainment daily. For a better grade of hotel, restaurant, and nightlife, you must go to Palma. Personally, I prefer to stay in Palma and commute to the beaches out here.

If you're going to stay here or commute to these beaches, there is frequent bus service (in season) from Palma via Bus 15 (leaving from the cathedral) and Bus 23 and 26 Expreso (both leaving from the Plaça Espanya). The fare is about 150 ptas. ($1.50). For full details call the E.M.T. office at 29-08-55.

WHERE TO STAY

The hotel offerings along here are vast and almost exclusively of the package-tour variety. Prices vary greatly throughout the year, depending on the season and how business is going. Due to the abundant offerings, hotels tend to come and go. Below is a handful of hotels that have managed to stick around awhile. Remember to ask for a discount, especially off-season.

Expensive

HOTEL RIU BRAVO, Carrer Misión de San Diego, s/n (no street number), 07620 Platja de Palma, Majorca. Tel. 971/26-63-00. Fax 971/26-57-54. Telex 68693. 199 rms. A/C TEL
$ Rates (including breakfast and IVA): 6,135–9,775 ptas. ($61.35–$97.75) single; 9,670–15,500 ptas. ($96.70–$155) double. AE, V. **Parking:** Available.

The Riu Bravo, set several blocks back from the beach, has a distinctive facade with round balconies. Within are luxuriously appointed public areas studded with marble. Although the guest rooms are not on a par with the public areas, they are pleasant enough, with tile floors, country-print wallpaper, and dark-wood furnishings from a few decades ago. The hotel has a swimming pool.

Moderate

AYRON PARK, Carrer Trasimè, 7, 07600 El Arenal, Majorca. Tel. 971/26-06-50. Fax 971/26-56-75. Telex 69103. 103 rms. TEL
$ Rates (including breakfast, dinner, and IVA): 4,300–5,300 ptas. ($43–$53) single; 7,500–9,500 ptas. ($75–$95) double. No credit cards. **Parking:** Available. **Closed:** Nov–Mar.

The guest rooms here are large but basic, and the facilities include a pool and a tennis court.

HOTEL ALEXANDRA, Avda. Pins, 15, 07610 C'an Pastilla, Majorca. Tel. 971/26-23-50. Fax 971/26-23-20. 164 rms. TEL
$ Rates (including breakfast): 4,500–7,200 ptas. ($45–$72) single; 5,300–11,000 ptas. ($53–$110) double. AE, DC, V. **Parking:** On premises.

A cut above the largely homogenized hotel offerings in this area, the Alexandra has guest rooms with terraces. The large pool on the lobby level features a bar and a sea view; a set of stairs takes you across the street to the beach. A second, smaller pool is on the fifth floor by the solarium. The restaurant serves a buffet breakfast. The hotel has a barbershop, a beauty parlor, and two pools.

HOTEL ROYAL CUPIDO, Carrer Marbella, 32, 07620 Platja de Palma, Majorca. Tel. 971/26-43-00. Fax 971/20-12-67. Telex 68504. 197 rms. TEL

$ Rates (including IVA): 6,000–11,400 ptas. ($60–$114) single; 7,500–14,300 ptas. ($75–$143) double. AE, EURO, MC, V. **Parking:** Available.

⭐ Another good choice awaits here behind a rather uninviting blank white facade. All the guest rooms have terraces with sea views, and the hotel has a pool.

Budget

HOTEL JAVA SOL, Carrer Goleta, s/n (no street number), 07610 C'an Pastilla. Tel. 971/26-27-76. Fax 971/26-30-85. 250 rms. TEL

$ Rates (including breakfast): 4,700–6,000 ptas. ($47–$60) single; 6,100–9,700 ptas. ($61–$97) double. AE, DC, EURO, MC, V. **Parking:** Available.

Yet another Sol entry, this hotel is a block from the beach, with simply furnished guest rooms boasting terraces and sea views. There is also a pool.

HOTEL NEPTUNO, Laud, 34, 07620 Platja de Palma, Majorca. Tel. 971/26-00-00. Fax 971/49-22-50. Telex 68751 CHLL-E. 105 rms. TEL

$ Rates (including breakfast and IVA): 3,700–5,800 ptas. ($37–$58) single; 4,800–8,100 ptas. ($48–$81) double. No credit cards. **Parking:** Nearby. **Closed:** Nov–Dec.

Ⓢ Right across the street from the beach, the Neptuno has public areas that are more antiquated than its comfortable guest rooms with terraces. The facilities include a pool and a solarium, and there is access to a tennis court and mini-golf.

HOTEL NIAGARA, Padre Bartolomé Salvá, 5, 07620 Platja de Palma, Majorca. Tel. 971/26-09-00. Fax 971/26-09-08. 140 rms. TEL

$ Rates (including breakfast and IVA): 2,500–5,300 ptas. ($25–$53) single; 4,400–9,500 ptas. ($44–$95) double. EURO, MC, V. **Parking:** Nearby. **Closed:** Nov–Feb.

This gleaming white hotel has recently refurbished its facade, pool, and public areas with lots of marble. The guest rooms were left untouched but are clean and comfortable and furnished in a Spanish style of yesteryear.

ES TRENC

About 25 miles (40km) southeast of Palma near La Rapita is Es Trenc, a beauty of a beach. To get there you'll drive through the flat, cultivated Majorcan plains studded with working windmills. After La Rapita, follow the signs for "Ses Covetes." From where you park the car, it's a short walk to a beach almost as long and broad as the one at Platja de Palma but without a single hotel. At one end are thatched beach umbrellas and lounge chairs; at the other end it's just you and your towel. And along the entire beach there is, blessedly, just one snack bar. The sand is fine, soft, and white and the water clear and clean. Fringed by a pine forest and sand dunes, this beach is so secluded that people have long favored it for nude bathing, although its status as a nudist beach remains unofficial (unlike Ibiza, Majorca has always been conservative in matters of public undress).

ILLETAS, PALMA NOVA & MAGALLUF

West of Palma is a series of small, sandy coves—Illetas, Palma Nova, and Magalluf. Frequent in-season bus service runs from the center of Palma to both Illetas and Arenal. At Palma Nova there is almost no beach to speak of—just a thin strip of sand. Magalluf has a curving bay with a respectable beach and offers rides on glass-bottom boats, waterskiing, and parasailing.

WHAT TO SEE & DO

Between Palma Nova and Illetas is **Port Portals,** where the yacht set park their major-league vessels. Along the marina are some fancy shops and restaurants and some pleasant places to enjoy an al fresco drink or ice cream while contemplating the flotilla of pleasure craft harbored nearby.

For children, **Aquapark** (tel. 13-08-11), near Magalluf on the road toward Cala Figuera, offers swimming pools and water slides and rides. Open May to October daily from 10am to 6pm. Admission is 1,550 ptas. ($15.50) for adults and 900 ptas. ($9) for children 5 to 12; children under 5 are free. From Palma's Plaça de España there is half-hourly bus service on Playasol buses 2 and 3.

WHERE TO STAY

ANTILLAS SOL, Carrer Violeta, 1, 07182 Magalluf, Majorca. Tel. 971/13-15-00. Fax 971/13-02-05. 329 rms. TEL **Bus:** 21 or 22.
$ **Rates** (including breakfast): 4,600–7,700 ptas. ($46–$77) single; 6,000–12,000 ptas. ($60–$120) double. AE, DC, EURO, MC, V. **Parking:** Public parking nearby.

At a slight remove from the in-town sprawl, this hotel offers newly renovated guest rooms with marble baths, carpeting, telephones, and terraces. Just beyond the large pool is a solarium on the sand, and beyond that is access to the beach. In conjunction with the Hotel Barbados Sol next door, it offers tennis, mini-golf, and an indoor pool in winter.

HOTEL MELIÀ DE MAR, Carretera de Illetas, 7, 07015 Illetas, Majorca. Tel. 971/40-25-11. Fax 971/40-58-52. Telex 68892. 133 rms, 11 suites. A/C MINIBAR TV TEL **Bus:** 21 or 22.
$ **Rates:** 18,000–20,000 ptas. ($18–$20) single; 23,000–25,800 ptas. ($230–$258) double. AE, DC, EURO, MC, V. **Parking:** On premises.

A prime five-star choice in Illetas, the Melià de Mar features guest rooms that are well appointed and suites that have terraces and sea views. The hotel has a tennis court, facilities for water sports, and indoor and outdoor pools.

SÓLLER

For a complete change of pace, consider the 18-mile (30km) trip to Sóller in a vintage wooden train operated by **Ferrocarriles Sóller** (tel. 75-20-51). There are about five departures daily, leaving from the Estación Plaça España. En route, it passes through the fruit-growing Sóller Valley, famous for its oranges. Of interest in Sóller are the cathedral and the bank building next door, designed by a pupil of Gaudí.

CHAPTER 10

AROUND MAJORCA

1. DEIA [DEYÁ] & THE WESTERN COAST

2. PORT DE POLLENÇA & THE NORTH

3. THE EASTERN COAST

From the rugged drama of its wild west coast to the level serenity of its central plains, Majorca packs a wide variety of scenery into 1,405 square miles (3,640 square km). Inland are the virile vistas of the Sierra de Tramontana, where the island reaches its highest peak at Puig Mayor (4,750 feet [1,445m]), the bucolic orange- and lemon-grove valleys of the Sóller region, and the mountainside artists' refuge at Deyá. Similarly varied is the 250-mile-long (400km-long) coastline that runs from the tame, white-sand beaches of the north and south to the jagged, cliff-tucked coves of the west.

Overland, the longest distance from one point to another on the island is a little over 50 miles (80km) north to south and slightly more than that east to west.

The island's cleanest and most peaceful seaside havens are outside the Palma Bay area. In the southwestern corner of the island, try the beaches of Camp de Mar and the port of Andraitx. Also nearby is the beautiful beach at San Telmo, opposite the uninhabited island of Dragonera.

Southeast of Palma are a number of wonderful beaches with crystal-clear water beginning at Cala Blava in the eastern corner of Palm Bay and continuing along the Platja d'es Trenc (see "Easy Excursions from Palma de Majorca" in Chapter 9) to Sant Jordi.

The eastern coast from Cala Santanyi north to Cala Ratjada is notched with charming lagoon-type *calas* (coves), often with sandy beaches and stands of pines. At Porto Cristo, 37.5 miles (60km) east of Palma, is a lovely beach on a beautiful horseshoe-shaped bay. Also over here are several impressive caves whose illuminated stalactites and stalagmites conjure some melodramatic optical illusions.

In the north, a chain of beaches stretches for miles and miles along the bays of Alcudia and Port de Pollença (Puerto de Pollença). Here the sand is whiter than that anywhere else on Majorca and the pines provide not only shade but also a pretty scenic accent. The water is generally shallow, warm, and clean, and the beaches are long enough to offer some privacy even when the area hotels are fully occupied.

North of Port de Pollença, the virtually virgin Formentor Peninsula combines all of Majorca's best features—pine forests, plunging cliffs, silken sand, and water so turquoise that you'll think it must be painted fresh daily.

GETTING AROUND

BY BUS From Palma there are numerous half- and full-day bus tours to all corners of the island for under 7,000 ptas. ($70). Contact any travel agency or your hotel reception desk for details. In addition, there is regularly scheduled bus and train service to some of the

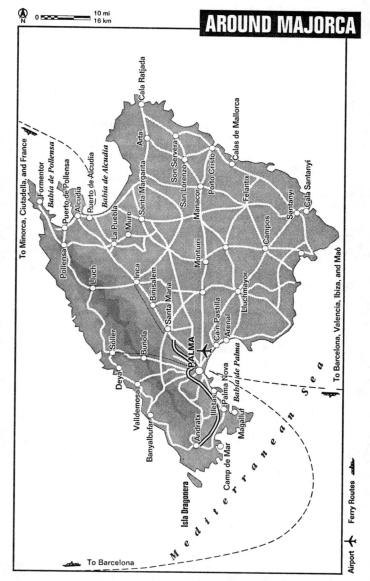

0 — 10 mi
16 km

To Minorca, Ciutadella, and France

To Barcelona, Valencia, Ibiza, and Maó

Formentor
Babia de Pollensa
Puerto de Pollensa
Alcudia
Puerto de Alcudia
Babia de Alcudia
Cala Ratjada
Arta
Son Servera
Calas de Mallorca
San Lorenzo
Porto Cristo
Manacor
Felanitx
Santanyi
Cala Santanyi
Pollensa
Lluch
La Puebla
Muro
Santa Margarita
Montuiri
Campos
Inca
Binisalem
Santa Maria
Can Pastilla
Arenal
Lluchmayor
Soller
Buñola
PALMA
Deya
Valldemosa
Illetas
Palma Nova
Babia de Palma
Magalluf
Andratx
Banyalbufar
Camp de Mar
Isla Dragonera

M e d i t e r r a n e a n   S e a

To Barcelona

Airport ✈   Ferry Routes ⚓

interior cities (see "Orientation" in Chapter 9 for details). From Port de Pollença there is frequent bus service to Pollença, Inca, Palma, and Alcudia in the summer. Details are available at the tourist office.

BY CAR   Renting a car is by far the best way to explore the island, as many of Majorca's special treats lie off the beaten path of mass tourism. At this writing rates begin at about 5,300 ptas. ($53). Atesa, Avis, BC Betacar, and Europcar are among the most economical and all have offices at the airport, in Palma, and elsewhere on the island.

Hours at the in-town offices vary markedly throughout the year, so your best bet is to call first or deal with the airport offices, whose hours are more consistent year round.

Atesa: At the airport (tel. 26-61-00), open daily from 7:30am to 11:30pm; also at Paseo Marítimo, 25 (tel. 45-66-02).

Avis: At the airport (tel. 26-09-10), open May to October daily 24 hours and November to April daily from 7:30am to 12:30am; also at Paseo Marítimo, 16, Palma (tel. 73-07-20).

BC Betacar & Europcar: At the airport (tel. 26-38-11), open May to October 24 hours daily and November to April daily 7am to midnight; also at Paseo Marítimo, 19, Palma (tel. 45-48-00).

ORGANIZED TOURS   A host of organized bus tours is available to all important points of the island through **Sidetours,** S.A., Paseo Marítimo, 16, Palma (tel. 28-39-00 for information; 73-76-16 for reservations). Most hotels carry their list of excursions and will happily make the arrangements for you.

BOAT EXCURSIONS   The offering of island cruises changes dramatically throughout the year, so either ask at your hotel or take a stroll down to the Paseo Marítimo to the dock opposite the auditorium, where you'll find conspicuous signboards announcing cruises, departure times, and prices.

1. DEIA (DEYÁ) & THE WESTERN COAST

Majorca's most imposing mountains run along the western coast, where from time to time the road zigzags narrowly through sloping pine forests. Although distances are short, the time required to cover them is considerably more than the mileage suggests, so leave yourself enough time to explore at leisure and savor the scenery.

The route indicated below under "What to See & Do" can be covered in one day if you get an early start. Or you can overnight in Deyá and spend the extra time taking photos at each of the numerous *miradores* (overlooks) along the way (each marked with a roadside sign depicting a camera) and traveling some of the rugged tertiary roads down to the private pleasures of remote rocky coves.

WHAT TO SEE & DO

After heading west out of Palma on the coastal highway, take the C-710 along the western coast. At kilometer 103 you'll come across the first in a series of **miradores,** this one looking down on a rocky cove at the juncture of two coastal mountains. Several kilometers farther along at Es Grau, where there is a restaurant/bar, some stairs lead up to a plunging panorama of tree-crowned cliffs. As you continue on past Estallench toward Banyalbufar, look back at the former to fully appreciate its picturesque cascade of orange-roofed, dun-colored houses. Between Estallench and Banyalbufar is a mirador with a ruined tower (don't bother to climb the ladder inside because there is no view from the top—the best view of the coast here is from the road). Banyalbufar is also best appreciated once you have passed it and can look back on its terraced splendor.

At Valldemossa, visit the ✪ **Real Cartuja** (tel. 61-21-06), the Carthusian monastery where Frédéric Chopin and George Sand spent two months in the winter of 1838 to 1839. Formerly the palace of King Martin I, it was given to the monks in the 14th century and expropriated by the government in 1835. The church itself is an 18th-century neoclassical structure. Cells 2 and 4 were inhabited by Chopin and Sand, but only a few items (a high-back chair, a small painting, and a French piano) remain here from their time; most of what they left behind was burned by the locals because they feared contagion by the tubercular Chopin. Also remaining is the Majorcan piano he used to compose several preludes. Several of Chopin's original scores and some original manuscript pages of Sand's *A Winter in Majorca,* a biting account of their time on the island, are on display. In another part of the monastery is a pharmacy dating from the late 17th century.

The Real Cartuja is open November through February on Monday to Saturday from 9:30am to 1pm and from 3 to 5:30pm; April to September on Monday to Saturday from 9:30am to 1pm and from 3 to 6:30pm; and March and October on Monday to Saturday from 9:30am to 1pm and from 3 to 6pm. Closed Christmas and New Year. Admission is 650 ptas. ($6.50).

Just shortly before you reach Deyá, you'll come to ✪ **Son Marroig** (tel. 63-91-58), the Majorcan refuge of Archduke Luis Salvador. Born in 1847, he fled from life at court in Tuscany and wandered throughout the Mediterranean on his yacht, writing numerous books about the area. In 1870 he bought the Son Marroig estate, whose tower dates from the 16th century. The highlights of this beautiful stone house today are the fully furnished salon with a coffered ceiling and the dining room filled with drawings, photographs of the archduke, a notable assemblage of Majorcan furniture and paintings, and a collection of ceramics from around the world. The views are the house's greatest asset, however, especially from the Carrara marble pavilion set in the gardens. The estate now belongs to the grandchildren of the archduke's private secretary, who inherited the mansion. Part of the estate is **Sa Foradada,** a small peninsula with a spectacular view that is 2 miles (3km) from the house and accessible only on foot. You must ask permission at the house to go there, and it will require not only climbing over a fence that keeps in the family sheep but also hiking somewhat strenuously up steep inclines.

Son Marroig is open on Tuesday to Saturday from 9:30am to 2pm and from 4:30 to 6pm (until 8pm in summer). Admission is 275 ptas. ($2.75).

Deyá, dramatically sheltered in a fertile valley on the slopes of a 4,000-foot mountain, is primarily an artists' and writers' hangout. It has two museums; a historic church; and several cafés, bars, restaurants, boutiques, and art galleries. Noted writer Robert Graves lived here for 45 years and is buried in the village church cemetery. Mike Oldfield, when he comes, has been known to play for hours in the local bars. Many other prominent people are also attracted by its beauty, intimacy, and upscale bohemian atmosphere.

En route from Deyá to Cala de Sa Calobra, you will pass through the dramatic northern reaches of the **Sierra de Tramontana,** whose white-rock peaks above the tree line suggest a Mediterranean rendition of the Alps. ✪ **Cala de Sa Calobra** itself is the king of Majorcan coves, embracing waters of fierce turquoise. From here a foot path partially tunneled through the face of the cliff leads to the Torrent de Pareis, where people splash in the surf that washes up on the small pebble beach.

Inland from here is the **Monastery de Lluch** (tel. 51-70-25), about 27.5 miles (44km) from Palma. Originally a 17th-century hostel for pilgrims, it is now the sanctuary of the Virgin of Lluch, the island's patron saint, known as "La Moreneta," because, like Catalonia's Virgin of Montserrat, she is black. In the chapel behind the church altar stands a 13th-century statue of La Moreneta topped with a halo and a crown rimmed with emeralds. The altar lighting for the statue is the work of Gaudí.

The church is open daily from 8am to 8pm; admission is free. Daily at noon and at sunset the famed boys' choir sings. The monastery's museum, containing a collection of fans, vestments, traditional costumes, ceramics, glass, Nativity scenes, instruments, paintings, and traditional Majorcan furnishings and jewelry, is open daily from 10am to 5:30pm (until 6:30pm in summer); admission is 225 ptas. ($2.25) for adults; children under 12 free.

WHERE TO STAY

The following hotels in and around Deyá, some 19 miles (30km) from Palma, are tranquil bases from which to explore the western coast. They are also very popular, so reserve well in advance.

EXPENSIVE

HOTEL ES MOLÍ, Carretera Valldemosa, 07179 Deyá, Majorca. Tel. 971/63-90-00. Fax 971/63-93-33. Telex 69007 ES MOLÍ-E. 70 rms and suites. A/C TEL
$ Rates (including breakfast and IVA): 11,600–12,600 ptas. ($116–$126) single; 18,500–20,500 ptas. ($185–$205) double; 17,500–19,000 ptas. ($175–$190) per person per day in suite. AE, DC, EURO, MC, V. **Parking:** Available. **Closed:** Nov–Mar.

✪ At one end of diminutive Deyá, Es Molí is built into the slope of a hill. Although less opulent than La Residencia (see below), it exudes a comparable sense of refuge amidst its beautiful gardens. Most of Es Molí's spacious, carpeted guest rooms have terraces from which to contemplate the surrounding scenic beauty, and their attractive furnishings are mainly Majorcan.

Weather permitting, guests can dine on the outdoor terrace or in the simple, elegant dining room serving international cuisine with local accents. Other facilities include a heated, spring-water swimming pool; a tennis court; and free transport to a secluded beach nearby.

HOTEL LA RESIDENCIA, Son Moragues, 07179 Deyá, Majorca. Tel. 971/63-90-11. Fax 971/63-93-70. 49 rms and suites. A/C TEL
$ Rates (including breakfast): 10,500–17,500 ptas. ($105–$175) single; 17,500–30,500 ptas. ($175–$305) double; 29,000–40,000 ptas. ($290–$400) suite. AE, DC, EURO, MC, V. **Parking:** Available.

⭐ This charming four-star hotel created from two old manor houses of the 14th and 16th centuries attracts such five-star guests as Michael Douglas and Peter Bogdanovich. In 1988, *Architectural Digest* saw fit to feature its stylish accommodations in one of its issues.

The guest rooms have tile floors, area rugs, canopy beds, antique and reproduction furnishings from the mainland and Majorca, marble baths, and beamed ceilings—TVs are available on request. The artwork throughout is by natives or longtime island residents.

The hotel's elegant El Olivo restaurant, serving "market cuisine," has earned one Michelin star and is popular with both guests and the public at large. It is open for lunch and dinner in winter and for dinner only in summer. The hotel also has a lighted tennis court and resident tennis pro (except in August), a pool with fresh spring water, a poolside grill, private access to the sea, and a massage service.

BUDGET

MONASTERY DE LLUCH, Plaça de los Peregrinos, 07315 Lluch, Majorca, about 3 miles (5km) from Escorca. Tel. 971/51-70-25 or 51-70-50. Fax 971/51-70-96. 87 rms (over half with bath).

$ **Rates** (including IVA): 1,900 ptas. ($19) double with bath, 1,450 ptas. ($14.50) per day for 3 days or more; 1,975 ptas. ($19.75) quad without bath, 1,600 ptas. ($16) per day for 3 days or more; 2,600 ptas. ($26) quad with bath, 1,925 ptas. ($19.25) per day for 3 days or more; 2,950 ptas. ($29.50) room for six with bath, 2,500 ptas. ($25) per day for 3 days or more; heating supplement in winter of 575 ptas. ($5.75) per day. EURO, MC, V. **Parking:** Available.

Near Puig Major north of Deyá, this monastery offers inexpensive year-round accommodations with a humble charm for those who don't mind being at an isolated remove from tourist life (see "What to See & Do" above for details on the monastery). Bear in mind that this is a functioning monastery with nine priests in residence—guests are expected to maintain a certain respect and quiet decorum. Some of the guest rooms have kitchens, and these can accommodate up to six. For those without kitchens, there are two restaurants.

PENSION MIRAMAR, Ca'n Oliver, s/n (no street number), 07179 Deyá, Majorca. Tel. 971/63-90-84. 9 rms (2 with bath).

$ **Rates** (including breakfast and dinner): 3,750 ptas. ($37.50) single; 6,500 ptas. ($65) double without bath, 7,000 ptas. ($70) double with bath. No credit cards. **Parking:** Available. **Closed:** Nov–Feb.

⑤ To get to this economical hilltop outpost, take the road leading up between Bar Las Palmeras and Christian's Bar along the main road from Palma. The Miramar's guest rooms are very basic but clean, and guests without a private bath share two modern baths; the rooms do have sinks. At least a century old, this former village house has a cozy dining room, beamed ceilings, a lounge with wicker rockers, and Majorcan furnishings throughout. From the outdoor terrace you can glimpse the sea in the distance (hence the name Miramar, "view of the sea").

WHERE TO DINE

There are a handful of restaurants in Deyá. Here are two of my favorites:

C'AN XELINI, Carrer Archiduque Luis Salvador. Tel. 63-91-39.
   Cuisine: INTERNATIONAL. **Reservations:** Recommended in summer and on weekends all year.
$ **Prices:** Appetizers 475–3,000 ptas. ($4.75–$30); main courses 1,300–3,750 ($13–$37.50). EURO, MC, V.
   Open: Dinner only, Thurs–Tues 7:30pm–midnight. **Closed:** Jan–Feb.

Located on the main road in town and occupying a house that is over 100 years old, C'an Xelini is actually two restaurants in one. The upstairs Bodega is intimate and informal and has an outdoor terrace; in winter its fireplace and candles create a very special ambiance. The larger, more formal dining area downstairs features ceiling fans, wrought-iron chandeliers, and cushioned benches. The menu includes at least half a dozen fondues and grilled meats. The pastas are homemade, and there are a number of daily specials.

RESTAURANTE JAIME, Carrer Archiduque Luis Salvador, 13. Tel. 63-90-29.
   Cuisine: MAJORCAN/SPANISH. **Reservations:** Not required.
$ **Prices:** Appetizers 425–2,100 ptas. ($4.25–$21); main courses 1,000–1,700 ptas. ($10–$17); menu del día 1,600 ptas. ($16). No credit cards.
   Open: Summer, lunch Tues–Sun 12:30–3pm; dinner Tues–Sun 7:30–10:30pm. Winter, lunch Tues–Sun 12:30–3pm; dinner Tues–Sun 7:30–10pm. **Closed:** Two weeks in Nov and 2 weeks in May.

Just a few doors down from C'an Xelini (see above) and one flight up, this family-style place serves mostly grilled meats and fish and features daily Majorcan specialties. Although the service is rough around the edges, the food is good and the prices are right. A fine winter dish is the pork loin rolled in cabbage leaves and stuffed with sausage and raisins. A must for dessert is the almond cake served with almond ice cream.

---

2. PORT DE POLLENÇA & THE NORTH

40 miles (65km) NE of Palma

GETTING THERE **By Bus** Buses leave from Palma's Estació Central Plaça España. For information call 75-22-24.

By Car You can continue on from Deyá (see above) along the C-710 all the way to Port Pollença.

ESSENTIALS Port de Pollença's **tourist office** is located at Plaça Miquel Capllonch, 2 (tel. 53-46-66), and is open May to October on Monday to Friday from 9am to 1pm and from 4 to 7pm and Saturday from 9am to 1pm; closed holidays. In an emergency, if you need an ambulance, the police, or the fire brigade, call 53-04-37 (this is the number for the municipal police). The *locutório de Telefónica* (central telephone office), at Paseo Saralegui by the marina, is open May to October daily from 10am to 1pm and from 4 to 9pm (until 10pm in June to October).

The bay at Port de Pollença is large, graceful, and rimmed with mountains—in short, it's a knockout, especially at sunset. Pleasure boats are anchored everywhere, and this haven is blessedly devoid of high-rise construction. Let's hope it stays that way.

If you don't need hundreds of souvenir shops and dozens of clubs and discos within a five-block radius, you'll like it here, some 40 miles (65km) from the perpetual motion of Palma and its nearby beaches. A series of low-rise hotels, private homes, restaurants, and snack bars line the very attractive beach, which is somewhat narrow at its northwestern end but has some of the island's finest, whitest sand and warmest, clearest water. For several miles along the bay there is a pleasant pedestrian promenade. There is only one luxury hotel in the area, however, and that is out on the Formentor Peninsula.

Tons of fine white sand were imported to the beach at the southeastern end of Pollença Bay to create a broad ribbon of sun- and sea-bathing space stretching for several kilometers along the bay's beautiful, clear waters. Windsurfing, waterskiing, and scuba diving are among the water sports offered in the area.

WHAT TO SEE & DO

SIGHTS The plunging cliffs and rocky coves of Majorca's northwestern coast are a stunning prelude to Port de Pollença. From the **Mirador des (del) Colomer** is an expansive view of the striking Californialike coast that stretches from Punta de la Nau to Punta de la Troneta and includes El Colomer (Pigeon's Rock), named for the nests in its cave.

But it is the 12.5-mile (20km) stretch of winding, at times vertiginous, road leading from Port de Pollença to the tip of the ✪ **Formentor Peninsula** that delivers the island's most intoxicating scenic visions. The cliffs over 650 feet (200m) high and spectacular rock-rimmed coves embrace intense turquoise waters. About halfway along this road is the **Cala de Pi de la Posada,** where you will find the Hotel Formentor and a lovely bathing beach. Continuing on to the end you'll come to the lighthouse at **Cabo Formentor.**

Wednesday is **market day** in Port de Pollença, so head for the town square (there's only one) from 8am to 1pm and browse through the fresh produce, leather goods, embroidered tablecloths, ceramics, and more. Bargaining is part of the fun. Sunday is market day in the town of Pollença.

Alcudia Bay is a long stretch of narrow, sandy beach with beautiful water backed by countless hotels whose hordes rather overwhelm the beach in peak season. The nightlife is more abundant and varied here than in Port de Pollença.

Between Port de Alcudia and Ca'n Picafort is the **Parc Natural de S'Albufera,** Carretera Alcudia-Artá, Km. 27, 07458 C'an Picafort (no phone). A wetlands area of lagoons, dunes, and canals covering some 1,975 acres (800 hectares), it attracts birdwatchers and other assorted nature enthusiasts. To date, more than 200 species of birds have been sighted here, among them heron, owl, and osprey, and, in the warbler family, the moustached, willow, and fan-tailed varieties. The best times to visit are spring and fall when migratory birds abound. Spring, too, offers a marvelous display of flora. The park is open daily, except Christmas, from October 1 to March 30 from 9am to 5pm and from April 1 to September 30 from 9am to 7pm. Visits are free, but you must get a permit at the reception center, where all motorized vehicles must be left. From there you can proceed on foot, horseback, or bicycle. Binoculars are available for rent. Detailed information and itineraries are provided at the reception center.

In the town of Pollença, about 4 miles (6km) from Port Pollença, is an 18th-century stairway leading up to an *ermita* (hermitage). Consisting of 365 stairs, it is known as the **Monte Calvario** (Calvary); but you can also reach the top by car via Carrer de las Cruces, which is lined with 10-foot-high (3m-high) concrete crosses.

At **Cala San Vicente,** between Pollença and Port de Pollença, is a pleasant, small sandy cove with some notable surf. Several small hotels and restaurants provide the necessary amenities.

TOURS For those who prefer the perspective from the sea, various **boat excursions,** including glass-bottom-boat outings, are offered in Pollença Bay. These boats as well as boats to Formentor leave from Port de Pollença's Estación Marítima several times daily in summer and on a limited basis in winter. Ask at your hotel or the marina itself for the latest schedule.

Borrás Excursiones Marítimas, Port de Pollença (tel. 53-05-70), offers fishing and sport excursions. To rent a windsurfer, catamaran, or light sailing boat, or to take instruction in their use, contact **Bellini,** Carrer Médico Llopis 9, Port de Pollença (tel. 53-32-95), from April to October. For information on the waterskiing school, check at the Hotel Illa D'Or or the Bar Katy along the water between the Hotel Illa D'Or and town.

Organized excursions on **horseback** are available at Rancho Grande, Pollença Road (tel. 86-54-80).

WHERE TO STAY

The hotels in the Port de Pollença area are mostly small and happily lacking in the mass-tourism sameness that prevails on the island's southern coast.

EXPENSIVE

HOTEL FORMENTOR, Formentor Peninsula (postal address: 07470 Port de Pollença, Majorca). Tel. 971/86-53-00. Fax 971/86-51-55. Telex 68523. 127 rms and suites. A/C MINIBAR TV TEL

$ Rates (including breakfast): 14,500–21,500 ptas. ($145–$215) single; 22,200–35,000 ptas. ($222–$350) double; 37,000–49,000 ptas. ($370–$490) suite. AE, DC, EURO, MC, V. **Parking:** Available. **Closed:** Nov–Mar.

Set on 5.5 square miles (15 square km) of grounds, this is one of Europe's most exclusive hotels. At once elegant and unpretentious, it is an oasis of peace and quiet, a paradise for sun-lazing. When it was built in the late 1920s, all construction materials had to be transported to the site by sea because the road was not built until the next decade. The guest rooms are tastefully appointed in a country style, with area rugs and gracious furnishings.

The Grill Room restaurant is open to hotel guests and to the public at night for informal dining, but in the more elegant upstairs dining room jackets and ties are required. On the upper terrace there is live music nightly, which makes it a most pleasant place for pre- and postdinner sipping. Other facilities include a pool, tennis courts (two lighted) and a resident tennis pro, horseback riding, and a well-tended beach with its own bar and restaurant.

MODERATE

HOTEL CAPRI, Anglada Camarasa, 69, 07470 Port de Pollença, Majorca. Tel. 971/53-16-00. Fax 971/53-33-22. Telex 69708 ILDO E. 33 rms. TEL
$ Rates (including breakfast and IVA): 4,000–5,300 ptas. ($40–$53) single; 7,500–9,700 ptas. ($75–$97) double. MC, V. **Parking:** Not available. **Closed:** Nov–Apr.

This is a bright white entry on the water near the town center. The furnishings in its pleasant guest rooms (about half with terraces) have a certain passé charm. If you're more interested in space than a sea view, you'll find the interior rooms larger. The first-floor bar has a great view from its outdoor terrace.

HOTEL DAINA, Atilio Boveri, 2, 07470 Port de Pollença, Majorca. Tel. 971/53-12-50. Fax 971/53-33-22. Telex 69708 ILDO E. 67 rms. TEL
$ Rates (including breakfast and IVA): 4,300–6,300 ptas. ($43–$63) single; 7,700–13,000 ptas. ($77–$130) double. AE, EURO, MC, V. **Parking:** Not available. **Closed:** Dec–Feb.

Right in the heart of town, this is one of the few hotels in Port de Pollença with a pool. The one here is further unique in that it juts out into the sea, is filled with sea water, and has a sandy beach on either side. The Daina's guest rooms are attractively furnished in a Spanish style and have equally attractive, freshly refurbished baths. About a quarter of them have sea views, and the sixth-floor rooms are air-conditioned.

HOTEL ILLA D'OR, Paseo Colón, 265, 07470 Port de Pollença, Majorca. Tel. 971/86-51-00 or 971/86-51-04. Fax 971/86-42-13. 120 rms. TEL
$ Rates (including breakfast and IVA): 5,600–7,500 ptas. ($56–$75) single; 9,700–15,000 ptas. ($97–$150) double. AE, DC, EURO, MC, V. **Parking:** Nearby.

To paraphrase Conrad Hilton, the three most important things about a hotel are location, location, and location—and few hotels can beat the Illa D'Or on that score. Ensconced at the quiet northwestern end of Pollença Bay, it is a vivid white presence with a certain colonial charm. Its terrace bar, where the Mediterranean waters lap gently as you sip your drink, is the best seaside bar in all of Majorca. At sunset you can sit here and watch the mountains behind the bay fade to purple against the pink-orange sky. Another nice thing about staying here is that you can walk the kilometer or so into town along a stone path at the very water's edge. Location aside, however, its combination of comfort, meticulous housekeeping, and warm, friendly service make it one of the best choices in town. It's also ideal for families with children.

Dating from 1929, the 80 guest rooms in the Illa D'Or's original structure contain traditional Majorcan furniture and appointments.

The furnishings in the newer wing are mundanely modern. Many of the rooms have terraces and sea views, and a third are air-conditioned. All meals are served in the friendly, airy dining room, and light lunches are served on the seaside terrace. Half and full board are available.

BUDGET

HOSTAL GALEÓN, Londres, s/n (no street number) (Apartado de Correos 18), 07470 Port de Pollença, Majorca. Tel. 971/86-57-03. Fax 971/53-26-54. 43 rms.

$ Rates (including breakfast and IVA): 1,700–2,700 ptas. ($17–$27) single; 2,600–4,100 ptas. ($26–$41) double. V. **Parking:** Nearby. **Closed:** Nov 26–Mar.

If you're having trouble finding something in town, this is a fall-back. Located at the southwestern end of Port de Pollença along the road to Alcudia, the Galeón offers guest rooms that are lackluster and a bit worn here and there, but the rates are very reasonable. All units have showers only (no tubs).

HOTEL RAF, Paseo Saralegui, 84, 07470 Port de Pollença, Marjorca. Tel. 971/86-51-95. 30 rms.

$ Rates (including breakfast and IVA): 2,800–3,570 ptas. ($28–$35.70) single; 4,700–6,500 ptas. ($47–$65) double. EURO, MC, V. **Parking:** Nearby. **Closed:** Nov–Mar.

This is a central choice across the street from the newly enhanced southwestern stretch of beach. The large, rather charming guest rooms are colorfully decorated and feature simple wood furnishings.

HOTEL RESIDENCIA EOLO, Plaça Ingeniero Gabriel Roca, 2, 07470 Port de Pollença, Majorca. Tel. 971/53-15-50. Fax 971/53-42-50. 52 rms. TEL

$ Rates (including breakfast and IVA): 2,000–3,850 ptas. ($20–$38.50) single; 4,000–6,000 ptas. ($40–$60) double. EURO, MC, V. **Parking:** Nearby.

Right in the middle of town and a stone's throw from the beach, the Eolo is nicely furnished and comfortable. Some of the guest rooms have ample terraces; all have showers (no tubs).

HOTEL RESIDENCIA SIS PINS, Anglada Camarasa, 77, 07470 Port de Pollença, Majorca. Tel. 971/53-10-50. Fax 971/53-40-13. 50 rms. TEL

$ Rates: 2,700–4,500 ptas. ($27–$45) single; 3,700–12,000 ptas. ($37–$120) double. DC, EURO, MC, V. **Parking:** Nearby. **Closed:** Nov–Mar.

A hacienda-style facade with flower-bedecked arches marks the entrance to the Sis Pins, which sits along the water close to the town center. Some of its rather functional guest rooms have terraces. The lobby lounge is quite comfortable and feels much like someone's living room.

WHERE TO DINE

The numerous restaurants in Port de Pollença and the surrounding area offer both traditional island dishes and culinary accents from abroad. Along the Passeig Vora Mar leading from the Hotel Illa D'Or into town are numerous small, informal restaurants by the sea offering sandwiches, salads, and full meals.

EXPENSIVE

DAUS, Escalonada Calvari, 10, Pollença. Tel. 53-28-67.
Cuisine: MAJORCAN/SPANISH. **Reservations:** Recommended.

$ Prices: Appetizers 650–1,300 ptas. ($6.50–$13); main courses 1,600–6,000 ptas. ($16–$60). AE, EURO, MC, V.
Open: Lunch Wed–Mon 12:30–3:30pm; dinner Wed–Mon 7:45–11:30pm (later in summer).

⭐ Located in the town of Pollença several kilometers from Port de Pollença, Daus sits at the bottom end of the 365 steps of Pollença's Monte Calvario (see "What to See & Do" above). If you're in the mood for a romantic meal, this is the place to come. The entranceway, adorned with a white drape and a large urn with a candle, sets the tone. The stone ceilings of its two dining areas attest to its former function as the *bodega* (wine cellar) of the Jesuits. Soft, live, classical music accompanies dinner on Wednesday, Friday, and Sunday except in July and August. You get all this and good food, too, as well as a very sophisticated level of service.

The menu, which changes every several months, is rich in such Majorcan specialties as lamb, rabbit, and caldereta de langosta, the most pricey dish. Some fixed offerings include arroz negro (rice with shrimp and cuttlefish in its own ink), dorada (sea bass) stuffed with monkfish and shrimp, and roast baby lamb. Outstanding among the homemade desserts is the crema catalana.

STAY RESTAURANT, Muelle Nuevo, Estació Marítima, s/n (no street number), Port de Pollença. Tel. 86-40-13.
Cuisine: SPANISH/INTERNATIONAL. **Reservations:** Recommended in July.

$ Prices: Appetizers 550–2,000 ptas. ($5.50–$20); main courses 1,650–3,500 ptas. ($16.50–$35). AE, EURO, MC, V.
Open: Jan–Apr and Nov, lunch Tues–Sun 12:30–4pm; dinner Tues–Sun 7:30–11pm. Dec, lunch Tues–Thurs 12:30–4pm; dinner Fri–Sun 7:30–11pm. June–Sept, lunch daily 12:30–4pm; dinner daily 7:30–11pm.

One of the pricier restaurants in town, Stay offers an ample selection of appetizers and some unique pasta offerings. Among the entrees, the house specialties include grilled, marinated chicken; grilled or broiled lobster; caldereta de langosta (lobster soup); arroz marinera (a fish soup with rice); and parrillada de mariscos (a platter of grilled prawns, shrimp, crab, and more). The menu changes substantially about every two months, however, so surprises are always in store. Many of the desserts are homemade. The open-air terrace offers a more informal and economical menu including such items as hamburgers and grilled sardines.

MODERATE

BAR/RESTAURANTE LA VICTORIA, Ermita de la Victoria, Alcudia. Tel. 54-71-73.
Cuisine: MAJORCAN/SPANISH. **Reservations:** Recommended on weekends.

$ Prices: Appetizers 450–1,000 ptas. ($4.50–$10); main courses 900–2,500 ptas. ($9–$25). AE, EURO, MC, V.
Open: Lunch daily 12:30–4pm; dinner daily 6:30–10:30pm.
Closed: Mon in winter and Nov.

At lunch La Victoria offers both scenic food for the soul and tasty fare for the palate. Perched high up on the Alcudia Peninsula, its outdoor terrace surveys all of Pollença Bay and the Formentor Peninsula. Inside is a two-tiered dining room. The menu is weighted with grilled meat and fish dishes, but there are a number of Majorcan specialties, such as sopas mallorquinas, frito mallorquín, and pescado à la mallorquina (fish and potatoes topped with vegetables). The lechona (suckling pig) is excellent—crispy on the outside, sweet, tender, and succulent on the inside.

Note: You can combine a luncheon visit to La Victoria with bathing at one of the two pretty sand beaches at Mal Pas. The water is marvelous. Also, as you drive up to La Victoria, you'll pass a series of rocky coves. If you don't mind parking your towel on a rock, these are fine for sunbathing, too, and command wonderful views of the deep-turquoise waters of Pollença Bay. This restaurant is also great for watching the sunset or having dinner by the light of the full moon.

BEC FI RESTAURANTE, Avenida Anglada Camarasa, 91, Port de Pollença. Tel. 53-10-40.
   Cuisine: MAJORCAN/SPANISH. **Reservations:** Required in Aug.
$ **Prices:** Appetizers 1,000–2,000 ptas. ($10–$20); main courses 1,000–2,900 ($10–$29). AE, DC, EURO, MC, V.
   Open: Lunch Tues–Sun 1–3:30pm; dinner Tues–Sun 7–10:30pm. **Closed:** Dec–Jan.

This is one of Port de Pollença's best restaurants, with a simple indoor dining area and a small outdoor patio sheltered with palm trees. The specialties are meat and fish prepared on a grill fueled by local encina (holm oak) wood.

CA VOSTRA, Carretera Port de Pollença-Alcudia, Port de Pollença. Tel. 86-55-46.
   Cuisine: MAJORCAN. **Reservations:** Recommended July–Aug.
$ **Prices:** Appetizers 450–1,500 ptas. ($4.50–$15); main courses 750–3,000 ptas. ($7.50–$30); menu del día 1,700 ptas. ($17). No credit cards.
   Open: Lunch daily noon–4pm; dinner daily 7pm–midnight. **Closed:** Wed in winter.

One of the cellar genre of restaurants, Ca Vostra has a beamed ceiling and wine barrels along the walls. According to the locals, it is the most traditionally Majorcan of Port de Pollença restaurants. The hearty, unpretentious food is in keeping with the rustic, red-and-white-checkered tablecloth ambiance. The frito mallorquín (a conglomeration of lamb innards sautéed with potatoes, peppers, garlic, and bay leaves) is not for everyone, but those who enjoy liver and such might want to give this traditional dish a try. Also good is the tumbet, a local-style ratatouille. Other house specialties include caldereta de rape (angler fish soup), caldereta de langosta (quite economical here), paella with lobster, and civet de conejo (rabbit marinated in red wine).

RESTAURANTE LA LONJA DEL PESCADO, Muelle Pesquero, s/n (no street number), Port de Pollença. Tel. 53-00-23.
   Cuisine: SEAFOOD. **Reservations:** Recommended for dinner in summer.

$ Prices: Appetizers 525–1,300 ptas. ($5.25–$13); main courses 675–4,700 ptas. ($6.75–$47). EURO, MC, V.

Open: June–Aug, lunch daily 12:30–4pm; dinner daily 7:30–11:30pm. Feb–May, lunch Thurs–Tues 12:30–4pm; dinner Thurs–Tues 7:30–10:30pm. **Closed:** Dec–Jan.

Another top Port de Pollença restaurant, La Lonja serves top-flight seafood flown in fresh daily from Galicia. The upstairs dining room, where lunch is served, overlooks the port. The menu selection, small but select, stars the caldereta de langosta.

BUDGET

CAFETERIA NEPTUNO, Carretera de Formentor, 13, Port de Pollença. Tel. 53-29-54.

Cuisine: SPANISH. **Reservations:** Not required.

$ Prices: Appetizers 325–1,000 ptas. ($3.25–$10); main courses 500–1,400 ptas. ($5–$14); tapas 300–900 ptas. ($3–$9). AE, EURO, MC, V.

Open: Daily 9:30am–midnight. **Closed:** Thurs in Nov–Jan.

This economical eatery a block from the beach specializes in tapas. If your appetite calls for something more, there are sandwiches, platos combinados for 500 to 1,400 ptas. ($5 to $14), and a menu del día for 1,000 ptas. ($10).

LOS PESCADORES, Passeig Vora Mar, 45. Tel. 53-41-01.

Cuisine: SPANISH/INTERNATIONAL. **Reservations:** Not required.

$ Prices: Appetizers 400–1,800 ptas. ($4–$18); main courses 675–1,900 ptas. ($6.75–$19). EURO, MC, V.

One of the best of the informal eateries along the seaside Passeig de Vora Mar, Los Pescadores offers good food at reasonable prices, plus an upstairs dining room whose balcony offers a fetching vista.

EVENING ENTERTAINMENT

Although the nightlife offering in Port de Pollença is rather meager—most people make the 6.5-mile (10km) trip to Alcudia—there are a few places in town with lots of atmosphere both in and out of tourist season. In addition to the following, there are numerous bars, pubs, and assorted watering holes along the waterfront and in some of the small streets in the center of town.

AÑORANZA, Carrer Juan XXIII, 22. Tel. 53-10-52.

Añoranza is a cozy, friendly bar where every night in the summer and Friday and Saturday in winter at 11:30pm the owners Juan and Manolo break out their guitars and sing. From time to time patrons, too, get up and sing and dance. It's all very informal and lots of fun. Open daily from 9:30pm to 3am.

DISCOTHEQUE CHIVAS, Carrer Médico Llopis, 5. Tel. 53-15-29.

For dancing, try this modern, smallish place with the standard flashing colored lights and loud music. Although the crowd is predominantly young, those in their 30s, 40s, and even 50s do put in an appearance, especially in the wee hours. Open in summer daily from 11pm to 5am; in winter on Friday, Saturday, and Sunday.

Admission (including one drink): 800 ptas. ($8).

NEW ANIARA, Formentor, 6. No phone.
Just around the corner from Añoranza (see above), this bar is owned by brothers of Juan and Manolo. One of the new breed of bars with a billiard table, sofa seating, and taped rock music, it attracts a somewhat younger crowd. Open daily from 9:30pm until "late."
Admission: Free.

3. THE EASTERN COAST

Less majestic than Majorca's western coast, the eastern coast is mostly rolling hills and farmland that meet the sea in a series of rocky coves, many now overpowered by high-rise construction. The upper portion of the east coast is easily explored from a base in Port de Pollença, the lower portion from a base in Palma.

WHAT TO SEE & DO

You can combine a visit to the Cuevas de Artá with a swim at the adjacent **Platja de Canyamel,** one of the nicest beaches along the eastern coast.
   Inca, in the center of the island, is Majorca's leather-manufacturing center. You may or may not find a bargain at its factory outlets, which primarily offer seconds, so check prices in Palma before coming. Most of the outlets are open on Monday to Friday from 9:30am to 7pm and on Saturday from 9:30am to noon.
   FÉVE, Plaça España, 9, Palma (tel. 75-22-45), operates the "Leather Express" train service between Palma and Inca.

MAJORICA PEARL FACTORY AND STORE, Carrer B-2, s/n (no street number). Tel. 55-02-00.
In Manacor, you can visit the 100-year-old Majorica pearl factory and store, whose selection of simulated pearl jewelry is the largest on the island. The handmade Majorica pearls are formed around a natural mineral core that is coated with layers of a secret mixture of fish scales to simulate the sheen of real pearls. Over 300 artisans work diligently to shape, polish, string, and inspect the pearls one by one. Their production consumes the scales of more than 100 million fish annually. Beware of the sly fakes sold under such similar names as "Majorca," "Mallorca," or "Majorque," however; the genuine article, guaranteed for 10 years, carries a red tag with "Perlas Majorica" inscribed in gold and a quality-control number. Sold in *agencias oficiales* (official agencies) in some 45 countries and hundreds of airport shops around the world, Majorica pearls are, of course, more attractively priced here at the source.
Admission: Free.
Open: Factory Mon–Fri 9am–12:30pm and 3–6:30pm; Sat–Sun 10am–1pm. Store Mon–Fri 9am–7pm; Sat–Sun 10am–1pm; holidays 10am–6pm. **Closed** (factory and store): Christmas Day.

CUEVAS DEL DRACH [CAVERNS OF THE DRAGON], near Porto Cristo. Tel. 57-00-02 or 57-07-74.

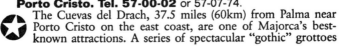

   The Cuevas del Drach, 37.5 miles (60km) from Palma near Porto Cristo on the east coast, are one of Majorca's best-known attractions. A series of spectacular "gothic" grottoes with amazing stalactite and stalagmite formations, they are a truly memorable experience, especially when teamed with a floating classical-music concert. While visitors sit in the cavernous darkness, three boats trimmed with lights—one carrying the musicians—cross one of the world's largest underground lakes. In all, the one-hour visit covers about half a mile of strikingly illuminated subterranean splendor.

Admission: 700 ptas. ($7).

Open: Nov–Mar, visits with concert daily on the hour 11am–3pm, visits without concert daily at 4 and 5pm. Apr–Oct, visits with concert daily on the hour 10am–5pm.

CUEVAS DE ARTÁ, near the Platja de Canyamel. Tel. 56-32-95.

You may think that when you've seen one cave you've seen them all. But the Cuevas de Artá, near the Platja de Canyamel, while similar to the Cuevas de Drach, offer a more intimate and, in some ways, more impressive display. During the 45-minute visit, you meander among cavernous rooms reaching 145 feet (45m) in height, while formations variously resembling a virgin with child and a pipe organ suggest that you have strayed into some surrealistic underground cathedral.

Admission: 650 ptas. ($6.50).

Open: Apr–Oct, daily 9:30am–7pm. Nov–Mar, daily 9:30am–5pm.

IBIZA TOWN

A party town extraordinaire, Ibiza annually stages a dazzling summer spectacle that truly lights up the night. By day, the all-night clubbers rest up on the island's beaches. At night, they don their provocative fashions and outrageous coifs and strut their freewheeling stuff through the Ibiza Town alleys lined with the come-ons of trendy tourism—bars, boutiques, sidewalk cafés, and stylish restaurants where you might spot such vacationing celebrities as Roman Polanski, Goldie Hawn, and Julio Iglesias.

Although Ibiza Town (population 28,000) is the island's capital and only true urban entity, it's not a resort town but a tourist port. There is no beach here, just a marina brimming with yachts and other pleasure boats. Visitors typically stay at the nearby beach resorts of Figueretas and Playa d'en Bossa and come into town primarily to shop and play the night away. These two resorts are of the concrete-jungle, tour-group ilk, with little to recommend them except the beaches that they now overwhelm. If you want to avoid the overcrowded sensation of their too-many hotels, consider staying in town and commuting out to the sand and the sea. It's merely a matter of a mile or two.

Founded by the Carthaginians 645 years before Christ, the town of Ibiza rises vertically from the port and forms a romantic mound of twinkling lights at night. The old barrios of the city's upper reaches contain the cathedral, the city hall, and numerous noble mansions of earlier eras. In the small interior villages (and occasionally in town) you'll see the grandmothers of the island draped in the traditional long dresses and scarfs of another time.

Every year the island's local population of over 70,000 plays host to a contingent of tourists numbering over one million, most of whom pour in between June 15 and September 15. Because Ibiza is tolerant of mankind's myriad eccentricities and can cater to them all, you never know just what awaits around the corner—but you can bet it won't be boring!

1. ORIENTATION

GETTING THERE

A mere 35-minute flight away from Barcelona, Ibiza is accessible by air and sea from Palma de Majorca (35 miles [56km]), Valencia (105

WHAT'S SPECIAL ABOUT IBIZA

A Special Hotel

☐ The Hotel Hacienda in Na Xamena on the northern end of the island—an idyllic oasis of tranquillity and beauty favored by an upscale clientele in search of true recreation and relaxation.

Nightlife

☐ Pachá and Amnesia, two trendy discos for those who like to party hearty until the wee hours.

Sights

☐ The cathedral, cobblestone streets, and vintage mansions of Ibiza Town's historic center.

☐ Ibiza Town's Archeological Museum and nearby necropolis, giving some impressive insights into the island's prehistory.

☐ Es Vedrá rock off Cala d'Hort, an imposing, mysterious, and mesmerizing geological formation.

Coves/Beaches

☐ The prettiest and most pristine coves and beaches are found along the northern coast of the island from Cala d'Eubarca to Cala Llonga.

---

miles [169km]), Barcelona (175 miles [282km]), and many European cities.

BY PLANE Iberia and Aviaco, a subsidiary of Iberia (tel. toll free 800/SPAIN-IB), service Ibiza via Barcelona, and several European carriers provide direct service from various European cities.

For **Iberia Airlines** reservations, call 30-09-54. Iberia's in-town office at Paseo Vara de Rey, 15 (tel. 30-31-90), is open April to mid-September Monday to Friday from 9:30am to 1:15pm and from 4:30 to 7:45pm and on Saturday from 8:30am to 1:15pm; from mid-September through March open Monday to Friday from 9:30am to 1:15pm and from 4 to 7:45pm and on Saturday from 8:30am to 1pm; closed holidays.

BY FERRY & HYDROFOIL Trasmediterránea, Avenida Bartolomé Vicente Ramón, s/n (no street number) (tel. 971/31-41-73), offers ferry service between Ibiza and Valencia, Barcelona, and the other Balearic islands. The four-hour trip from Palma runs from 3,850 ptas. ($38.50) for a seat to 11,000 ptas. ($110) for a cabin. Fares from both Barcelona and Valencia run from 5,200 ptas. ($52) to 15,000 ptas. ($150). If the crossing is direct, the ferry from Barcelona takes 9 hours; from Valencia, 6½ hours. Tickets are available at Trasmediterránea or at any travel agency. The Trasmediterránea office in Ibiza Town is open all year on Monday to Friday from 9am to 1pm and 4:30 to 6:45pm and on Saturday from 9am to noon; closed holidays. The office at the Estación Marítima in the port opens two hours before the departure of its ferries.

As ferry and hydrofoil services tend to change annually, check current schedules before planning your itinerary.

Note: Space on ferries and planes is extremely tight in July and

August. If you're planning to come during those months, book everything well in advance.

ARRIVING

BY PLANE Every hour on the half hour there is daily **bus service** from Es Codolar airport into Ibiza Town. (Buses depart *for* the airport from the ticket kiosk at Avenida Isidor Macabich, 24, daily every hour on the hour from 7am to 10pm.) The fare for the 5.5-mile (9km) ride to or from the airport is 100 ptas. ($1).

A **taxi** from the airport to the center of town is 1,300 ptas. ($13); supplements apply at night and on Sunday and holidays. The fare from the airport to the Hotel Hacienda at the northern end of the island is 3,500 ptas. ($35).

At the airport, you can **change money** at the Banco Exterior de España from April 1 to October 31 daily from about 8:30am to 10pm; in winter, hours revert to normal banking hours (see "Fast Facts: Ibiza" below).

For **airport information,** call 30-03-00.

BY FERRY & HYDROFOIL Ferries and hydrofoils arrive in the port of Ibiza Town in the heart of the city. From nearby you can catch a bus or taxi to any point on the island.

TOURIST INFORMATION

The **tourist office,** Vara de Rey, 13 (tel. 30-19-00), is open Monday to Saturday from 9:30am to 1:30pm and from 5 to 7pm and on Saturday from 10:30am to 1pm; closed holidays.

Two handy publications that provide detailed information on all aspects of island life are "Ibiza Spotlight" and "Your Master Guide to Ibiza," both available at bookstores, newsstands, and hotels.

CITY LAYOUT

"D'Alt Vila" (Upper Town) is sheltered within the old city walls that date from five different eras: Phoenician in the area of Carrer Major near the cathedral; Byzantine on Carrer de Joan Roman; Roman here and there; Arab along Carrer de Sant Josep; and Christian, from the time of Felipe II, in the newer sections. Visually and architecturally—not to mention panoramically—D'Alt Vila is the most interesting area of Ibiza Town and houses numerous pensions, shops, and restaurants. At the end of Carrer Conquista is the house of the last Arab king of Ibiza (look through the gate of house no. 8). Also in D'Alt Vila are the Ayuntamiento (Town Hall), whose magnificent belvedere looks out over the sea; the archeological museum; and the cathedral (see "What to See & Do" below).

If you exit D'Alt Vila through the Portal Nou, you'll see the graceful silhouette of **Puig des Molins,** site of the Carthaginian and Roman necropolis dating back to the beginning of the 7th century B.C. More than 4,000 hypogeum-type tombs were carved into the rock of this hill, and many of the world's leading archeologists have come here to study them. Most of the treasures on display in the archeological museum were unearthed here.

At the eastern end of Ibiza Town by the marina is **Sa Penya,** the former seafaring district that was long home to local fishermen and sailors. Unfortunately, the upper reaches of this neighborhood have become rather unsavory and only the picturesque, whitewashed structures of the lower streets along the water continue to house the shops, boutiques, restaurants, and bars for which the entire quarter was once duly famous.

Near the western end of the marina is the **Paseo Vara de Rey,** the town's brief, central boulevard that, along with its extension, Avenida de España, comprises what might loosely be termed Ibiza's business district.

GETTING AROUND

Ibiza Town is small enough that you can get around easily on foot—there is no public transportation within the city. However, should you want to go to other parts of the island, there are **taxi** stands at the bus terminal, at the port terminal, and at the end of the Paseo Vara de Rey. For a radio cab in Ibiza Town, call 30-70-00 or 30-66-02.

Ibiza taxis do not have meters, but a list of official prices for specific routes is available from every driver. Supplements are charged at night, on holidays, and for luggage.

For information on the comings and goings of boats, airplanes, and buses, check the daily listings in *La Prensa de Ibiza* and *Diario de Ibiza*.

FAST FACTS: IBIZA

Most of the information you need for planning your trip to Ibiza is in "Fast Facts: Barcelona" in Chapter 3. The following information is specific for Ibiza.

Business Hours   Time in Ibiza bends to humans rather than the other way around, so hours are erratic, subject to weather, whim, tourist demand, or whatever. Generally speaking, however, stores are open Monday to Friday from 10am to 1:30 or 2pm and from 5 to 8:30pm (though in the peak summer months hours extend well beyond this). On Saturday in the off-season most are open in the morning only.

Banks are generally open Monday to Friday from 9am to 2pm and on Saturday from 9am to noon, but there are numerous *oficinas de cambio* (exchange offices) open all day.

Office hours are typically Monday to Friday from 9am to 1:30pm and from 4:30 to 6 or 7pm.

Restaurant hours are generally daily from 1 to 4pm and from 8 to 11pm, but patrons are often allowed to linger well past midnight.

Consulates   The Consulate of the United Kingdom, Avenida Isidor Macabich, 45, 1st Floor (tel. 30-18-18), is open on Monday to Friday from 9am to 2pm and on Saturday from 9:30am to noon. The nearest U.S. Consulate is in Palma de Majorca (see "Fast Facts: Palma de Majorca" in Chapter 9).

Currency Exchange   In addition to banks, there are numerous *oficinas de cambio* (exchange offices) in town. You can also change money at most travel agencies and hotels.

Electricity   Most tourist lodgings have 220-volt electricity, but you will still find some 125-volt outlets, so check first.

Emergencies　For medical assistance in English call Dr. Vicente Riera Mayans, Vara de Rey, 26 (tel. 31-16-75). For Red Cross assistance or an ambulance, call 30-12-14. In case of fire, call 31-30-30. For the police, dial 091.

Holidays　In addition to all Spanish national holidays (see "When to Go" in Chapter 2), Ibiza Town observes the following local holidays: the Focs de San Joan from June 21 to 24 and town fairs from August 2 to 8.

Language　Ibicenco, the island's dialect of Catalan, shares official status with Spanish (see "Fast Facts: Barcelona" in Chapter 3). The local name for Ibiza is "Eivissa."

Lost Property　There is a Lost and Found Office at the Municipal Police headquarters at Carrer Vicente Serra, 25 (tel. 31-58-61).

Newspapers　*La Prensa de Ibiza* and *Diario de Ibiza* are the leading Spanish-language dailies. *Ibiza Now,* the island's English-language newspaper, is published fortnightly.

Pharmacies　Any closed pharmacy displays in its window the location of the nearest open one. *La Prensa de Ibiza* and *Diario de Ibiza* also list the pharmacies open around-the-clock that day.

Post Office　The central post office is located at Carrer Madrid, 21–23 (tel. 31-13-80) and is open on Monday to Friday from 9am to 8pm and on Saturday from 9am to 1pm. Other post offices around the island are in San Antonio de Abad, San José, and Santa Eulàlia; they are open on Monday to Friday from 9am to 2pm and on Saturday from 9am to 1pm. You can also buy stamps at any estanco (tobacconist).

Safety　Whenever you're traveling in an unfamiliar city or area, stay alert. Be aware of your immediate surroundings. Wear a moneybelt and keep a close eye on your possessions. Be particularly careful with cameras, purses, and wallets, all favorite targets of thieves and pickpockets.

Telephone　The local area code is 971 (do not dial the 9 when calling from outside Spain). You can make international calls from most public phones, but you'll need a heavy supply of coins. Since hotels often tack a surcharge of 25% or more onto long-distance calls, it is best to go to one of the numerous telephone centers around the island for your international conversations. Rates are substantially lower at night and on holidays.

The national telephone company (CTNE or Compañía Telefónica Nacional de España) offers service from its kiosk on Avenida Santa Eulalia by the marina in summer daily from 10am to 2pm and 3pm to midnight; in winter daily from 10am to 2pm and 4 to 9:30pm; closed in November or January.

To make an international call, first dial 07, wait for the tone, then dial the country code, city (or area) code, and phone number.

Television/Radio　There are three Spanish-language radio stations on Ibiza—Radio Popular (AM 837), Popular FM Ibiza (FM 89.1), and Radio Ibiza-SER (FM 98.1). There are numerous Spanish-language and Catalan-language TV stations. TVs with satellite hookups are becoming increasingly common throughout the island and offer a variety of global programming in many languages. Check *La Prensa de Ibiza* for daily listings.

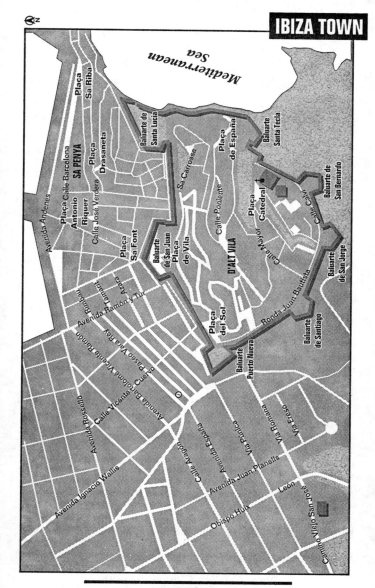

2. ACCOMMODATIONS

Most visitors staying in town (about a kilometer from the nearest beach) opt for rented apartments or small pensions, so there are no mass-tourism monstrosities to impinge on the intimate charm of the island's capital. On the other hand, there is also none of the select, stellar hostelries that stud the inland hilltops and the coast.

The posted rates at most lodgings are the official maximums the places can charge. Often you can negotiate at least a 10% discount—sometimes more in the off-season. For the purposes of this guide, "expensive" hotels charge 10,000 ptas. ($100) and up for a double room; "moderate" hotels, 7,500 to 10,000 ptas. ($75 to $100); and "budget" lodgings, 2,000 to 7,500 ptas. ($20 to $75).

Note: Unless otherwise indicated, all accommodations have private bath or shower, all hotels are open year round, and all rates given include service charge but *not* IVA.

If you wish to rent an apartment, a house, or a luxury villa, contact **Ibiza House Renting,** Carrer Avicena, 1, 07800 Ibiza (tel. 971/30-62-13 or 971/30-05-12; fax 971/30-51-79). It's open Monday to Friday from 9:30am to 1:30pm and from 5 to 8pm, Saturday from 10am to 1:30pm.

EXPENSIVE

IN IBIZA TOWN

HOTEL ROYAL PLAZA, Carrer Pedro Francés, 27–29, 07800 Ibiza. Tel. 971/31-00-00. Fax 971/31-40-95. Telex 69433 RYPA E. 117 rms. A/C MINIBAR TV TEL
$ Rates: 7,000–12,200 ptas. ($70–$122) single; 11,000–18,500 ptas. ($110–$185) double; 20,000–35,000 ptas. ($200–$350) suite. AE, DC, EURO, MC, V. **Parking:** Available.

Located three blocks from the port, this is a comfortable, modern, businesslike hotel from the sleek, clean lines of its marble lobby to the brown-and-beige decor of its carpeted guest rooms, most of which have terraces. From the sunbathing deck on the roof there are magnificent views of the port and the old, walled section of Ibiza Town.

For reservations, contact Marketing Ahead, 433 Fifth Ave., New York, NY 10016 (tel. 212/686-9213; fax 212/686-0271).

Dining/Entertainment: The Plaza Snack Bar/Restaurant serves snacks daily from 11:30am to midnight, lunch from 1:30 to 4pm, and dinner from 7 to 11:30pm. The breakfast buffet is served in Le Relais daily from 7 to 11am. The adjoining bar is open daily from 8am to 11pm.

Services: Room service.

Facilities: Small L-shaped swimming pool with a view of the old city.

EL PALACIO IBIZA, Carrer Conquista, 2, 07800 Ibiza. Tel. 971/30-14-78. Fax 971/39-15-81. 7 suites. MINIBAR TV TEL
$ Rates (including breakfast): 17,000–29,000 ptas. ($170–$290) single; 18,500–31,500 ($185–$315) double. AE, DC, EURO, MC, V. **Parking:** Available. **Closed:** Nov–Apr.

Subtitled the "Hotel of the Movie Stars," this unusual hostelry occupies a thousand-year-old piece of real estate in the heart of Ibiza Town's D'Alt Vila. Each of its suites is named after a famous Hollywood star and features a corresponding decor, including some very valuable movie memorabilia. Some of the suites have showers only (no tubs), but all are superbly luxurious and offer splendid views. Room service and turndown service are thoughtful touches.

Breakfast is served in the lovely garden. At the cozy bar you'll find the occasional celebrity and much talk of films present, past, and future. In short, you'll have a singular, highly select holiday experience.

IN FIGUERETAS & PLAYA D'EN BOSSA

Figueretas and Playa d'en Bossa, the beaches closest to Ibiza Town, are virtually a continuation of the capital and bursting at their overexploited seams with lackluster hotels. A notable cut above the throng of package-tour institutions are the two seaside hostelries below.

HOTEL LOS MOLINOS, Ramón Muntaner, 60 (Apartado 504), 07800 Figueretas. Tel. 971/30-22-50. Fax 971/30-25-04. Telex 68850. 147 rms. A/C MINIBAR TV TEL

$ Rates: 4,800–8,500 ptas. ($48–$85) single; 9,000–14,000 ptas. ($90–$140) double. AE, DC, EURO, MC, V. **Parking:** Available. **Closed:** Nov–Apr.

Among the waterfront properties of Figueretas, Los Molinos gets high marks for its beautifully landscaped setting and lovely pool area with access to a small beach. Two-thirds of the guest rooms have terraces and sea views, but most of the singles, which are somewhat cramped, face the street.

Dining/Entertainment: There is a restaurant on the premises.
Services: Room service.
Facilities: Swimming pool, beauty parlor, water sports from the hotel jetty (you can even fish from the rocks surrounding the garden).

HOTEL TORRE DEL MAR (Apartado 564), Playa d'en Bossa, 07800 Ibiza. Tel. 971/30-30-50. Fax 971/30-40-60. Telex 68845. 217 rms. A/C TV TEL

$ Rates: 7,000–12,000 ptas. ($70–$120) single; 10,000–17,500 ptas. ($100–$175) double. AE, DC, EURO, MC, V. **Parking:** Available. **Closed:** Nov–Apr.

A little farther out but still only 1 mile (1.5km) from Ibiza Town, the Torre del Mar is the top hotel on the Playa d'en Bossa. Its lobby lounges and bar studded with baroque and brocade accents are quite elegant. The cheery guest rooms here are well appointed and have terraces; half have sea views.

Dining/Entertainment: There is a restaurant on the premises.
Services: Room service.
Facilities: Outdoor and indoor pools, sauna, tennis court, massage, weight room, playground, small nearby beach.

MODERATE

HOSTAL RESIDENCIA EL CORSARIO, Carrer Poniente, 5, or Santa María, 12, 07800 Ibiza. Tel. 971/30-12-48. 14 rms (12 with bath).

$ Rates: 5,000–7,000 ptas. ($50–$70) single without bath; 8,000–9,000 ptas. ($80–$90) double with bath. AE, DC, EURO, MC, V. **Parking:** Nearby. **Closed:** Nov–Mar.

This quaint inn shares an old corsair's residence with its restaurant (see "Dining" below). Located within the old city walls, it has lovely arbored courtyards with olive trees and a good deal of antiquated charm. Some of the guest rooms feature antique furnishings.

Room 13 has three beds, beamed ceilings, arched doorways, and a wonderful view of the harbor. Rooms 1 and 2 share an outdoor terrace. Room 15 is in a newer part of the building and has the best view of all. Room 10 is a single with the same great view. One room, known as the "estudio," has four beds. Try to avoid Room 5—it's the hottest and has no view. Reservations are a must in summer.

LA VENTANA HOTEL, Sa Carrossa, 13 (Apartado 1360), 07800 Ibiza. Tel. 971/30-15-48. Fax 971/39-01-45. 13 rms.

$ Rates: 7,000–8,500 ptas. ($70–$85) small double; 8,300–9,800 ptas. ($83–$98) large double. AE, DC, EURO, MC, V. **Parking:** Nearby. **Closed:** Nov–Holy Week.

Located in D'Alt Vila, this charming hostelry occupies a traditional *ibicenco* house that was stylishly restored in 1984. The guest rooms, all doubles, are bright and cheerful, and owner Catherine Bagnis-Vogel makes guests feel like they're staying in someone's home rather than in a hotel. The lobby bar, which feels more like a living room than a hotel lounge, works on the honor system—take what you want and pay later. The third-floor rooms have the best views; six of the seven largest rooms have balconies. The fine view of the port from the large outdoor terrace is shared by everyone.

BUDGET

HOSTAL/APARTAMENTOS EL PUERTO, Carrer Carlos III, 22, 07800 Ibiza. Tel. 971/31-38-27. Fax 971/31-74-52. 96 rms, 70 apts. TEL

$ Rates: 3,000–4,800 ptas. ($30–$48) single; 3,600–7,500 ptas. ($36–$75) double; 3,300–7,500 ptas. ($33–$75) studio apt; 4,000–9,700 ptas. ($40–$97) one-bedroom apt for two, 375–700 ptas. ($3.75–$7) third-person supplement. EURO, MC, V. **Parking:** Nearby.

Just a few blocks from the port, El Puerto has rooms and apartments that feature simple wood furnishings. There are 12 single rooms and 10 studio apartments. Half the rooms and all the apartments have terraces. The apartments also have fully equipped kitchenettes. There is a lot of sunbathing space around the pool.

HOSTAL RESIDENCIA APARTAMENTOS RIPOLL, Carrer Vicente Cuervo, 10–14, 07800 Ibiza. Tel. 971/31-42-75. 15 rms (none with bath), 16 apts.

$ Rates: 1,800–3,300 ptas. ($18–$33) single; 3,000–3,300 ptas. ($30–$33) double; 3,500–7,300 ptas. ($35–$73) apt for two or three. Showers 350 ptas. ($3.50). No credit cards. **Parking:** Nearby.

The reception desk here is one flight up. While the guest rooms are merely adequate, all the one-bedroom apartments are very comfortable and have terraces, modern kitchens, complete baths, and sofa-beds in the sitting rooms. There are 10 doubles and several triples; the rooms have sinks, but you'll have to pay an extra charge each time you take a shower.

HOSTAL RESIDENCIA ARAGÓN, Carrer Aragón, 54, 07800 Ibiza. Tel. 971/30-60-60. 10 rms (none with bath).

$ Rates (including IVA): 2,500 ptas. ($25) single; 4,700 ptas. ($47) double; 6,200 ptas. ($62) triple; 7,300 ptas. ($73) quad. No credit cards. **Parking:** Nearby.

Within easy walking distance of the town center and Figueretas beach, the Aragón is the best low-priced pension in town. Its entrance is one flight up, and its atmosphere is very homey. Triples and quads are available. Some rooms have TVs, and all have sinks.

HOSTAL RESIDENCIA MONTESOL, Paseo Vara de Rey, 2, 07800 Ibiza. Tel. 971/31-01-61. 55 rms. TEL

$ Rates: 3,000–3,900 ptas. ($30–$39) single; 4,500–5,700 ptas. ($45–$57) double with shower, 5,000–6,700 ptas. ($50–$67) double with bath. EURO, MC, V. **Parking:** Nearby.

Adjacent to the popular café of the same name (see "Dining" below), the Montesol has guest rooms that are right on the marina and have white tile flooring throughout. Although all are clean and comfortable, there is a dearth of charm. All rooms have toilets.

HOSTAL RESIDENCIA PARQUE, Carrer Vicente Cuervo, s/n (no street number), 07800 Ibiza. Tel. 971/30-13-58. 34 rms (some with bath).

$ Rates: 2,100–2,500 ptas. ($21–$25) single; 4,500–5,700 ptas. ($45–$57) double. No credit cards. **Parking:** Nearby. **Closed:** Dec.

Located in the center of town near the old city walls, the Parque has guest rooms that are small and friendly but largely functional. All the double rooms are equipped with private baths; the singles have sinks only. The seven corner rooms have terraces, but this means added noise at night.

HOSTAL RESIDENCIA SOL Y BRISA, Avenida Bartolomé Vicente Ramón, 15, 07800 Ibiza. Tel. 971/31-08-18. 19 rms (none with bath).

$ Rates (including IVA): 1,000–1,500 ptas. ($10–$15) single; 1,800–2,500 ptas. ($18–$25) double. No credit cards. **Parking:** Nearby.

The Sol y Brisa offers very basic accommodations just a few blocks from the port. Here, too, the reception area is one flight up. The guest rooms (all with sinks) are small, clean, and, thanks to the tiled flooring, surprisingly friendly. Those that have been recently refreshened are especially cheery, so request one of those if possible. Some of the baths are brand new, and the remaining ones are scheduled to be done over.

3. DINING

Although similar dishes turn up on menus throughout the Balearic Islands, the dishes are often rendered with distinctive local twists— except, of course, the *ensaimada,* the pastry of choice on each island. My favorite *ibicenco* confection, however, is *flao,* a kind of cheesecake made with herbs, a hint of mint, and honey.

In some Ibiza restaurants, coarse peasant bread, olives, and alioli (garlic mayonnaise) are an automatic prelude to meals. One distinctive local dish you should try is *sofrit pages*—sautéed pork, lamb, and chicken simmered with potatoes, peppers, and whole garlic cloves. But seafood is clearly the island's culinary forte, and although many of the fish may be unfamiliar to you—such as denton, rape, besugo, dorada, and emperador—they are as commonplace here as sole, cod, and halibut are in the United States.

Among the island's home-brewed spirits are *frígola,* a sweet, aromatic liqueur made with wild thyme; *palo,* a somewhat bitter apéritif made from carob; and *hierbas ibicencas,* a liqueur combining anis and numerous herbs.

Most of Ibiza's restaurants offer a similar range of prices, with entrees running from 1,000 to 4,000 ptas. ($10 to $40), so you can eat reasonably or expensively almost anywhere. That being the case, it makes sense to eat judiciously in the island's better restaurants than to try to save money in the "less expensive" places that offer little imagination and low quality. Real bargain eating amounts to having a sandwich in a bar or a quick bite in a cafeteria and at one of the food stands that abound in the tourist centers. Service is usually included in the prices, but IVA is *not.* Many restaurants offer economical three-course luncheon menus del día, including bread and house wine. At cafeterias, tapas bars, and other informal eating establishments, it often costs less to eat at the bar than at a table.

EXPENSIVE

EL BRASERO, Carrer Barcelona, 4. Tel. 31-14-69.

Cuisine: SPANISH/CONTINENTAL. **Reservations:** Recommended June–Sept.

$ Prices: Appetizers 625–2,000 ptas. ($6.25–$20); main courses 1,625–3,000 ptas. ($16.25–$30). EURO, MC, V.

Open: Daily 8pm–12:30am. **Closed:** Nov–Apr.

This romantic bistro-type restaurant with ornamental wrought-iron railings offers both indoor and outdoor dining. Most patrons opt for the former to view the funky nightlife pageant as it parades by.

The Brasero's menu is a mixture of Spanish and international fare. The breast of duck with Armagnac sauce is delicious, as are the "Formen-terafish" prepared in a variety of ways and the rabbit stuffed with mushrooms. For the rest, it's mainly fish.

EL PORTALÓN, Plaça dels Desamparats, 1 & 2. Tel. 30-39-01.

Cuisine: SPANISH/INTERNATIONAL. **Reservations:** Recommended July–Sept.

$ Prices: Appetizers 800–1,700 ptas. ($8–$17); main courses 1,100–4,000 ptas. ($11–$40); menu del día 2,500–3,000 ptas. ($25–$30). AE, DC, EURO, MC, V.

Open: Lunch Mon–Sat 12:30–3:30pm; dinner daily 8pm–12:30am. **Closed:** Mid-Jan to mid-Feb.

El Portalón offers romantic patio dining in D'Alt Vila as well as indoor intimacy in a rustic, Old World setting. The menu gathers together a more or less standard offering of meat and fish dishes accented with some typical Spanish fare. At lunch, it offers an additional, lighter, more moderately priced menu with most dishes costing under 1,500 ptas. ($15).

SAUSALITO, Plaza Sa Riba, 5 (at the eastern end of the port). Tel. 31-01-66.
  Cuisine: MEDITERRANEAN. **Reservations:** Recommended in summer.
$ Prices: Appetizers 675–1,500 ptas. ($6.75–$15); main courses 1,300–2,500 ptas. ($13–$25). AE, EURO, MC, V.
  Open: Dinner only, daily 8pm–2am. **Closed:** Nov–Mar.

An Ibiza institution run by emigré Frenchman (via Algeria) Alain Mion, Sausalito serves Mediterranean cuisine to an international clientele in a bistro setting. On the walls are photos of famous stars (not the usual celebrity-poses-with-restaurant-owner shots, but actual movie stills). Daily meat and fish specials complement a well-rounded standard menu featuring roast baby lamb; confit of duck; and baby chicken "Sausalito" stewed with onions, black pepper, white wine, and vinegar.

MODERATE

EL CORSARIO, Carrer Poniente, 5, or Santa María, 12. Tel. 30-12-48.
  Cuisine: SEAFOOD/SPANISH. **Reservations:** Recommended in summer.
$ Prices: Appetizers 525–1,500 ptas. ($5.25–$15); main courses 1,700–2,300 ptas. ($17–$23). AE, DC, EURO, MC, V.
  Open: Dinner only, Mon–Sat 8pm–midnight. **Closed:** Nov–Holy Week.
Installed in the former home of a corsair built at the turn of the 16th century, El Corsario specializes in all manner of fresh fish from the market. Apéritifs served on the outdoor terrace are accompanied by a splendid harbor view.

POMELO, Carrer La Virgen, 53. Tel. 31-31-22.
  Cuisine: SPANISH. **Reservations:** Not required.
$ Prices: Appetizers 500–1,800 ptas. ($5–$18); main courses 800–2,000 ptas. ($8–$20). AE, EURO, MC, V.
  Open: Dinner only, daily 7pm–1:30am. **Closed:** Nov–Holy Week.
This bright, friendly place on a trendy shopping street serves steak tartare and a large selection of meat dishes. Specialties of the house are roast lamb and escalopines. Grab an outdoor table for people-watching.

RESTAURANT BAR CAN'ALFREDO, Paseo Vara de Rey, 16. Tel. 31-12-74.
  Cuisine: SPANISH/IBIZENCAN. **Reservations:** Not required.
$ Prices: Appetizers 525–1,600 ptas. ($5.25–$16); main courses 1,600–2,700 ptas. ($16–$27); menu del día 1,300–2,200 ptas. ($13–$22). AE, DC, EURO, MC, V.
  Open: June–Sept, Mon–Sat 1pm–midnight; Sun 1–5pm. Sept–June, Mon–Sat 1–5pm and 8pm–midnight; Sun 1–5pm.
Right in the heart of town, this small, simple, unpretentious place with only a dozen tables is very popular with locals and visiting celebrities (note photos of them with owner Alfredo Riera). The ibicenco specialties here include burrida de ratjada (skate stew with almonds, garlic, and potatoes) and bullit de peix (fish-and-potato stew).

BUDGET

CAP DES FALCO, Las Salinas. No phone.
Cuisine: INTERNATIONAL. **Reservations:** Not required.
$ Prices: Appetizers 350–650 ptas. ($3.50–$6.50); main courses 600–2,700 ptas. ($6–$27). No credit cards.
Open: Summer, Tues–Sun 1:30–11pm (lunch served 1:30–5pm and dinner served 8:30–11pm). Winter, lunch Tues–Sun 1–5pm; dinner Tues 8:30–11pm. **Closed:** Jan–Feb and 10 days in Nov.

Although this seaside entry has a hint of the hippy era about it, it has been around only a few years. All is very lazy and laid back here amid the salt flats. It is, however, a bit hard to find. As you head south out of Ibiza Town, there is a barely discernible dirt road off to the right just before the turnoff to the left for Escavallet Beach. Follow it as it winds through the salt flats and at the end you'll find Cap des Falco.

If you stick to the tuna, avocado, or tomato-and-mozzarella salads, you can eat cheaply. For an entree, try the grilled rabbit or the filet mignon.

SPECIALTY DINING: SNACKS & TAPAS

BAR SES BOTES, Carrer Isidoro Macabich, 16. Tel. 31-27-66.
Cuisine: TAPAS. **Reservations:** Not required.
$ Prices: Tapas 275–350 ptas. ($2.75–$3.50) per plate. No credit cards.
Open: Mon–Sat 6am–2am; Sun 6pm–2am. **Closed:** 3 weeks in Jan.

At this traditional Spanish tapas bar, several plates of tapas can make a quick, light meal. Choose among squid, mushroom, kidney, pork, potato salad, and gambas al ajillo (shrimp in garlic and olive oil).

CAFÈ MAR Y SOL, Carrer de Lluís Tur i Palau (at the edge of the port). Tel. 31-07-71.
Cuisine: SNACKS/SANDWICHES/ICE CREAM. **Reservations:** Not required.
$ Prices: Tapas 250–1,000 ptas. ($2.50–$10); pizzas 550–825 ptas. ($5.50–$8.25); sandwiches 250–575 ptas. ($2.50–$5.75). No credit cards.
Open: Daily 8am–2am.

In the trendy scheme of things, the Mar y Sol is in constant competition with the Montesol (see below), just across the street. The people-watching from the outdoor terrace is equally fine here, but indoors the winsome wrought-iron tables, tapestry seat cushions, and decorative wooden accents make it more pleasant than the Montesol.

Snacks, sandwiches, and ice-cream creations are served, and next door is a small bakery where you can buy pastries to accompany your afternoon coffee or tea. As with most Spanish cafés, prices here vary slightly depending on whether you do your consuming at the bar, at an indoor table, or at an outdoor table.

CAFETERIA MONTESOL, Paseo Vara de Rey, 2. Tel. 31-01-61.

Cuisine: SNACKS/SANDWICHES. **Reservations:** Not required.
$ Prices: Tapas 175–350 ptas. ($1.75–$3.50); sandwiches 275–500 ptas. ($2.75–$5); assorted light bites 175–1,750 ($1.75–$17.50). No credit cards.
Open: Daily 8am–2am.

At the western end of the marina, the Montesol is a 30-plus-year-old Ibiza tradition where tourists come to people-watch and locals to gossip and gab. In fact, the patrons at its sidewalk tables usually constitute a spectacle in their own right. Both indoors and out, the Montesol serves snacks and sandwiches. Next door is the Hostal Residencia Montesol (see "Accommodations" earlier in this chapter).

---

4. WHAT TO SEE & DO

MUSEO ARQUEOLÒGICO DE IBIZA [ARCHEOLOGICAL MUSEUM], Plaza Catedral, s/n (no street number), and Vía Romana, s/n (no street number). Tel. 30-12-31 or 30-17-71.

⭐ Installed in the former arsenal of the city fortress, this museum's collection (including the most important assemblage of Punic remains in the world) chronicles Ibiza's ancient days rather comprehensively. Artifacts include Phoenician tombstones and bronze dolls from 1000 to 800 B.C.; clay figurines of Tanit (the Phoenician fertility goddess) and Best (god of fertility); and assorted jewelry, pottery, beads, and amphorae. Upstairs are Roman artifacts and a smattering of Muslim and Christian objects, including a 13th-century wooden Christ figure and some corsair cannons. Explanations and identifications, when given, are in Spanish or Catalan, so pick up an English-language brochure to get the most out of your visit.

Note: At this writing, the museum was closed for renovation. Admission and hours are to be determined when it reopens. Check the current status with the tourist office.

MUSEO PUIG DES MOLINS, Vía Romana, s/n (no street number). Tel. 30-12-31 or 30-17-71.

⭐ The Museo Puig des Molins was built on the site of the necropolis that was the city's cemetery from about 654 B.C. (the accepted date for Ibiza's founding) to the 1st century A.D. Objects found on the site are displayed here, including many figurines, amphorae, and other assorted artifacts.

Admission: 225 ptas. ($2.25).
Open: Summer, Mon–Sat 10am–1pm and 5–8pm. Winter, Mon–Sat 10am–1pm and 4–7pm. **Closed:** Holidays.

SANTA MARIA DE LAS NIEVES CATEDRAL, Plaza Catedral. No phone.

This cathedral's glaringly inappropriate name ("Saint Mary of the Snows") was bestowed by the general who ordered its construction in gratitude for his successful bid to wrest Ibiza from the Arabs. When he prayed for victory, he vowed to name the church in honor of the virgin whose feast day followed most closely on the heels of his triumph: Saint Mary of the Snows was the one.

The cathedral's original Gothic beauty, hidden beneath a series of baroque embellishments, is now being painstakingly unmasked. Exhibited in the sacristía and museo are gold and silver ceremonial objects and religious vestments.

As you leave the cathedral, follow Carrer Universidad de Ibiza past a hole in the wall on the right (the remains of a Phoenician cistern) and beyond the city walls to a terrace that will afford an expansive view of the harbor and the island.

Admission: Catedral free; sacristía and museo 75 ptas. (75¢).

Open: Summer, Sun–Fri 10:30am–1pm and 4–5:30pm; Sat 10:30am–1pm. Winter, daily 11am–2pm. **Closed:** Holidays.

---

5. SAVVY SHOPPING

Shopping is just one of the many vacation indulgences that make Ibiza famous. From the stands that spring up nightly at the edge of the marina to the trendy boutiques of Carrer de la Virgen, you can indulge your consumer vices in everything from cheap costume jewelry to fancy clothes and fine handcrafts.

ACCESSORIES

LUCKY LIZARD, Mestre Joan Mayans, 2. Tel. 31-47-06.

Connoisseurs of chic, fun footwear and bold accessories will love Beverly Feldman's original Ibiza Town store (see "Savvy Shopping" in Chapter 6 as well). Open Monday to Saturday from 10am to 1:30pm and from 6 to 10pm; closed November through Holy Week.

S'ESPARDENYA, D'Ignasi Riquer, 29, D'Alt Vila. Tel. 30-54-16.

The Ibiza branch of Barcelona's La Manual Alpargatera (see "Savvy Shopping" in Chapter 6), S'Espardenya features handmade espadrilles ranging from the simple to the glitteringly stunning. From June through September it's open on Monday to Saturday from 11am to 2:30pm and from 5 to 11pm; in October, April, and May, the hours are Monday to Saturday from 11:15am to 2:30pm and from 5:30 to 10:30pm. It's closed from November through Holy Week.

CERAMICS

CERAMICAS "ES TEST," Carrer de Mar, 15. No phone.

This shop carries a limited yet high-quality selection of Ibizan ceramics, including reproductions of some of the Punic statues in the archeological museum. But the main attractions here are the traditional black-and-white Ibizan figures by Luis Amor that are far superior to the standard, mass-produced variety sold in most other shops. Also outstanding are the beautiful plates by Gabrielet, an Ibizan artist now living in Formentera, and his pupil, Toniet. Open on Monday to Saturday from 10am to 1:30pm and 5 to 7pm (until midnight June through September). Closed from January to Holy Week.

IMPRESSIONS

Every year the Spanish police decide that they must cut down on
the floating population of escapists, who regard the island as a
slightly more accessible Tahiti, and a purge takes place.
Deportation is usually carried out on grounds of moral
insufficiency. . . . Annually Ibiza's Bohemian plant is pruned back
to the roots, and with each new season it produces a fresh crop.
—NORMAN LEWIS, THE CHANGING SKY, 1959

FASHION

Fashion has been an important Ibiza industry since the late 1960s, when the nonconformist fashion philosophy known as "ad lib" took hold here, rooted in the first Ibizan creations combining elements of the traditional *pitiusa* attire of the natives and the natural, free-flowing garments of the hippies who flocked here in the 1960s. In recent years Ibizan designs have become much more sophisticated and complex, but the nonconformist spirit has not wavered.

Indifferent to the fashion fads of the moment, Ibiza's highly romantic creations encourage an independent, improvisational way of dressing that mixes and matches fashion concepts to create a look that is distinctly individual.

JOY BORNE, Carrer Josep Verdera, 14. Tel. 31-09-72.

This is fashion central for the outrageous clothes and accessories that have come to be associated with this sybaritic island. The flowing, froufrou designs here are adorned with feathers, sequins, and beads and are priced in accordance with their fancifulness. Open daily from 10am to 1:30pm and from 5 to 10pm (until midnight June through September; closed February to Holy Week).

MANGO, Riambau, 2, and Luis Tur Palau, 20. Tel. 31-64-20.

This is part of a nationwide chain of stores offering casual but stylish fashions at affordable (albeit not bargain) prices. Mango is open on Monday to Saturday from 10:30am to 1:30pm and from 5:30 to 10pm.

PAULA'S, Carrer de la Virgen, 4. Tel. 31-12-23.

At the pinnacle of the Ibizan fashion industry is Armin Heinemann, who designs not only the fashions at Paula's but also the fabrics, prints, and perfumes. His clothing and hats are of a dramatic crêpe de chine that he developed himself, and the styling and workmanship throughout are strictly that of haute couture. The prices are up there, too. Paula's carries some men's fashions as well and displays all in a richly elegant Victorian setting. Open on Monday to Friday from 11am to 1pm and from 6:30 to 9:30pm; closed from mid-October to mid-May.

Stateside, look for Paula's fashions in a shop called Ibiza at 46 University Place in New York (tel. 212/533-4614) and in Paula's Maria at 8840 Beverly Boulevard in Beverly Hills (tel. 213/273-2600).

TYKE, Carrer Josep Verdera, 10 and 12. Tel. 31-02-26.

This shop showcases women's fashions by Tyke, an American designer and long-time Ibiza resident. At no. 10 you'll find more mainstream designs; at no. 12, the more romantic fashion expressions of the island. Tyke is open Monday to Saturday from 10:30am to 2pm and from 5 to 10:30pm (evening hours are 7pm to midnight June through September). It's closed from December through March.

LEATHER

PEDRO'S, Carrer Anníbal 8 (at the corner of Conde Rosselón). Tel. 31-30-26.

Pedro Planells is a master with leather. His shop really has no name but by now might sport a small sign saying simply "Pedro's." All of his top-quality creations are highly original, are sewn by hand, and can be custom made. He also fashions desks, doors, chandeliers—and just about anything you can think of—in leather and silver. His clients include many well-heeled jet-setters and, on occasion, even King Juan Carlos of Spain. Considering the quality materials, imagination, hard work, and care that go into each of Pedro's pieces, they are most fairly priced.

Hours here are very flexible indeed, subject to the whims of Pedro's artistic temperament. From June through September you can usually find him here daily from 10am to 1:30pm and from 3:30 to 8:30pm; in other months, you'll just have to try your luck. The shop is usually closed in February.

SANDAL SHOP, Plaça De Vila, 2. Tel. 30-54-75.

Just inside the walled city, this shop purveys fine leather goods made by its own artisans. The selection of belts, some with semiprecious-stone buckles, is beautiful; the leather bags and brief-cases are attractive and durable; and the sandals can be custom-made. Summer hours are Monday to Friday from 10:30am to 2pm and from 5:30 to 11:30pm, Saturday from 10:30am to 2pm and from 6 to 11:30pm; winter hours are Monday to Saturday from 11am to 1:30pm and from 5:30 to 7pm. Closed in January and February.

6. EVENING ENTERTAINMENT

In summer, Ibiza swings around the clock. To keep pace with the all-night clubbers, all you need are money and transportation, for most begin their evening in Ibiza Town and then later head out to the discos of the moment elsewhere on the island.

At dusk, the marina area blossoms with vendors selling jewelry, scarves, and assorted handcrafts. Nearby, the string of bars lines up stool to stool. Just stroll along and pick one, two, three, or more strategic perches from which to watch the world at play.

Two of the brightest stars in the Ibiza night in recent years have been Amnesia and Pachá.

AMNESIA, Carretera Sant Antoni (San Antonio)-Ibiza, km. 2.5. Tel. 19-80-64.

Attracting a predominantly younger crowd with musical offerings and spacious multilevel dance floors, Amnesia occasionally stages wild parties. Much of the space is open air, with canopies and awnings spread out here and there and small, scattered pools. Snacks are served. Open daily from midnight to 6am; closed from October to mid-June.

Admission (including one drink): 3,500 ptas. ($35).

LA CANTINA [A.K.A. TEATRO PEREYRA], Conde Rosellón, 3. Tel. 30-10-04.

A few blocks from the marina, this reincarnation of the Teatro Pereyra is now a lively music bar with a Bourbon Street feel about it. The visiting bands play soul, funk, jazz, and rock, and owner Eric Harmsen, who plays a mean piano, joins in most nights. The crowd is often moved to dancing in the aisles. La Cantina also serves snacks, breakfast, and dinner. The place is open daily from 10am to 5am; music begins at 11pm.

Admission: Free, but there's a 550-pta. ($5.50) minimum.

CASINO DE IBIZA, Paseo Juan Carlos I (Paseo Marítimo), s/n (no street number). Tel. 31-33-12.

Here gamblers will find the usual gaming tables and slot machines in a quiet, modern setting. You need your passport to get in. The adjoining nightclub offers live cabaret entertainment several nights a week from May to October. It opens at 9:30pm, and the show begins at 10:15pm. The slot-machine room is open in summer daily from 6pm to 6am, in winter daily from 6pm to 5am. The casino's summer hours are daily from 10pm to 5am; winter hours are daily from 10pm to 4am.

Admission: Slot machines free; casino 600 ptas. ($6); 2,750 ptas. ($27.50) for show, including one drink and casino admission. Men are not permitted to wear shorts in the casino.

PACHA, Paseo Marítimo, s/n (no street number). Tel. 31-36-12 or 31-09-59.

Frequented by the beautiful people of all ages in their ultrachic clothes and kinky coifs, this spacious split-level disco near the casino (see above) has several dance floors and numerous bars. In summer, overheated dancers can cool off in the swimming pool. Unfortunately, the music is primarily of the droning disco and rap variety reminiscent of the pounding cadences of jackhammers. Pacha is open May through October daily from midnight to 6am and November through April on Friday and Saturday only.

Admission (including one drink): 3,000 ptas. ($30).

AROUND IBIZA

Many different Ibizas await beyond the trademark trendiness of Ibiza Town. Some are trendy in other ways, others are very traditional; some are enticingly secluded, still others are so overrun with bargain-basement tour groups that you'll want to avoid them. Whatever your pleasure, though, you're bound to find it somewhere.

Except, of course, if you're looking for mountains. Ibiza has no mountain ranges, just large lumps in the landscape. A petite 1,550 feet (475m) at its highest point, its finest contours are those of its craggy, cliff-rimmed coasts, sheltering a wealth of inviting coves and bays often graced with fine sand, pine trees, and Spanish cedars. Ibiza also has the only river in the Balearics.

Its total area is 230 square miles (572 square km), and it measures 25 miles (41km) long and 12.5 miles (20km) wide.

Along its 375-mile (600km) coast are over 100 beaches of varying sizes, shapes, and sexual persuasions. Salinas, because of its large expanse and proximity to Ibiza Town, is the most popular. Nearby Es Cavallet is a nude beach. Popular in the north is the beach at Portinatx; in the south, the most popular is Cala d'Hort. The island's longest beach is Playa d'en Bossa. Its most dangerous is that at Cala Nova, where the undertow is fierce when the sea simmers with whitecaps. Almost every tourist beach offers the full array of amenities—bars, restaurants, pedalboats, lounge chairs, umbrellas, windsurfers, and facilities for other assorted water sports.

Inland, the island scenery tends to pine-clad hills, valleys of almond trees (attractively abloom in February), fig trees, orange and lemon groves, carob trees, wild herbs and flowers, and many memorable vistas across the hills to the sea. Scattered here and there are palm trees, Arab waterwheels, and charming windmills.

At Roca Llisa, the posh community where Roman Polanski has his house, is the island's sole golf course with 27 holes.

GETTING AROUND THE ISLAND

BY ORGANIZED TOUR **Viajes Meliá,** Paseo Vara de Rey, 7, Ibiza Town (tel. 30-39-00), offers bus and boat tours around Ibiza and to Formentera. Among them is an all-day bus tour of the island taking in the major points of interest and including a swim at one of the beaches. The cost is 2,700 ptas. ($27). A day's tour by boat and bus of Formentera costs 5,000 ptas. ($50). Tours are offered from May to October; hotel pickups can be arranged.

BY BUS The **bus station** in Ibiza Town is at Avenida Isidoro Macabich, 42 (tel. 31-56-11). Buses depart from two locations along this street—in front of the main terminal at no. 42 and in front of the

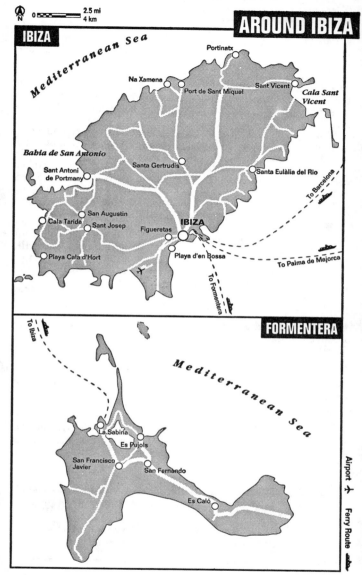

ticket kiosk at no. 24. In summer there is frequent and extensive bus service throughout the island with one-way fares reaching a maximum of 300 ptas. ($3). Schedules and routes are available at the main terminal and at bus stations around the island. You must buy your tickets before boarding, except when journeying from Ibiza Town to Playa d'en Bossa/Cala Llonga.

La Prensa de Ibiza, *Diario de Ibiza*, and *Ibiza Now* publish comprehensive, up-to-the-minute information on bus and ferry services.

BY CAR Driving around the island is easy and pleasant and lets you explore the many different faces of Ibiza to decide which one suits you best. Three main roads radiate from Ibiza Town and then branch out to the island's northern, southern, and western extremes. The network of secondary and tertiary roads is the most developed in the south and west, making the picturesque coves here readily accessible. The splendid coves and beaches of the north and east are often accessible only by boat.

If you're interested in renting a car (which I strongly recommend), Avis and BC Betacar/Europcar have offices at the airport and elsewhere on the island:

Avis: At the airport (tel. 30-29-49), open May through October daily 24 hours, reduced hours the rest of the year; Avenida Santa Eulàlia del Rio, 17, Ibiza Town (tel. 31-31-63), open on Monday to Saturday from 9am to 1pm and from 5 to 8pm and on Sunday from 9am to 1pm.

BC Betacar/Europcar: At the airport (tel. 30-31-84), open May through October daily 24 hours and November through April on Monday to Friday from 7:30am to 11:30pm; Carrer Carlos III, Ibiza Town (tel. 31-09-66), open on Sunday to Friday from 9am to 1:30pm and from 4 to 7:30pm and on Saturday from 10am to noon (closed Saturday and Sunday in winter).

At presstime, Avis offered the lowest base rate of 5,400 ptas. ($54) per day, but because rates are highly volatile, be sure to shop around.

BY BOAT **Marbella Charter,** S.A., Puerto Deportivo Marina Botafoch, Local 209/211, 07800 Ibiza (tel. 971/31-32-10 or 971/31-40-10; fax 971/31-39-10), rents a variety of motorboats that will enable you to explore the island's coast for quiet, secluded coves and beaches. Rates run from 45,000 to 200,000 ptas. ($450 to $2,000) per day, with discounts offered for longer rentals of up to one month or more.

Jacques Dupuy takes a minimum of 4 and a maximum of 15 passengers on excursions of one day or more aboard his magnificent 68-foot sailboat, *Ibiza*. For up to eight passengers it costs 80,000 ptas. ($800) per day with a crew and lunch; for eight or more it costs 8,000 ($80) per person. Contact **Barco Ibiza** (tel. 971/30-26-12; fax 971/30-26-29).

1. SANT ANTONI DE PORTMANY (SAN ANTONIO ABAD) & THE SOUTHWESTERN COAST

In the western part of Ibiza, about 9 miles (15km) from the capital, the innate beauty of Sant Antoni Bay has been much sinned against by the crimes of construction committed in the name of mass tourism. Known to the Romans as Portus Magnus, the town of Sant Antoni has been packaged for tourism since the 1950s and has recently become Ibiza's "hooligan headquarters" ("hooligans" are primarily working-class Brits on package holidays who turn into the hard-drinking, sex-crazed, vandalizing vacationers dreaded by civilized tourists and local hotel and bar owners). The fact that the local population of several thousand swells to some 45,000 in summer gives some indication of the abuse the town suffers annually.

Things improve as you follow the coast around to the east and south, where a number of the coves have not yet been as ravaged and many hotels cater to families.

WHAT TO SEE & DO

From Sant Antoni's marina, **boats** depart for Formentera and Ibiza and offer various island tours, including excursions on glass-bottom boats. The offerings change from year to year, so check at the marina or contact **Cruceros San Antonio, S.A.,** Calle Progreso, 6, 1st Floor, Sant Antoni (tel. 34-34-71).

On the town's outskirts are the **underground Chapel of Santa Inés,** a national monument, and the **"Seis Fontanelles"** caves with interesting wall paintings.

Sant Josep **(San José)** is an inland town of about 1,000 inhabitants some 9 miles (15km) from the capital and gives its name to an administrative district containing one of the most ruggedly beautiful stretches of Ibizan coastline (from Cala Bassa to Cala Vadella), the famous Es Vedrá rock, the island's highest peak at Atalayassa (1,550 feet [475m]), and the salt flats.

Offshore at the popular southern beach of Cala d'Hort is the intriguing **Es Vedrá rock** where, in times of hardship and hunger, the Ibicencos would go, at great personal risk, to gather seagull eggs for survival. A Carmelite priest once recorded mystical revelations and meetings with "unearthly beings surrounded by light" while meditating on the island. Gigantic circles of light, up to 50 meters in diameter, have allegedly emerged from the sea here at times, discouraging fishermen from working the area. It is said that a strong magnetic force emanating from Es Vedrá attracts such strange phenomena. Photographers and romantics take note: After June 15 the sunrise here is especially dramatic, illuminating Es Vedrá while the surrounding hills remain in darkness.

WHERE TO STAY

Besides Ibiza Town, Figueretas, and Playa d'en Bossa, this is the most developed part of the island, with hordes of mediocre tour-group hotels crowding Sant Antoni and scarring parts of the coast to the southwest. A recent downturn in mass-tourism traffic has prompted their prices to plummet and, along with them, their standards, so if you plan to stay in package-tour digs, pick and choose with care. On the other hand, there are also a handful of choice, little hotels inland that are absolute heaven.

EXPENSIVE

APART.HOTEL VICTORIA, off the road toward Cala Tarida (Apartado 304), 07820 Sant Antoni, Ibiza. Tel. 971/ 34-09-00. Fax 971/34-25-72. 29 apts, 6 suites. A/C TV TEL
$ Rates: 9,500–37,000 ptas. ($95–$370) suite for two; 11,000–16,000 ptas. ($110–$160) apt for two. EURO, MC, V. **Parking:** Available.

This peaceful, secluded, hacienda-style retreat about 1 mile (2 km) from Port des Torrent is perched on a hilltop overlooking the bay of Sant Antoni. All the modern units are luxuriously appointed and have at least one terrace each. The rooms are categorized as minisuites, suites, and luxury suites; the first have showers only (no tubs). Five of the six apartments are large enough to accommodate up to six people; all of them have large kitchens.

Dining/Entertainment: The very pretty restaurant here serves up a fine view along with its French cuisine.

Services: Laundry.

Facilities: Indoor pool, fitness room, sauna, massages, private helipad.

HOTEL VILLAGE, Urbanización Caló den Real (along the road toward Cala Tarida), 07830 Sant Josep, Ibiza. Tel. 971/80-00-34. Fax 971/80-02-27. 20 rms, 3 suites. MINIBAR TV TEL

$ Rates (including breakfast and IVA): 9,700–13,000 ptas. ($97–$130) single; 14,000–19,000 ptas. ($140–$190) double; 20,000–26,000 ptas. ($200–$260) junior suite; 24,000–33,000 ptas. ($240–$330) suite. Half board available. AE, DC, EURO, MC, V.
Parking: Available.

Another of the island's small, select hotels, the Village is 15 miles (24 km) west of Ibiza Town. Just beyond the elegant white-marble entrance is an inviting bar/lounge. From the hotel's elevated perch, a walkway leads down to a rocky beach by the sea, where there are platforms equipped with lounge chairs and a small bar.

The white marble extends throughout the property and into the luxurious double guest rooms, with a touch of gray marble added in the baths. All the accommodations have large beds, area rugs, and terraces. Six rooms face the mountains rather than the sea. Room no. 40 has an especially large terrace with a sea view.

Dining/Entertainment: The very stylish restaurant offers international fare with a Spanish accent.

Services: Room service.

Facilities: Three tennis courts, sauna and whirlpool, fitness room, putting green.

PIKES, Apartado 104, 07820 Sant Antoni de Portmany, Ibiza. Tel. 971/34-22-22. Fax 971/34-23-12. 22 rms and suites. A/C MINIBAR TEL TV

$ Rates (including continental breakfast): 16,500–30,000 ptas. ($165–$300) double; 27,000–60,000 ptas. ($270–$600) suite. 15% discount for individual occupancy. Children under 12 accepted only if accompanied by a nanny. AE, DC, EURO, MC, V.
Parking: Available on premises. **Closed:** Jan–Apr.

A series of signs guides you through the maze of dirt roads leading to this luxurious refuge. Forged from a complex of 600-year-old farm buildings, it has combined all manner of 20th-century creature comforts with a good many of the farm's original charms. Celebrities such as Sade, George Michael, Julio Iglesias, Joan Baez, and Grace Jones have enjoyed this setting of sophisticated informality.

The rooms are all different—but all are very stylishly and, in some cases, sensually decorated. All but two twin-bedded rooms feature queen- or king-size beds.

Dining/Entertainment: The hotel's restaurant is a series of small, intimate rooms offering sedate, cushioned comfort. There is a breakfast nook outside.

Services: Room service.
Facilities: There's a pool on the grounds, and the management will organize boating, diving, golfing, and horseback excursions.

MODERATE

CLUB HOTEL TARIDA BEACH, Playa Cala Tarida, 07830 Sant Josep, Ibiza. Tel. 971/80-04-72. Fax 971/80-04-12. 407 studios. TEL
$ Rates (including breakfast): 4,700–7,200 ptas. ($47–$72) per person. Children staying in parents' room are charged 30%–50% of the normal per-person rate. Half and full board available. DC, EURO, MC, V. **Parking:** Available. **Closed:** Oct–Apr.

The Club Hotel Tarida Beach makes up a small, comfortable community unto itself. The transient population spans the generations, including young people, families, and elderly couples from the Continent.

The very clean and comfortable accommodations have dual living and sleeping areas (with double sofa-beds) that can be separated by means of folding doors; additional beds can also be added. The units have kitchens.

Guests can enjoy the several restaurants, the snack bar, the TV rooms with satellite hookups, the nightly poolside entertainment, and the disco. Services include a supermarket, laundry facilities, a beauty parlor, and a multilingual day-care center with classes for children offered on Monday to Saturday from 10am to 1pm and 4 to 6:30pm.

Available for guests' use are two swimming pools; two tennis courts; two squash courts; saunas; a very clean 100-foot-long (300m-long) beach with facilities for waterskiing, sailing, and diving; plus boats sailing from here to Sant Antoni, Formentera, and Ibiza.

Reservations can be made through Insotel, Carrer Aragó 71, 07800 Ibiza Town (tel. 971/39-00-68; fax 971/30-13-51; telex 68867 VIPY E).

HOTEL APARTAMENTOS NEREIDA, 07829 Cala de Bou, Ibiza. Tel. 971/34-33-62. 72 apts, 64 studios. TEL
$ Rates (including breakfast, dinner, and IVA): 2,800–5,500 ($28–$55) per person. Children 2–11 stay in parents' unit at 50%–100% discount. EURO, MC, V. **Parking:** Available. **Closed:** Nov–Apr.

On Sant Antoni Bay, this complex offers apartments, each with two terraces, a bedroom with twin beds, a sitting room with a sofa-bed, and a sink and stove with dishes and cooking utensils. The studios each have a terrace, a bed-sitting room with two beds and convertible sofa, and a stove. The furnishings are of plain but pleasant pine. The hotel has a seaside pool, children's playground, restaurant, bar, cafeteria, and snack bar.

Reservations can be made through Insotel, Carrer Aragó 71, 07800 Ibiza Town (tel. 971/39-00-68; fax 971/30-13-51; telex 68867 VIPY E).

LES JARDINS DE PALERM, Apartado 62, 07830 Sant Josep, Ibiza. Tel. 971/80-03-18. Fax 971/80-04-53. 8 rms, 1 suite. TV TEL

$ Rates (including breakfast): 16,500–26,500 ptas. ($165–$265) double; 27,500–38,500 ptas. ($275–$385) suite. AE, DC, EURO, MC, V. **Parking:** Available. **Closed:** Nov–Feb.

⭐ Located along a side road leading up from the village of Sant Josep (San José), Les Jardins de Palerm is a charmingly intimate hotel conjured from a 17th-century hacienda-style *finca* (farm). Staying here is rather like being a guest at someone's country home. Scattered patios and garden terraces harbor cozy nooks for curling up with a book or just daydreaming.

The guest rooms, all decorated differently, are comfortably rustic and charmingly romantic with terraces, ceiling fans, beamed ceilings, and the occasional antique.

The restaurant here is a favorite among locals; reservations are imperative, especially in summer, when it functions outdoors. In winter, the seating moves indoors to a series of diminutive rooms, one of which has a delightful fireplace capped with a log mantle. The hotel also has a swimming pool.

BUDGET

RESTAURANT DEL CARMEN, José Marí Tur (Apartado 180), 07830 Sant Josep, Playa Cala d'Hort, Ibiza. Tel. 908/14-26-61. 9 rms.

$ Rates: 5,500 ptas. ($55) per person single or double. EURO, MC, V. **Parking:** Available. **Closed:** Nov–Holy Week.

On the quiet, remote Cala d'Hort at the western end of the island, opposite Es Vedrá rock, this simple hostelry offers clean and comfortable guest rooms, most with terraces. All have twin beds and small sofa-beds suitable for children. Call in February or March for May bookings and as early as possible for July, August, and September.

The hotel restaurant serves a standard menu of Spanish and international dishes, featuring fresh fish, pastas, paella, and lobster. Appetizers run from 400 to 1,300 ptas. ($4 to $13) and main courses from 475 to 3,200 ptas. ($4.75 to $32). This is also a good choice for lunch if you're just visiting the beach.

WHERE TO DINE

Many of Ibiza's finest restaurants are tucked away in quiet coves or in the countryside, so you really need a car to sample the full range of the island's culinary savoir-faire.

CANA JUANA, Sant Josep, about 9 miles (14km) from Ibiza Town along the road to Sant Josep (San José). Tel. 80-01-58.

Cuisine: INTERNATIONAL. **Reservations:** Strongly recommended as tables are few.

$ Prices: Appetizers 900–2,100 ptas. ($9–$21); main courses 1,000–3,200 ptas. ($10–$32). AE, EURO, MC, V.

Open: Dec 30–May 31, Tues–Sun 1–3pm and Tues–Sat 8:15pm–midnight. June 1–Oct 15, daily 8:15pm–midnight. **Closed:** Oct 16–Dec. 29.

⭐ Chef Juana Biarnes and her husband, J. Michel Bamberger, have turned a centuries-old country house into a wonderfully cozy, intimate dining experience—one that gastronomically distinguishes itself from other island offerings. Studded with Catalan specialties, the menu typically offers a few select fish dishes and an assortment of inventive meat dishes and appetizers. Some regular entries include codfish with spinach, raisins, and pine nuts; confit de canard with beans; country bread topped with tomatoes, olive oil, and anchovies or cured ham; potatoes with a sea-urchin sauce; merluza (hake) steamed with vegetables atop a sauce of special olive oil and 25-year-old sherry vinegar; and dorada (a local fish) dressed with vinegar, olive oil, garlic, and lamb's lettuce. Unusual among the tasty selection of homemade desserts is a uniquely light yogurt mousse teamed with raspberry coulis. An extensive offering of Spanish wines complements the fine fare.

Before distinguishing herself as a chef, Juana made her mark as Spain's first female newspaper journalist and photographer. Now her fine restaurant is itself newsworthy and enjoys a following of very loyal clients whose names are embroidered on their own personal napkins—among them is the king of Spain's father, the Count of Barcelona.

EL RINCON DE PEPE, Sant Mateu, 6, Sant Antoni de Portmany. Tel. 34-06-97.
Cuisine: TAPAS/SNACKS. **Reservations:** Not required.
$ Prices: Tapas 275–550 ptas. ($2.75–$5.50); platos combinados 550–900 ptas. ($5.50–$9); main courses 500–1,750 ptas. ($5–$17.50). No credit cards.
Open: Daily 11am–2am. **Closed:** Sun 4–7pm in July and Aug and Nov–Holy Week.

This is a great place for tapas (mostly seafood), but you can also choose among hamburgers, hot dogs, salads, and hearty entrees. The food is simple and good, the atmosphere pleasant, and the bar an attractive arrangement of tile and wood.

SA TASCA, San Augustín, off to the right along the road from Sant Josep (San José) to Sant Agusti (San Agustín). Tel. 80-00-75.
Cuisine: CONTINENTAL/IBICENCO. **Reservations:** Required for dinner in summer.
$ Prices: Appetizers 675–1,600 ptas. ($6.75–$16); main courses 1,400–2,500 ptas. ($14–$25). AE, EURO, MC, V.
Open: June to mid-Sept, Tues–Sun noon–midnight. Rest of year, Tues–Sun 1–4pm and 7:30–11:30pm.

Invitingly charming, Sa Tasca has a large open-air dining area and several small interior dining rooms (some with a fireplace) that are used in the winter and retain all the Old World character of this 200-year-old Ibizan house. The extensive international menu is sprinkled with ibicenco specialties and a special market menu that changes every two or three months. Fish and meat flambés prepared tableside are permanent house specialties.

2. THE NORTHERN COAST

The north remains largely untainted by the scourge of mass tourism, except for a handful of coves. Here you'll find some of the island's prettiest countryside, with fields of olive, almond, and carob trees and the occasional *finca* raising melons or grapes.

WHAT TO SEE & DO

Near the Hotel Hacienda is the **Taller de Arte** (no telephone), where Joaquín Mateo creates and sells paintings, ceramics, and bronze sculptures of great grace and striking visual appeal. Open in April through October daily from 10am to 1pm and 4:30 to 8pm.

Off the road leading into Port de Sant Miquel (Puerto de San Miguel) is the **Cova de "Can Marca,"** about 300 feet (100m) from the Hotel Galeón. There is a fine view of the bay from the snack bar. After a stunning descent down stairs that cling to the face of the cliff, you enter a cave that's over 100,000 years old and forms its stalactites and stalagmites at the rate of about 0.4 inch (1cm) per 100 years. A favored hiding place for smugglers and their goods in former days, today it's a beautifully orchestrated surrealistic experience— including a sound-and-light display—not unlike walking through a Dalí painting. Many of the limestone formations are delicate miniatures. The half-hour tour is conducted in several languages for groups of up to 70. From Holy Week to the end of October, tours are offered daily every half hour from 10am to 7pm. Admission is 525 ptas. ($5.25) for adults and 275 ptas. ($2.75) for children.

At the island's northern tip is **Portinatx,** a pretty series of beaches and bays now marred by a string of souvenir shops and haphazardly built hotels. For a taste of its original, rugged beauty, go past all the construction to the jagged coast along the open sea.

Every Saturday throughout the year there is a **flea market** just beyond Sant Carles (San Carlos) on the road to Santa Eulàlia (you'll know where it is by all the cars parked along the road). Open from about 10am until 8 or 9pm, it offers all kinds of clothing (both antique and new), accessories, crafts, and the usual odds and ends of a combination craft fair and flea market.

If you want to escape to a lovely beach that remains a stranger to hotel construction, head for **Playa Benirras** just north of Port de Sant Miquel (Puerto de San Miguel). An unpaved but passable road leads out to this small, calm, pretty cove where lounge chairs are available and pedalboats are for rent. There are also snack bars and restaurants here.

If you want to go **horseback riding,** contact C'an Mayans, Santa Gertrudis (tel. 63-68-84). Outings of from one to three hours cost 2,500 ptas. ($25) per hour and times are arranged to suit clients. Riding classes also are available.

A beautiful drive is that from Sant Carles (San Carlos) along the coast to Cala Sant Vicent (San Vicente).

SHOPPING IN SANTA GERTRUDIS

Santa Gertrudis, just off the main road between Ibiza Town and Sant Miquel (San Miguel), is a small village containing several shops offering high-quality handcrafts, antiques, jewelry, artwork, and more. Below are some long-standing establishments that have seen numerous others come and go:

CASI TODO, Plaza de la Iglesia, Santa Gertrudis. Tel. 19-70-23.
Casi Todo, literally meaning "almost everything," is an aptly

named shop that is a browser's paradise. Antiques and all manner of interesting odds and ends find their way here. It's located in the main square. Open in summer daily from 11am to 2pm and from 6 to 10pm; open the rest of the year daily from 11am to 6pm. Closed for several days at Christmas.

GALERIA CAN DAIFA, no address, Santa Gertrudis. Tel. 19-70-42.

This shop offers unique antique and modern jewelry, antique lamps, paintings, sculptures, and other assorted items both old and new. Open in May through October daily from 6pm to midnight; during other months daily from 5 to 10pm. Closed from November through April.

TE CUERO, Plaza del Banco, s/n (no street number). No phone.

Te Cuero specializes in fine leather goods from the island and carries unusual belts, wallets, skirts, and pants. It also offers belt buckles; scarves; and, at times, a glimpse of the world's oldest bonsai specimen, the pride and joy of shop owner Klaus, a transplanted German. His petite marvel is over 1,000 years old and documented in the *Guinness Book of World Records*. Open in summer on Monday to Saturday from 6 to 11pm and in winter on Monday to Saturday from 11am to 2pm and 5 to 9pm. Closed for two weeks in January.

WHERE TO STAY

The hotel offerings are much more limited in the north than in the traditional pockets of tourism in the south and west. Nevertheless, the island's finest hotel, the five-star Hacienda, is perched here above Na Xamena Bay. Port de Sant Miquel, Cala Sant Vicent, and Portinatx—former tranquil, seaside havens—in recent years have become increasingly pockmarked with package-tour hotels.

EXPENSIVE

HOTEL HACIENDA, Na Xamena, 07815 Sant Miquel (San Miguel), (Apartado 423) Ibiza. Tel. 971/33-30-46. Fax 971/33-31-75. Telex 69322 HHNX. 53 rms, 10 suites. A/C MINIBAR TV TEL

$ Rates: 15,000–22,000 ptas. ($150–$220) single; 18,500–33,000 ptas. ($185–$330) double; 24,000–35,000 ptas. ($240–$350) junior suite; 27,000–90,000 ptas. ($270–$900) suite. AE, DC, EURO, MC, V. **Parking:** On premises. **Closed:** Nov–Holy Week or late Apr.

More than a place to stay, the Hotel Hacienda is a state of mind. Set in a dense pine grove atop a promontory on Na Xamena Bay, this singular, sybaritic retreat in the Moorish style is favored by such personalities as Goldie Hawn, Tony Roberts, and Adnan Khashoggi in his more carefree days. Some 90% of the Americans who come to Ibiza opt for this hideaway, the island's only five-star property and a member of the Relais et Châteaux network. At once luxurious and laid back, it is also favored by honeymooners seeking a paradise of privacy. To me, its rare blend of luxury, informality, personalized service, and exclusivity make it one of the world's most appealing and soothing of lodgings.

Capricious and eccentric of layout, the hotel boasts numerous nooks and crannies that offer constant surprises and are tailor-made for sitting and doing absolutely nothing. The focal point of the hotel's call to leisure is the large, gracious pool around which, weather permitting, breakfast, lunch, and dinner are served. Any guest who has spent more than 365 days in the hotel is awarded a silver medal—54 have been granted so far. I guess it's true what they say about a satisfied customer!

The Hacienda's light, airy guest rooms are varied of decor, and more than 20 now offer Jacuzzis. Top of the line is the two-bedroom Presidential Suite (no. 607), a real stunner with a sea view from the separate shower and tub in the master bath as well as from the Jacuzzi out on the terrace. All rooms have one of the finest sunset views in the annals of travel.

For reservations, contact Marketing Ahead, 433 Fifth Ave., New York, NY 10016 (tel. 212/686-9213; fax 212/686-0271).

Dining/Entertainment: The hotel's fine restaurants (one pool-side; another, more formal one upstairs) were the recipients of the 1988 "Golden Fork Award" bestowed by the International Food, Wine & Travel Writers Association. The varied menu is, in the words of General Manager Ernesto Ramón Fajarnés, "only an indication" of what's available. For example, a fine pepper steak flambéed with cognac is not on the menu but almost always available on request. Similarly, available for up to 12 people is an authentic Carthaginian meal served in the restaurant's special alcove. In keeping with the family tradition of chronicling the island's history, Don Ernesto has personally documented the authenticity of a dozen or so recipes of that remote period. Summer evenings by the pool there is often musical entertainment.

Services: Room service, turndown service.

Facilities: A heated indoor pool and two outdoor pools; a tennis court; bicycle rentals and suggested itineraries; discounts at the island's challenging 27-hole golf course; horseback riding and boat rentals arranged on request.

MODERATE

HOTEL CARTAGO, 07815 Port de Sant Miquel (Puerto de San Miquel), Ibiza. Tel. 971/33-30-24. 196 rms.
$ Rates (including breakfast and IVA): 4,000 ptas. ($40) single; 7,500 ptas. ($75) double. AE, DC, EURO, MC, V. **Parking:** Available.

The Cartago is very similar to its counterpart next door, the Hotel Galeón (see above). Together these two massive hotels have procured a good view for themselves but in turn have destroyed the view for others from below because they are quite out of proportion to this lazy little bay. The rooms here are slightly inferior to those at the Galeón. The Cartago also has tennis courts and water sports.

HOTEL GALEÓN, 07815 Port de Sant Miquel (Puerto de San Miquel), Ibiza. Tel. 971/33-30-19. 182 rms and suites.
$ Rates (including IVA): 4,000 ptas. ($40) single; 6,500 ptas. ($65) double; 8,700 ptas. ($87) suite. AE, DC, EURO, MC, V. **Parking:** Available. **Closed:** Nov–Apr.

The Hotel Galeón is one of two cliff-hanging hotels overlooking this lovely bay. All the guest rooms have terraces and sea views, but beyond that, this is your basic dormitory-style tourist accommodation—simple, clean, comfortable, and rather nondescript. The same applies to the restaurant. The facilities include tennis courts and water sports.

BUDGET

HOTEL CALA SAN VICENTE, 07469 Cala Sant Vicent,
Ibiza. Tel. 971/33-30-55. Fax 971/33-30-55. 116 rms. TEL
$ Rates (including breakfast, dinner, and IVA): 2,800–5,300 ptas.
($28–$53) per person single or double. No credit cards. **Parking:** Available. **Closed:** Nov–Apr.

The second Insotel hostelry at Cala Sant Vicent, this one has similarly functional rooms and virtually the same facilities as the Imperio Playa.

You can also make reservations through Insotel, Carrer Aragó 71, 07800 Ibiza Town (tel. 971/39-00-68; fax 971/30-13-51; telex 68867 VIPY E).

HOTEL IMPERIO PLAYA, 07469 Cala Sant Vicent, Ibiza.
Tel. 971/33-30-55. Fax 971/33-30-55. 210 rms. TEL
$ Rates (including breakfast, dinner, and IVA): 2,800–5,300 ptas.
($28–$53) per person single or double. No credit cards. **Parking:** Available. **Closed:** Nov–Apr.

Cala Sant Vicent (San Vicente) is a pretty bay on the northeastern tip of the island, and the winding drive out here through the lovely pine forests is beautiful. The wide, 1,150-foot-long (350m) beach curves at the foot of some steep hills dotted with traditional houses. The sand and water are lovely, and the beach is among the best cared for on the island. (Windsurfing, waterskiing, and pedalboats are available at the beach.)

Of the several package-tour hotels on the beach, the Imperio Playa and the Hotel Cala San Vicente (see below) are the best. The public lounges here at the Imperio Playa are spacious; the guest rooms are functional and friendly. Guests enjoy the restaurant, bar, snack bar, disco, beauty parlor, boutiques, pool, tennis court, and children's playground.

You can also make reservations through Insotel, Carrer Aragó 71, 07800 Ibiza Town (tel. 971/39-00-68; fax 971/30-13-51; telex 68867 VIPY E).

WHERE TO DINE

As in the matter of hotels, there are fewer restaurants in the northern part of the island than to the south and west, but those that are here are rather exceptional.

RESTAURANTE AMA LUR, Carretera Sant Miquel, km.
2.3, Santa Gertrudis. Tel. 31-45-54.
Cuisine: BASQUE. **Reservations:** Required in July–Aug.
$ Prices: Appetizers 900–2,200 ptas. ($9–$22); main courses 2,000–2,500 ptas. ($20–$25). AE, EURO, MC, V.
Open: June–Nov, daily 8pm–midnight. Mar–May, Thurs–Tues 8pm–midnight. **Closed:** Dec–Feb.

Installed in a 200-year-old farmhouse, Ama Lur has several small interior dining areas and a stylish al fresco terrace. The cuisine is "modernized, enhanced" Basque and includes such unusual dishes as filet of sole with artichokes and magret of duck with figs in a raspberry-vinegar sauce.

RESTAURANTE CAN GALL, Carretera Ibiza–San Juan,
km. 11.6. Tel. 33-29-16.

Cuisine: SPANISH/IBICENCO. **Reservations:** Strongly recommended for dinner in July–Aug and Sun lunch in winter.

$ **Prices:** Appetizers 475–1,500 ptas. ($4.75–$15); main courses 700–2,300 ptas. ($7–$23). AE, EURO, MC, V.

Open: Lunch Wed–Mon 1–3:30pm; dinner Wed–Mon 8–11:30pm (until midnight in summer). **Closed:** Nov 20–end of Dec.

⭐ Located in the countryside in a 125-year-old farmhouse, Can Gall is a rustic restaurant offering largely Spanish dishes sprinkled with some local fare. Among the house specialties are cochinillo de San Lorenzo (suckling pig), a delicious grilled quarter chicken, suckling rabbit, and a savory bean stew. In winter, the menu features game and, at Sunday lunch, sofrito pages (chicken, lamb, and pork sautéed with sausage).

3. SANTA EULÀLIA & THE EASTERN COAST

Nine miles (14km) from Ibiza Town on the estuary of the island's only river is Santa Eulàlia del Río. Crowning the Puig de Missa at the town's entrance is a typical, gleaming white ibicenco fortress church of the 16th century. Its *porche*, which provides shelter from the sun, reflects the Arab architectural influence on the island. Prettier, more tranquil, and less plastic than Sant Antoni, Santa Eulàlia predominantly attracts middle-class northern Europeans and is more of a family resort.

WHERE TO STAY

HOTEL S'ARGAMASSA SOL, Urbanización S'Argamassa, 07182 Santa Eulàlia del Río. Tel. 971/33-00-51. Fax 971/33-00-76. 230 rms. TEL

$ **Rates** (including breakfast and IVA): 4,500–7,000 ptas. ($45–$70) single; 6,000–11,000 ptas. ($60–$110) double. AE, DC, EURO, MC, V. **Parking:** Available. **Closed:** Nov–Apr.

⭐ The Hotel S'Argamassa Sol is one of the best bets in the area. A brief walk from a sandy beach, the hotel, with its own small dock, is 2 miles (3km) outside the town of Santa Eulàlia del Río. Its guest rooms all have baths, terraces, and sea views. Although a bit stark, these rooms are clean and comfortable. A lobby lounge and bar, swimming pool, games room, TV room, playground, restaurant, lit tennis court, and waterskiing from the hotel dock complete the offering.

For reservations, contact Marketing Ahead, 433 Fifth Ave., New York, NY 10016 (tel. 212/686-9213; fax 212/686-0271).

WHERE TO DINE

DOÑA MARGARITA, Paseo Marítimo s/n (no street number). Tel. 33-06-55.

Cuisine: SPANISH/CATALAN. **Reservations:** Recommended in summer.

$ Prices: Appetizers 450–2,000 ptas. ($4.50–$20); main courses 800–2,700 ptas. ($8–$27). AE, DC, EURO, MC, V.

Open: Summer, Tues–Sun 1–3:30pm and 8–11:30pm. Winter, daily 1–4pm; Fri–Sat also 8–11:30pm. **Closed:** 4 weeks around Nov–Dec.

One of the best restaurants in town, Doña Margarita is located on the curved seaside promenade in Santa Eulàlia. The cuisine is traditional Spanish with some Catalan accents, such as esqueixada de bacalla. The extensive menu fluctuates greatly from day to day depending on the market offerings. Some staples among the meat dishes include entrecôte, roast lamb, and veal stew. The fish dishes are more market-sensitive. The outdoor terrace offers a splendid view of the bay.

4. AN EXCURSION TO FORMENTERA

Formentera is a convenient and fun one-day excursion. You can see the ocean from any point on the island. Some say the island has the best beaches in the Mediterranean—the opinion has much merit. Formentera has been declared a "World Treasure" by UNESCO, one of four places thus honored due to its special character as an ecological and wildlife preserve. This designation implies an indirect control by UNESCO of activities that could jeopardize the island's ecological well-being.

Meanwhile, day trippers from Ibiza have fun sampling its long, sedate beaches and solitary coves before returning to Ibiza's ebullience in the evening.

Historically, Formentera's political fate has been much the same as Ibiza's—subject to the same succession of conquering cultures. The southernmost of the Balearic Islands, Formentera has a total area of 30 square miles (82 square km), excluding the two interior lakes (Estany Pudent and d'es Peix). The island is flat except for the two plateaus, Es Cap de Barbaria and La Mola. Its population of approximately 5,000 triples in the summer. The island's scrub pines and dune beaches are reminiscent of parts of Long Island's Hamptons and sections of the New England coast, albeit with the important added attractions of milder temperatures and dazzling Mediterranean waters in varying shades of aquamarine.

When you arrive, visit the **tourist office kiosk** at the dock, which has maps and general information about the island.

GETTING THERE

BY HYDROFOIL **Flebasa Lines** offers frequent, daily hydrofoil service to Formentera in summer. The 20-minute round-trip journey costs 2,500 ptas. ($25) for adults and 1,250 ptas. ($12.50) for children 3 to 10 (children under 3 free). Ticket windows are located in the town's central marina at the northern end of Avenida Santa Eulàlia.

BY FERRY In summer, regular ferry service to Formentera is frequent (check daily listings in *La Prensa de Ibiza, Diario de Ibiza,* and *Ibiza Now*); round-trip fares for the one-hour trip run about 2,100 ptas. ($21) for adults and 1,050 ptas. ($10.50) for children 6 to 12 (children under 6 free).

GETTING AROUND

On Formentera, you can rent a car, various forms of two-wheeled motorized transport, or a bicycle at the port of La Sabina. Two-wheeled traffic is common on the island, and the trunk roads have separate bike lanes to accommodate it. I recommend getting your own wheels and sampling several beaches before settling in at the one that most appeals. When you arrive at La Sabina, all the vehicle-rental offices will be open: **Bicycles** rent for about 500 ptas. ($5) per day, **mobilettes** for about 1,500 ptas. ($15), and **motorbikes** for about 3,500 ptas. ($35).

You can also take a **taxi** to the beach of your choice; rates run from 1,000 ptas. ($10) to Es Pujols to 2,500 ptas. ($25) to the far end of Playa Mitjorn. If you do this, be sure to arrange a return pickup or call well in advance for a return taxi (tel. 32-00-52 in La Sabina or 32-00-16 in Es Pujols) because it may take 20 minutes until it gets to you. When you arrive at La Sabina, taxis will be waiting.

THE BEACHES

Along Platja de Mitjorn, which is several kilometers long, the current is stronger and things get dangerous faster than on the Es Calo side of the island, which is, however, more rocky. To help you find the beach that will suit you best, here is a quick survey of what's most accessible to the day tripper, beginning at the easternmost end of the island farthest from La Sabina.

If you follow the main trunk road down the island to the eastern end of **Platja de Mitjorn,** you will see signs for Club La Mola Hotel and Club Maryland that will eventually lead you to **Es Copinyar beach,** which is very pleasant and long and offers the services of several snack bars and restaurants. On the other side of this end of the island, which is very narrow at this point, is the beach near the town (just a few buildings, really) of **Es Caló.** As you head back toward La Sabina, it is on your right just beyond the "town" and indicated by a simple, faded wooden sign and a cement-block walkway leading down to the sea (watch for bikes and Vespas parked along the road). Although the beach is rocky, the cliffs in the background add drama, and there are numerous sandy areas where you can settle in with a good book. When you get hungry or thirsty, there's a small snack bar.

Heading again along the main trunk road toward La Sabina, you will see a sign for "Las Dunas Playa," which will lead you to the adjoining beaches of **Las Dunas** and **Els Arenals.** The road out is bumpy at best, but the mile-long beach with thatched umbrellas is worth the jostle. The water here remains shallow quite far out, with few rocks. There is also a restaurant for food and drink. The remaining, more westerly portions of Platja de Mitjorn are less appealing.

At **Cala d'es Pujols** you'll find one rock-rimmed cove next to a sandy cove lined with shops, bars, and other tourist amenities abutting the beach. This is much the same as what you'll find on some of Ibiza's more crowded beaches—there is really no need to come to Formentera for it.

By far Formentera's pièce de résistance beach-wise is the **Platja de Ses Illetas,** stretching along the slender northern tip of the island. As you leave La Sabina, take the "Pujols" turnoff to the left and continue straight, entering the dirt road when the paved road curves right toward **Es Pujols.** This road, which passes the salt flats, gets very bumpy but remains navigable at slow speeds until it terminates in a restaurant/bar (there are also several others along the way). The sea and sand are idyllic here, with beaches on either side of the slender finger of land trailing soft and white out into the Mediterranean. When the waters on one side are rough, they are calm on the other. All along you will see yachts moored out in the blue-green waters of the curving coves. In the annals of sea and sand, one couldn't ask for more.

WHERE TO STAY

If you wish to spend a night or two on Formentera, the **Insotel Group** has several hotels along Platja de Mitjorn in varying price ranges. For information and reservations, contact their central office at Carrer Aragón, 71, 07800 Ibiza Town (tel. 971/39-00-68; fax 971/30-13-51; telex 68867 VIPY E).

CHAPTER 13

MAÓ (MAHÓN)

A polite, provincial city, Maó (Mahón) is a curious hybrid of bay-windowed Georgian town houses and unpretentious Spanish structures sharing a warren of narrow streets. Unlike most other port cities in the world, Maó has no district of vice, no seamy side to balance its propriety.

It has been the capital of Minorca since the British saw the potential of its deepwater channel as a naval base during the War of the Spanish Succession (1702–14) and managed to have the island ceded to them under the Treaty of Utrecht in 1713. Although Spain regained possession in 1782, the Napoleonic threat in the Mediterranean gave rise to a new British base under the command of Admirals Nelson and Collingwood. While the British legacy has blended with the Spanish, it is still distinguishable, especially in such architectural features as the Georgian sash windows sometimes still referred to locally as *winderes*.

Situated atop the cliffs of a natural harbor on Minorca's southeastern shore, Maó is prettiest when viewed from the port. Its population is nearly 22,000, and it is the focal point of island commerce.

As the capital and the city closest to the airport, Maó is the center for most tourist services. But Ciutadella (Ciudadela), the long-ago capital, runs a close second in terms of tourist activity, and many of the entries in "Fast Facts: Maó" below mention both these cities, which flank the island like urban bookends.

1. ORIENTATION

GETTING THERE

BY PLANE **Aviaco** (tel. 26-02-72 in Palma, tel. 36-90-15 in Maó) offers direct flights from Palma and Barcelona.

BY FERRY There are also **ferries** from Palma, Barcelona, Ibiza, and Valencia that sail into Maó Port. The trip from Barcelona is about seven to eight hours aboard a moderately luxurious liner. For about the same cost as a chair in the lounge, you can purchase a bunk in a quad cabin (see Chapter 2 for prices).

Trasmediterránea, Estació Marítima, Maó Port (tel. 36-29-50), is open Monday to Friday from 8am to 1pm and 5 to 7pm, Saturday from 8:30am to noon, and Sunday from 3 to 4:30pm, but all ferry arrangements are just as easily made at any travel agency.

WHAT'S SPECIAL ABOUT MINORCA

Views
☐ The sweeping vista from Cap de Cavalleria on the northern end of the island.

Beaches
☐ The numerous secluded beaches around the island that require some effort to get to—often a four-wheel-drive vehicle or even a boat—but reward the effort with resounding tranquillity and sumptuous beauty.

Activities
☐ Chartering a boat and discovering beaches and coves inaccessible by road.

☐ Hiking both inland and along the coast.

Nightlife
☐ La Cova d'en Xoroi, a bar/disco installed in a series of cliffside caves in Cala En Porter.

☐ The ports of Maó and Ciutadella, where evening strolls are leisurely and diverting.

ARRIVING

The airport, 3 miles (5km) from Maó, has no money-exchange facilities and no bus service. To get anywhere by bus, you have to take a taxi into Maó and catch the buses that radiate from there throughout the island. There is no bus service from the port, either. Visitors must take a cab or walk up a rather steep hill into town.

TOURIST INFORMATION

The **tourist office** in Maó at Plaça de S'Esplanada, 40 (tel. 971/36-37-90), is open Monday to Friday from 9am to 2pm and from 5 to 7pm and on Saturday from 9:30am to 1pm; closed holidays. For airport information, call 36-01-50. The tourist information booth at the airport (tel. 36-01-50, ext. 1115) is open May to October daily from 8am to 2pm; closed the rest of the year. The Maó Town Council offers a toll-free information service at 900/30-05-84.

For information on flight and ferry schedules, consult the *Minorca Diario Insular*.

Some publications worth picking up are *12 Walks in Minorca* and *More Walks in Menorca* by Dodo Mackenzie (600 ptas. [$6] each) and the *Archaeological Guide to Minorca* by a trio of Spanish authors sponsored by the Consell Insular de Minorca (1,000 ptas. [$10]), available at most bookstores.

CITY LAYOUT

The **Plaça de la Constitución,** with its neoclassical Casa Consistorial, is the nucleus of Maó. Nearby in **Plaça Alfonso III** is a sculpture commemorating the king who took Minorca from the Moors in 1287. Also in this plaza is the notable Ca'n Mercadal, a Minorcan mansion of 1761 now housing the Biblioteca Pública.

The **port** is the city's northern boundary and is lined with restaurants and shops. From here, the **Costa de Ses Voltes** winds its way to **Plaça d'Espanya** at the edge of the town nucleus, composed of narrow, crisscrossing streets. Marking the other extreme of "center city" is the **Plaça de S'Esplanada,** where the tourist office is located.

Like Ibiza Town, Maó has no beach and is not a resort city but rather a center for shopping and nightlife. Nearby **Es Castell (Villacarlos),** a virtual continuation of the capital stretching east along the port, comes closer to being a resort, but it also has no beach. You'll find some of the island's more popular hotels there, however, and at Cales Fonts you'll find a very popular nightlife niche. **Cala Mesquida** and **Punta Prima** offer two fine beaches nearby.

GETTING AROUND

Taxis do not have meters here. Official lists posted at the airport and the port indicate fares to various points on the island; prices vary from other departure points. The fare from the airport to Maó is approximately 950 ptas. ($9.50), with supplementary charges levied on Sunday, holidays, at night, and for luggage. There are taxi stands in every town. For a radio taxi call 36-71-11 or ask at your hotel for local taxi service.

FAST FACTS: MAÓ

Most of the information you'll need for planning your trip to Maó can be found in previous chapters. The following information is specific to Maó and, in some cases, Ciutadella.

Business Hours Banks are open June through September Monday to Friday from 9am to 2pm; hours are extended to Saturday during the rest of the year. Shops are generally open Monday to Saturday from 10am to 1:30pm and 5 to 8pm. Restaurants, bars, and discos have very "flexible" hours that correspond to demand, so in the shoulder-season months (May, June, September, and October) hours may deviate substantially from those indicated in this book.

Consulates The British Vice Consular office is at Torret, 28, San Luís (tel. 36-64-39). The nearest U.S. Consulate is in Palma de Majorca (see "Fast Facts: Palma de Majorca" in Chapter 9).

Currency Exchange You can exchange money at most banks during normal banking hours, but travel agencies, car-rental companies, and many stores and hotels will also change money for you after hours or on weekends.

Electricity Maó uses primarily 220 volts, but some 125-volt outlets are still to be found.

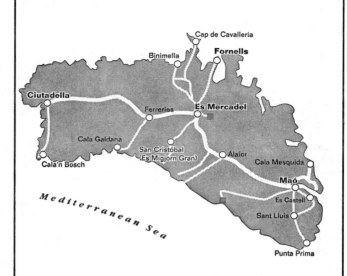

MAÓ (MAHÓN)/MINORCA

MINORCA

Cap de Cavalleria

Binimella

Fornells

Ciutadella

Ferreries

Es Mercadel

Cala Galdana

San Cristóbal
(Es Migjorn Gran)

Alaíor

Cala'n Bosch

Cala Mesquida

Maó

Es Castell

Mediterranean Sea

Sant Lluis

Punta Prima

MAÓ (MAHÓN)

Port de Maó

C. Fornels

Av. Dr. García

Muelle Comercial

Pl. de la Constitución

Pl. Miranda

C. Sant Sebastian

C. Madrid

Av. Fort de l'Eau

Pl. Espanya

C. Verge del Carme

C. Ciutadella

Conde de Cifuentes

Pl. Reial

Camins Castell

Costa de la Figuera

Josep María Quadrado

Parque El Freginal

Es Castell

Pl. de S'Esplanada

Av. Joseph Anselem

Cos de Gracia

Verge de Gracia

C. de la Infanta

Av. Minorca

C. Dr. Camis

Emergencies For hospital attention or an ambulance, call 36-35-00, 36-12-21, or 36-11-80 in Maó; 36-06-87 or 38-19-93 in Ciutadella. The Red Cross numbers in the two cities are 36-11-80 and 38-19-93, respectively. The police in Maó can be reached at 091; in Ciutadella at 38-10-95. In the event of fire, call 36-39-61 in Maó or 38-07-87 in Ciutadella.

Holidays Besides the nationwide holidays (see "When to Go" in Chapter 2), the following fiestas honoring local patron saints are observed throughout the island: On September 7, 8, and 9 Maó stages horse processions in the streets; on June 16, 23, and 24 much the same occurs in Ciutadella; August 11 and 12 in Alaior; July 24 and 25 in Es Castell (Villacarlos); August 23 and 24 in Ferreries; July 15 and 16 in Es Mercadal; August 25 and 26 in Sant Lluís; and July 8, 9, and 10 in Es Migjorn Gran.

Language See "Fast Facts: Barcelona" in Chapter 3. "Menorca" is the prevailing, Spanish spelling of the island's name. The local dialect of Catalan is Menorquín. Signs and maps can be confusing because some are in Spanish, some in Menorquín, and some in a linguistic mix of both.

Newspapers The local Spanish- and Catalan-language daily is *Minorca Diario Insular*. A monthly English-language magazine called *Roqueta* provides information on what's happening on the island. Also available locally is the English-language *Majorca Daily Bulletin*. As in Ibiza and Majorca, foreign papers are readily available.

Pharmacies For the daily listing of pharmacies open around the clock, consult the *Minorca Diario Insular*.

Post Office The post office in Maó is at Bon Aire, 15 (tel. 36-38-92); open Monday to Friday from 9am to 9pm and on Saturday from 9am to 2pm; closed holidays. In Ciutadella the post office is at Plaça des Born, 9 (tel. 38-00-81); hours are Monday to Friday from 9am to 2pm and Saturday from 9am to 1pm; closed holidays. Both offer telegram, fax, and telex services. Most upscale hotels also offer telex and fax services.

Safety Whenever you're traveling in an unfamiliar city or area, stay alert. Be aware of your immediate surroundings. Wear a moneybelt and keep a close eye on your possessions. Be particularly careful with cameras, purses, and wallets, all favorite targets of thieves and pickpockets. All in all, though, Menorca remains largely crime-free.

Telephone There are telephone booths all over the island. Many bars also have telephones available for public use with meters indicating the number of units for which you must pay. Local calls require a minimum of three 5-pta. coins.

In Maó you can make international calls at the Locutorio de Telefónica at the northeastern edge of Plaça de S'Esplanada daily from 10am to 1pm and from 5 to 9pm; in Ciutadella, at the Locutorio de Telefónica at the southern end of Plaça dels Pins daily from 10am to 1pm and from 5:30 to 9:30pm.

Television/Radio Several national Spanish-language TV stations and several regional Catalan-language stations broadcast to the island year round. In summer TV3 broadcasts the news in English, French, German, Italian, and Dutch.

2. ACCOMMODATIONS

In July and August hotel space is at a premium, so book well in advance. The hotel offerings in town range from pensions to the four-star Port Mahón. There are no luxury hotels to compare with the upper-echelon accommodations of Ibiza and Majorca, however, as Minorca is the sleeper of the Balearic Islands in tourist terms and caters primarily to package-tour travelers from Britain and Germany.

The posted rates at most lodgings are the official maximums the places can charge. Often you can negotiate at least a 10% discount—sometimes more in the off-season. For the purposes of this guide, "expensive" hotels charge 11,000 ptas. ($110) and up for a double room; "moderate" hotels, 5,000 to 11,500 ptas. ($59 to $115); and "budget" lodgings less than 5,000 ptas. ($50).

Note: Unless otherwise indicated, all accommodations have private bath or shower, all hotels are open year round, and all rates given include service charge but *not* IVA.

EXPENSIVE

HOTEL PORT-MAHÓN, Avenida Fort de L'Eau, 13, 07701 Maó, Minorca. Tel. 971/36-26-00. Fax 971/35-10-50. 74 rms. A/C MINIBAR TV TEL
$ Rates (including IVA): 9,700–12,000 ptas. ($97–$120) single; 15,000–20,000 ptas. ($150–$200) double; 22,700–30,000 ptas. ($227–$300) suite. AE, DC, EURO, MC, V. **Parking:** Nearby.
Perched on a cliff above the port, the Port-Mahón represents a bit of Old World elegance surrounded by well-maintained gardens and charmingly captivating public spaces. Built in the 1950s, this grand dame of Minorca hotels has a colonial English mien steeped in Spanish graciousness. All the guest rooms have been newly redone, but they are somewhat small; some have terraces and sea views. The restaurant has a lovely view of the port, and there is a very inviting piano bar. The hotel also has a swimming pool and offers room service and turndown service.

HOTEL RESIDENCIA CAPRI, Sant Esteve, 8, 07703 Maó, Minorca. Tel. 971/36-14-00. Fax 971/35-08-53. 75 rms. A/C MINIBAR TV TEL
$ Rates: 8,200 ptas. ($82) single; 11,000 ptas. ($110) double; 15,000 ptas. ($150) triple; 18,000 ptas. ($180) quad. AE, DC, EURO, MC, V. **Parking:** Nearby.
Located in the center of Maó, the Capri is a Best Western affiliate that has recently been renovated throughout and offers some nice amenities, such as real hairdryers in the guest rooms. As it is geared more to businesspeople than tourists, it offers no pool but includes such extras as room service until midnight, turndown service, and babysitting upon request.

MODERATE

HOSTAL BINIALI, Ctra. S'Uestrà, Binibeca, 50, 07710 Sant Lluís, Minorca. Tel. 971/15-17-24. Fax 971/15-03-52. 9 rms. TEL

$ **Rates:** 8,500–10,000 ptas. ($85–$100) single; 9,700–12,000 ptas. ($97–$120) double. AE, DC, EURO, MC, V. **Parking:** On premises. **Closed:** Nov–Apr.

Located just outside Sant Lluís along the road to Binibeca (a flurry of flags signals the entrance about 0.6 mile [1km] along the road on the left when coming from Sant Lluís), this tranquil, elegantly rustic inn occupies a converted 18th-century farmhouse. Each of its very charming guest rooms has a sizable terrace and features—as do the public rooms of the inn—Minorcan antiques. The inviting baths feature lovely tile-work. The restaurant serves meals outdoors on a shaded terrace or indoors in a cozy dining room. The pool is in a lovely garden setting. All in all, this is a retreat offering lots of peace, comfort, and quaintness within easy reach of Binibeca beach and the facilities and activities of Maó.

HOTEL AGAMENON, Paraje Fontanillas, 18, 07720 Es Castell (Villacarlos), Minorca. Tel. 971/36-21-50. Fax 971/36-21-54. 75 rms and suites. TEL

$ **Rates:** 4,700–6,500 ptas. ($47–$65) single; 6,000–9,000 ptas. ($60–$90) double; 8,500–11,000 ptas. ($85–$110) suite. AE, DC, EURO, MC, V. **Parking:** Available. **Closed:** Nov–Apr.

Go beyond the Almirante (see below) along the Maó–Es Castell (Villacarlos) road and take the first turn off to Es Castell (Villacarlos) and then bear left to reach this gleaming white, five-story structure in a quiet setting. All the Agamenon's sizable guest rooms are pleasant and have terraces overlooking the sea. The hotel has a pool, a restaurant, and a bar with terrific views of the port.

HOTEL DEL ALMIRANTE (also known as the Collingwood House), Carretera de Es Castell (Villacarlos), along the road from Maó to Es Castell, 07700 Maó, Minorca. Tel. 971/36-27-00. Fax 971/36-27-04. 40 rms (20 with bath, 20 with shower).

$ **Rates** (including breakfast): 3,500–5,000 ptas. ($35–$50) single with shower; 5,300–8,000 ptas. ($53–$80) double with shower, 5,500–8,200 ptas. ($55–$82) double with bath. No credit cards. **Parking:** Available. **Closed:** Nov–Apr.

A decidedly English ambiance prevails at this small, cozy inn whose main building is the former residence of Lord Collingwood, who was chief admiral of the British Mediterranean Squadron and close friend of Admiral Nelson. It dates from the early 18th century and combines an English Georgian style with Minorcan accents of the period. At various times it has served as a convent, the home of a German sculptor, and the German embassy.

Since 1964, it has been a hotel with 30 "bungalow" rooms of recent vintage complementing the older rooms in the house proper, which contains an assortment of antiques, memorabilia from the British Empire, and the occasional tasteless modern furnishing. Upstairs is an eccentric parlor with an old upright piano. Rooms 7, 8, and 9 in the old house have some antique furnishings and the finest views, but all the guest rooms are immaculate and well kept. Guests can enjoy the swimming pool and bar.

HOTEL REY CARLOS III, Cala Corp, 07720 Es Castell **(Villacarlos),** Minorca. Tel. **971/36-31-00.** Fax 971/36-31-05. 87 rms. TEL

$ **Rates** (including IVA): 5,000–6,000 ptas. ($50–$60) single; 6,700–9,000 ptas. ($67–$90) double. MC, V. **Parking:** Available. **Closed:** Nov–Apr.

⭐ Just a few blocks from the Agamenon (see above), the Rey Carlos greets you with old-fashioned charm. All the spacious guest rooms, spread across three floors, are doubles with sea views from their terraces. The decor varies from room to room, but each is clean and pleasant. All the first-floor rooms have new baths; the remaining rooms will soon follow suit. The facilities include a pool and a restaurant. Overall, this is a very good choice in a great setting.

BUDGET

RESIDENCIA JUME, Concepción, 6, 07701 Maó, Minorca. Tel. **971/36-32-66.** Fax 971/35-48-34. 35 rms.

$ **Rates:** 1,600–1,800 ptas. ($16–$18) single; 3,200–3,500 ptas. ($32–$35) double; 1,100–1,700 ptas. ($11–$17) additional per bed in triple and quad. No credit cards. **Parking:** Nearby. **Closed:** Dec 15–Jan 7.

💲 This very clean, comfortable, and commendable in-town option has spacious, cheerful guest rooms; a TV sitting room by the reception area; and a cafeteria.

3. DINING

The majority of the capital's restaurants are gathered around the port and serve lovely maritime vistas with their meals.

The most popular Minorcan dishes are the *calderetas,* rich soup/casseroles of fish, shellfish, or the local spiny lobster. Although common to all the Balearic Islands, the calderetas of Minorca enjoy a special cachet. King Juan Carlos of Spain is reported to have a special fondness for them and often sojourns to Fornells to indulge.

Minorca's *escopinyes* ("venus" clams) also are touted, along with the whole range of its Mediterranean fish and shellfish, which nowadays command high prices. More typical and economical local fare are *oliagua* (tomato-based vegetable soup), baked eggplant, partridge-and-cabbage casserole, and *formatjades* (pastry turnovers) with various fillings.

Traditional Minorcan cured sausages include the spreadable *sobrasada, camot* (large black sausage), and *carnixua* (coarsely cut salami-type sausage). Another local specialty is Maó cheese.

As with all the Balearic Islands, meals in Minorca are generally not cheap because almost everything must be flown in. And even the local fish is quite expensive. All the better restaurants are more or less on a par when it comes to price, with entrees costing from 1,000 ptas.

($10) to 8,000 ptas. ($80) for *langosta* (lobster). At moderate restaurants, entrees run from 700 to 3,000 ptas. ($7 to $30). Since generally speaking the price differential among the island's restaurants is minimal, it makes sense to eat judiciously in the island's better restaurants than to try to save money in the "less expensive" places that offer little imagination and low quality. Eating cheaply means grabbing a sandwich, tapas, or snack at a bar or pub or some pizza or pasta at one of the numerous pizzerias. As with the hotels, service is usually included in the prices, but IVA is *not*. Many restaurants offer economical three-course luncheon menus de día, including bread and house wine. At cafeterias, tapas bars, and other informal eating establishments, it often costs less to eat at the bar than at a table.

Most of the island's classiest and priciest restaurants are in Maó and Fornells, along with one or two first-class offerings in Ciutadella.

For trivia buffs, here's an interesting culinary footnote: Mayonnaise (*mahonesa* in Spanish) was supposedly invented in Maó (Mahón).

EXPENSIVE

GREGAL RESTAURANT BAR, Mártires del Atlante (also called Anden de Levante), 43. Tel. 36-66-06.

Cuisine: SEAFOOD/INTERNATIONAL. **Reservations:** Not required.

$ Prices: Appetizers 650–1,750 ptas. ($6.50–$17.50); main courses 925–5,700 ptas. ($9.25–$57). AE, DC, EURO, MC, V.

Open: Lunch, daily 1–3:30pm. Dinner, daily 8–11:30pm.

This small, pleasant restaurant with a beamed ceiling and checkered tablecloths specializes in seafood. Some of the day's wares are on display for the choosing. Gregal also serves meat and fowl dishes in a Spanish, Catalan, French, and international vein, along with a sprinkling of Greek dishes including dolmades, taramosalata, and moussaka.

JAGARO RESTAURANT, Moll de Llevant, Port de Maó. Tel. 36-46-60 or 36-23-90.

Cuisine: ECLECTIC. **Reservations:** Recommended; reserve the day before in July–Aug.

$ Prices: Appetizers 700–1,800 ptas. ($7–$18); main courses 1,100–7,000 ptas. ($11–$70); menus del día from 2,100–5,300 ptas. ($21–$53). AE, DC, EURO, MC, V.

Open: Sept–June, lunch daily 1–4pm; dinner daily 8pm–midnight. July–Aug, daily 1pm–midnight.

Jagaro's offers dining in an atrium setting or amidst an elegant array of wood and greenery.

The menu, Minorca's most varied and interesting, includes many unusual house specialties. Among them are carparcho de mero (grouper) with a green-mustard sauce; ensalada templada con cigalitos y setas (a bed of lettuce topped with warm prawns and wild mushrooms); red pepper stuffed with cuttlefish; a unique variation of gazpacho containing melon and shrimp; *mosaico de verduras* (a plate of grilled fresh vegetables); Iranian caviar; goose liver; and a long list of seafood dishes including caldereta de langosta, ortigas (sea anemones), and caldereta de marisco y pescado. Fish here is primarily prepared one of two ways—al horno (baked) or al espalda (baked first with wine, then topped with a wine-and-garlic sauce).

The meat offering in summer includes duck magret in an orange sauce, confit of duck, and small "hamburgers" of magret and foie gras served with a sweet-and-sour sauce. All the desserts are homemade, including the honey and almond ice creams and sorbets. The wine list is mostly Spanish and offers reds dating from 1935. And as if all this weren't enough, the service is impeccable and the red wines are decanted. For 9 years now owner Jaime Garriga has been offering a very sybaritic dining experience for those with a gourmet palate and budget.

RESTAURANTE ROCAMAR, Cala Fonduco, 32. Tel. 36-56-01.

Cuisine: SPANISH/MINORCAN. **Reservations:** Recommended.

$ Prices: Appetizers 750–1,500 ptas. ($7.50–$15); main courses 1,100–3,500 ptas. ($11–$35); menu del día 2,200 ptas. ($22); children's menu with entrees under 1,500 ptas. ($15). EURO, MC, V.

Open: Lunch daily 1–3:30pm; dinner daily 8:30–11pm. **Closed:** Nov and Mon in winter.

Located at the western end of the port, Rocamar is deemed the island's best restaurant by most locals; a Michelin recommendation seconds that notion. Situated on the first (to Americans, second) floor of the Hostal Rocamar, the restaurant boasts a classically elegant decor with lots of wood.

The menu stresses seafood. Top choices are caldereta de langosta (lobster), fish stew with thyme sauce, and salmon with green-pepper sauce. Meat entrees include lamb, rabbit, and magret. Live music accompanies evening meals on Monday, Tuesday, Wednesday, Friday, and Saturday.

MODERATE

BAR RESTAURANTE ESPAÑA, Carrer Victori, 48–50, Es Castell (Villacarlos). Tel. 36-32-99.

Cuisine: SPANISH. **Reservations:** Not required.

$ Prices: Appetizers 350–1,200 ptas. ($3.50–$12); main courses 500–1,900 ptas. ($5–$19); menu del día 800–900 ptas. ($8–$9). EURO, MC, V.

Open: Lunch daily 1–4pm; dinner daily 7:30–11:30pm. **Closed:** End of Dec to Feb.

Established more than 45 years ago, the Bar Restaurante España is likely the oldest ongoing restaurant on the island. No doubt it owes its continued success to consistently offering good value for the money. A specialty of the house among the fresh fish featured on the menu is *cigalas à la americana* (prawns in a spicy sauce). A high percentage of the clientele is foreign, and owners Lorenzo Porcel and his wife, Magdalena, keep a close watch on things to ensure customer satisfaction.

PILAR RESTAURANT, Forn, 61. Tel. 36-68-17.

Cuisine: MINORCAN. **Reservations:** Required in Aug.

$ Prices: Appetizers 750–1,600 ptas. ($7.50–$16); main courses 1,500–2,000 ptas. ($15–$20); menu del día 2,100 ptas. ($21). AE, EURO, MC, V.

Open: Apr–Nov, lunch Mon–Sat 1:30–3:30pm; dinner Mon–Sat 8–11pm. Dec–Mar, lunch Mon–Sat 1:30–3:30pm.

At this small, stylish restaurant in the center of Maó, you'll feel you're dining in somebody's home. Even the small kitchen where owner-chef Pilar Pons works her culinary wonders looks more like a domestic kitchen than a restaurant kitchen. There are about half a dozen tables indoors and another half a dozen spread around the rear patio in summer. A smattering of antique furnishings and impressionistic artwork contribute to the coziness.

The menu is understandably limited, but that does not apply to the quality and care taken in preparation. The market-fresh cuisine is largely menorquín with innovative variations. Try the berenjenas rellenas (stuffed eggplant) and conejo à la menorquina (rabbit in an onion-and-thyme sauce), *calamares rellenos* (stuffed squid), and *cap roig* (scorpion fish). For dessert, try the *pastel de nueces con chocolate* (walnut cake with chocolate).

BUDGET

AMERICAN BAR, Plaça Reial, 8. Tel. 36-18-22.
   Cuisine: SPANISH/INTERNATIONAL. **Reservations:** Not required.
$ Prices: Appetizers 350–900 ptas. ($3.50–$9); main courses 650–1,300 ptas. ($6.50–$13); menu del día 900 ptas. ($9). No credit cards.
   Open: Winter, Mon–Sat 6:30am–10pm. Summer, Mon–Sat 6:30am–11pm.

The American Bar is as close as Maó comes to a diner. Located in the heart of the central shopping district, it offers a square meal in a no-nonsense indoor or outdoor setting. The down-home Spanish menu is sprinkled with such international footnotes as lasagna, spaghetti, and hot dogs. It also serves snacks and ice cream.

LA TROPICAL, Carrer Lluna, 36. Tel. 36-05-56.
   Cuisine: SPANISH/MINORCAN. **Reservations:** Not required.
$ Prices: Appetizers 175–900 ptas. ($1.75–$9); main courses 500–2,200 ptas. ($5–$22); pizzas 700–1,000 ptas. ($7–$10); menu del día 1,300 ptas. ($13). MC, V.
   Open: Daily 8am–midnight.
La Tropical is a three-in-one eatery. You can have snacks at the bar, platos combinados in the informal dining room, or full-fledged restaurant fare in the more formal dining area. The restaurant offers a good selection of Minorcan specialties, including a reasonably priced fish-and-shellfish caldereta. There is also a daily market menu and an assorted selection of Spanish and international dishes. You can order snacks at the bar.

4. WHAT TO SEE & DO

There is really little need to spend much time in Maó, except perhaps to shop in the center of town or spend your evenings in the restaurants and bars along the port. The **Cathedral of Santa María,** however, does have an unusual organ whose inner workings, built in Barcelona, are the work of Swiss artisan Johan Kyburz; its outer cabinetry and sculpture are the work of Maó artists. Inaugurated in 1810, it consists of 4 keyboards and 3,210 pipes, 215 of them wooden and the rest metal. In summer, special daily half-hour concerts are held at 11am to show off its special musical charms. Admission is 250 ptas. ($2.50). At other times there is no charge for visiting the church and organ (the cathedral is open daily from 8am to 6pm).

Just off the Plaça de S'Esplanada on Carrer Conde de Cifuentes is the **Ateneo Científico, Literario y Artístico,** essentially a retired men's club but with a small, offbeat museum boasting "the most comprehensive collection of dried seaweeds in southern Europe." The museum is open Monday through Saturday from 10am to 1pm and 4 to 6pm.

Off the Maó–Es Castell (Villacarlos) road is a marked turnoff for the *taula* and *talayot* of Trepucó. The taula (see the section on archeological highlights under "Ciutadella & the West" in Chapter 14) one of the island's largest, probably dates from the middle of the millennium before Christ.

From Cales Fonts in Es Castell (Villacarlos) there are **boat excursions** around Maó Harbor and to surrounding bays leaving daily in summer between 2:30 and 3pm; the cost is 1,000 ptas. ($10) for adults, half price for children. From the ports of Maó and Ciutadella, **Lineas de La Cruz** offer several daily boat excursions to secluded beaches and coves as well as glass-bottom-boat outings. For bookings in Maó contact the Aquarium (tel. 35-05-37); in Ciutadella, contact the shop Es Pont (tel. 38-63-98).

Both motorboats and sail boats can be chartered with or without a crew and with or without waterskiing equipment for a minimum of one day at 215, S.A., Andén de Levant, 215, Port de Maó (tel. 35-00-13; fax 36-50-95); rates range from 6,000 ptas. ($60) per day for a Zodiac 3.50 to over 100,000 ptas. ($1,000) for a Rinker Fiesta Vee 260. Discounts are offered on charters of more than three days. In May, June, and September, the company offers an excursion (with crew) for four that circles the island at a cost of about 20,000 ptas. ($200) per person.

Menorca Aquasport Charter, S.L., Moll de Llevant, 300, Port de Maó (tel./fax 36-97-46), offers half-day, full-day, and extended rentals of all manner of boats and yachts with or without crew. Rates begin at 6,000 ptas. ($60) for a half-day rental of a sailing dinghy to over 120,000 ptas. ($1,200) for a full-day rental of a power cruiser without skipper.

Maó itself and the adjacent Es Castell (Villacarlos) have no beaches. Some fine sandy property is not far away, however, both to the north and to the south.

North of Maó is **Cala Mesquida,** one of the best beaches on the island. After turning off the road toward Cala Llonga, follow the "Platja" or "Playa" signs through the sleepy fishing village and continue along the dirt track to this beautiful long beach flanked by rocky bluffs, one of which is topped with the ruins of a tower. There are no snack stands or restaurants here, but there are some in the village. Also north of the capital en route to Sant Antoni is **Golden Farm** the Georgian mansion where Admiral Lord Nelson and Lady Hamilton allegedly cohabited.

South of Maó is Sant Lluís, a small town of whitewashed two-story buildings. **Punta Prima,** a large, sandy beach known to have some rigorous surf, is below Sant Lluís to the east. A full complement of bars and eateries caters to bathers nearby. Another attractive beach in this area is at **Cala de Binibeca.** The sand is lovely, white, and fine here, and there is a very inviting thatch-roofed bar/restaurant terraced across the rocks.

At kilometer-stone 4 of the Maó-Ciutadella road, a marked turnoff to the left leads to the **Talatí de Dalt.** From the small parking indentation, some rudimentary steps in the stone wall facilitate your climbing over it so you can follow a rudimentary path to the taula, hypostylic chambers, and subterranean caves of this prehistoric village. Most noteworthy is the taula with a pilaster leaning on the capital stone. As it's not there for support, one can surmise that it was a vertical stone that broke loose and toppled into its present position.

5. SAVVY SHOPPING

Maó offers the most extensive and most sophisticated shopping on the island. The primary shopping streets that wind their way through the heart of town are Sa Ravaleta (with a series of open-air terraces in the middle), Carrer Nou, Carrer Hanover (also called Costa de Sa Plaça), and Carrer del Dr. Orfila (also called Carrer de Ses Moreres).

Between Ferreries and Ciutadella along the Maó-Ciutadella highway are large factory outlets offering leather goods, Majorica pearls, and Lladró porcelain.

LOOKY BOUTIQUE, Carrer de Ses Moreres, 43. Tel. 36-06-48.
Here you'll find some of the island's most stylish and sophisticated leather goods manufactured in its factory in Ciutadella. The offering includes shoes, handbags, leather clothing for men and women, and luggage. Open on Monday to Friday from 10am to 1:30pm and from 5 to 8pm and on Saturday from 10am to 1:30pm.

There is also a shop in Ciutadella at José María Quadradro 14 (tel. 38-19-32) and another in Fornells at Paseo Marítimo 23 (tel. 37-65-45).

PATRICIA, Carrer de Ses Moreres, 31. Tel. 36-91-78.
Patricia also offers leather goods of its own local fabrication, featuring stylish coats, jackets, and suede skirts and suits. Open on Monday to Friday from 9:30am to 1:30pm and from 5 to 8pm and on Saturday from 9:30am to 1:30pm.

Shops can also be found in Ciutadella at Camino Santandria/Ronda Baleares (tel. 38-50-56) and at Fornells, Carrer Poeta Gumersindo Riera 1 (tel. 37-65-73).

ES PORTAL, Sa Ravaleta, 23. Tel. 36-30-36.
This shop features designer fashions for both men and women, including creations by Adolfo Domínguez, Sybilla, Moschino, Victorio & Lucchino, Armani jeans, and Jr. Gaultier. If you've been to Ibiza, you'll recognize the fashions of designer Armin Heinemann of Paula's in Ibiza Town. Es Portal also carries unique accessories and shoes. Summer hours are Monday to Friday from 10am to 1:30pm and from 5:30 to 9pm and Saturday from 10am to 1:30pm; winter hours are Monday to Friday from 10am to 1:30pm and from 5 to 8:30pm and Saturday from 10am to 1:30pm.

TOLEDO, Carrer Nou, 17. Tel. 36-57-84.

Toledo sells primarily Lladró and Majórica pearls along with crystal, silver, and assorted gift items. Open on Monday to Friday from 9:30am to 1:30pm and from 5 to 8pm and on Saturday from 9am to 2pm.

---

6. EVENING ENTERTAINMENT

The nightlife offering in the port of Maó stretches piecemeal along the port. The tone is more upscale and subdued than that in Ciutadella (see Chapter 14). The principal diversion of an evening is conversation with friends over a few drinks, accompanied by a little music, at an outdoor terrace or at a bar.

For dancing, there are several discos in town and in the neighboring developments (ask around for the newest and trendiest). One curious spot at the eastern extremity of the port is the **Aquarium Pub,** Andén de Ponente, 73 (tel. 35-05-37), with aquariums lining the walls, a billiard room, and loud music. It claims to be open daily from 9am to 8pm, but in truth it seems to open and close on a whim.

One of the most pleasant places to spend an evening is at **Cales Fonts** in nearby Es Castell (Villacarlos) (take the last exit for Es Castell). This snug little cove is rimmed with diminutive whitewashed houses that from May to October blossom with boutiques, assorted eateries, and informal entertainment. At least a dozen open-air restaurants and several snack bars are strung along the Cales Fonts waterfront, so just stroll along, look at the menus and plates of food on the tables, and choose what looks best. Most of these establishments offer a mixture of Spanish and international cuisine and, of course, stress seafood.

Two places that deliciously deviate from the mainstream here are the **Restaurante Pizzería La Caprichosa,** Muelle Cales Fonts, 44 (tel. 36-61-58), at the far end of the cove, and **Groucho Crêperie,** Cales Fonts (no phone), at the near end. The former has grilled fish and meat dishes ranging from 700 to 1,400 ptas. ($7 to $14), basic pasta dishes for under 900 ptas. ($9), and outstanding pizzas from 600 to 975 ptas. ($6–$9.75). It's open May through October daily from 1 to 3:15pm and from 7pm to past midnight; closed Sunday at lunch. At Groucho Creperie, the crêpes come savory, sweet, flambéed, or with ice cream, each for under 600 ptas. ($6). It's open March 15 to October 15 daily from 6pm to 3am.

AROUND MINORCA

Maó and Ciutadella are the urban cornerstones of Minorca. The former, the current capital, is more British of aspect and subdued of demeanor. The latter, the former capital, is more earthy and flamboyantly Spanish. In tandem they represent the two cultural faces of the island.

Physically speaking, Minorca is 34 miles (55km) long and an average of 10 miles (16km) wide. It is the second largest of the Balearic archipelago and the one farthest from the Spanish mainland. Of the Balearic Islands, Minorca has best preserved its natural habitat. Much of its 175-mile (282km) coastline remains undeveloped and, in some cases, accessible only by all-terrain vehicle, by boat, or on foot. Those who make the effort are amply rewarded with virgin vistas of crystal-clear water and shimmering white sand.

Beyond that, much of Minorca's enchantment lies in a landscape that variously echoes the English countryside, the highlands of Scotland, and the rocky, arid terrain of certain parts of Spain's Andalucía region. From the pinnacle of its most dazzling and dramatic scenic beauty at Cap de Cavalleria in the north, the island's terrain tapers off to the softer, gentler landscapes of the south that, in certain lights, take on overtones of Thomas Hardy's ominous moors.

All across the island are dry-stone walls that recall the Arab presence and the agricultural strength of the island in the days before tourism. Once they sheltered field after field of staple crops from the *tramontana* (a vicious north wind); now only a handful of them keep watch over a few meager acres of rape and corn.

Tourism is the economic beacon of tomorrow, and in one or two places around the island it's already beginning to shine rather too brightly. Fortunately, the island seems to have taken note of the sins of rampant exploitation committed against parts of Majorca and Ibiza and is attempting to steer a more rational and far-sighted course into its touristic future.

GETTING AROUND

BY ORGANIZED TOUR   Several bus and boat tours are offered from May to October. For full information, contact **Ultramar Express,** Vassalo, 31, Maó (tel. 36-16-16); open Monday to Friday from 9am to 1pm and from 4 to 7:30pm and on Saturday from 9am to 1pm.

BY BUS   Transportes Minorca, S.A., José María Quadrado, 7, Maó (tel. 36-03-61), and Carrer Barcelona 8, Ciutadella (tel. 38-03-93), operates buses servicing the island and departing Maó from either the Plaça de S'Esplanada or in front of the station itself near this plaza and departing Ciutadella from the Plaça de S'Esplanada (Plaça Colón) near the central Plaça d'es Born. The Maó station opens half an hour before departure times because some routes require advance purchase of tickets (check which these are). Otherwise, tickets are sold on board the buses leaving from the plazas. The schedules are highly volatile, so pick up the latest one at the tourist office or the station itself or check the listings in *Roqueta*. One-way fares range from 90 to 400 ptas. (90¢ to $4).

BY CAR Since most of the island's better beaches are off the major public transportation routes and the island's major arteries, renting a car will greatly enrich your stay. You can also rent a motorbike or bicycle, but some of the remote roads can get rather bumpy. Real explorers will want to rent an all-terrain vehicle. There are several rental-car agencies at the airport that also have offices in Maó and at various points around the island:

Atesa: At the airport only (tel. 36-62-13), open daily from 8am until the last flight of the night.

Avis: At the airport (tel. 36-15-76), open May to October daily from 7:30am to 10:30pm, the rest of the year daily from 8am to 9pm; Plaça de S'Esplanada, 53, Maó (tel. 36-47-78), open in summer only, daily from 9am to 1pm and 4:30 to 7pm.

BC Betacar/Europcar: At the airport (tel. 36-64-00), open in summer daily from 8am to 11pm and in winter daily from 8am to 9:30pm; Plaça de S'Esplanada, 8, Maó (tel. 36-06-20), open Monday to Saturday from 8am to 1pm and from 4 to 8pm and on Sunday from 9am to 1pm and from 5 to 7pm.

At presstime, base rates began at about 4,500 ptas. ($45) per day, but special rates apply for rentals of more than one week and special promotional rates are available from time to time, so shop around.

There are only about half a dozen gas stations scattered around the island, so try to keep the tank topped off. Only one station in Maó and (sometimes) one in Ciutadella are open after 9pm, and only selected ones are open on a rotating basis on weekends and holidays.

1. CIUTADELLA & THE WEST

Located at the western end of the island, Ciutadella has a typically Mediterranean air about it. Lining the narrow streets of the old city are noble mansions of the 17th and 18th centuries and numerous churches. It was the capital until 1722, when the British chose Maó instead, largely because its harbor channel is eminently more navigable than the one at Ciutadella. Subsequently, the British built the main island road to link the two cities.

Like Maó, Ciutadella perches high above its harbor, which is smaller than Maó's. The seat of Minorca's bishopric, Ciutadella pontificates while Maó administrates. Its population is 19,000— again, just a few thousand less than Maó's head count.

Known as "Medina Minurka" under the Muslims, Ciutadella retains some Moorish traces despite the 1558 Turkish invasion and destruction of the city. An obelisk in memory of the city's futile defense against that invasion stands in the pigeon-filled Plaça d'es Born (Plaza del Born), the city's main square overlooking the port.

The **tourist office** (tel. 38-10-50), housed in a mobile unit parked in the Plaça d'es Born, is open May to October daily from 9am to 1:30pm. In the afternoon from 5 to 9pm it stations itself in the various tourist developments around Ciutadella on a rotating basis.

You can **change money** and **rent a car** at Friend's Cars, Plaça d'es Born, 27 (tel. 38-60-67); open Monday to Friday from 9am to 2pm and from 5 to 9pm, on Saturday from 9am to 2pm; in July to September it's also open on Sunday from 11am to 1pm.

GETTING THERE & GETTING AROUND

Ferry service runs between Majorca and Ciutadella. See any travel agency for information.

All along Plaça de S'Esplanada (Plaça Colón) at the edge of Plaça d'es Born are **bus stops** serving various parts of the island. Destinations and departures are clearly marked, and there is a ticket kiosk in the square.

WHAT TO SEE & DO

Ciutadella's municipal center of gravity is the **Plaça d'es Born,** which contains two magnificent palaces (the Conde de Torresaura and Casa Salort, now a theater), the Real Alcázar (now the Town Hall), and the San Francisco Church. In the center of the square stands an obelisk commemorating the heroic but ineffectual defense of this former capital against the Turkish invasion in 1558.

Leading off this square is Carrer Mayor, where on the right you'll find the **Palacio Salort,** privately owned but uninhabited and open to the public July to October Monday to Saturday from 10am to 2pm; admission is 200 ptas. ($2). Part of this palace dates from the 16th century and the rest from the 19th. The facade is neoclassical, but the arcades facing the Plaça d'es Born are in a Renaissance style. On the ceiling of the main entrance you can see the coats of arms of the Salort and Martorell families, the latter having enlarged the house to its current size in 1813. Of particular note in this two-story structure are the French tapestries, English chairs, and Louis XV– and Louis XVI–style console tables. Downstairs are a patio garden and a garage with a vintage 1920s Buick on display, the second car to come to Ciutadella.

Farther along this same street is the **cathedral,** which was built in a Gothic style atop a former mosque upon the orders of King Alfonso III of Aragón some 700 years ago; its neoclassical facade dates from 1813, however. Completely sacked in 1936 at the onset of the Civil War, its current aspect is the result of subsequent restoration. Notable are its fine vaulting and the width of the nave flanked on either side by six chapels. The choir, formerly in the center of the nave, was moved to either side of the episcopal chair during the post–Civil War restoration.

From the aristocratic Plaça d'es Born to the quaint Plaça d'Alfonso III stretches a pedestrian zone lined with shops. While some Maó shops have branches here, the shopping is generally better in the capital.

The surrounding streets make up the heart of the old town and are lined with whitewashed houses dabbed with accents of color.

As with Maó, the pulse of life in Ciutadella emanates from the port, where the fishermen's quays are animated with sailboats and yachts and a wide range of restaurants, terrace bars, handcraft stalls, boutiques, pubs, and the occasional discotheque. Ciutadella doesn't have a beach either, but there are some good ones in the vicinity, along with a number of other worthwhile sights.

Some 2.5 miles (4km) before reaching Ciutadella on the main

Maó-Ciutadella road, there is a well-marked track leading south to the **Naveta des Tudons,** a two-story tomb from the Bronze Age containing the remains of about 50 bodies. In 1968 the naveta (so called because it's shaped like an upturned boat) was restored and excavations carried out that turned up invaluable prehistoric artifacts including arms, jewelry, and crockery. Another track nearby leads to a prehistoric cave with pillars and niches in the wall similar to those described below at Cala Morell.

Some 5 miles (8km) northeast of Ciutadella at **Cala Morell,** along a well-marked road, is one of the most important groups of prehistoric caves on Minorca. One of them has an isolated pilaster cut separate from the rock face with a horn-shaped capital, and another has high-relief ornaments decorating its facade and framing the trapezoidal portal. Also found here are numerous hollows, usually oval in shape, about half a meter up the cliff sides. Speculation is that they were receptacles for offerings to the dead entombed here. Not all these caves were exclusively burial chambers, however; some served as dwellings as well, but it is unclear whether they ever served both purposes simultaneously.

If you continue along the road past the caves down to the playa, you'll come to one of the island's prettier, more peaceful bays, framed with cliffs and unusual rock formations. There is a small sand beach here, as well as cement platforms for sunbathing and a snack bar and restaurant. Housing developments are rapidly cropping up on the hillside—so far they blend in nicely.

South of Ciutadella at **Cala de Santandria** and **Cala Blanca** are two small bays with vest-pocket beaches and a smattering of hotels and hostels (see "Where to Stay" below), snack bars, restaurants (see "Where to Dine" below), and shops.

On the island's southwestern coast between Son Xoriguer and Cala Galdana, a series of aboriginal beaches sheltered by pinewoods includes the sandy double bay of **Son Saura** and the lovely inlets of **Cala Turqueta** and **Macarella.**

ARCHEOLOGICAL HIGHLIGHTS

Archeologists posit that Minorca was first inhabited as long as 7,000 years ago by a strong, athletic race that relinquished its caves to construct underground villages. Scattered across the island's countryside are significant archeological remnants dating back over 3,000 years that have, unfortunately, been largely neglected. Collectively, however, these numerous *talayots, taulas, navetas,* and prehistoric cave villages make up a valuable open-air museum. Thought to have some link with similar remains in Sardinia, they are believed to date primarily from the Talayot Culture of the second millennium B.C.

Talayots are the round rock mounds found all over Minorca. Were they watchtowers as some suggest? Probably not—they have no interior stairway and only a few are found along the coast. The best-preserved one is at Torello, near Maó airport, which you can drive up to (but it's closed to the public). The megalithic **taulas** are huge Stonehenge-esque, T-shaped stone structures about 12 feet (4m) high and apparently peculiar to Minorca. Dating from pre-Roman times, their purpose is unknown, and they are almost always found alongside a talayot.

The **navetas,** dating from 1400 to 800 B.C., are stone constructions in the shape of inverted boats (hence the name derived from *nave,* Spanish for "boat"). Many have false ceilings, and often you can walk inside. Perhaps the island's best known is the **Naveta d'es Tudons** near Ciutadella, a funerary building belonging to the Talayotic Age (1500–1400 B.C.).

Another archeological must on Minorca is the prehistoric village of **Torre d'en Gaumes** (see "Central & Southern Areas" below) with its notable variety of monuments. Also of interest are **Trepucó** and **Talati de Dalt** near Maó, and the Paleo-Christian basilica at Son Bou (again see "Central & Southern Areas" below).

For further details, pick up the "Guide to the Archeological Sites of Minorca" and "Archeological Itineraries" available free at the island's tourist offices.

WHERE TO STAY

In general, the hotel offerings in and around Ciutadella are on a par with those in and around Maó. Along the coast from Los Delfines to Cala Blanca are a number of tourist resorts with fine beaches, and in Ciutadella itself there are several commendable hostelries, some bordering on the luxurious. At night, many of the travelers staying at the nearby beaches head into Ciutadella to enjoy the fine restaurants and nightlife.

EXPENSIVE

PATRICIA HOTEL, Paseo Sant Nicolau, 90–92, 07760 Ciutadella, Minorca. Tel. 971/38-55-11. Fax 971/48-11-20. 44 rms. A/C MINIBAR TV TEL

$ Rates: 7,750–9,700 ptas. ($77.50–$97) single; 11,500–15,000 ptas. ($115–$150) double. AE, DC, EURO, MC, V. **Parking:** Nearby.

This is one of Ciutadella's more luxurious hotels. Located near the Plaça d'es Born, it is primarily a businessperson's enclave, but is just a kilometer from the beach at Playa de La Caleta. The carpeted guest rooms are done in pleasant pastels and feature large baths, and the hotel offers a cafeteria.

MODERATE

HOTEL ALMIRANTE FARRAGUT, Cala'n Forcat, 07760 Ciutadella, Minorca. Tel. 971/38-28-00. 472 rms.

$ Rates: 3,500–5,200 ptas. ($35–$52) single; 4,900–10,000 ptas. ($49–$100) double. EURO, MC, V. **Parking:** Available. **Closed:** Nov–Apr.

Located 3 miles (5km) outside Ciutadella on a small rocky inlet in the development of Los Delfines, the Almirante Farragut has large, amorphous public areas. The guest rooms, however, are pleasant enough, with patio flooring, baths (50 singles have shower only), and terraces with views of the inlet or the open sea.

The facilities include two saltwater pools for adults, one pool for children, bars, a restaurant, a cafeteria, a disco, a TV and video room, tennis courts, mini-golf, shops, a beauty parlor, a supermarket, a diving school, and access to the bay.

HOTEL ESMERALDA, Paseo Sant Nicolau, 175, 07760 Ciutadella, Minorca. Tel. 971/38-02-50. 161 rms. TEL

$ Rates: 4,000–6,000 ptas. ($40–$60) single; 6,500–9,200 ptas.

($65–$92) double. EURO, MC, V. **Parking:** Available. **Closed:** Nov–Apr.

The Esmeralda is Ciutadella's answer to Maó's Hotel Port-Mahón. Similarly located at the mouth of the harbor, it's about 15 minutes away from the nearest beach. The guest rooms, while large, are sparsely furnished, but the baths are big and bright (though some have showers only—no tubs). Some rooms have terraces, and some boast sea views. The hotel also has a pool.

MEDITERRANI, Cala Blanca (Apartado de Correos 1), 07760 Ciutadella, Minorca. Tel. 971/38-42-03. Fax 971/38-61-62. Telex 69528 BOJU E. 180 rms. TEL

$ Rates (including breakfast and IVA): 4,500–7,500 ptas. ($45–$75) single; 7,000–12,500 ptas. ($70–$125) double. EURO, MC, V. **Parking:** Available. **Closed:** Nov–Apr.

The best of the package-group hotels on the island, the Mediterrani is a brief walk from the small, sandy beach at Cala Blanca. Its public areas are well laid out, its very pleasant guest rooms are simply but invitingly outfitted with tiled floors and terraces, and the property is so well cared for that I thought it was brand new when, in fact, it was in its sixth season. The facilities include a pool, bar, dining room, TV lounge, games room, and tennis court.

BUDGET

HOSTAL MADRID, Carrer Madrid, 60, 07760 Ciutadella, Minorca. Tel. 971/38-03-28. 14 rms. TEL

$ Rates: 1,800–2,300 ptas. ($18–$23) single; 3,500–4,300 ptas. ($35–$43) double. No credit cards. **Parking:** Nearby. **Closed:** Nov–Apr.

Tucked away on a residential street near the Hotel Esmeralda, the Hostal Madrid offers three floors of comfortable guest rooms (no elevator), all with balconies. Guests can enjoy the pool and the bar/cafeteria. Playa des Degollador, a 10-minute walk away, is the nearest beach. The hotel is also a short walk into town and to the port.

HOSTAL RESIDENCIA CIUTADELLA, Carrer Sant Eloy, 10, 07701 Ciutadella, Minorca. Tel. 971/38-34-62. 17 rms. TEL

$ Rates: 2,000–2,700 ptas. ($20–$27) single; 3,400–4,500 ptas. ($34–$45) double; 4,500–5,600 ptas. ($45–$56) triple. MC, V. **Parking:** Nearby.

This solid in-town choice near Plaça Alfonso III just off the main shopping street has sizable guest rooms and floor-length windows fronting a rather quiet street. The floors are tiled and the upholstered furnishings covered in cheery, floral prints. The rooms are spread across three floors, but there is no elevator.

HOTEL ALFONSO III, Camí de Maó, 53, 07760 Ciutadella, Minorca. Tel. 971/38-01-50. 52 rms. TEL

$ Rates: 1,600–1,900 ptas. ($16–$19) single with shower; 3,300–3,700 ptas. ($33–$37) ptas. double with shower, 3,800–4,500 ptas. ($38–$45) double with bath. AE, DC, EURO, MC, V. **Parking:** Available.

The Alfonso III sits at the far end of the main shopping street leading off Plaça d'es Born and offers simple, dormitory-style accommodations at economical rates. Twenty guest rooms have showers only (no tubs). There are a dining room and a cafeteria/snack bar.

HOTELS CALA BONA and MAR BLAVA, Urbanización Son Oleo, 07760 Ciutadella, Minorca. **Tel. 971/38-00-16.** 44 rms.

$ Rates: 2,500–3,000 ptas. ($25–$30) single; 3,800–5,000 ptas. ($38–$50) double. No credit cards. **Parking:** Nearby. **Closed:** Nov–Mar.

These two neighboring hotels under the same management are at a cozy half-kilometer remove from the center of Ciutadella. Stairs lead down to the pretty, rock-rimmed bay below for sunbathing by the sea. The decor throughout both hotels is ad hoc but homey.

The guest rooms in both are clean and comfortable, all with sea views. The rooms at the Mar Blava are more cramped; the 18 rooms at the Cala Bona are nice and bright. Triples and quads are available. The bar, pool, reception area, and outdoor terrace are all at the Mar Blava.

WHERE TO DINE

The port of Ciutadella offers a great selection of restaurants for all palates and prices. Beyond that, there are some commendable choices in and around town.

EXPENSIVE

CASA MANOLO, Marina, 117–121, Port de Ciutadella. **Tel. 38-00-03.**
Cuisine: SPANISH/MINORCAN. **Reservations:** Required in summer.
$ Prices: Appetizers 300–1,000 ptas. ($3–$10); main courses 950–6,500 ptas. ($9.50–$65). AE, DC, EURO, MC, V.
Open: Lunch daily 1–4pm; dinner daily 8–11pm. **Closed:** Dec 10–Jan 10.

Situated at the far end of the port where all the bigger yachts are docked, Casa Manolo tops the list of Ciutadella restaurants in quality and cost, offering very good value for the money. King Juan Carlos has been known to drop in here from time to time for the fresh seafood and lobster specialties. Spanish and local cuisine are featured, including such house specialties as arroz de pescado caldoso (a kind of fish paella but with more broth) and *caldereta de langosta* (lobster-based bouillabaisse). The outdoor dining area is small and sophisticated; the indoor area is carved out of rock. Owner Manuel Plens-Guiu presides over it all with great care and attention.

MODERATE

CAS QUINTU, Plaza Alfonso III, 4, Ciutadella. **Tel. 38-10-02.**
Cuisine: SPANISH/MINORCAN. **Reservations:** Not required.
$ Prices: Appetizers 500–2,000 ptas. ($5–$20); main courses 700–3,500 ptas. ($7–$35); menu del día 1,000 ptas. ($10). AE, EURO, MC, V.
Open: Lunch, daily 1–4pm. Dinner, daily 7:30–11pm. Bar, daily 9am–1am.

Cas Quintu offers informal tables by the bar or a more handsome and formal setting in the back. Seafood is the specialty, and the day's fare is on display near the bar. The calderetas share top billing with other traditional Spanish fish dishes. There is also a seasonal menu with an assortment of Spanish and Minorcan dishes, among them several meat offerings.

ES CALIU GRILL, Carretera Cala Blanca, Ciutadella. Tel. 38-01-65.

Cuisine: SPANISH. **Reservations:** Not required.

$ Prices: Appetizers 300–950 ptas. ($3–$9.50); main courses 700–2,000 ptas. ($7–$20). AE, DC, EURO, MC, V.

Open: May–Oct, lunch daily 1–4pm; dinner daily 7:30pm–12:30am. Oct–May, lunch Fri–Sun 1–4pm; dinner Fri–Sun 7:30pm–12:30am.

Along the main road between Cala Santandria and Cala Blanca, Es Caliu is the place to come when you've had your fill of seafood. Specializing in grilled meats of the first and freshest quality, it offers veal, pork, rabbit, quail, and spit-roasted suckling pig and lamb. But beyond fine food, you get a very special ambiance here. Above the bar hang hams and garlic braids, and off to the side are stacked wine barrels. The family-style tables and benches are made of cut and polished logs. The outdoor terrace is roofed and smothered with cascading flowers; indoors there are two rustic dining areas, one with a fireplace.

RESTAURANT EL COMILON, Plaça de S'Esplandad (Plaça Colón), 47, Ciutadella. Tel. 38-09-22.

Cuisine: FRENCH. **Reservations:** Recommended on Sat.

$ Prices: Appetizers 675–1,700 ptas. ($6.75–$17); main courses 500–2,200 ptas. ($5–$22); menus del día 1,100–1,500 ptas. ($11–$15). DC, EURO, MC, V.

Open: May–Oct, lunch daily 1–3:30pm; dinner daily 8–11pm. Oct–May, lunch daily 1–3:30pm; dinner Mon–Sat 8–11pm.

This is an upscale eatery featuring fresh seafood—mostly grilled—and dishes with a French accent, including entrecôte with either a roquefort, pepper, or Normandie sauce (a sweet-and-sour sauce made with apples, whiskey, honey, and vinegar). The tournedos belle époque are served with fresh vegetables. The dozen or so indoor tables are topped with pink linen, and there is covered patio dining in the back.

BUDGET

BAR TRITON, Muelle Ciutadella. Tel. 38-00-02.

Cuisine: TAPAS. **Reservations:** Not required.

$ Prices: Tapas and sandwiches 300–800 ptas. ($3–$8); platos combinados 450–2,100 ptas. ($4.50–$21). No credit cards.

Open: Daily 4:30am–midnight (until 2am in summer).

A fine tapas spot, Triton, in the port, offers a wide range of snacks, including sausages; tortillas (Spanish omelets); meatballs; and a dozen or so seafood tapas, among them baby octopus, stuffed squid, and escupiñas (Minorcan clams). On the wall inside are photos and illustrations of the port before it was a haven for holidaymakers. As in those days, fishermen still make up an important part of the clientele, and you'll often find the local men engaged in a friendly afternoon game of cards.

FUNKY JUNKIE, Es Pla de Sant Joan, 15, in the port. Tel. 38-55-97.

Cuisine: AMERICAN. **Reservations:** Not required.

$ Prices: Hamburgers 275–1,100 ptas. ($2.75–$11); sandwiches 275–650 ptas. ($2.75–$6.50); main courses 550–1,900 ptas. ($5.50–$19). AE, EURO, MC, V.

Open: Apr–Oct, daily 11am–4pm and 7pm–4am. Nov–Mar, Thurs–Sun 7pm–3am.

Billing itself as "Junk-Food Heaven" and "Home of the Junker— The Best Junk Food from Around the World," Funky Junkie is owned and operated by Ed Wall—a transplanted Philadelphian who makes fast friends with his customers and is always glad to see a fellow American—and his Minorcan wife, Lali. Ed also knows a lot about the island and can fill you in on the latest nightspots. Meanwhile, his fast-food eatery serves up 17 versions of a hamburger with Ed's special sauce, club sandwiches, Philadelphia steak sandwiches, Sloppy Joes, spareribs, and some Italian and Mexican dishes. Naturally, the food doesn't taste the same as that back home, but Ed's hospitality is 100% American.

LA GRANJA, Plaça de S'Esplanada (Plaça Colón), 48, Ciutadella. Tel. 38-40-81.

Cuisine: TAPAS AND LIGHT BITES. **Reservations:** Not required.

$ Prices: Tapas 250–850 ptas. ($2.50–$8.50) a plate, depending on how much you want. No credit cards.

Open: Mon–Sat 10am–11pm (until 1am in summer).

Popular with both locals and tourists, La Granja is a stylish, modern tapas bar offering both indoor and outdoor "grazing." You'll find no menu here, only a verbal explanation, offered in diverse languages by owners Tolo and Gila, of the selection of fresh, high-quality tapas and sandwiches available that day, some of which are on appetizing display. A recent addition to the repertoire are vegetarian tapas (all fresh vegetables), which can be teamed with cereals.

EVENING ENTERTAINMENT

Ciutadella is more popular with the younger crowd than Maó. At night its port blossoms with handcraft stands and diverse musical establishments in addition to the bars and restaurants that are open all day. Also in the vicinity are a number of popular discos.

AL PAIRO, along Es Pla de Sant Joan, Port de Ciutadella. Tel. 38-62-88.

A small, smoky, cave bar one flight up, Al Pairo offers South American music that starts anytime between 11:30pm and 1am. It's open in summer daily from 9pm to 4am, in winter on Friday and Saturday only from 9pm to 4am.

ALADINO, Port de Ciutadella. No phone.

Aladino is a cave bar with darts, billiards, loud music, and a largely young crowd. From June to September, Aladino is open daily from 8:30pm to 4am; from September to June, it's open Friday to Saturday from 8:30pm to 3am.

BAR LA ESCALERA, Carrer de Pere Capllonch, s/n (no street number). Tel. 38-52-42.

This is the first place you'll come to as you descend the steps down to the port. Like many other nightspots around the island, it's installed in a cave and has a billiard table and loud music. The crowd is largely offbeat. Open daily from 9pm to 4am.

CAFÉ DE PARIS, San Sebastian, 8, Ciutadella. No phone.

For those who like their music sedate and their ambiance upscale and sophisticated, the art deco echoes here make a pleasant setting for a drink and conversation. You can take your pick among many small, intimate conversational areas or perch yourself at the gracefully curving bar at the entrance. There is no billiard table or no loud music—just a pleasant place to sit and chat. The crowd is mostly local. The Café de Paris, located near the cathedral, is open daily from 6:30pm to whenever.

CHIC, Santandria. Tel. 38-63-59.

A little farther out of Ciutadella than Mannix (see below), Chic is one of a chain of discos throughout Spain—and a disco is a disco is a disco. From May to October, Chic is open daily from 11pm to 6am; from October to May it operates on weekends only from 11pm to 6am.

Admission: 1,000 ptas. ($10).

HADDOCK BAR, next to the Bar Triton, Port de Ciutadella. Tel. 38-49-68.

Here you'll find outdoor tables, a small indoor bar, and a billiard table downstairs. The loud music is a mixed bag of popular Spanish and international tunes. The crowd is similarly mixed. Open daily from 8pm to 4am.

LATERAL, across the way from Al Pairo. No phone.

This is the port's disco. A subterranean, cellar atmosphere prevails downstairs. Upstairs is a terrace bar and, yes, a billiard table. Lateral attracts a mixed crowd. Summer hours are daily from 10pm to 5am; winter hours are Friday and Saturday only from 10pm to 5am.

MANNIX, along Cala Degollador just outside Ciutadella. Tel. 38-47-27.

This disco in the standard mold features music of the 1960s. It's open in July to September daily from midnight to 5am; from September to July, hours are Friday to Sunday from midnight to 5am.

Admission (including one drink): 1,000 ptas. ($10).

ZONA B, Es Pla de Sant Joan, s/n (no street number), Port de Ciutadella. Tel. 38-43-20.

This bar can arguably be said to have the loudest music of all, although the competition is fierce. Again, there are billiards upstairs. Open in summer daily from 9pm to 4am, in winter on Friday and Saturday only from 9pm to 4am.

---

2. CENTRAL & SOUTHERN AREAS

Topographically and climatically, this is the more tranquil part of the island. The beaches are more accessible, and the winds blow less strongly—as a result, tourism has taken a firmer foothold here than in the north. Santo Tomás, Cala Galdana, Playa de Son Bou, Cala Bosch, and Punta Prima are some of the focal points for travelers.

WHAT TO SEE & DO

Mercadal, a town of several thousand inhabitants at the foot of Monte Toro, is a picturesque ensemble of white houses with grace notes of color. Among its claims to local fame are two types of almond confectionery—*carquinyols* (small, hard cookies) and *amargos* (a kind of macaroon). The place to get some is **Pastelería Villalonga Ca's Sucrer,** Plaça Constitución 11, Mercadal (tel. 37-51-75), open in summer on Tuesday to Saturday from 9:30am to 1:30pm and from 5 to 8:30pm, from 4:30 to 8pm in winter; also open on Sunday in winter from 11am to 2pm.

Just down the street from this pastelería is a shop called **Es Ventall** (tel. 37-55-27), with a limited but interesting selection of decorative items, clothing, accessories, fans, designer T-shirts, and costume jewelry. Owner Biel Mercadal and his wife design many of these things themselves and scout the island for the work of local artisans. Es Ventall is open on Monday to Saturday from 10am to 2pm and 6 to 10:30pm; in winter on Monday through Friday from 5 to 8:30pm and on Saturday from 9am to 2pm.

From Es Mercadal, you can take a road 2.5 miles (4km) up to **Monte Toro,** the island's tallest mountain at 1,170 feet (357m), crowned with a sanctuary that is a place of pilgrimage for Minorcans. The winding road leads to a panoramic view of the island's rolling green countryside dotted with *fincas* (farm estates), trim fields, and stands of trees. From this vantage point you can also clearly see the contrast between the flatter southern part of the island and the lumpier northern region. The hilltop sanctuary includes a small, simple church with an ornate gilded altar displaying the image (reportedly found nearby in 1290) of the Virgin Mare de Déu d'el Toro, the island's patron saint. In 1936 the church was destroyed, but the statue was saved from the flames and a new church built. The church is open daily from early morning to sunset; admission is free. In the courtyard of the sanctuary is a bronze monument to those Minorcans who left for North America in the 18th century, while the island was still a British colony, and founded the town of St. Augustine in Florida. The large statue of Christ commemorates the Civil War dead. There is a snack bar with a pleasant terrace here.

About halfway along the road from Alaior to Playa Son Bou is a turnoff to the left to **Torre d'en Gaumes,** the largest prehistoric village on Minorca. Uncovered here during excavations in 1974 was a beautiful bronze Egyptian statue of Imhotep, architect of the world's first pyramid and god of medicine, dating from 650 B.C. Most notable here now are the enclosure of the taula, the hypostilic chamber, the central talayot, and the system for collecting rainwater by means of open channels and hollows cut out of the rock.

Playa Son Bou is a stunning beach defaced by two outsize hotels. Although still enchanting, the mile-long, narrow, sandy beach and clear, turquoise waters are now often crowded, even in the off-season; in July and August they're best avoided. At the eastern end of the beach just beyond the two monster hotels are the ruins of a Paleo-Christian basilica most probably dating from the 5th or 6th century. Visible in the cliffs beyond are some cave dwellings, some of which appear quite prosperous, with painted facades and shades to keep out the noonday sun.

To the east in Cala En Porter is a most unique nightspot. Embedded in a series of caves within a sheer cliff face rising from the sea, **La Cova d'en Xoroi** (tel. 37-72-36) is a conglomeration of bars, terraces, intimate nooks and crannies, and a disco floor. For sheer drama, the setting can't be beat. As you walk down the entrance stairway, all magnificently unfolds before you. Then you come to the dance floor overlooking the sea at the cliff's edge—there's no window, just a railing. Prehistoric vessels were found inside these caves, which, according to legend, were once the refuge of a Moor called Xoroi who had abducted a local maid and made his home here with her and their family. So unusual is this place that by day it's a tourist sight. From May through October you can visit it daily from 11am to 1:30pm and from 4 to 9pm; admission is 275 ptas. ($2.75) and includes a refreshment. It's open for drinks and dancing in May on Friday and Saturday and June through September nightly from 11pm to 5am. Cover charge is 1,500 ptas. ($15), including one drink. Don't miss it!

Shortly before the turnoff for Es Migjorn Gran along the Maó-Ciutadella road is a sign indicating the **Club Hípico/Riding School,** also known as the *Picadero de Menorca* (tel. 37-18-52), which organizes excursions on horseback for groups of 8 to 10 people. These six-hour rides include a barbeque lunch and cost about 6,300 ptas. ($63) per person. You can also ride by the hour on the stable grounds for about 1,600 ptas. ($16) per hour. To make arrangements, it is best to visit the stables during the day or call the number above in the evening. If you don't speak Spanish, ask someone at your hotel to make arrangements for you.

WHERE TO STAY

Most of the hotels in this area cater to tour groups. Some are better than others.

HOTEL LOS CONDORES SOL, Playa de Santo Tomás, s/n (no street number), 07749 Es Migjorn Gran, Minorca. Tel. 971/37-00-50. Fax 971/37-03-48. Telex 69047 HCON E. 188 rms. TEL

$ Rates (including breakfast): 4,500–7,000 ptas. ($45–$70) single; 6,000–11,200 ptas. ($60–$112) double. AE, DC, EURO, MC, V. **Parking:** Available. **Closed:** Nov–Apr.

Right next door to the Santo Tomás, this Sol group property features an abundance of stone, wood, and tiles creating a friendly, hacienda atmosphere. The attractive guest rooms have pretty balconies with wooden doors, louvered shutters, and sea views. Guests have use of the pool, shops, beauty parlor, mini-golf, and dining room.

HOTEL LOS GAVILANES SOL, Urbanización Cala Galdana, s/n (no street number), 07750 Ferreries, Minorca. Tel. 971/37-31-75. Fax 971/37-31-75. Telex 69046 HGAV E. 357 rms. TEL

$ Rates (including breakfast): 4,700–7,500 ptas. ($47–$75) single; 6,500–11,500 ptas. ($65–$115) double. Children 2–6 get 25% discount. AE, DC, EURO, MC, V. **Parking:** Available.

The original beauty of Cala Galdana has been substantially marred by tourist construction, but you can enjoy the best end of its sandy, crescent beach and beautiful turquoise waters by staying at the Gavilanes. A member of the Sol hotel group, this one offers sizable, functional guest rooms and the standard amenities of a large tour-group hotel. The facilities include a pool, a children's playground, TV and games rooms, a gift shop, a supermarket, and water sports.

HOTEL LORD NELSON, Playa Santo Tomás, 07749 Es Migjorn Gran, Minorca. Tel. 971/37-01-25. Fax 971/37-01-96. 145 rms. TEL

$ Rates (including IVA): 5,000–6,600 ptas. ($50–$66) single; 6,600–9,450 ptas. ($66–$94.50) double. MC, V. **Parking:** Available. **Closed:** Nov–Apr.

This more intimate property has an attractive swimming pool bordering the dunes of the beach. All the compact but comfortable guest rooms have terraces with at least partial sea views. There are also 32 bungalow accommodations where three can stay for the price of two.

HOTEL SANTO TOMÁS, Playa Santo Tomás, 07749 Es Migjorn Gran, Minorca. Tel. 971/37-00-25. Fax 971/37-03-52. 85 rms and suites. A/C MINIBAR TV TEL

$ Rates (including IVA): 5,300–8,500 ptas. ($53–$85) single; 11,000–17,000 ptas. ($110–$170) double; 15,500–35,000 ptas. ($155–$350) suite. AE, DC, EURO, MC, V. **Parking:** Available. **Closed:** Nov–Apr.

One of my favorite Minorca hotels, the Santo Tomás, a Best Western affiliate, not only has seniority on this beach but also offers a level of quality, comfort, and convenience that's hard to beat anywhere else on the island. In fact, it's the only four-star hotel on the island located on the beach. Its dining room, bar, and other communal spaces have the bright, breezy feel of a lazy summer retreat.

The pleasant guest rooms have recently been redone and upgraded to offer such amenities as radios, real hairdryers, and very attractive furnishings and appointments. The majority have terraces with sea views.

The facilities include a swimming pool (an especially nice one surrounded by a terrace garden dotted with thatched umbrellas), a seaside bar and barbecue, a rudimentary mini-golf course, and a smattering of water sports offered on Santo Tomás Beach.

Reservations can be made through Best Western in the United States (tel. toll free 800/528-1234) or through Best Western in Barcelona (tel. 3/430-14-41).

HOTEL VICTORIA PLAYA, Playa Santo Tomás, 07749 Es Migjorn Gran, Minorca. Tel. 971/37-02-00. Fax 971/37-02-77. 266 rms. TEL

$ Rates (including breakfast and IVA): 4,000–7,500 ptas. ($40–$75) single; 5,700–12,500 ptas. ($57–$125) double. DC, MC. **Parking:** Available. **Closed:** Nov–Apr.

All the Victoria Playa's guest rooms have terraces, sizable baths, patio flooring, and a light, cheery decor. The public areas and bar are geared to tour groups; overall, the hotel has an institutional feel about it, with hallways that recall those of college dorms. The hotel has a swimming pool.

WHERE TO DINE

Some of the best dining in this area is offered in the inland villages rather than along the coast. Mercadal, in particular, has a few choice restaurants.

CA N'OLGA, Pont Na Macarrana, near Carrer d'es Sol, Es Mercadal. Tel. 37-54-59.

Cuisine: MEDITERRANEAN. **Reservations:** Recommended on weekends.

$ **Prices:** Appetizers 850–1,400 ptas. ($8.50–$14); main courses 1,000–2,500 ptas. ($10–$25). AE, DC, EURO, MC, V.

Open: Mar–May and Oct–Dec, Fri–Sun 1:30–3pm and 7:45–11pm. June–Sept, Fri–Sun 7:45–11:30pm. **Closed:** Jan–Feb.

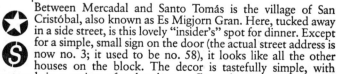 A stylish, sophisticated spot that attracts a similar clientele, Ca N'Olga is warm, winsome, and intimate. Occupying a typical white-stucco Minorcan house some 150 years old, this restaurant offers dining on a pretty outdoor patio or at a handful of indoor tables.

The eclectic menu changes frequently with the market offering. The day I was there the menu included quail with onion-and-sherry vinegar and osso buco. Some standard dishes that tend to appear regularly are cap roig (scorpion fish), *cabrito* (baby goat), some kind of fish terrine, and mussels au gratin. Among the homemade desserts you'll often find fig ice cream and chestnut pudding.

COSTA SUR, Playa de Santo Tomás. Tel. 37-03-26.

Cuisine: INTERNATIONAL. **Reservations:** Not required.

$ **Prices:** Appetizers 500–1,400 ptas. ($5–$14); main courses 650–2,300 ptas. ($6.50–$23). AE, EURO, MC, V.

Open: Dinner only, daily 7–11pm. **Closed:** Nov–Apr.

The sophisticated aspirations of Costa Sur are hampered by its rather stark decor. The menu is equally divided between seafood and meat dishes, and the house prides itself on its cheese soufflé, salmon crêpe, pepper steak, and *suquet de rape* (fish stew). It also serves a smattering of pasta dishes.

58, S'ENGOLIDOR, Carrer Major, 3, Es Migjorn Gran (San Cristóbal). Tel. 37-01-93.

Cuisine: MINORCAN. **Reservations:** Required on weekends and in June–Aug.

$ **Prices:** Appetizers 500–650 ptas. ($5–$6.50); main courses 950–1,900 ptas. ($9.50–$19). EURO, MC, V.

Open: May–Oct, Tues–Sun 8–11pm. Nov–Apr, Fri–Sun 8–11pm.

Between Mercadal and Santo Tomás is the village of San Cristóbal, also known as Es Migjorn Gran. Here, tucked away in a side street, is this lovely "insider's" spot for dinner. Except for a simple, small sign on the door (the actual street address is now no. 3; it used to be no. 58), it looks like all the other houses on the block. The decor is tastefully simple, with artwork in a variety of styles shown off to advantage against crisp white walls. A series of small rooms contain a few tables each, and outdoors there are two patio dining areas where you can sometimes smell the herbs growing in owner José Luis's garden, which provides some of the fruits and vegetables on his menu.

The menu is limited but varied, with many Minorcan specialties, such as oliaigua, eggplant stuffed with fish, baked pork chop with potatoes and tomatoes, roast lamb, and a very savory rabbit–and–wild-mushroom stew.

Upstairs there are four very cozy guest rooms to let (available January to November) with bright, modern baths and some attractive antique furnishings. With breakfast they rent for 2,900 ptas. ($29) for a single and 3,500 ptas. ($35) for a double; discounts are offered for extended stays.

RESTAURANT MOLÍ D'ES RECO, Es Mercadal. Tel. 37-53-92.
  Cuisine: MINORCAN. **Reservations:** Recommended in summer.
  $ Prices: Appetizers 375–2,200 ptas. ($3.75–$22); main courses 650–3,800 ptas. ($6.50–$38); menus del día 1,100–1,600 ptas. ($11–$16). AE, EURO, MC, V.
  Open: Lunch daily 1–4pm; dinner daily 7–11pm.

Easily spotted by the windmill that inspired its name, Molí d'es Reco has a pleasant outdoor patio but a rather plain indoor dining area. Overall, the place is a bit touristy, but it offers hearty Minorcan fare including stuffed eggplant, oliaigua amb tomatecs (a soup with tomato, onion, parsley, green peppers, and garlic), snails with spider crab, partridge with cabbage, and *calamares à la menorquina* (stuffed squid with an almond-cream sauce).

RESTAURANTE BAR SA PLAÇA, Carrer d'Enmig, 2, Es Mercadal. Tel. 37-50-48.
  Cuisine: SPANISH. **Reservations:** Not required.
  $ Prices: Appetizers 525–2,100 ptas. ($5.25–$21); main courses 900–1,600 ptas. ($9–$16); menus del día 1,000–1,300 ptas. ($10–$13). EURO, MC, V.
  Open: Summer, daily 6am–1am. Winter, daily 6am–midnight.
  Closed: Feb.

This budget alternative under the same ownership as Molí d'es Reco (see below) serves traditional Spanish fare in a lively family setting with an odd-lot assortment of tables indoors and out. It's clearly a local favorite not only for dining but also for snacks.

3. FORNELLS & THE NORTHERN COAST

The road leading north from Mercadal to Fornells runs through some of the island's finer scenery. On the northern coast, the tiny town of Fornells snuggles around a bay filled with boats and windsurfers and lined with restaurants and a few shops. Built up around four defense edifications—the Talaia de la Mola (now destroyed), the Tower of Fornells at the harbor mouth, the fortress of the Island of Las Sargantanas (the Lizards) situated in the middle of the harbor, and the now-ruined Castle of San Jorge or San Antonio—Fornells today is a flourishing fishing village noted for its upscale restaurants featuring savory lobster calderetas.

WHAT TO SEE & DO

In Fornells you can rent small sailboats, windsurfers, waterskis, kayaks, motorboats, fishing gear, and mountain bikes at **Servináutica Menorca,** S.C., Carrer Mayor 27–31 (tel. 97-66-36).

West of Fornells is **Platja Binimel.la,** a beautiful beach (unofficially nudist) that's easily accessible by car. Its long, curving, sandy cove is peacefully set against undulating hills. A snack bar is the sole concession to civilization.

By far the most splendid panorama here is that seen from the promontory at **Cap de Cavalleria,** the northernmost tip of the island, marked by a lighthouse. Getting there requires some effort, however. At a bend in the road leading to Platja Binimel.la, a signpost indicates the turnoff to Cap de Cavalleria through a closed gate leading to a dirt road. Simply open the gate, close it behind you, and continue on. Since all beaches in Spain are public, no one may impede access to them. Landowners can, however, discourage visitors by making access difficult. Since many of the roads leading to Minorca's undeveloped beaches are similarly closed by gates, the prevailing custom is simply to open them, proceed on through, and close them behind you. It is important that you close them, because often these gates keep livestock confined to certain areas. As you follow the long dirt road (negotiable in a regular car or on a motorbike) out to Cap de Cavelleria, you'll come across several more sets of gates and travel through beautiful countryside that's somewhat reminiscent of the Scottish Highlands, with cultivated fields and scattered, grand fincas. Shortly before the lighthouse is a "parking area" down to the left. You'll have to pick your way across the scrub and rocks for the splendid views. The best one is from a circular tower in ruins up to the right of the lighthouse. Now brace yourself for a staggeringly beautiful vista encompassing the whole of Minorca—a veritable symphony of dramatic cliffs and jewel-blue water.

WHERE TO STAY

There are no mass-tourism hotels in Fornells, only a few small places to stay.

HOSTAL S'ALGARET, Plaça S'Algaret, 7, 07748 Fornells, Minorca. Tel. 971/37-65-52. 23 rms. A/C TEL

$ Rates (including IVA): 3,500 ptas. ($35) single; 6,600 ptas. ($66) double. AE, EURO, MC, V. **Parking:** Nearby. **Closed:** Nov–Mar.

The large, comfortable guest rooms here feature tiled floors; very basic furnishings; large, modern baths; and sizable terraces.

HOSTAL IRIS, Carrer Major, 17, 07748 Fornells, Minorca. Tel. 971/37-63-92. Fax 971/37-67-07. 17 rms. A/C MINIBAR TEL

$ Rates: 3,000–6,500 ptas. ($30–$65) single; 4,500–9,700 ptas. ($45–$97) double. EURO, MC, V. **Parking:** Available.

Just a few doors away from the Hostal S'Algaret (see above), this hotel has guest rooms that are spacious and very inviting, some with terraces. The facilities include a pool, solarium, snack bar, lounge, and guest dining room. You can rent a TV for your room if you wish.

WHERE TO DINE

Fornells is noted for its fine seafood restaurants specializing in the Minorcan calderetas. King Juan Carlos has been known to sail in here when he wants to savor some, and in peak summer season people phone up their favorite Fornells restaurant days in advance with their orders.

CAN MIQUEL, Paseo Marítimo, s/n (no street number). Tel. 37-66-23.
    Cuisine: SEAFOOD. **Reservations:** Recommended in July–Aug.
$ **Prices:** Appetizers 350–2,200 ptas. ($3.50–$22); main courses 700–8,100 ptas. ($7–$81). EURO, MC, V.
    Open: Lunch Tues–Sun noon–4pm; dinner Tues–Sat 8–10pm. **Closed:** Nov–Feb.

Moderate in its prices and modest in its checkered-tablecloth decor, Can Miquel offers the usual Fornells fare. The lobster calderetas are priced by weight, and you can choose your own lobster if you like.

ES CRANC, Carrer de Ses Escoles, 29. Tel. 37-64-42.
    Cuisine: SEAFOOD/MINORCAN. **Reservations:** Required in summer.
$ **Prices:** Appetizers 400–1,500 ptas. ($4–$15); main courses 725–6,500 ptas. ($7.25–$65). EURO, MC, V.
    Open: Nov and Mar to mid-Apr, daily 1:30–3:30pm. Mid-Apr to Oct, daily 1:30–4pm and 8pm–whenever. **Closed:** Dec–Feb.

The consensus among Minorcans is that Es Cranc serves the best caldereta. Located several blocks from the harbor near the church, this first-class eatery in a rustic, homey setting would have to be good to thrive at a remove from the prime waterfront action.

Besides the selection of calderetas, the house specialties include paella and arroz caldoso (the local, juicier version of paella). The top-of-the-line calderetas and arroces here feature the spider crab (cranc), from which the restaurant takes its name, or the langosta (spiny lobster). Another dozen and a half seafood dishes and a dozen meat dishes complete the offering.

ES PLA, Pasaje des Pla (along the water). Tel. 37-66-55.
    Cuisine: SEAFOOD/MINORCAN. **Reservations:** Recommended in summer.
$ **Prices:** Appetizers 650–2,500 ptas. ($6.50–$25); main courses 1,200–7,000 ptas. ($12–$70); menu del día 2,600 ptas. ($26). AE, DC, EURO, MC, V.
    Open: Lunch daily 1–3:30pm; dinner daily 7:30–10:30pm.

This is the king's choice in Fornells. Large and informally elegant, Es Pla is an upper-crust restaurant where you can eat indoors or out. There is also a long, stainless-steel bar for sipping premeal apéritifs. The daily fish specials and caldereta de langosta are the main attractions.

S'ALGARET RESTAURANT, Plaça S'Algaret, 7. Tel. 37-65-52.
    Cuisine: TAPAS. **Reservations:** Not required.
$ **Prices:** Tapas 200–400 ptas. ($2–$4) per plate. AE, DC, EURO, MC, V.
    Open: Summer, daily 8am–midnight. Winter, daily 9am–10pm.

Adjacent to the hostel of the same name (see "Where to Stay" above), S'Algaret is popular with the locals and one of the few economical alternatives in Fornells. Here you can nibble on tapas, sandwiches, a varied selection of tortillas (Spanish omelets), and a smattering of *platos combinados*.

S'ANCORA, Rosario, 23 (in the port). Tel. 37-66-20.

Cuisine: SEAFOOD/SPANISH. **Reservations:** Not required.

$ Prices: Appetizers 675–1,700 ptas. ($6.75–$17); main courses 800–8,000 ptas. ($8–$80); menu del día 2,200 ptas. ($22). AE, DC, EURO, MC, V.

Open: Lunch daily noon–4pm; dinner daily 7–11pm.

One of the priciest Fornells restaurants, S'Ancora is large and friendly, with indoor and outdoor dining (upstairs offers a particularly nice view). As with most of the other restaurants in the area, the specialty here is caldereta. The other specialty is *langosta* (lobster) prepared half a dozen different ways. The rest of the fish and seafood dishes have a decidedly Spanish accent. There are also a dozen or so meat and fowl dishes.

A. SPANISH/CATALAN VOCABULARY

BASIC PHRASES

ENGLISH	SPANISH	CATALAN
Pardon	Perdón	Perdó
Excuse me	Perdone usted	Perdoni
Please	Por favor	Si us plau *or* Per favor
Thank you	Gracias	Gràcies
Thank you very much	Muchas gracias	Moltes gràcies
Good morning	Buenos días	Bon dia
Good afternoon	Buenas tardes	Bona tarda
Good night	Buenas noches	Bona nit
See you tomorrow	Hasta mañana	Fins demà
Good-bye	Adiós *or* Hasta la vista	Adéu *or* A reveure
Yes	Sí	Sí
No	No	No
I don't understand	No entiendo	No ho entenc
Do you speak . . . ?	Habla usted . . . ?	Parla . . . ?
Catalan	catalán	català
Spanish	español	espanyol
English	inglés	anglès
My name is . . .	Me llamo . . .	Em dic . . .
What is your name?	Cómo se llama?	Com es dieu?
How are you?	Cómo está usted?	Com està?
I'm fine	Estoy bien	Estic bé
Very well	Muy bién	Molt bé
Not so good	No muy bien	Estic malament
Good weather	Buen tiempo	Bon temps
Bad weather	Mal tiempo	Mal temps
Do you have . . . ?	Tiene algo . . . ?	En té de . . . ?
a cheaper one	más barato	més bon preu
a larger one	más grande	més gran
a smaller one	más pequeño	més petit
another color	de otro color	un altre color
What do you want?	Qué quiere usted?	Que vols?
I am looking for . . .	Busco . . .	Cerco . . .
I need . . .	Necesito . . .	Necessito . . .

ENGLISH	SPANISH	CATALAN
I would like . . .	**Quisiera . . .**	**Voldria . . .**
A little	**Un poco**	**Una mica**
A lot	**Mucho**	**Força**
Too much/too many	**Demasiado**	**Massa**
How much?	**Cuánto?**	**Quant?**
Where is . . . ?	**Dónde está . . . ?**	**On és . . . ?**
How do I get to . . . ?	**Para ir a . . . ?**	**Per anar a . . . ?**
On the left	**A la izquierda**	**A l'esquerra**
On the right	**A la derecha**	**A la dreta**
What time do you serve . . . ?	**A qué hora se sirve . . . ?**	**A quina hora es pot . . . ?**
breakfast	**el desayuno**	**esmorzar**
lunch	**la comida**	**dinar**
dinner	**la cena**	**sopar**
Do you have a vacant room?	**Tiene alguna habitación libre?**	**Té alguna habitació lliure?**

COMMON WORDS

ENGLISH	SPANISH	CATALAN
miss	**señorita**	**senyoreta**
mister/sir	**señor**	**senyor**
madam/lady	**señora**	**senyora**
morning	**mañana**	**matí**
midday/noon	**mediodía**	**migdia**
evening	**tarde**	**tarda**
night	**noche**	**nit**
yesterday	**ayer**	**ahir**
today	**hoy**	**avui**
tomorrow	**mañana**	**demà**
day	**día**	**dia**
week	**semana**	**setmana**
bakery	**panadería**	**forn** or **fleca**
bank	**banco**	**banc**
bookshop	**librería**	**llibreria**
exchange (money)	**cambio**	**canvi**
haircut	**cortar el cabello**	**tallar els cabells**
hairdresser	**peluquero**	**perruquer**
pastry shop	**pastelería**	**pastisseria**
pharmacy	**farmacia**	**farmàcia**
bad	**mal**	**malament**
cheap	**barato**	**barat**
expensive	**caro**	**car**
open	**abierto**	**obert**
closed	**cerrado**	**tancat**
large	**grande**	**gran**
small	**pequeño**	**petit**
right (correct)	**correcto**	**correcte**
hot	**calor** or **caliente**	**calor** or **calenta**
cold (temperature)	**frío**	**fred**
weather	**tiempo**	**temps**

ENGLISH	SPANISH	CATALAN
early	**temprano**	**aviat**
late	**tarde**	**tard**
near	**cerca**	**prop**
far	**lejos**	**lluny**
more	**más**	**més**
tall	**alto**	**alt**
to call/telephone	**llamar**	**trucar**
to dye	**teñir**	**tenyir**
to pay	**pagar**	**pagar**
to eat	**comer**	**menjar**
to drink	**beber**	**beure**
to order	**pedir**	**demanar**
bill/check	**cuenta**	**compte**
price	**precio**	**preu**
money	**dinero**	**diners**
traveler's check	**cheque de viajes**	**xec de viatge**
blouse	**blusa**	**brusa**
pants	**pantalones**	**pantalons**
shirt	**camisa**	**camisa**
shoes	**zapatos**	**sabates**
to try on	**probar**	**emprovar** *or* **provar**
book	**libro**	**llibre**
guidebook	**guía**	**guia**
newspaper	**periódico**	**periòdic** *or* **diari**
magazine	**revista**	**reviste**
map	**mapa**	**mapa**
post office	**oficina de correos**	**oficina de correus**
postcard	**tarjeta postal**	**targeta postal**
stamps	**sellos**	**segell**
border	**frontera**	**frontera**
driver's license	**carnet de conducir**	**carnet de conducir**
Customs	**aduana**	**duana**
Customs duties	**derechos de aduana**	**drets de duana**
passport	**pasaporte**	**passaport**
ambulance	**ambulancia**	**ambulància**
bandage	**vendaje**	**embenat**
cold (illness)	**resfriado**	**refredat**
cough	**tos**	**tos**
dentist	**dentista**	**dentista**
diarrhea	**diarrea**	**diarrea**
dizziness	**mareo**	**mareig**
doctor	**médico**	**doctor**
fever	**fiebre**	**febre**
headache	**dolor de cabeza**	**mal de cap**
hospital	**hospital**	**hospital**
indigestion	**indigestión**	**indigestió**
sick	**enfermo**	**malalt**
toothache	**dolor de muelas**	**mal de queixal**

ENGLISH	**SPANISH**	**CATALAN**
bathroom	**baño**	**bany**
bed	**cama**	**llit**
hot water	**agua caliente**	**aigua calenta**
room	**habitación**	**habitació**
sink	**lavabo**	**lavabo**
downstairs	**a bajo**	**a baxi** *or* **sota**
upstairs	**arriba**	**a dalt** *or* **dalt**

DAYS OF THE WEEK

Monday	**lunes**	**dilluns**
Tuesday	**martes**	**dimarts**
Wednesday	**miércoles**	**dimecres**
Thursday	**jueves**	**dijous**
Friday	**viernes**	**divendres**
Saturday	**sóbado**	**dissabte**
Sunday	**domingo**	**diumenge**

NUMBERS

one	**uno**	**u** *or* **un**
two	**dos**	**dos** *or* **dues**
three	**tres**	**tres**
four	**cuatro**	**quatre**
five	**cinco**	**cinc**
six	**seis**	**sis**
seven	**siete**	**set**
eight	**ocho**	**vuit**
nine	**nueve**	**nou**
ten	**diez**	**deu**
eleven	**once**	**onze**
twelve	**doce**	**dotze**
thirteen	**trece**	**tretze**
fourteen	**catorce**	**catorze**
fifteen	**quince**	**quinze**
sixteen	**dieciséis**	**setze**
seventeen	**diecisiete**	**disset**
eighteen	**dieciocho**	**divuit**
nineteen	**diecinueve**	**dinou**
twenty	**veinte**	**vint**
thirty	**treinta**	**trenta**
forty	**cuarenta**	**quaranta**
fifty	**cincuenta**	**cinquanta**
sixty	**sesenta**	**seixanta**
seventy	**setenta**	**setanta**
eighty	**ochenta**	**vuitanta**
ninety	**noventa**	**noranta**
one hundred	**cien** *or* **ciento**	**cent**
one thousand	**mil**	**mil**
half	**medio**	**mig** *or* **mitjà**
third	**tercio**	**terç**
quarter	**cuarto**	**quart**
fifth	**quinto**	**cinqué**

MENU TRANSLATIONS

ENGLISH	SPANISH	CATALAN
fruit	fruta	fruita
apple	manzana	poma
banana	plátano	banana
grapes	uvas	ram
melon	melón	meló
orange	naranja	taronja
peach	melocotón	préssec
pear	pera	pera
strawberries	fresas	maduixes
vegetables	verdura	verdura
asparagus	espárragos	espàrrecs
beans	judías	mongetes
carrots	zanahorias	pastanagues
mushrooms	setas	bolets
olives	aceitunas	olives
onions	cebollas	cebes
peas	guisantes	pèsols
potatoes	patatas	patates
rice	arroz	arròs
beef	carne de buey or carn de vaca	carne de bou
chop	chuleta	xuleta
escalope	escalopa	escalopa
game	caza	caça
lamb (roast)	cordero (asado)	xai (rostit)
liver	hígado	fetge
pork (roast)	cerdo (asado)	porc (rostit)
rabbit (roast)	conejo (asado)	conill (rostit)
snails	caracoles	cargols
veal (roast)	ternera (asada)	vedella (rostita)
clams	almejas	cloïses
codfish	bacalao	bacallà
eel	languila	anguila
lobster	langosta	llagosta
oysters	ostras	ostres
prawns (shrimp)	gambas	gambes
salmon	salmón	salmó
shellfish	marisco	marisc
sole	lenguado	llenguado
trout	trucha	truita (de riu)
tuna (tunny)	atún	tonyina
turbot	rodaballo	rèmol
dessert	postre	postres
cakes/pastries	pastelería	pastisseria
ice cream	helado	gelat
beer	cerveza	cervesa
coffee	café	café
milk	leche	llet
mineral water	agua mineral	aigua mineral
tea	té	té
water	agua	aigua
wine	vino	vi

ENGLISH	SPANISH	CATALAN
breakfast	**desayuno**	**esmorzar** or **desdejuni**
lunch	**comida** or **almuerzo**	**dinar**
dinner	**cena**	**sopar**
bread	**pan**	**pa**
butter	**mantequilla**	**mantega**
cheese	**queso**	**formatge**
garlic	**ajo**	**all**
salt	**sal**	**sal**
sugar	**azúcar**	**sucre**
bottle	**botella**	**ampolla**
glass	**vaso**	**got**
fork	**tenedor**	**forquilla**
knife	**cuchillo**	**ganivet**
spoon	**cuchara**	**cullera**
hors d'oeuvres	**entremeses**	**entremesos**
pasta	**pasta**	**pasta**
soup	**sopa**	**sopa**
salad	**ensalada**	**amanida**
menu	**carta**	**carta**
tip	**propina**	**propina**
waiter	**camarero**	**cambrer**

B. METRIC MEASURES

LENGTH

1 millimeter (mm)	=	.04 inches
1 centimeter (cm)	=	.39 inches
1 meter (m)	=	39 inches
1 kilometer (km)	=	.62 mile

To convert kilometers to miles, multiply the number of kilometers by 0.62. Also use to convert speeds from kilometers per hour (kmph) to miles per hour (m.p.h.).

To convert miles to kilometers, multiply the number of miles by 1.61. Also use to convert speeds from m.p.h. to kmph.

CAPACITY

1 liter (l)	=	33.92 ounces	= 1.06 quarts
1 Imperial gallon	=	1.2 U.S. gallons	

To convert liters to U.S. gallons, multiply the number of liters by 0.26.

To convert U.S. gallons to liters, multiply the number of gallons by 3.79.

To convert Imperial gallons to U.S. gallons, multiply the number of Imperial gallons by 1.2.

To convert U.S. gallons to Imperial gallons, multiply the number of U.S. gallons by 0.83.

WEIGHT

1 gram (g)	=	0.035 ounces
1 kilogram (kg)	=	35.2 ounces
	=	2.2 pounds
1 metric ton	=	2,205 pounds

To convert kilograms to pounds, multiply the number of kilograms by 2.2.

To convert pounds to kilograms, multiply the number of pounds by 0.45.

AREA

1 hectare (ha)	=	2.47 acres
1 square kilometer (km²)	=	247 acres

To convert hectares to acres, multiply the number of hectares by 2.47.

To convert acres to hectares, multiply the number of acres by 0.41.

To convert square kilometers to square miles, multiply the number of square kilometers by 0.39.

TEMPERATURE

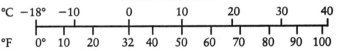

To convert degrees Celsius to degrees Farenheit, multiply °C by 9, divide by 5, then add 32 (for example: 20°C × 9/5 + 32 = 68°F).

To convert degrees Farenheit to degrees Celcius, subtract 32 from °F, multiply by 5, then divide by 9 (example: 85°F − 32 × 5/9 = 29.4°C).

INDEX

GENERAL INFORMATION

SIGHTS & ATTRACTIONS

BARCELONA & ENVIRONS

IBIZA

MAJORCA

MINORCA

ACCOMMODATIONS

BARCELONA

IBIZA

MAJORCA

Key to Abbreviations: *B* = Budget; *E* = Expensive; *I* = Inexpensive; *M* = Moderate; * = Author's favorite; $ = Super-value choice

MINORCA

RESTAURANTS

BARCELONA & ENVIRONS

Key to Abbreviations: B = Budget; E = Expensive; I = Inexpensive; M = Moderate; * = Author's favorite; $ = Super-value choice.

IBIZA

MAJORCA

MINORCA

Now Save Money on All Your Travels by Joining FROMMER'S ® TRAVEL BOOK CLUB
The World's Best Travel Guides at Membership Prices

FROMMER'S TRAVEL BOOK CLUB is your ticket to successful travel! Open up a world of travel information and simplify your travel planning when you join ranks with thousands of value-conscious travelers who are members of the FROMMER'S TRAVEL BOOK CLUB. Join today and you'll be entitled to all the privileges that come from belonging to the club that offers you travel guides for less to more than 100 destinations worldwide. Annual membership is only $25 (U.S.) or $35 (Canada and all foreign).

The Advantages of Membership

1. Your choice of three free FROMMER'S TRAVEL GUIDES. You can pick two from our FROMMER'S COUNTRY and REGIONAL GUIDES (listed under Comprehensive, $-A-Day, and Family) and one from our FROMMER'S CITY GUIDES (listed under City and City $-A-Day).
2. Your own subscription to **TRIPS & TRAVEL** quarterly newsletter.
3. You're entitled to a **30% discount** on your order of any additional books offered by FROMMER'S TRAVEL BOOK CLUB.
4. You're offered (at a small additional fee) our **Domestic Trip Routing Kits**.

Our quarterly newsletter **TRIPS & TRAVEL** offers practical information on the best buys in travel, the "hottest" vacation spots, the latest travel trends, world-class events and much, much more.

Our **Domestic Trip Routing Kits** are available for any North American destination. We'll send you a detailed map highlighting the best route to take to your destination—you can request direct or scenic routes.

Here's all you have to do to join:
Send in your membership fee of $25 ($35 Canada and foreign) with your name and address on the form below along with your selections as part of your membership package to FROMMER'S TRAVEL BOOK CLUB, P.O. Box 473, Mt. Morris, IL 61054-0473. Remember to check off 2 FROMMER'S COUNTRY and REGIONAL GUIDES and 1 FROMMER'S CITY GUIDE on the pages following.

If you would like to order additional books, please select the books you would like and send a check for the total amount (please add sales tax in the states noted below), plus $2 per book for shipping and handling ($3 per book for all foreign orders) to:

FROMMER'S TRAVEL BOOK CLUB
P.O. Box 473
Mt. Morris, IL 61054-0473
1-815-734-1104

[ ] YES. I want to take advantage of this opportunity to join FROMMER'S TRAVEL BOOK CLUB.
[ ] My check is enclosed. Dollar amount enclosed_____*
(all payments in U.S. funds only)

Name_____

Address_____

City_____ State_____ Zip_____

To ensure that all orders are processed efficiently, please apply sales tax in the following areas: CA, CT, FL, IL, NJ, NY, TN, WA, and CANADA.

*With membership, shipping and handling will be paid by FROMMER'S TRAVEL BOOK CLUB for the three free books you select as part of your membership. Please add $2 per book for shipping and handling for any additional books purchased ($3 per book for all foreign orders).

Allow 4-6 weeks for delivery. Prices of books, membership fee, and publication dates are subject to change without notice.

Please Send Me the Books Checked Below

FROMMER'S COMPREHENSIVE GUIDES
(Guides listing facilities from budget to deluxe, with emphasis on the medium-priced)

	Retail Price	Code		Retail Price	Code
☐ Acapulco/Ixtapa/Taxco 1993–94	$15.00	C120	☐ Jamaica/Barbados 1993–94	$15.00	C105
☐ Alaska 1990–91	$15.00	C001	☐ Japan 1992–93	$19.00	C020
☐ Arizona 1993–94	$18.00	C101	☐ Morocco 1992–93	$18.00	C021
☐ Australia 1992–93	$18.00	C002	☐ Nepal 1992–93	$18.00	C038
☐ Austria 1993–94	$19.00	C119	☐ New England 1993	$17.00	C114
☐ Austria/Hungary 1991–92	$15.00	C003	☐ New Mexico 1993–94	$15.00	C117
☐ Belgium/Holland/ Luxembourg 1993–94	$18.00	C106	☐ New York State 1992– 93	$19.00	C025
☐ Bermuda/Bahamas 1992–93	$17.00	C005	☐ Northwest 1991–92	$17.00	C026
			☐ Portugal 1992–93	$16.00	C027
☐ Brazil, 3rd Edition	$20.00	C111	☐ Puerto Rico 1993–94	$15.00	C103
☐ California 1993	$18.00	C112	☐ Puerto Vallarta/ Manzanillo/ Guadalajara 1992–93	$14.00	C028
☐ Canada 1992–93	$18.00	C009			
☐ Caribbean 1993	$18.00	C102			
☐ Carolinas/Georgia 1992–93	$17.00	C034	☐ Scandinavia 1993–94	$19.00	C118
			☐ Scotland 1992–93	$16.00	C040
☐ Colorado 1993–94	$16.00	C100	☐ Skiing Europe 1989– 90	$15.00	C030
☐ Cruises 1993–94	$19.00	C107			
☐ DE/MD/PA & NJ Shore 1992–93	$19.00	C012	☐ South Pacific 1992–93	$20.00	C031
			☐ Spain 1993–94	$19.00	C115
☐ Egypt 1990–91	$15.00	C013	☐ Switzerland/ Liechtenstein 1992–93	$19.00	C032
☐ England 1993	$18.00	C109			
☐ Florida 1993	$18.00	C104	☐ Thailand 1992–93	$20.00	C033
☐ France 1992–93	$20.00	C017	☐ U.S.A. 1993–94	$19.00	C116
☐ Germany 1993	$19.00	C108	☐ Virgin Islands 1992–93	$13.00	C036
☐ Italy 1993	$19.00	C113	☐ Virginia 1992–93	$14.00	C037
			☐ Yucatán 1993–94	$18.00	C110

FROMMER'S $-A-DAY GUIDES
(Guides to low-cost tourist accommodations and facilities)

	Retail Price	Code		Retail Price	Code
☐ Australia on $45 1993–94	$18.00	D102	☐ Israel on $45 1993–94	$18.00	D101
			☐ Mexico on $50 1993	$19.00	D105
☐ Costa Rica/ Guatemala/Belize on $35 1993–94	$17.00	D108	☐ New York on $70 1992–93	$16.00	D016
☐ Eastern Europe on $25 1991–92	$17.00	D005	☐ New Zealand on $45 1993–94	$18.00	D103
			☐ Scotland/Wales on $50 1992–93	$18.00	D019
☐ England on $60 1993	$18.00	D107			
☐ Europe on $45 1993	$19.00	D106	☐ South America on $40 1993–94	$19.00	D109
☐ Greece on $45 1993– 94	$19.00	D100			
			☐ Turkey on $40 1992– 93	$22.00	D023
☐ Hawaii on $75 1993	$19.00	D104			
☐ India on $40 1992–93	$20.00	D010	☐ Washington, D.C. on $40 1992–93	$17.00	D024
☐ Ireland on $40 1992– 93	$17.00	D011			

FROMMER'S CITY $-A-DAY GUIDES
(Pocket-size guides with an emphasis on low-cost tourist accommodations and facilities)

	Retail Price	Code		Retail Price	Code
☐ Berlin on $40 1992–93	$12.00	D002	☐ Madrid on $50 1992– 93	$13.00	D014
☐ Copenhagen on $50 1992–93	$12.00	D003	☐ Paris on $45 1992–93	$12.00	D018
☐ London on $45 1992– 93	$12.00	D013	☐ Stockholm on $50 1992–93	$13.00	D022

FUNDACIÓ CAIXA DE CATALUNYA

La Pedrera

La Pedrera

FROMMER'S TOURING GUIDES
(Color-illustrated guides that include walking tours, cultural and historic sights, and practical information)

	Retail Price	Code		Retail Price	Code
☐ Amsterdam	$11.00	T001	☐ New York	$11.00	T008
☐ Barcelona	$14.00	T015	☐ Rome	$11.00	T010
☐ Brazil	$11.00	T003	☐ Scotland	$10.00	T011
☐ Florence	$ 9.00	T005	☐ Sicily	$15.00	T017
☐ Hong Kong/Singapore/ Macau	$11.00	T006	☐ Thailand	$13.00	T012
			☐ Tokyo	$15.00	T016
☐ Kenya	$14.00	T018	☐ Venice	$ 9.00	T014
☐ London	$13.00	T007			

FROMMER'S FAMILY GUIDES

	Retail Price	Code		Retail Price	Code
☐ California with Kids	$17.00	F001	☐ San Francisco with Kids	$17.00	F004
☐ Los Angeles with Kids	$17.00	F002			
☐ New York City with Kids	$18.00	F003	☐ Washington, D.C. with Kids	$17.00	F005

FROMMER'S CITY GUIDES
(Pocket-size guides to sightseeing and tourist accommodations and facilities in all price ranges)

	Retail Price	Code		Retail Price	Code
☐ Amsterdam 1993–94	$13.00	S110	☐ Minneapolis/St. Paul, 3rd Edition	$13.00	S119
☐ Athens, 9th Edition	$13.00	S114			
☐ Atlanta 1993–94	$13.00	S112	☐ Montréal/Québec City 1993–94	$13.00	S125
☐ Atlantic City/Cape May 1991–92	$ 9.00	S004			
			☐ New Orleans 1993–94	$13.00	S103
☐ Bangkok 1992–93	$13.00	S005	☐ New York 1993	$13.00	S120
☐ Barcelona/Majorca/ Minorca/Ibiza 1993–94	$13.00	S115	☐ Orlando 1993	$13.00	S101
			☐ Paris 1993–94	$13.00	S109
☐ Berlin 1993–94	$13.00	S116	☐ Philadelphia 1993–94	$13.00	S113
☐ Boston 1993–94	$13.00	S117	☐ Rio 1991–92	$ 9.00	S029
☐ Cancún/Cozumel/ Yucatán 1991–92	$ 9.00	S010	☐ Rome 1993–94	$13.00	S111
			☐ Salt Lake City 1991–92	$ 9.00	S031
☐ Chicago 1993–94	$13.00	S122			
☐ Denver/Boulder/ Colorado Springs 1990–91	$ 8.00	S012	☐ San Diego 1993–94	$13.00	S107
			☐ San Francisco 1993	$13.00	S104
			☐ Santa Fe/Taos/ Albuquerque 1993–94	$13.00	S108
☐ Dublin 1993–94	$13.00	S128			
☐ Hawaii 1992	$12.00	S014	☐ Seattle/Portland 1992–93	$12.00	S035
☐ Hong Kong 1992–93	$12.00	S015			
☐ Honolulu/Oahu 1993	$13.00	S106	☐ St. Louis/Kansas City 1993–94	$13.00	S127
☐ Las Vegas 1993–94	$13.00	S121			
☐ Lisbon/Madrid/Costa del Sol 1991–92	$ 9.00	S017	☐ Sydney 1993–94	$13.00	S129
			☐ Tampa/St. Petersburg 1993–94	$13.00	S105
☐ London 1993	$13.00	S100			
☐ Los Angeles 1993–94	$13.00	S123	☐ Tokyo 1992–93	$13.00	S039
☐ Madrid/Costa del Sol 1993–94	$13.00	S124	☐ Toronto 1993–94	$13.00	S126
			☐ Vancouver/Victoria 1990–91	$ 8.00	S041
☐ Mexico City/Acapulco 1991–92	$ 9.00	S020	☐ Washington, D.C. 1993	$13.00	S102
☐ Miami 1993–94	$13.00	S118			

Other Titles Available at Membership Prices

SPECIAL EDITIONS

	Retail Price	Code		Retail Price	Code
☐ Bed & Breakfast North America	$15.00	P002	☐ Where to Stay U.S.A.	$14.00	P015
☐ Caribbean Hideaways	$16.00	P005			
☐ Marilyn Wood's Wonderful Weekends (within a 250-mile radius of NYC)	$12.00	P017			

GAULT MILLAU'S "BEST OF" GUIDES
(The only guides that distinguish the truly superlative from the merely overrated)

	Retail Price	Code		Retail Price	Code
☐ Chicago	$16.00	G002	☐ New England	$16.00	G010
☐ Florida	$17.00	G003	☐ New Orleans	$17.00	G011
☐ France	$17.00	G004	☐ New York	$17.00	G012
☐ Germany	$18.00	G018	☐ Paris	$17.00	G013
☐ Hawaii	$17.00	G006	☐ San Francisco	$17.00	G014
☐ Hong Kong	$17.00	G007	☐ Thailand	$18.00	G019
☐ London	$17.00	G009	☐ Toronto	$17.00	G020
☐ Los Angeles	$17.00	G005	☐ Washington, D.C.	$17.00	G017

THE REAL GUIDES
(Opinionated, politically aware guides for youthful budget-minded travelers)

	Retail Price	Code		Retail Price	Code
☐ Able to Travel	$20.00	R112	☐ Kenya	$12.95	R015
☐ Amsterdam	$13.00	R100	☐ Mexico	$11.95	R016
☐ Barcelona	$13.00	R101	☐ Morocco	$14.00	R017
☐ Belgium/Holland/ Luxembourg	$16.00	R031	☐ Nepal	$14.00	R018
			☐ New York	$13.00	R019
☐ Berlin	$11.95	R002	☐ Paris	$13.00	R020
☐ Brazil	$13.95	R003	☐ Peru	$12.95	R021
☐ California & the West Coast	$17.00	R121	☐ Poland	$13.95	R022
			☐ Portugal	$15.00	R023
☐ Canada	$15.00	R103	☐ Prague	$15.00	R113
☐ Czechoslovakia	$14.00	R005	☐ San Francisco & the Bay Area	$11.95	R024
☐ Egypt	$19.00	R105			
☐ Europe	$18.00	R122	☐ Scandinavia	$14.95	R025
☐ Florida	$14.00	R006	☐ Spain	$16.00	R026
☐ France	$18.00	R106	☐ Thailand	$17.00	R119
☐ Germany	$18.00	R107	☐ Tunisia	$17.00	R115
☐ Greece	$18.00	R108	☐ Turkey	$13.95	R027
☐ Guatemala/Belize	$14.00	R010	☐ U.S.A.	$18.00	R117
☐ Hong Kong/Macau	$11.95	R011	☐ Venice	$11.95	R028
☐ Hungary	$14.00	R118	☐ Women Travel	$12.95	R029
☐ Ireland	$17.00	R120	☐ Yugoslavia	$12.95	R030
☐ Italy	$13.95	R014			